Presented to the library of
Jackson Community College
by the Rotary International
Group Study Exchange Team
from Sydney, Australia
                    October 1974.

H. Burnett
Paul Wordsworthy.

Bob Lee

Brian Freeman.

Bob Wells
Keith Farmer.

Australia

OSMAR WHITE   JOHN KEITH WILLEY

Illustrated

ROSS   BRIAN CARROLL
RENNIE ELLIS & OTHERS

Photography by
JOHN CARNEMOLLA, MICHAEL MORCOMBE,
ALLAN KLEIMAN & OTHERS

LANSDOWNE PRESS

First published 1974
by Lansdowne Press,
(A division of IPC Books Limited),
37 Little Bourke St, Melbourne, 3000.
© Lansdowne Press
ISBN 0 7018 0435 1
Typeset by Dudley E King, Linotypers, Melbourne
Printed and bound in Hong Kong

INTRODUCTION
A LAND OF CONTRAST

Australia—a great and ancient land mass, washed by three oceans and stretching almost from the equator to the roaring forties. A land of diversity, of contrasts and contradictions that mock the phrase 'typically Australian' and the untutored visions of rolling plains supporting gum trees, sheep, kangaroos and lean men with wide brimmed hats.

For here, too, are soft green hills, vine festooned jungles, densely forested mountains and snow covered peaks, the blazing red domes and pinnacles of ancient inland ranges, fertile coastal plains, millions of square miles of desert and sombre heathlands—an enormous scenic spectrum. While the greatest variety of scene lies close to the coasts, behind the mountains and forests and well bred geometry of agriculture is the brooding heart of the land, an eternal presence of ochre and earth colours, of fantastic alien shapes and an unbelievable monotony of desert and plain.

The band of highlands down the eastern flank of Australia, formed by a great wrinkling of the earth's crust many millions of years ago, is a vast carapace of broken tablelands and peaks. It shelters and waters the civilised east, provides its superb diversity of scenery and the richness and safety of its pastoral land.

This is home to most Australians, the city dwellers and the people of the closely settled rural areas. The three biggest cities, Sydney, Melbourne and Brisbane, sprawl across the lush coastal plain that pushes up sugar crops in the tropical north and rich grass for the pampered dairy herds of the south. To add to the blessing of the fortunate east the seaboard is indented with river estuaries and inland waterways, lined by thousands of miles of wide beaches and ennobled by rugged cliffs and headlands and, occasionally, mountains which stray from the range to meet the sea.

In the north it is flanked, too, by the Great Barrier Reef, a 1,200 mile long buttress of brilliantly-coloured coral heads and ledges, tropical and continental islands, clear, warm waters and an abundance of marine and bird life.

Behind the coastal strip the mountains thrust and roll in blue hazed grandeur, densely clothed, sometimes in lush rainforest but mostly in smaller eucalypts and acacias, cut in the more spectacular regions by ravines, gorges and escarpments, pouring water to the coast in short, sharp rivers and down to the more gradual landward slopes into lazy brown rivers which wind, gum lined through rich plateau lands. But gradually the rivers dry up and are replaced by wandering channels that become rivers only after heavy rain, the trees space out until, finally, they become a rarity. The red desolation of the outback takes over, cut by great saw toothed ridges and towering masses that are like no other mountains on earth. Then, more than 1,500 miles west, the coastal pattern in reverse rolls green lands into the Indian Ocean.

This huge physical spectrum is host to an enormous range of unique and distinctive animal life. There are over 150 marsupial animals which carry their young in inbuilt cradles, among them the kangaroo and koala, the emblems of Australian wildlife, and the Tasmanian 'Tiger', one of the rarest animals in the world. There are the egg laying mammals, antiquated rarities, the echidna and the platypus. The kookaburra's droll laughter is the friendliest and most recognisable sound from within an incredible variety of bird life. Shy lyrebirds, rewarding the patient with a glimpse of their beauty in the

5

southern forests, soaring wedgetailed eagles, dancing brolgas, emus and parrots—all have lent individuality to Australia.

But the most unremitting factor in the Australian landscape is the gum tree. In its many guises and varieties it is the scenic link in the Australian vastness. Perhaps monotonous en masse, but each with an individual strength and beauty, these living representatives of a distant past have survived and thrived in Australia. The smell of eucalyptus is so much the essence of rural Australia that it can bring tears to the eyes of sophisticated expatriates.

Australians have brought their country, in less than 200 years, from the mists of antiquity to a leadership among nations. They have tamed the land and made it work for them; they have forged great industrial development from natural resources that are, as yet, only marginally exploited; they have built great cities and achieved one of the world's highest living standards; they have, for a country of 12 million people, made a big impact in the arts, in science, in industry and in sport.

But this is a book, not of people, but of their background—the Australian country and coastline. It is a book which has aimed at capturing and delineating the beauty of the land and its infinite variety, the backdrops before which the busy drama of Australian life is being played.

Facts and Figures

Australia is the flattest continent in the world, with an average elevation of only 1,000 feet above sea level, compared with a world average of 2,300 feet. Almost three-quarters of the island continent is an ancient plateau, the Great Western Plateau, averaging about 1,000 feet. Another large division is the central eastern lowlands, extending north-south with an average height of less than 500 feet. Even the eastern highlands have only an average altitude of less than 3,000 feet, and no peak rises above 7,500 feet.

It is the driest continent—about 70 percent of Australia has a rainfall of less than 20 inches a year, nearly 60 percent received less than 15 inches and about 40 percent less than 10 inches. The total annual run off of Australian rivers is less than the St Lawrence River in North America. The greatest surface run off is from tropical Australia, and it is a hopeful indicator of future development that the northern water resources are practically unharnessed, while the waters of the south are substantially committed for use in hydroelectricity and irrigation projects. Australia lacks the extensive inland river systems of the mountainous continents, its largest system being the Murray River and its tributaries, but there are artesian bores under 60 percent of the continent which support stock on the arid inland plains.

Australia's size (2,964,741 square miles), global siting (straddling the Tropic of Capricorn) and physical features give it a varied climate. Slightly more than half of Queensland, 33 percent of Western Australia and 81 percent of the Northern Territory lies within the torrid zone. Central and southern Queensland are sub-tropical and further south are the warm, temperate regions of New South Wales, South Australia and Western Australia and the cooler areas of Victoria, south-west Western Australia and Tasmania.

Australia's claim to be a land of sunshine is borne out by the average daily hours of sunshine for the capital cities: Darwin 8·4; Perth 7·8; Brisbane 7·5; Canberra 7·2; Adelaide 6·9; Sydney 6·7; Melbourne 5·7 and Hobart 5·6. The mean temperatures of the hottest and coldest months in the capitals are: Darwin 85·3 (77·1); Brisbane 76·9 (58·7); Perth 74·6 (55·4); Adelaide 73·4 (51·9); Sydney 71·6 (53·3); Canberra 68·3 (41·7); Melbourne 67·7 (48·9); Hobart 61·7 (46·2).

In most areas January is the hottest month, although in Tasmania and Victoria February is hottest and in the tropical north, because of the increased cloudiness of the wet season from December to March, temperatures are highest in November.

In the drier inland the range of temperatures from early morning to afternoon increases with the distance from the coast. During the hot summers of the northern inland temperatures often go over 110°F. The most consistently hot area is inland from Port Hedland, Western Australia, where at Marble Bar from October 1923 to April 1924 there were 160 consecutive days with temperatures rising to at least 100°F.

The average annual rainfalls of the capitals, and the number of days on which rain occurs, are: Darwin 60·48 (97); Sydney 47·75 (150); Brisbane 44·89 (124); Perth 34·89 (121); Melbourne 25·83 (141); Hobart 24·83 (163); Adelaide 20·77 (121).

In the north, mainly on the eastern seaboard, forests and vegetation are those of the moist tropics. Further south, east of the Great Dividing Range particularly, the vegetation is of the warm temperate zone. Inland the progressively drier elements restrict growth to the river fringes, and there are extensive treeless areas.

Australia's long isolation as a landmass has resulted in a vegetation predominantly different from the rest of the world. The relatively arid conditions which came to prevail intensified the struggle for existence and led to the development of a large range of plant life adapted to the environment. These plants form the main part of Australia's flora, with eucalypts and wattles predominating.

Eucalypts have about 500 species. They thrive in cold or heat, wet or dry, the richest soil or infertile sand. The most majestic species are the Victorian mountain ash, the tallest hardwood in the world, and the karri and jarrah of Western Australia. Eucalypts provide nearly all of the general purpose hardwoods, and much of the country's paper.

Wattles (acacia) are pod-bearing plants, represented in Australia by over 600 species. Australia also has thousands of species of wildflowers. Each state has its own large range of endemic groups, with Western Australia the most lavishly endowed.

Australia's wildlife is remarkable for the presence of many unique animals and the absence of several orders known in other countries. The severance of land bridges with other continents left Australia as an island sanctuary for its large population of marsupials, which produced a differentiation of many types.

Nearly half of the approximately 230 species of mammals recorded in Australia are marsupials. The remainder comprise the placental mammals and the rare species of monotremes. These are the only egg-laying mammals known and are considered by some zoologists to be descendants from ancient forms which evolved from mammals to reptiles.

The platypus is a living fossil; a furred creature which lays eggs, suckles its young, has webbed feet and a ducklike bill. It inhabits the watercourses of eastern Australia. Spiny ant-eaters are land dwellers, they carry a protective coat of spines and have a tubular snout and long narrow tongue for catching ants and other insects. When alarmed they use their spade-like claws to dig into the ground, and on soft ground they appear to sink into the earth.

Marsupials vary markedly in size and general appearance—they range from kangaroos exceeding 6 feet in height to insectivorous species smaller than a house mouse. Throughout their wide diversity of habit and environment they share a common feature—the possession of a pouch to accommodate the young.

As well known as the kangaroo, and perhaps even more popular, is the koala, a solemn and inoffensive tree dweller which lives on the leaves of certain species of Eucalypt. Other tree-dwelling marsupials include the cuscus of the tropics, tree-climbing kangaroos and many types of possums. The relatively few carnivorous marsupials include insect-eating 'mice', large native cats and the Tasmanian 'Devil' and Tasmanian 'Tiger'. The 'Tiger' is almost a legendary creature, believed by some naturalists to survive still in the wild parts of Tasmania.

The dingo, a wild dog, is believed to have evolved from Asiatic dogs which accompanied the ancestors of the Australian Aboriginal on their migrations by sea. Australia's range of native placental mammals is restricted to species of rodents and bats, while marine mammals include whales, seals and the dugong, or sea cow.

There are about 700 bird species in Australia, with some 530 species considered to be endemic. It is the home of 60 known species of parrots and 70 species of honeyeater. The best-known birds are those of unique characteristics or beauty and include the beautiful, superbly vocal lyrebird, the black swan, the emu, the cassowary, the stately brolga, the kookaburra, the mound-building brush turkey, mallee fowl and scrub fowl, the Cape Barren Goose, and the bush callers—whipbirds, bellbirds and magpies.

Reptiles include over 200 kinds of lizards, 140 snake types, two crocodiles, freshwater tortoises and marine turtles.

Australia's main mineral deposits are in two broad regions—The Precambrian rocks of Western Australia and South Australia, Northern Territory and parts of Queensland and New South Wales contain most metalliferous deposits—iron, lead, zinc, silver, copper, uranium, nickel and gold.

The mineralised Palaeozoic and Mesozoic rocks—containing gold, now mostly worked out, a few large areas of copper, lead, silver, zinc, and smaller amounts of other metals—extend round the east of the continent. Most of Australia's known black coal occurs in the eastern states, while there are large deposits of brown coal in Victoria. Significant oil and natural gas discoveries have been made at a number of places throughout Australia.

Mineral and farm products have always constituted the bulk of Australia's exports, and today they account for about 80 percent of exports. While the rural sector of the economy has been relatively static, the treasure house of mineral wealth uncovered in the last ten years has brought a new era of industrial and economic development.

Australia has become one of the world's biggest exporters of iron ore, mostly from reserves of at least 15,000 million tons of high grade ore in the north-west ranges, the Hamersleys and Opthalmias. The latest boom is in nickel, where what could prove to be the world's biggest deposits have been found at Kambalda in Western Australia. Bauxite, from Weipa in Queensland, is another new mineral to add to the silver, lead, zinc and copper extractions that have been the mainstay of Australian mining.

Manufacturing now employs some 1·3 million people—in over 60,000 factories. The greatest growth has been in metals, chemicals and engineering, and, on a population basis, Australia is now as highly industrialised as the United States.

Wool is still the greatest source of rural wealth. Australia produces about 30 percent of the world's wool, and the industry exports about 90 percent of its clip to provide about 30 percent of all export receipts. Beef and veal exports are only exceeded by Argentina.

Wheat production is the third rural mainstay, but irrigation is playing a big part in a new look in agriculture—with products like cotton, sorghum and rice joining the well-established cereal, fruit and sugar growing industries.

New South Wales

THE SENIOR STATE

Oldest, most populous, most industrialised of Australia's six States, New South Wales has sunshine to match that of California and the northern shores of the Mediterranean, for it lies in similar latitudes. Pervading sunshine and blue skies are its climatic norms.

Physically it is part of the pattern of eastern Australia, a 309,433 square mile slice of the continent.

First is the coastal plain, the thousand mile strip of fertile land, a mere twenty to fifty miles wide, but containing within it some of the State's finest dairying, fruitgrowing, farming and forest country. Here too are the State's three biggest cities: Sydney, Newcastle and Wollongong. Where the coastal strip meets the Pacific Ocean, New South Wales has a glorious seafront of bold headlands, estuaries, sunswept lagoons and golden beaches.

As a backdrop to this coastal plain stands the Great Dividing Range, the escarpment that runs down eastern Australia like a gigantic backbone. Within it lie the Blue Mountains, a holiday playground famed for its crisp-edged bracing air and its immense valleys, their sheer walls dropping away for two thousand feet and more—a land of waterfalls, cascades and glens festooned with moss and maidenhair and overhung by treeferns.

In the southern part of New South Wales, the Great Dividing Range rises to the 7,314 feet of Mount Kosciusko, Australia's highest point and monarch of the Australian Alps.

Beyond the ranges come three great tablelands, New England, Central and Southern, and the plains that extend westwards beyond them. This is the garden and granary of New South Wales, where wheat thrives, merino sheep produce their once-golden fleece, vegetables and fruit proliferate. The slow flowing rivers that take the melting snows of the Great Dividing Range westward have been tapped for the Murrumbidgee Irrigation Area and the farms of the Riverina, the land between the rivers. Prosperous inland towns dot the western tablelands and plains.

Gradually the fertile plains give way to the arid Outback, the land of vast distances, where stocking rates are measured in square mile to the sheep, where people concentrate in a few oases. Here lies that extraordinary city, Broken Hill, fourth largest in the State, but set 739 miles from the State capital at Sydney, the only reason for its location being that it straddles the world's richest, most massive single deposit of silver, lead and zinc.

OPERA HOUSE FROM CIRCULAR QUAY

SYDNEY–
COSMOPOLITAN
CAPITAL

The beautiful city of Sydney thrusts and arches itself around a fine confusion of bays and inlets. Its towers of commerce and white sailed opera house gleam down into the waters of the breathtakingly beautiful harbour. It sparkles back, seemingly unsullied by the constant passage of ferries, ocean going ships, workboats and other maritime miscellany. On weekends it becomes white canopied with the sails of a thousand yachts.

Overhead the great iron bridge rumbles with the chronic indigestion of big city traffic.

This is Australia's oldest, biggest and most fascinating city. It is sprawling, lusty, sometimes grimy, always noisy, but it has, on the whole, made the most of its beautiful setting. Its waterside houses peep down through their gardens to tranquil inlets lined with pleasure craft; city workers look up from their desks to see ocean liners gliding through the harbour; the coastal suburbs to the north and south fringe eighteen miles of golden surf beaches—Manly, Dee Why, Avalon, Palm Beach, Coogee, Maroubra.

To the south and south-west its industries spread in a grey and grimy ring that pumps life into the commercial arteries from 16,000 factories.

Its nightlife, centred on the legendary Kings Cross, is lively, loud and attractive; its culture vigorous and *avante garde*; its citizens friendly, outgoing and sport crazy.

This is the heart of New South Wales, the most populous State with 4,430,000 people, and the leading primary, mineral and manufacturing producer.

The other major industrial areas are black spurs on the green flank of the coast. Newcastle, 100 miles north of Sydney, is a coal and steel city and the seaboard heart of the rich Hunter Valley. Wollongong-Port Kembla, 50 miles south of Sydney, is the main heavy industry city in Australia.

The State encompasses hundreds of miles of ocean beaches, beautiful river, lake and mountain scenery, an expanse of harsh, flat interior plain, a sub-tropical north coast, and a belt of snow covered highlands in the south.

The topography falls into the four natural north-south divisions common to the eastern states: the narrow and fertile coastal plains, the tablelands of the Great Dividing Range, 30 to 100 miles wide and rising to high mountain regions in the north and south, the undulating western slopes of the range and the dry plains of the far west.

A COLONIAL HERITAGE

From its inconspicuous beginnings as a dumping-off spot for British convicts, the eighteenth century settlement at Port Jackson grew into a gracious colonial town under the guiding hand of Lachlan Macquarie, its fifth Governor. Today echos of the past are found in the well-preserved Georgian and Victorian buildings that still dot the modern metropolis of Sydney.

One of the first areas settled was The Rocks district near the wharves where the square-riggers used to tie up. At first it was a squalid waterfront area of cramped streets and seamen's taverns and it carried a most unsavoury reputation. Jack London and Joseph Conrad both commented on The Rocks in their writings. However, by the mid-nineteenth century merchants and notable professional men had set up home in the area and it acquired a new face of respectability. Many of the streets still retain their colonial flavour and a walking tour through The Rocks conjures up historic images of Sydney. Argyle Place especially, with its little cottages and terrace houses and its leafy trees has a village green atmosphere. George Street, the oldest street in Australia, was originally called Sergeant Major's Row. The colony's first jail was here and also the site for public executions. Later it became part of Sydney's Chinatown. These days it is a typical big city street with all the trappings of twentieth century commercial development.

Amongst the early convicts Governor Macquarie discovered Francis Greenway, an exceptionally talented architect, whom he set to work designing buildings whose lasting beauty still causes gasps of delight. St James Church in King Street, with its classical proportions and copper sheathed spire is one of Greenway's finest examples of Georgian-styled architecture. The nearby law courts in Queen's Square were originally designed by Greenway as convict barracks. Macquarie was so pleased with them that he granted the convict a full pardon. Parliament House and the Old Mint in Macquarie Street, Victoria Barracks in Oxford Street, Elizabeth Bay House and Vaucluse House all offer remarkable insights into the building style of the times.

In the latter half of the nineteenth century the simple and tasteful Georgian styles gave way to the more baroque Victorian architecture with its emphasis on ornamentation. Rows of terrace houses with two and three storeys and balconies embellished with cast iron lace were built in the inner city suburbs. Hundreds of them still survive to give Sydney's hilly streets a character that is typical of the city's beginnings.

AN OLD BUILDING AT THE ROCKS

SUBLIME SUBURBIA

The great attraction of many of Sydney's suburbs is that they overlook the harbour or the Pacific Ocean and consequently take on the look of expensive holiday resorts. On the city side of Port Jackson a succession of bays runs from the Bridge towards the Heads. Each of these inlets forms its own suburb. In those nearer to the city, like Elizabeth Bay and Rushcutters Bay, tall apartment buildings and flats predominate, but as you get further east into Double Bay, Point Piper and Vaucluse, the city hill-and-dale streets take on the look of well-bred domesticity. The houses are large and comfortable and have been there for some years and the residents obviously take pride in their gardens. Many of the people who are prominent in Sydney's business and social life have made their homes in these areas.

A mile or two inland, past urbane Bellevue Hill and Woollahra, is Paddington, a district of great architectural charm. 'Paddo', as it is affectionately called, has often been described as the soul of Sydney. Rows and rows of Victorian terrace homes face the narrow streets and give them a peculiarly sculptured look that speaks of the past. The area is mostly populated by people who take special delight in living there and restoring the old houses in an effort to preserve its identity. Bistros and wine bars, galleries and ateliers, antique shops and boutiques can all be found scattered amongst the terraces.

In the south and west of the city are the industrial areas, now absorbing European personality as the centres of the various migrant populations, and the spreading red-roofed suburbia of the western suburbs. The western city of Parramatta, Australia's second oldest city, now has its history overlaid by the veneer of modern commerce. The southern suburbs stretch down to Botany Bay, George's River and Port Hacking, where hills and river reaches give the suburbs a more individual appearance.

The most favoured suburbs are those of the north shore, where the houses strive to face the twin deity of harbour and ocean and the steeply scarped sandstone hills, cleft with ridges of rock, allow for individuality of siting and design. In waterside suburbs like Cremorne, Mosman, Castlecrag and Clontarf, palatial homes hide behind sub-tropical vegetation. Many have yachts and speedboats moored at private piers.

Huge American-style shopping centres throughout the suburbs cater to the housewife's every need, and luxurious Rugby League clubs provide comprehensive entertainment facilities for their thousands of suburban members.

TERRACE HOUSES AT PADDINGTON

▲ WATERFRONT HOMES ON SYDNEY HARBOUR   ▼ HARBOUR SUBURB OF MANLY

A FRIENDLY, BUSTLING CITY

There is something about the city streets of Sydney and the bustling people who animate them that makes you want to linger and stroll those extra couple of blocks to soak it all up. The atmosphere is gregarious, and unlike other big cities, one does not feel alienated, but very much a part of it all. In the department stores, some of them with more than twenty acres of floor space, the service may not always be super efficient, but it's friendly and there is often this sense that you are being served not by a salesgirl paid to be polite, but rather by someone you've known before. Multi-floor stores like Farmers and David Jones are a world of their own and it is easy to spend half a day just browsing around.

Shopping arcades are also a feature of downtown Sydney and kaleidoscopic thoroughfares like the Imperial Arcade and Her Majesty's Arcade, both running between Pitt and Castlereagh Streets, are packed with specialty shops, boutiques and snack bars offering everything from imported Italian handbags to freshly baked Danish pastries.

Martin Place is the official heart of Sydney. The General Post Office is here and so are most of the banks. On Thursday at 12.30 p.m. a mounting of the guard ceremony takes place at the marble Cenotaph. In front of the G.P.O. flower sellers do a lively trade from their well-stocked barrows and colourful magazine kiosks display reading material from all over the world. Streams of late model cars are continually turning out of Martin Place and nosing down the narrow and sometimes confusing streets. They jockey for positions with the buses and taxis that are forever shuttling passengers up and down the city blocks.

At the end of the day the lowered sun hits the plate glass windows of the office buildings and casts a golden hue over the streets. It's the peak hour, and thousands of people clutching shopping bags and brief cases and the evening paper hurry towards the underground railway stations or the ferries at Circular Quay, while the continual traffic rumble on the great iron bridge reaches a throbbing crescendo as the choked canyons of the city disgorge traffic bound for the north shore suburbs. The day is over, but the night still holds promise.

MARTIN PLACE, THE OFFICIAL HEART OF SYDNEY

SYDNEY EXPRESSWAY

MORE THAN A MILLION PEOPLE VISIT SYDNEY'S 10 DAY
ROYAL AGRICULTURAL SHOW AT EASTER

COASTAL MAGNIFICENCE

Prevailing breezes, fresh from their trip across the Pacific Ocean, soon meet the barrier of the Great Dividing Range and deposit their moisture load upon the coastal plains. Rivers here are short but numerous and reliable. So the thousand mile coastal strip of New South Wales is fertile, picturesque and productive.

Sydney sits on the edge of this fertile coastal strip. For six hundred miles to the north the Pacific Highway sits between mountain and sea until crossing into the neighboring State of Queensland. To the south, the Princes Highway makes a similar, shorter journey into Victoria.

Rivers are the landmarks along these highways.

Going north, the Hawkesbury is the first of them. It carves its way through rugged country, in marked contrast to the fertile slopes of the Hunter Valley, where the coastal plain widens out to 150 miles, an area that produces some of the State's best table wines.

The mountains come closer to the sea again north of the Hunter, but they still leave room for the broad flats of the Manning, Hastings and Macleay Rivers. Dairy farms line the rivers, fishing villages dot the coast.

Northwards the climate becomes more tropical. Banana plantations begin to make their appearance. Coff's Harbour is conscious enough of the banana's place in its economy to have built 'the biggest banana in the world', a concrete monster in full natural colour.

Grafton, where the Clarence River punctuates progress, is tropical enough to be famous for its jacarandas.

In the valleys of the Richmond and Tweed, the most northerly of the New South Wales rivers, crops of sugar, bananas, papayas and pineapples give the countryside an increasingly tropical look.

South from Sydney is the Illawarra Country, its name taken from the aboriginal 'high place near water'. The mountains come close to the sea indeed; some of the best coastal views in Australia are to be seen from roadside lookouts here.

The big steel centre of Wollongong–Port Kembla, third largest city in the State, provides contrast to the dairying vistas that dominate the Illawarra.

To the south, the coastal plain becomes a land of tall timber, fishing villages, with a tourist highlight in historic old ghost town of Boydtown.

SOUTH COAST SEASCAPE

FISHING FLEET AT NAROOMA, SOUTH COAST

ROCK FISHING ON FAR NORTH COAST
HAWKESBURY RIVER, N.S.W.

RICH COUNTRY NEAR TARCUTTA, SOUTHERN N.S.W.

RUGGED DIVIDING RANGE

The Australia–long Great Dividing Range, which separates the coastal strip from the rolling plains beyond, comes closest to Sydney in the Blue Mountains, which rise from the flats of the Nepean River only forty miles from the city.

Nature has moulded the Blue Mountains into an area that is curiously different, sometimes startlingly grand, even awe-inspiring. Streams here do not trickle off the central humpbacked ridge, they plunge, spray veiled over sheer thousand foot cliffs. Down in the glens and gorges, cascades rush in splashing ribbons of silver through mighty stands of timber, natural boulder-strewn amphitheatres here and there patched pale green with carpets of moss, grottos choked with ferns.

Beyond the Blue Mountains, Jenolan Caves display what can be achieved by the tireless industry of minute submarine animals, a stupendous geological upheaval and the patient and beautifying sculpturing of the elements.

As the Great Dividing Range moves south in New South Wales, it creeps higher, finally to reach Australia's highest point in the 7,314 feet of Mt Kosciusko, grandest of the Snowy Mountains. Snow covers these mountains from June to October, and ski enthusiasts flock to sophisticated resorts like Thredbo, Crackenback, Smiggins' Hole and Fall's Creek for the season.

As the snows melt for another summer, the streams become torrents filling the dams of the Snowy Mountain Scheme, a gigantic engineering project that has turned the eastward flowing rivers back through tunnels under the mountains to water the vast inland areas.

Not all New South Wales mountains have been disciplined into taking their place in the tidy line of the Great Dividing Range. Far to the north-west of Sydney, the Warrumbungles just rise abruptly from the otherwise featureless plain of the central west.

When the Warrumbungle volcanoes were active, lava was squeezed up through vents like toothpaste from a tube, eventually leaving vertical pillars towering into the air, in formations like Belougery Spire, the Breadknife, the Needle, Crater Bluff, Tonduran Spire and Bluff Mountain.

The Great Dividing Range has dictated the pattern of New South Wales roads and railways. Only occasionally does a road clamber up through the passes to join the coastal strip with the plains beyond the ranges. Such roads are almost invariably scenic bonanzas.

BRIDAL FALLS, BLUE MOUNTAINS

THE THREE SISTERS, KATOOMBA, BLUE MOUNTAINS

THREDBO ALPINE VILLAGE

FISHING A SNOWY MOUNTAINS STREAM

SKIING, N.S.W. ALPS

WHERE EMU ROAM

Beyond the fertile tablelands and slopes lie the great western plains of New South Wales, where Australia's national emblem, the kangaroo and the emu, roam. In this spacious land you begin to understand the true meaning of Australia's vast inland.

The Darling River meanders south-westwards through it all, bound for its rendezvous with the Murray.

In the north, the country is so flat that road and railway planners could use their rulers to draw their line of march between Nyngan and Bourke, a distance of 200 miles. Towns here have musical names like Bourke, Brewarrina, Cobar and Nyngan.

Bourke, on the Darling, is the metropolis of the north-west, with no less than 3,300 people. A sealed road of 490 miles to Sydney now makes a mockery of all the old jokes about 'Back o' Bourke', once the epitome of isolation.

In the days of the Murray-Darling paddle steamers, Bourke was a major port, the riverboats originally taking wool downstream for export through South Australia, before Sydney recaptured the trade with a river-railway transport combination. Boats on the Darling today are more likely to carry fishermen, pitting their wiles against cod, golden perch, catfish and bream.

To the south, the Darling comes near enough to the mining city of Broken Hill to supply it with water,

THE CITY OF BROKEN HILL

through a 70 mile pipeline. Built over the world's richest silver-lead-zinc deposit yet discovered, 'The Hill' has a reputation as a rip-roaring town which makes its own rules.

The Silver City Highway, which streaks northwards across New South Wales from the Victorian to the Queensland border, connects Broken Hill with Tibooburra, most north-westerly and therefore most remote of all towns in New South Wales, but not far from the Wild Dog Fence that keeps marauding Queensland dingoes away from New South Wales sheep. On its way north the Silver City Highway passes through the ghost town of Milparinka, whence the Mount Browne gold rush once brought two thousand hopeful miners.

Broken Hill may be hundreds of miles from the sea, but it does have a first class beach resort. Menindee Lakes, due east of the city, were until 1960 just a series of broad, shallow basins into which the Darling would overflow in times of flood. A dam on the river now keeps them full, providing 40,000 acres of water surface to be enjoyed by the people and the seagulls of the West Darling country, as the area between the river and the South Australian border is called.

From Menindee Lakes, the Darling continues its journey to Wentworth, where it finally combines its waters with the Murray to provide Australia with its most stately stream.

EMUS, N.S.W. CENTRAL WEST

COUNTRYSIDE NEAR MENINDEE, WESTERN N.S.W.

THE GOLDEN WEST

Although the eastern face of the Great Dividing Range is rugged, to the west it fades away only gradually in table lands and plains.

The Golden West, which begins immediately west of the Blue Mountains, is a region of green stands of lucerne (alfalfa) and other improved pastures, fields of thriving wheat, sheep and cattle grazing, apple and cherry orchards, bustling towns and cities.

This is the country that saw Australia's first gold rushes in the 1850s. Gone now are the bearded, swaggering diggers in their moleskin trousers, Wellington boots and cabbage tree hats. Some of the towns that thrived on gold, such as Bathurst, have managed to hook their star to more permanent sources of wealth. Others, like Lucknow and Hill End, are just shadows of their former selves.

North of the Golden West lies the New England Tableland, high country in which sheep, dairy cattle, apples, cherries, maize, peas, potatoes and cabbage prosper.

New South Wales has one of its main educational centres on the New England Tableland, at Armidale, headquarters of the University of New England and Armidale Teachers' College.

Between the Lachlan and Murray Rivers, in the southern section of the inland slopes, the Riverina basks in the sun, a rich pastoral and agricultural region of wide open plains, sheep and cattle pastures, irrigation schemes, wheatfields and vineyards.

One special part of the Riverina is the Murrumbidgee Irrigation Area, sitting astride the main canal that channels off the Murrumbidgee River at Berembed Weir, 25 miles east of Narrandera, gateway to the MIA. Here irrigation makes possible the spreading miles of orchards, vineyards, cotton and rice fields, the picturesque willow and poplar lined canals, the wineries and fruit and vegetable canneries, the scent of the fruit trees in blossom, the grape harvest, the shaded parklands and the prosperous towns.

So great is the profusion of crops grown in the MIA that the work of harvesting goes on all year round. The warm January sun brings melons, nectarines and plums to a golden ripeness. Peaches, pears and prunes are ready for the pickers in February and March. And so it goes on until November comes and it is time to get in the oats crop.

SHEEP GRAZE NEAR PARKES, N.S.W.
THE CITY OF TAMWORTH, N.S.W.

SOUTHERN TABLELANDS SCENE

THE ARTIFICIAL LAKE BURLEY GRIFFIN GIVES CANBERRA A FOCUS

MANY HARVESTS

New South Wales is one of the best endowed of the Australian states.

While the glamour of Australia's new rush to mineral riches in the 1960s was concentrated elsewhere, the mines of New South Wales continued to provide some forty per cent of Australia's total mineral production: black coal from the Hunter Valley, the Illawarra and the Lithgow area; silver-lead-zinc from the lodes of Broken Hill; rutile and zircon from the mineral sands of the central and northern coasts; tin and copper deposits developed in recent years.

Second among the State's great natural resources are its 24 million acres of forest. Hardwood trees such as ironbark, tallowwood, blackbutt and turpentine yield some of the world's most durable and decorative timbers. The native eucalypt has adapted itself to differing environments ranging from the State's semi-tropical jungles to its semi-desert lands.

New South Wales produces over forty per cent of Australia's total factory output. Massive steelworks at Newcastle and Port Kembla use Australian ore to produce iron and steel that are low in price, high in quality. Much of this production is later worked into wire, pipes, motor-vehicles, agricultural equipment, rails and railway rolling stock, internal combustion engines, hardware, radio and electrical appliances, fine precision instruments and aircraft.

Non-ferrous metal industries are also well represented, with emphasis on bronze and copper alloys. Along with them have come heavy chemical industries, producing essential industrial acids and gases, as well as ammonia and caustic soda. The State has acquired its own efficiency in the spheres of instrument technology, electronics and radar, three-quarters of all requirements now being made on the spot.

Yet New South Wales still recognises that the produce of the land remains of vital importance to the State's economy and well-being. Eastwards to the seaports flow the products of the farms and pastures.

In both size of flocks and quality of fleece, New South Wales is the leading State for sheep and wool.

Sheep also play their part in the State's food production, as do the beef cattle and dairying industries, the latter mainly confined to the fertile coastal plains.

Agricultural as well as pastoral, New South Wales has a wide enough variety of soil and climate to produce such diverse crops as sugar cane, bananas, pineapples, passionfruit, grapes, rice, cotton, citrus, stone fruits, cherries, apples. And as the modern concrete silos and steel elevators along the railway lines indicate, ideal conditions for wheat are widespread throughout the State.

M.I.A. BEAN CROP

CROP DUSTING AT WEE WAA COTTON FIELD

BLASTING, SNOWY MOUNTAINS

MINING, BROKEN HILL

WHEAT CROP, WESTERN N.S.W.

THE SETTLEMENT AND DEVELOPMENT OF SYDNEY

In 1770 the eastern coast of Australia was discovered by explorer Captain James Cook, in his 369 ton ship *Endeavour*. He sailed into Botany Bay and named the new territory New South Wales, claiming it in the name of the King of England. Twelve miles further north along the coast he discovered another huge natural harbour which he did not enter but named Port Jackson.

Eighteen years later Captain Arthur Phillip sailed into Botany Bay after an eight month voyage from England. Phillip was at the head of the First Fleet, a convoy of eleven ships—two King's ships, six convict transports and three store ships—to set up a penal settlement where the British government could transport its unwanted convicts. He found Botany Bay unsuitable, and, following Cook's charts, sailed for Port Jackson.

Later Phillip wrote: 'We got into Port Jackson early in the afternoon, and had the satisfaction of finding the finest harbour in the world, in which a thousand sail of the line may ride in the most perfect security . . . The different coves were examined with all possible expedition. I fixed on the one that had the best spring of water, in which the ships can anchor so close to the shore that at a very small expense quays may be made at which the largest ships may unload. This cove which I honoured with the name of Sydney, is about a quarter of a mile across at the entrance, and half a mile in length.'

The British flag was unfurled at Sydney Cove on 26 January 1788, a day now commemorated nationally as Australia Day.

From the beginning it was a struggle. Amongst the 1,000 or so convicts and marines there were very few skilled labourers either in farming or the trades and tools were in short supply. At first the settlement was housed in tents, then later, under the direction of the ships carpenters, rough buildings were constructed. Finally a convict with the necessary skills started manufacturing bricks from clay deposits near where Paddy's Market is today.

Early attempts at growing food were not very successful and the colony had to depend on supplies from England to sustain it. The Second Fleet arrived in 1790 with a further 770 convicts but its storeship had been wrecked en route, 247 prisoners had died between England and New South Wales and the rest were in a bad condition. This further added to Sydney's food problems and the incidence of scurvy mounted. The Third Fleet arrived with another 1,468 convicts the following year.

By then grants of land had been given to convicts whose time had expired, and although there was a general ignorance of farming methods, 150 of these people had started farms.

When Phillip returned to England in 1792 he had established friendly relations with the aboriginal natives and he left behind him a settlement of about 4,000 people.

During the next seventeen years Sydney had a succession of eight governors and military commanders. One of them was William Bligh, famous for his role in the mutiny on the *Bounty*. Bligh had even less luck in his relationships with the men of the N.S.W. Corps in Sydney. They too mutinied over Bligh's attempts to destroy their monopoly of the rum trade and they placed him under arrest and ran the colony to their own advantage.

In 1805 John Macarthur, a free settler, was granted 5,000 acres near Camden where he experimented in breeding sheep for wool.

The result was the famous Australian Merino strain and in time it was to bring great prosperity to the economy.

As a city Sydney was neglected by its governors and it grew up in a most haphazard way. It was not until Governor Macquarie's term of office, 1809-1821, that the city, under his leadership, started developing an identity it could be proud of. Many people consider him the founder of modern Sydney. He promoted education and erected fine public buildings and churches, many of them designed by convict architect Francis Greenway. The Supreme Court was established in 1814 and the first bank, the Bank of N.S.W. was granted its charter in 1817. A large hospital was built, asylums founded and road building increased. Macquarie also encouraged exploration, and in 1813 a way was found across the Blue Mountains which opened up the Western Plains for settlement. By 1825 the population of N.S.W. was 33,675 and Sydney was becoming a major shipping and trading centre for the South Pacific. The city was first lit by oil lamps in 1826 and then gas in 1841. A mail delivery service went into operation in the 1830s. In 1838 the colony had $2\frac{3}{4}$ million sheep and exported over $4\frac{1}{2}$ million pounds of wool. In 1840 the transportation of convicts stopped and there was a general increase in free immigration. Gold was discovered near Bathurst in 1851 and the subsequent rushes brought thousands more people into Sydney which prospered accordingly. In 1852 the University of Sydney was opened and by 1860 the population of the city reached 100,000 people and many lasting buildings were being erected. The first electric telegraph started operation in 1858 and electric street lights replaced the gas lamps in 1890.

Responsible Government was granted in 1855 and in the latter part of the century the community started developing a strong sense of Australian nationalism. Federation was granted in 1900 and the Commonwealth of Australia established on 1 January 1901. Sydney, as the principal city of the Commonwealth, continued to flourish in the new century and quickly grew into a heavily industrialized metropolis.

PLACES OF INTEREST IN SYDNEY

HISTORIC

St James Church King Street and Queens Square. A fine old Georgian styled church designed by convict architect Francis Greenway and built in 1819. Its spire is sheathed in copper.

Hyde Park Barracks Queens Square. Originally designed by Greenway as convict quarters and now serves as law courts. Many additions have been made to the original building.

Parliament House Macquarie Street. The central building was originally part of the Rum Hospital. It was built in 1811-1816 and first occupied by State Legislature in 1829. Open weekdays, phone 2 0351 for information.

Richmond Villa Located behind Parliament House facing the Domain. A beautifully preserved Victorian Gothic House built in 1849 and now the headquarters of the N.S.W. Parliamentary Country Party. Its architect was Mortimer Lewis.

The Old Mint Macquarie Street. This typical wide verandahed colonial building was also part of the old Rum Hospital built in 1811-1816 by three settler businessmen in payment for monopoly of the colony's rum trade. Between 1855 and 1926 the building was part of the Royal Mint.

University of Sydney Parramatta Road. The university's Great Hall is Sydney's best example of Gothic Revival architecture. It is especially noted for its superb hammer-beamed roof. The architect was Edmund Blacket.

St Andrews Cathedral Anglican. Bathurst Street. Also designed in Gothic Revival style by Blacket.

St Marys Cathedral Roman Catholic. Cathedral Street. Another example of Gothic Revival, this time designed by William Wardell.

Greenway's obelisk Macquarie Place. Historic stone marker from which the colony's roads were measured.

Royal College of Physicians 145 Macquarie Street. Built in 1848 as a gracious, two-storeyed residence. Extra floors were added later.

General Post Office Martin Place. A monumental building taking 22 years to complete from its beginnings in 1865. The architectural style is Renaissance, the architect James Barnet, whose image actually appears sculptured into a panel on the Pitt Street side.

Town Hall George Street. A fine example of Victorian architecture including a grand ornamented tower. This building is the seat of government of the City of Sydney. Its galleried concert hall holds 2,500 people and houses one of the world's finest pipe organs.

Lands Department Building Loftus Street. More Victorian grandeur with an unusual onion-shaped dome on its tower. Designed by James Barnet in 1877.

Conservatorium of Music Macquarie Street. Erected in 1819 as Government House stables and is now the city's centre for the teaching of music. Open 9 a.m.-9 p.m. weekdays and 9 a.m. to noon on Saturdays.

Darlinghurst Court House Taylor Square, Darlinghurst. Designed in the Greek Revival style by Mortimer Lewis and erected in 1837.

The Old Gaol Forbes Street, Darlinghurst. Now the East Sydney Technical College. Enclosed by huge convict built wall whose stones still bear the marks of the convict masons. Of several buildings the Round House is most interesting. Open to visitors 9 a.m.-5 p.m. Phone 31 0266 for information.

Elizabeth Bay House Onslow Avenue, Elizabeth Bay. Built in 1832 for the Colonial Secretary, it was the scene of many memorable

Circular Quay at the turn of the century

gatherings of intellectuals and artists. Designed by John Verge, it is one of the finest examples of colonial architecture still standing. At present it is divided into flats but it is still possible to see the entrance hall with its spiral staircase and spectacular domed ceiling.

Victoria Barracks Oxford Street, Paddington. Immensely long building designed in the Georgian tradition by Major George Barney in 1841. Visitors welcome any day, conducted tours each Tuesday at 11 a.m. include witnessing changing of the guard ceremony. Phone 31 0455, Ext. 517, for information.

Vaucluse House Wentworth Avenue, Vaucluse. Fully restored former home of William Charles Wentworth, famous explorer and politician responsible for the N.S.W. Constitution. Open daily 10 a.m.-5 p.m.

The Rocks Northern end of George Street near Circular Quay West. Waterfront area once known throughout the South Pacific for its sailor's pubs, prostitutes and bawdy life. In 1855 it had thirty-seven taverns of which two still operate. Later it became a choice residential area for some of the colony's elite and it still retains much of its original architectural character. Suggested walking tour: Turn up Argyle Street from Lower George Street, pass the old bond stores, go under The Cut which was begun in 1843, and continue to Argyle Place, a square faced by Georgian and Victorian cottages and the 130 year old Garrison Church. The Rocks' Historical Museum is in the same area and is open from 2.30 p.m. to 5 p.m. on Saturdays and Public Holidays. Climb the stone stairs to Observatory Park, which dates from 1858. Look for the Agar Steps and descend into Kent Street. Walk north past the terrace, past Argyle Place again and into Lower Fort Street where you'll find the old Hero of Waterloo Hotel and some excellent Georgian buildings, especially Bligh House at No 43. Continue on until you reach George Street North. Here, behind the Sailor's Home, you will find Cadman's Cottage which was built in 1816 and is now the oldest house in Sydney. It is best viewed from the Overseas Terminal. Governor Phillip, the founder of Sydney, first landed nearby and a plaque, in front of the Maritime Services Building, commemorates the place.

GENERAL

Australia Square George and Pitt Streets. Australia's tallest building—50 levels, 600 ft. high—soars above a plaza with open air cafes and a fountain. The Skywalk lookout deck is open from 10 a.m. till 10 p.m. every day. Admission—adults $1.00, children 20c. Summit Restaurant revolves on the top of the tower and diners get panoramic views of the harbour. Shopping levels include many specialty shops.

A.M.P. Building Circular Quay. Observation Deck 26 storeys high is open 9 a.m. to 5 p.m. Monday to Saturday, 10 a.m. to 5 p.m. Sundays, 7 p.m. to 10 p.m. Saturdays and Sundays. Conducted tours 11 a.m. and 2.30 p.m. Admission—adults 20c, children 10c. Pensioners and school groups free. Occasional lunch hour plays in theatrette at 1.10 p.m. on weekdays.

Sydney Opera House Bennelong Point. This controversial and strikingly original building was begun in 1959 and is expected to be completed in 1972 at a cost of $85 million. It was designed by Danish architect Joern Utzon who won a competition which attracted over 200 entries from all over the world. His sail-like exterior, which is reminiscent of the yachts on the harbour created enormous technical problems and costs, all raised by state lotteries, have spiralled way above the original estimates of $7 million. After a long argument regarding a number of technical and functional issues the N.S.W. Government and Utzon parted ways when the Opera House was less than half completed and the project was taken over by a local architectural company. At the time of writing, tours have been discontinued because of safety hazards but construction can be viewed from an observation platform and pavilion.

State Government Office Block   Cnr. Phillip and Bent Streets. Known as the Black Stump, this unusual building is one of the tallest in Australia and houses many State Government Departments.

Australian Museum   Cnr. College and William Streets. A most comprehensive natural history museum with emphasis on Australiana. Includes exhibits on life of Australian aborigines. Open 10 a.m. to 5 p.m. Tuesdays to Saturdays, and Public Holidays; noon to 5 p.m. Mondays (10 a.m. to 5 p.m. in school holidays); 2 p.m. to 5 p.m. Sundays. Closed Good Friday and Christmas Day. Restaurant open same hours as the museum, but closed on Sundays.

Mining Museum   28 George Street North. One of the best collections of geological specimens, gemstones, fossils, and ores in the Southern Hemisphere.

Museum of Applied Arts and Science   Harris Street, Ultimo—near Central Station. Contains exhibits of glassware, ceramics, engineering, shipping and aviation. There is also a Planetarium. Open 10 a.m. to 5 p.m., weekdays, Saturdays and Public Holidays, 2 p.m. to 5 p.m. Sundays. Closed Christmas Day and Good Friday.

Nicholson Museum of Antiquities   University of Sydney, Parramatta Road. Ancient Greek, Roman and Egyptian exhibits of sculpture, jewellery, and utensils.

Cenotaph   Martin Place opposite the G.P.O. War memorial to servicemen and women who gave their lives for their country. Mounting of the guard ceremony each Thursday at 12.30 p.m. except during Christmas to New Year period.

Library of N.S.W.   Shakespeare Place. Includes General Reference Library, Mitchell Library and its famous collection of Australian books and documents, Dixson Library, Shakespeare Tercentenary Memorial Library and Mitchell and Dixson Galleries. Public Library open 10 a.m. to 10 p.m. Mondays to Saturdays; 2 p.m. to 6 p.m. Sundays and Public Holidays, closed Christmas Day and Good Friday.

Stock Exchange   20 O'Connell Street. Public Gallery open 10 a.m. to 5 p.m. weekdays. The best time to view operations is in the morning. Trading finishes at 3.30 p.m.

Church Missionary Society   Cnr. Bathurst and Kent Streets. Display of aboriginal craft including bark paintings, carvings, beading, boomerangs and spears. Purchases can be made. Open 8.30 a.m. to 5 p.m. weekdays.

History House   8 Young Street. Interesting collection of early documents, weapons and dress.

Fort Denison   A 114 year old island fortress in the middle of the harbour. Originally it was used as a convict prison and named Pinchgut by its hungry occupants. It still holds many interesting relics and can be visited with a special pass available from the Maritime Services Board, telephone 2 0545.

Sydney Harbour Bridge   Opened in 1932, and nicknamed 'the coathanger' by visitors from other states, this huge bridge has an arch 440 ft. high and measuring 1,650 ft. from pylon to pylon, making it the second largest single-span bridge in the world. Total length of the bridge with its approaches is 2¼ miles. The high water clearance is 170 ft. and average daily traffic flow 110,000 vehicles. The south-east pylon includes a lookout and a restaurant and is open daily from 9 a.m. to 6 p.m. There is an admission charge.

Paddy's Market   Haymarket, with entrance in Hay Street. Sydney's own 'flea market'. A colourful atmosphere and many stalls selling fascinating antique junk, unusual clothing and jewellery and many other offbeat things. A lot of fun. Open 11 a.m. to 5.30 p.m. Fridays only. Vegetable market is open Saturday morning also.

Taronga Park Zoo   Mosman. Over 5,000 animals in 70 acres of bushland and gardens overlooking the harbour makes Taronga Park one of the world's most fascinating zoos. Worth a visit for the Aus-

tralian section alone. Includes a reptile house, platypus viewing tank, aquarium, and aviaries. Open every day of the year from 9.30 a.m. to 5 p.m. Dolphin act twice daily at 11 a.m. and 3 p.m. in outdoor pools. Take ferry from No 5 wharf at Circular Quay.

Marineland   Manly. Killer sharks, giant rays, turtles, and many other fish. See underwater divers risk their lives hand feeding the creatures of the deep at 11.15 a.m., 3.15 p.m., and 8.15 p.m. An admission charge is made.

Take the Manly Ferry or speedy Hydrofoil from Circular Quay.

Kings Cross   Take bus from city along William Street. The centre of Sydney's night life—restaurants, night clubs, cabaret, strip tease, cocktail bars. Still swinging in the early hours of the morning. There are many odd-ball characters in the area and just walking the streets is great entertainment day or night.

Paddington   Take buses 389, 390, 378 or 379 from Elizabeth Street in the city. This inner suburb has a unique village atmosphere and hundreds of fine examples of terrace houses. It is well known for its characteristic architecture, art galleries, restaurants and interesting inhabitants.

CITY PARKS AND GARDENS

Of the 7,161 acres which comprises the City of Sydney proper, 880 acres are given over to parks and gardens.

Royal Botanic Gardens Farm Cove. Sixty-six acres of beautifully cared for gardens and parkland on the shores of Farm Cove, so called because it was the site of the first attempt at farming in Australia. In 1788 Governor Phillip grew vegetables in the area. The gardens contain many specimens of bushes, trees and flowers from all over the world, as well as hothouses for orchids and tropical ferns. Only a few minutes from the centre of the city, they are open from 7 a.m. to sunset. Cars can travel through the gardens on Mrs Macquarie's Road to a point looking out on to the harbour.

The Domain Just a few blocks east of Martin Place, The Domain is an expanse of open parkland adjoining the Botanic Gardens. On Sundays soap-box orators gather good natured crowds around them while they hold forth on all kinds of controversial subjects. It is some of the best free entertainment in Sydney.

Hyde Park Bordered by Elizabeth and College Streets and adjacent to the city, Hyde Park is the most central of Sydney's parks. In the early colonial days it was the scene of colourful horse racing meetings. Now it is a peaceful, 42 acre refuge from the continual pace of city life. Within its boundaries are the Anzac War Memorial, a one hundred foot high red granite building with a beautiful white marble interior open to the public from 10 a.m. to 4.30 p.m. Monday-Friday, 9 a.m. to 12 noon on Saturdays and 2 p.m. to 5 p.m. on Sundays. You can also see the magnificent bronze statues of the Archibald Memorial Fountain, the F. J. Walker Family Fountain, and Busby's Bore Fountain on the site of Sydney's first water supply.

Rushcutters Bay Park A large recreation and sports area leading on to the bay and its interesting marina for ocean-going yachts.

Cooper Park Manning Road, Double Bay, a bushland setting with picnic facilities, tennis courts and playgrounds.

Centennial Park A 480 acre area east of the city with facilities for horse riding and many spectator sports.

Nielsen Park Vaucluse, a popular swimming area in the harbour where you will see some of Sydney's best-known faces.

PARRAMATTA

Fifteen miles west of the city is Parramatta, the second oldest settlement in Australia, and the site of several colonial buildings of significance.

Old Government House This is the oldest remaining public building in Australia and one of the most historic. The main rooms are furnished in the style of the times and the house is open to the public on Tuesdays, Thursdays, Sundays and public holidays from 10 a.m. to 12.30 p.m. and 2 p.m. to 4.30 p.m.

Hambledon Cottage Hassall Street. Open for inspection 11 a.m. to 5 p.m. Wednesdays to Sunday.

Linden House and Lancers Barracks Smith Street. Linden House Museum has a weapon collection covering the period 1885-1960. Also on display are period uniforms and equipment.

Experiment Farm Cottage 9 Ruse Street, Harris Park (next to Parramatta) Australia's first wheat was grown here. Open weekdays 10 a.m. to 12.30 p.m. and 2 p.m. to 4 p.m., Saturdays 10 a.m. to 12.30 p.m., Sundays 2 p.m. to 5 p.m.

HOTELS, RESTAURANTS AND ENTERTAINMENT

ACCOMMODATION

Sydney has several international standard hotels, many luxury motels and hundreds of lesser hotels and guest houses providing good, clean accommodation. Reservations can be made for all of these through the N.S.W. Government Tourist Bureau, independent travel bureaux or direct with the accommodation itself. There are also serviced and furnished apartments, flats and holiday houses available through real estate agents.

Recommended first class accommodation
Wentworth Hotel, 61 Phillip Street, 2-0370.
Chevron Hotel, 81 Macleay Street, Potts Point, 35-0433.
Menzies Hotel, 14 Carrington Street, 2-0232.
Carlton Rex Hotel, 56 Castlereagh Street, 28-5541.
Australia Hotel, 45 Castlereagh Street, 2-0388.
Crest Hotel, Darlinghurst Road, Kings Cross, 35-2755.
Astor Motor Hotel, Cahill Expressway, Woolloomooloo, 35-5366.
Top of the Cross Travelodge, 110 Darlinghurst Road, Kings Cross, 31-0911.
Cosmopolitan Motor Inn, Knox Street, Double Bay, 36-6871.
Rushcutters Bay Travelodge, 110 Bayswater Road, Rushcutters Bay, 31-2171.
The Town House, 23 Elizabeth Bay Road, Elizabeth Bay, 35-3244.
Gazebo Hotel, 2 Elizabeth Bay Road, Kings Cross, 35-1999.
Chateau Commodore, 14 Macleay Street, Potts Point, 35-2500.
Texas Tavern Hotel, 44 Macleay Street, Kings Cross, 35-1211.

RESTAURANTS

Sydney has hundreds of restaurants catering to every taste and pocket and including traditional cuisines from France, Italy, India, Indonesia, America, Mexico, Hungary, Yugoslavia, Germany, Lebanon, Japan, Switzerland, Sweden, China, Greece, Spain. Styles range from luxurious chandelier settings to back street bistros. It is wise to book where possible.

Suggested

Argyle Tavern Argyle Street, 27-1613. Authentic early Sydney atmosphere in convict built bond store. Roasts a speciality. Dancing.

Doyles 11 Marine Parade, Watsons Bay, 337-2007. Fresh seafood served in cafe setting by the beach.

Chelsea 119 Macleay Street, Potts Point, 35-4333. Luxurious but intimate setting, superb French style cuisine, excellent service, dancing.

Caprice Sunderland Avenue, Rose Bay, 37-6787. Built entirely over the water, cocktail bar, dancing, luxurious atmosphere.

Coachmen 763 Bourke Street, Redfern, 69-5110. Highly recommended by the *New York Times*. Convict built house surrounded by gardens. Excellent wine list, cocktail bar, and dancing.

Captain Cook Floating Restaurant Rose Bay, 37-7941. Winner of 1970 Golden Plate Award, fully air conditioned, two cocktail bars, Lunch–dinner 7 days a week.

Beppi's 29 Yurong Street, East Sydney, 31-4558. Superb Italian food, excellent service.

Mamma Maria's 154 Brougham Street, Kings Cross, 31-4273. Good but inexpensive Italian food in noisy, friendly atmosphere. Cocktail bar.

Summit Australia Square Tower, 27-9777. Unique revolving

restaurant 47 floors above Sydney Harbour. Fantastic views as you eat. Cocktail bar.

The French Restaurant 379a Bourke Street, Taylor Square, 31-3605. Established since 1880, once a rendezvous for French officers. Old world decor, French cuisine, dancing.

Nagoya Sukiyaki House 186 Victoria Street, Kings Cross, 35-1711. Authentic Japanese food, decor and service. Food cooked at your table by kimono clad waitresses.

Patrick's 152 Jersey Road, Paddington, 32-2882. Good food and wine, fashionable meeting place for Sydney's young and sophisticated.

ENTERTAINMENT

You'll never be short of something to do at night in Sydney. There is entertainment on every level to suit every taste. Below are a few suggestions for a night you will remember.

Silver Spade Room, Chevron Hotel 81 Macleay Street, Potts Point, 35-0433. Sydney's biggest and best night club. A great atmosphere, two shows nightly, many of the greats of international show business play at the Silver Spade. Be sure to book.

Les Girls All Male Revue 2c Roslyn Street, Kings Cross, 35-6630. Sammy Lee's slick, fast moving production starring some of the worlds best female impersonators. Brilliant staging and costuming. Restaurant and V.I.P. cocktail bar. A night to both entertain and amaze you.

Whisky a Go Go 152 William Street, Kings Cross, 31-5164. A huge two level discotheque and night club. Three cabaret rooms, top bands, 20 gorgeous go-go girls dance in golden cages. Wine, dine and dance to rock music till 3 a.m., seven nights a week.

Texas Tavern Hotel 44 Macleay Street, Kings Cross, 35-1211. Unusual complex of cocktail bars, restaurants and entertainment rooms—The Red Garter has gay nineties atmosphere, Dixieland band and floor show; The Barn puts on two country and western style floorshows a night, The El Camino Real Restaurant serves authentic Mexican cuisine.

Music Hall Restaurant 156 Military Road, Neutral Bay, 90-8222. Wine and dine in old turn of the century style theatre and watch melodrama on stage. Join in the fun and hiss the villain. Includes singing waiters. Be sure to book.

Pink Pussycat 86a Darlinghurst Road, Kings Cross, 31-6715. Striptease with more strip than tease. Interesting line-up of acts, shows run continuously till 3 a.m. Admission $2.00.

The Bull 'n' Bush 113 William Street, Kings Cross, 31-4627. Restaurant with old time musical revue. The diners become part of the act. An uproariously funny night. Must book well in advance.

The Argyle Tavern 18 Argyle Street, Sydney, 27-1613. Restaurant with captivating colonial atmosphere. Located in 137 year old convict built bond store in Rocks area. Spit roasts, waitresses in period costume, lots of rollicking fun and singing of old bush songs. Dancing.

ART GALLERIES

Art Gallery of N.S.W. Art Gallery Road, Domain, 221-2100. Exhibitions of paintings and other art forms from Australia and overseas.

Native Art Gallery 13 Gurner Street, Paddington, 31-9441. Melanesian art, carvings, etc.

The Strawberry Hill Gallery 533 Elizabeth Street South, 609-1005. Various exhibitions.

Barry Stern 28 Glenmore Road, Paddington, 31-7676. Mixed exhibitions. Some of the best of the newer Australian art.

Bonython Art Gallery 52 Victoria Street, Paddington, 31-5087.

Changing exhibitions of some of the best known names in Australian art.

Rudy Komon Art Gallery   124 Jersey Road, Woollahra, 32-2533. Run by well-known art expert and dealer.

Gallery "A"   21 Gipps Street, Paddington, 31-9720. Has excellent reputation for high standard of Australian and overseas exhibitions.

Hollsworth Galleries   86 Holdsworth Street, Woollahra, 32-1364. Continuous exhibitions of paintings, graphics, and sculpture. Changes every three weeks.

Villiers Art Gallery   Bay Street, Double Bay, 328-1119. Paintings by famous Australian artists.

Abbia Gallery   133 New South Head Road, Edgecliff, 32-2431. Collection of African primitive art including bronzes, masks and artifacts.

David Jones Art Gallery   In the Elizabeth Street department store, 2-0664.

Blaxland Gallery   At Farmers department store, cnr Pitt and Market Streets. Changing exhibitions of all kinds of art and craft.

Watters Gallery   Known for its *avant-garde* exhibitions of new Australian artists.

Central Street Gallery   1 Central Street, 26-3116.

Clune Galleries   171 Macquarie Street, 221-2166.

Tapa Traders Gallery   Shop 1, 74 Archer Street, Chatswood, 412-2593. Melanesian artifacts from New Guinea, Solomon Islands and New Hebrides.

Primitive Art Gallery   253 Pitt Street, 61-4326. Shields, masks, drums, figures, pottery, etc from primitive cultures.

The Argyle Arts Centre   18 Argyle Street, in 137 year old Argyle Store and Bond. Displays of gold, silver, copper, leatherwork, fabrics, sculpture, pottery, etc. Artists and craftsmen on premises.

Macquarie Galleries   40 King Street, 29-5787.

Artarmon Galleries   479 Pacific Highway, Artarmon, 42-0321.

SPORTS

Sydney's climate makes outdoor sports especially popular and public recreation areas cater for all kinds of organised sport. There are many good public golf courses close to the city—Moore Park, Randwick, Bondi—and arrangements to play as guests at the excellent private golf clubs can be made—Royal Sydney Golf Club is the largest. There are championship tennis courts at White City and Rushcutters Bay and many other private and public centres. There are also ten pin bowling centres, riding schools and bridle paths, indoor and outdoor swimming pools, lawn bowls, squash courts, croquet greens, and ice skating. Boats for fishing, including game fishing, cruising and sailing can be hired at waterfront resorts.

Spectator sports include cricket, rugby, soccer, Australian Rules football, motor racing at Armaroo Park and Warwick Farm, night trotting at Harold Park, greyhound racing at Wentworth Park, and horseracing at Randwick, Rosehill and Warwick Farm racecourses. Further information from the daily papers, the telephone directory or the N.S.W. Government Tourist Bureau.

PRINCIPAL SURF BEACHES

North of the harbour   Manly, Queenscliff, Freshwater, Curl Curl, Deewhy, Long Reef, Collaroy, Narrabeen, Turimetta, Warriewood, Mona Vale, Bungan Beach, Newport, Bilgola, Avalon, Whale Beach, Palm Beach.

South of the harbour   Bondi, Tamarama, Bronte, Clovelly, Coogee, Maroubra, Malabar, Cronulla, Marley, Wattamolla.

THEATRES

Cinema   Ascot, 246 Pitt Street; Barclay, 681 George Street; Capitol, 12 Campbell Street, Haymarket; Century, 586 George Street; Embassy, 79 Castlereagh Street; Forum, 747 George Street; Gala, 236 Pitt Street; Liberty, 232 Pitt Street; Lido, 357 George Street; Lyceum, 210 Pitt Street; Mayfair, 75 Castlereagh Street; Paramount, 525 George Street; Paris, 205 Liverpool Street; Plaza, 600 George Street; Regent, 487 George Street; Roma, 628 George Street; Savoy, 29 Bligh Street; St. James, 109 Elizabeth Street; State, 49 Market Street; Town, 303 Pitt Street; Rapallo, 527 George Street.

Live   Ensemble, 78 McDougall Street, Milson's Point; Genesian, 420 Kent Street; New Theatre, 151 William Street; Metro Theatre, 28 Orwell Street, Potts Point; Old Tote Parade Theatre, Anzac Parade, Kensington; Playbox Theatre, 138 Phillip Street; Phillip Theatre, 150 Elizabeth Street; Independent Theatre, 269 Miller Street, North Sydney; Theatre Royal, 59 Castlereagh Street; Sir John Clancy Auditorium, University of N.S.W., Kingsford; Wayside Theatre, Hume Street, Kings Cross.

Theatre Restaurants   Music Hall Restaurant, 156 Military Road, Neutral Bay; Doncaster Theatre Restaurant, 266 Anzac Parade, Kensington; The Bull 'n' Bush, William Street, Kings Cross.

SHOPPING

Main Department Stores   David Jones', three city stores in Elizabeth Street, George Street, Market Street; Farmer's, cnr Pitt and Market Streets; Grace Bros, Broadway; McDowell's, King and George Streets; Walton's, George and Park Streets, Curzon's, Pitt through to George Street; Hordern Bros, Pitt Street; Mark Foys, Liverpool Street near Museum Station.

Duty Free Shops   78 Castlereagh Street and at Kingsford Smith Airport, Mascot. For people travelling overseas only.

Sydney has a great range of specialty shops and boutiques selling every kind of local and imported merchandise. There are eleven shopping arcades, most of them running off Pitt and Castlereagh Streets where you find the most concentrated retail area. The near city suburb of Double Bay also has many specialty shops, especially for men's and women's fashion. A Saturday morning visit to this colourful shopping centre can make quite a fascinating excursion.

PLACES TO VISIT OUT OF TOWN

HAWKESBURY RIVER

'On the Rhine, on the Mississippi, and on the Hawkesbury alike, there is created an idea that if the traveller would only leave the boat and wander inland, he would be repaid by the revelation of marvellous beauties of nature, beauties which have perhaps never yet met the eyes of man.' The fact that the 19th century writer Anthony Trollope grouped the Hawkesbury River with these two other great waterways suggests the impact its beauty had on him. In a hundred years that beauty has in no way diminished. The paddle steamers that once plied its broad reaches have given way to modern ferries, motor cruisers, houseboats and yachts, but the sculptured sandstone cliffs and the strangely haunting trees they harbour are still there and the thousands of acres of surrounding bushland have been shielded from the ravages of civilization.

The Hawkesbury enters the Pacific at Broken Bay, twenty miles north of Sydney and it is this region especially, with its adjacent Pittwater and the Cowan Creek and Berowra Creek tributaries, that has become Australia's most renowned holiday retreat and water recreation area. There are over 400 miles of shoreline and countless inviting inlets to be explored by boat. The fishing is excellent and facilities for water travellers are strategically placed along the way. Cruising boats are rented by:

Halvorsen Boats, Box 21, P.O. Turrumurra, N.S.W. Phone 47 9011. The Halvorsen fleet of over 60 motor cruisers ranges from 25-footers to 38-footers and is located at the beautiful land-locked harbour of Bobbin Head in the Ku-ring-gai Chase National Park. Cruisers include all facilities, sleep up to 9 people, and can be easily handled by inexperienced people. Rates vary according to size of cruiser and the season but go as low as $60 for 5 days. A detailed brochure is available from Halvorsen.

'Cruis Craft' Hire Cruisers, Box 18, Berowra Waters, N.S.W. Phone 610 1031. Fleet ranges from 4 berth 26-foot cruisers to 10 berth 36-footers. All facilities including hot showers on board. Rates from 5 days for $60., depending on time of the year. Brochure available.

Rent-a-Cruise of Australia, 10 The Plaza, Sailors Bay Road, Northbridge N.S.W. P.O. Box 56, Phone 95 5225. Rents houseboats it calls 'floating motel units' with fully self-contained luxurious accommodation for up to 6 persons. Hiring charges for the 33-foot vessels from $100 for 5 days and range upwards according to the time of the year.

KU-RING-GAI CHASE NATIONAL PARK

This magnificent area of 36,040 acres, which borders the southern banks of the Hawkesbury River, Cowan Creek, Pittwater and Broken Bay, was declared a national park in 1894 specifically 'to conserve the scenery and natural wonder of the sandstone bushland'. Today it is virtually a living museum of plants and animals native to the Sydney region. It also includes examples of very old aboriginal rock engravings. Take the Pacific Highway (No 1) north from Sydney to entrance near Mt Colah approximately 15 miles from the city. Enquiries to Superintendent, Ku-Ring-Gai Chase National Park, via Turramurra, 2074, Phone 47 9017.

THE BLUE MOUNTAINS

This scenic wonderland is part of the Great Dividing Range and rises from the coastal plains 40 miles west of Sydney. It encompasses 24 townships in an area of 520 square miles and contains some of the most spectacular mountain panoramas in Australia. The region was first penetrated in 1813 and is now extensively developed to cater for holiday-makers and tourists. Accommodation in the Blue Mountains includes hotels, motels, guest houses, holiday flats, cottages, cabins, caravan parks and camping grounds.

The mountains are broken by vast wooded valleys and precipitous gorges, waterfalls, caves (*see* Jenolan Caves) and startling rock formations. As well as an excellent road system there are hundreds of miles of bush tracks and trails that take travellers deep into the incredibly beautiful valleys. Above them hangs the vividly blue haze, a natural phenomenon from which the mountains get their name. Principal town is Katoomba, 68 miles from Sydney, elevation 3,336 ft. accessible from Sydney by road, small plane or fast, electric train. The town's name came from an aboriginal word meaning 'waterfalls' and some of the best in the area may be viewed from the lookouts and bush tracks (Try the 7 mile Prince Henry's Cliff Walk). With its sister town Leura, Katoomba has a population of 14,000 and facilities for swimming, golf, bowls, rock climbing, trotting, tennis, horse-riding, speedway racing, cinema and night clubs. There is also a Museum of Natural Art and some lovely gardens. Some of the most outstanding features nearby include Echo Point, a fantastic lookout across the Jamieson and Burragorang Valleys and the Three Sisters rock formation; the Leura Cascades, Katoomba Falls and Bridal Veil waterfall—all are floodlit between 7 p.m. and 9 p.m.; Sublime Point, Mt Solitary, Ruined Castle, Orphan Rock, Kings Tableland, Malaita Point, Eagle Hawk Rock, Cyclorama Point and Narrow Neck.

Many of these points of interest can be seen from the 5 mile Cliff Drive, which starts at the turn-off from the Great Western Highway on the western side of Katoomba.

Near Katoomba Falls a revolving restaurant gives diners superb views across the valleys. Here also is the terminal for the Scenic Railway and Skyway. The railway plunges passengers through an abandoned coal mine and down 750 feet to the bottom of the valley where they can explore the trails and fern grottos.

The Skyway is an aerial cable car that travels between cliff faces 1,000 ft. above the valley.

Fifteen-minute joy rides over the mountains are available at the Katoomba Airport. For the adventurous there are guides to take you on horseback safaris through the valleys. Other places worth visiting are Springwood—altitude 1,218 ft., pleasant year round climate, scenic walks and lookouts; Woodford—convicts' cell and whipping post at Ball's Camp; Blackheath—spectacular Blackheath Gorge, according to famous scientist Charles Darwin, the largest chasm on earth with perpendicular sides, 1,000 ft. waterfalls, annual Rhododendron Festival in November, many lookouts; Hazlebrook, Wentworth Falls, Lawson—all with waterfalls and scenic walks; 'Everglades'—a beautiful 12½-acre garden property in Denison Street, Leura with stonework terraces, exotic flowers cold climate arboretum. Access to the Blue Mountains from Sydney is along the Great Western Highway (No 32).

JENOLAN CAVES

Fifty miles from Katoomba, 113 miles from Sydney, these underground limestone caves are one of Australia's most remarkable geological phenomena. More than two million people have visited these awesome caverns since they were opened to the public over one hundred years ago. Surrounded by a 6,000 acre wildlife reserve, the caves, formed half a million years ago by water erosion and underground streams, have breathtaking pools and extraordinary stalactites and stalagmites. Expert guides lead parties through miles of illuminated caverns that were once the hideout of an escaped convict turned bushranger. Tours take about one and a half hours although some caves may be explored alone. Special photographic tours are available daily at 11 a.m. and 4 p.m. Regular inspection hours are: Morning 10.00, 10.15, 10.30, 11.00 a.m. Afternoon 1.30, 1.45, 2.00, 2.30, 4.00 p.m.; Evening 8.00 p.m.

The 6,000 acre Jenolan Caves Reserve has many nature trails along which all geological, botanical and zoological features are labelled and explained. Animal and birdlife includes rock wallabies, waterdragons, cunningham skinks, spiny anteaters, ring-railed possums, sugar gliders, wombats, grey kangaroos and the black swan, rock-warblers, superb lyrebirds, satin bowerbirds, king parrots, gang gang cockatoos, yellow robins, white-eared honeyeaters, fantailed cuckoos, wedge-tailed eagles and many others.

Accommodation is at the tudor styled, seventy-three year old Jenolan Caves House. Bar facilities and recreation rooms are available. Motorists should take the Great Western Highway from Sydney to the Jenolan Caves turnoff at the Lett River Bridge, 84 miles from Sydney. Trains leave Central Station, Sydney, on Monday, Wednesday, Friday, Saturday and Sunday mornings and link up with the Jenolan road-coach at Mt Victoria. Details of accommodation, cave inspection and packaged coach and train tours available in brochure form from New South Wales Government Tourist Bureau, 8-10 Martin Place, Sydney. Phone 2 0136.

THE ROYAL NATIONAL PARK

This 40,000 acre tract of natural forest and river scenery is located less than 20 miles south of Sydney and contains more than 700 species of Australian flora, nearly 250 different types of birds and many of Australia's unusual marsupials. Many walking tracks and 36 miles of good roads crisscross the park. From the hills in the south the Hacking River cuts the park in two and flows all the way to Port Hacking, its northern boundary. The park's eastern boundary is made up of ten miles of Pacific surf beaches and rocky headlands. At Garie and Wattamolla both rock and surf fishing are available and the latter has a natural lagoon swimming pool fed by a waterfall. The main town in the Royal National Park is Audley, a pretty village on the river with first class guest accommodation and a modern restaurant. Boats can be hired to enjoy the river scenery and often swans and wild ducks will follow rowers. Tea rooms, camping grounds and facilities for picnics are all available. The most interesting road is Lady Carrington Drive, which runs about six miles from Audley along the upper reaches of the river and traverses areas of towering rainforests and semi-tropical vegetation. Amongst the ferns and vines can be found the wonga pigeon, green catbird, lyrebird, blue kingfisher, rufous fantail, wallabies, possums and the flying phalanger.

How to get there *By train*—a train for the park leaves all city stations every weekday morning and there are several on weekends and holidays. Exact times are available at all railway stations. *By car*—travel south from Sydney along the Princes Highway and turn off at Loftus. If coming from the south turn off at Waterfall. *By launch*—Launches connect with trains at Cronulla and travel to Audley and return. Launches leave Cronulla at 10 a.m. and 2 p.m.

every day in January and alternate days in other months. Phone the N.S.W. Govt. Tourist Bureau, 2 0136 for details. Coach tours are also available.

AFRICAN LION SAFARI

At Warragamba, one and a quarter hours drive from Sydney, sixty lions and cheetahs roam at large in a large park. Visitors can drive through in their cars and meet the animals face to face. Game wardens patrol the park at all times and African curios and carvings are on sale. Admission: adults $1.00. Children 40c. Pensioners 25c. The park is open Monday to Saturday, 10 a.m. to 5 p.m., Sunday 9 a.m. to 5 p.m. To get there travel west from Sydney on Highway 32 and turn south near Penrith, or on Highway 31 and turn west at Liverpool. For further information write to African Lion Safari Pty Ltd, Warragamba, N.S.W. 2752, or phone Warragamba 74 1113 (STD-047).

BULLENS ANIMAL WORLD

Located at Wallacia near the Warragamba lion park, Animal World includes over four miles of road winding through villages representing many countries of the animal world. See herds of elephants, camels, buffalo, donkeys, mules, welsh and shetland ponies, llamas, deer, goat, bison, chimpanzees, monkeys, kangaroos and emus. There are many baby animals children can play with.
Enquires phone: Wallacia 129 or Ludenham 12.

AUSTRALIAN REPTILE PARK

Located at Gosford, 54 miles north of Sydney, the park is actually a research station set up to investigate aspects of Australian reptiles and to extract vemon from snakes for use in snakebite antidotes developed by the Commonwealth Serum Laboratories. Each year about 5,000 snakes are milked by hand and the dangerous operation is often watched by visitors. Reptiles on view at the park include taipans, death adders, tiger snakes, rattlesnakes, black snakes, cobras, boa constrictors, pythons and crocodiles. Visitors may also mingle with tame wombats and kangaroos. Travel to Gosford by electric train or drive via the Pacific Highway.

THE CENTRAL COAST

The area known as the Central Coast begins immediately north of the Hawkesbury River, just over 30 miles from Sydney, and extends to Budgewoi and Munmorah Lakes. It is made up of hundreds of square miles of mountains, forests, lakes, beaches, orchards and farmlands. Because of its location between Sydney and Newcastle it is known as the "playground of two cities". The main towns are Gosford and Wyong and the area has many holiday resorts and amenities for vacationers. Fishing of all kinds is very good and there are wildlife sanctuaries for the nature lover. Golf, water skiing and surfing are all well catered for. You get there by train, or by car on the Pacific Highway. A comprehensive colour brochure on the region is available from the N.S.W. Government Tourist Bureau, 8-10 Martin Place, Sydney 2000, Phone 2 0136.

THE ILLAWARRA COAST

This popular district begins 20 miles south of Sydney and extends down the coast about 150 miles to Durras Water. Illawarra is an Aboriginal word meaning 'high place near the sea' and the area is noted for its spectacular lookouts across seascapes and lush dairying country. Mountain ranges, rainforests, waterfalls, lakes and rivers have all helped make the Illawarra a very popular holiday area and many resorts, particularly near the magnificent beaches and lakes, attract a steady stream of vacationers. Outstanding features include the fantastic Blowhole at Kiama, the waterfalls at Minnamurra, the Bulli lookout, the huge Port Kembla Steelworks, Sublime Point lookout and Lake Illawarra. Main towns are Wollongong, Kiama, Nowra, Shellharbour and Ulladulla. You travel to the Illawarra via the Princes Highway. A comprehensive colour brochure on the region is available from the N.S.W. Government Tourist Bureau, 8-10 Martin Place, Sydney 2000, Phone 2 0136.

TOURS IN AND AROUND SYDNEY

There are numerous day and half-day organised coach tours of Sydney and the surrounding districts and also harbour and river tours which offer the most interesting and economical way of seeing a lot in a short time. Commentaries are given on route and prices start from as low as $3.00. The N.S.W. Government Tourist Bureau run a series of tours that includes visiting places such as the Hawkesbury River (includes a cruise), Lion Safari, Royal National Park, Illawarra Lakes, Blue Mountains, and the Jenolan Caves. There are also tours of Sydney by night, historic Sydney and the northern beaches. A booklet available from the Bureau details all the tours and their prices. Information also from Pioneer tours 2 0651, Redline 31 0886, Parlorcars 211 1611, Pykes 27 5633.

Sydney Harbour Ferries Pty. Ltd. operate an excellent Harbour Cruise which leaves from No 4 jetty, Circular Quay at 2.30 p.m. on Wednesdays, Saturdays, Sundays, Public Holidays and every day during January. Prices: adults 75c, Children 35c. The company also run a popular River Cruise up the Parramatta and Lane Cove Rivers which leaves from No 5 jetty, Circular Quay at 2.30 p.m. on Sundays and Public Holidays. Prices: adults 75c, Children 35c. Enquiries: Sydney Harbour Ferries Pty. Ltd., Circular Quay, Sydney 2000, Phone 27 5276.

There is also a three-hour Coffee Cruise of the main and Middle Harbour aboard the M.V. *Captain Cook*, with a commentary on points of interest by the tour hostess. The tour vessel departs from No 6 Circular Quay at 10 a.m. on Tuesdays and Thursdays and 1.15 p.m. on Saturdays, Sundays and Public Holidays. Prices: Adults $3.00, Children $1.50. Tickets are available at the gangway, or book through the N.S.W. Government Tourist Bureau. The M.V. *Captain Cook* is also available for private charter.

N.S.W. COASTLINE

Almost anywhere on the coast of New South Wales is a good spot to sit down for a picnic, absorb the view, take photographs, or catch a fish. Swimming, particularly surfing, is best kept for patrolled beaches, where life savers set up flags to show the safe areas and stand ready to pull you out and revive you if you get into difficulty.

NORTH FROM SYDNEY

North of Sydney, the coast divides conveniently into five sections; all reached by the Sydney to Brisbane Pacific Highway, part of National Highway No 1, the coastal route around Australia.

The Central Coast is nearest to Sydney. It begins on the northern shores of the Hawkesbury River, 30 odd miles from Sydney, and extends to Budgewoi and Munmorah Lakes. It covers hundreds of square miles of mountains, forests, lakes, beaches, orchards and farmlands. It faces the picturesque estuary of the Hawkesbury River, surrounds the winding foreshores of Brisbane Water (an inland lake emptying into Broken Bay opposite the mouth of the Hawkesbury), borders Tuggerah Lakes, and is fringed by a superb strip of ocean front. Situated midway between Sydney and Newcastle, and not very far from either, the Central Coast is a playground for both cities.

Gosford, on Brisbane Water, is the focal point of the area. Local attractions include the *Australian Reptile Park*, one mile north, where visitors may watch the operation of 'milking' 5,000 snakes a year for their venom. A steel and concrete dinosaur outside the park is 18 feet high and 90 feet from nose to tail tip.

Beach resorts in the area include Terrigal, Avoca, Wagstaff, Woy Woy, Ettalong, Pearl Beach, Patonga, Tuggerah Lakes, The Entrance, Budgewai, Toukley, Bateau Bay and Blue Lagoon.

Newcastle, predominantly an industrial city, has several beaches, one of them, Newcastle Beach, only 200 yards from the main street. Eight Newcastle beaches are patrolled daily from August to May.

Merewether, at the southern end of the long arc of sand commencing in the north of Bar Beach, can usually be depended on for good surf, and also has a large swimming pool. Bar Beach, named after a rock bar which protects it, is floodlit at night.

Dixon Park, midway between Bar Beach and Newcastle Beach, is a secluded spot where a good surf usually rolls. Another secluded beach, with easy walking distance of the city, is **Nobbys Beach.**

On the north side of Newcastle Harbour are **Stockton** and **North Stockton Beaches,** which are at the southernmost end of a 30 mile stretch of sand reaching north to Port Stephens.

The **Lower North Coast** begins at the twin towns of Forster and Tuncurry, a little north of Newcastle, and extends northwards to take in the country around the Manning, Hastings, and Macleay Rivers.

Port Macquarie is an historic seaside town in the region. Founded as a convict settlement in 1821, it still has some of its old buildings, notably **St Thomas' Church of England,** the third oldest church in Australia, designed by convict architect Francis Greenway and built between 1824 and 1828. The **Hastings District Historical Society Museum,** housed in convict-built quarters, has a collection of chains, cat o' nine tails, and other relics of the early days.

Other centres on the Lower North Coast include Taree, Kempsey, Wingham, Gloucester, Stroud and Wauchope. Beach resorts include Black Head, Camden Haven, Crescent Head, Crowdy Head, Forster, Grassy Head, Harrington, Hat Head, Old Bar, South West Rocks, Tuncurry. **Comboyne Plateau,** inland from Camden Haven, midway between Taree and Port Macquarie, is a spectacular upland where rich pockets of farming country intermingle with native rainforest, in which there are almost a hundred waterfalls and cascades.

Wallis Lake, a beautiful sheet of water 16 miles long and in places six miles wide, is a paradise for fishermen where flathead, bream, whiting and blackfish abound.

The **Mid North Coast** begins at Nambucca, extends northwards along the next hundred miles of surf swept golden beachlands to Yamba, at the mouth of the Clarence River, inland to the Jacaranda Festival City of *Grafton*, and the mountain timberlands of Dorrigo.

Coff's Harbour, Australia's largest timber port, has a strongly sub-tropical atmosphere, as befits its position among the banana plantations that penetrate every valley and contour every slope of the beautiful hills surrounding the town.

Beach resorts along the Mid North Coast include Coff's Harbour, Corindi Beach, Iluka, Minniewater, Mullaway, Mylestom, Nambucca Heads, Red Rock, Sawtell, Scott's Head, Urunga, Valla Beach, Woolgoolga, Wooli and Yamba.

Summerland, the **Far North Coast,** begins at Evans Head, and goes to the Queensland border. It includes Australia's most easterly point, **Cape Byron.** Perhaps its most spectacular feature is 3,795 feet **Mt Warning,** overlooking the whole panorama of the **Tweed Valley,** rich with canefields, banana plantations and lush dairy pastures.

Cities and towns in Summerland include Lismore, Kyogle, Casino and Coraki (all on the Richmond River), Murwillumbah (on the Tweed River). Beach resorts include Ballina, Brunswick Heads, Byron Bay, Evans Head, Fingal Head, Kingscliff and Tweed Heads.

SOUTH FROM SYDNEY

The **Illawarra** and **South Coast Riviera,** a land of panoramas, surf washed beach resorts, dairy meadows, streams and waterfalls, lakes and rivers, as well as Australia's third largest industrial city, Wollongong, a giant industrial complex, coal mines and a busy seaport. It all begins 20 miles or so south of Sydney.

The panoramas are best seen from such well known lookouts as **Sublime Point** (just off the Princes Highway 40 miles south of Sydney)), **Mt Keira Lookout** (a few miles further south overlooking Wollongong), **Saddleback Mountain** (4 miles from Kiama) and **Mt Cambewarra** (2,300 feet high, at the eastern end of Kangaroo Valley, near Nowra).

Lake Illawarra stretches from the Pacific Ocean between Port Kembla and Shellharbour to the foothills of the Illawarra Range, providing Wollongong and Port Kembla with a convenient, natural playground.

Port Kembla Steelworks may be inspected by arrangement with the Visitors' Reception Centre at the steelworks, providing a few days' notice is given.

Kiama, where the Blowhole is a major attraction, Austinmer, Bulli, Burrill Lake, Conjola, Durras Lake, Gerringong, Gerroa, Huskisson, Jamberoo, Minnamurra, Shellharbour, Stanwell Park, St Georges Basin, Sussex Inlet, Tabourie Lake, Thirroul, Ulladulla and Warrawong are all beach and lake resorts in the Illawarra and South Coast Riviera.

Wollongong Beach is right at the end of the city's main street. In all there are seventeen main surfing beaches in the Greater Wollongong area.

The **Far South Coast** of New South Wales begins near Bateman's Bay, goes south to the Victorian border. It is an amalgam of open ocean beaches and safe anchorages, mirror lakes and tranquil rivers, craggy cliffs and bold headlands, lush farmlands and enthralling bush scenery.

Bega, 'capital of the Far South Coast' is at the junction of the Bega and Brago Rivers, in the centre of a rich and fertile valley.

Bermagui is the chief port on the Far South Coast for commercial tuna boats, and a favourite spot for amateur fishermen of all ages.

Eden is another port favoured by many professional fishing boats.

Boydtown, an old ghost town seven miles south of Eden, recalls the days when whales were hunted along this coast. Benjamin Boyd built the town in 1843 as a seaport and whaling station. He believed it would become a major port. All that remains of his endeavours are Boydtown's church, now in ruins, the Sea Horse Inn (again in use as a hostelry), and a tower, which although intended as a lighthouse never helped a ship into port. One thing that does remain is Boydtown's beautiful beach, on Twofold Bay.

Other beaches are at Batehaven, Bateman's Bay, Bermagui, Dalmeny, Durras Lake, Eden, Merimbula, Narooma, Pambula, Tathra, Tuross Heads, Wallaga Lake and Wombyn Lake.

THE SOUTHERN HIGHLANDS

SNOWY MOUNTAINS

The Southern Highlands, approached from Sydney down the Hume Highway through the historic towns of **Camden** and **Picton,** begin in the Braemar-Mittagong country, some 70 odd miles south of Sydney, and continue to the country around Goulburn.

The region is one of lush grazing lands for sheep, stud beef and dairy cattle, and of thoroughbred horse studs, intermingled with stone and pome fruit orchards and flourishing vegetable gardens. Exotic deciduous trees thrive in the fresh upland climate, giving their best show in autumn, while hawthorn bushes and hedges bring a touch of old England to the landscape.

The invigorating climate of their 2,000 to 2,500 feet has made the Southern Highlands into a popular holiday spot for Sydney people, their favourite destinations being **Mittagong, Bowral, Moss Vale** and **Bundanoon.** Of these, only Mittagong is on the Hume Highway. Bowral, Moss Vale and Bundanoon, together with Sutton Forest, Exeter, Penrose, Wingello and Tallong, are on the Highland Way, which branches off the Hume Highway at Mittagong and rejoins it at Marulan. Other small centres, such as Robertson, Kangaloon, Glenquarry and Burrawang, and attractions such as **Fitzroy Falls** and **Kangaroo Valley,** are found on the picturesque roads leading from Bowral and Moss Vale to the Illawarra and South Coast districts.

Several well known festivals are staged within the Southern Highlands. One such is Bowral's popular **Tulip Time Festival,** held each October. A golfing festival, the **Golden Leaves Golf Festival,** is played yearly on a different course in the area in April, a time of the year chosen because of the autumn colours.

Mittagong nestles in the valley of the Nattai River near its source, beneath the rocky buttress of 2,790 feet high Mt Gibraltar, highest point in the region. Its **Dahlia Festival Week** is held each February. **Lake Alexandra** is ten minutes walk from town.

Moss Vale is centre of a scenic district. Fitzroy Falls, for instance, are only 11 miles away.

Bowral and district are particularly popular with hikers and horesriders. In October, tulips take over **Corbett Gardens,** and the grounds of institutions, schools and private homes throughout the town.

Berrima is an historic village, many of its old sandstone buildings, dating from the 1830s, still in good condition. The Surveyor-General Inn, named after Sir Thomas Mitchell, who founded the town in 1829, is the oldest continuously licensed hotel in Australia still trading within its original walls. 'The Historic Village of Berrima', a folder giving fairly detailed information, is available from New South Wales Government Tourist Bureaus.

Wombeyan Caves, 40 miles west of Mittagong, 117 miles from Sydney, have three limestone caves open for public inspection. The road from Mittagong runs through spectacular mountain country.

Goulburn is the largest and most important centre between Sydney and the Federal capital, Canberra. It is a fairly typical Australian inland city, a wool and stock selling centre, with some industry. Its main interest for visitors lies in its architecture. Buildings of an earlier age include its two cathedrals—**St Saviour's Church of England** and **St Peter and Paul's Roman Catholic Church** and its **Court House.** These contrast with such contemporary buildings as the Lilac Time Hall and the Workers' Club.

Each October, Goulburn stages its **Lilac Time Festival,** one of the largest festivals in the State.

The Snowy Mountains, part of the Great Dividing Range of eastern Australia, cover thousands of square miles of mountains and high plains in the south-east of New South Wales.

It is the land of Australia's highest peaks, its biggest national park, its only glacial lakes (four of them) and its most extensive snowfields.

Mt Kosciusko, named by Polish explorer Strzelecki in honour of his country's national hero, is the highest peak in Australia (7,314 feet). Other tall peaks, all higher by far than anywhere else in Australia, include Mt Townsend (7,251 feet), Mt Twynam (7,207 feet), North Ramshead (7,197 feet), Mt Carruthers (7,042 feet), Muellers Peak (6,987 feet) and Mt Northcote (6,986 feet).

In winter, snow sports are the main attraction of the Snowy Mountains. On the slopes of Kosciusko and on nearby peaks from June to October, there is mile upon glistening mile of smooth, deep snow. As well as slopes that offer an irresistible challenge to the expert, Kosciusko and nearby mountains have gentle nursery slopes for beginners.

Main centres for snow sports are Thredbo Alpine Village, Smiggin Holes, Wilson's Valley, Diggers Creek, Perisher Valley, Charlotte's Pass, Guthega (no commercial accommodation) and Kiandra, which claims to have been the birthplace of skiing as a sport in 1861.

More and more people are finding that the Snowy Mountains can be just as fascinating in summer when the ground is covered with so many varieties of wildflowers that the tourist brochures hardly exaggerate by describing them as a 'veritable carpet across the valleys'. The eucalyptus-scented mountain air gives an extra stimulus to the bracing summer climate.

Among summer attractions are trout fishing in stream and lake, boating, trail-riding on horseback, picnicking, golf, swimming, bushwalking, motoring, riding chairlifts, photographing the wildflowers.

Motorists driving between Sydney and Melbourne find the **Alpine Way** an interesting variation on the other routes. It can be done in two days with an overnight stop at Thredbo.

Cooma, a comfortable day's drive from either Sydney or Melbourne, is the headquarters town of the Snowy Mountains region. The Avenue of Flags in Centennial Park there represents 27 countries, in recognition of the birthplaces of many men from overseas who worked on the Scheme.

The **Snowy Mountains Hydro-Electric Scheme** is an $800 million dollar project involving 16 large dams and many smaller ones, seven power stations, almost 100 miles of tunnels, and more than 80 miles of aqueducts. Building all this involved construction of 1,000 miles of roads and tracks, and many towns, villages and work camps. The scheme has a capacity of nearly 4,000,000 kilowatts of electricity and supplies almost 2,000,000 acre feet of extra water for irrigation each year. The fundamental concept of the scheme is to prevent water on the eastern slopes of the ranges from flowing via the Snowy River into the sea, but to tunnel it back under the ranges into the Murrumbidgee and Murray Rivers, which flow westwards through Australia's dry interior.

Conducted coach tours of the Snowy Mountains Scheme operate daily from Cooma for one, two or three days. Private motorists may tour the area; lookout points with explanatory notice boards are situated at the principal dams and power stations. Inspections of Tumut 1 underground power station may be made several times daily.

Trout fishing is popular in the Snowy Mountains. **Lake Eucumbene** is open all year. Big brown and rainbow trout also abound in rivers and streams throughout the area.

Information on the Snowy Mountains and the Snowy Mountains Hydro-electric Scheme is available from Cooma Visitors' Centre, Centennial Park, Cooma; Kosciusko National Park Visitors' Centre, Sawpit Creek, Mt Kosciusko; Snowy Mountains Authority Information Centres at Cooma and Khancoban.

NEW ENGLAND

From the Moonbi Range, near Tamworth, the New England Tableland stretches 200 miles north to the Queensland border. New England is a high country by Australian standards, much of it over 3,000 feet. At Round Mountain, on its eastern rim, it rises to 5,280 feet.

Despite its altitude, much of New England is admirably suited for agriculture. The rich soils of the plateau receive more than 30 inches of rain annually, and have been intensively cultivated, especially around the main centres. These abundant, more closely settled areas are at their best from September to December, with sheep grazing in improved pastures, mile upon mile of apple and cherry orchards, prosperous dairy farms, acres of maize, peas, potatoes and cabbage, all thriving in the spring sunshine.

Autumn is also a pleasant season in New England, for the pioneers nostalgically planted their new gardens and roadsides with thousands of deciduous trees from Britain. In March and April, streets and parks glow with the russet-gold leaves from pinoak and claret ash, poplar and silver birch.

Armidale is well known as a city of churches and schools, with two magnificent cathedrals, St Peter's and St Mary's, a number of impressively styled churches, the University of New England, Armidale Teacher's College, Armidale High School, the Armidale School, Armidale Technical College, five or six other major schools and seven preparatory schools.

Points of interest in Armidale include: Hinton Benefaction Art Gallery (at Armidale Teachers' College), a restored mid-Victorian era Standard School at the Teachers' College, Folk Museum, Central Park (where there is a relief map showing tourist attractions of the city and district). In the nearby countryside are Dangar's Falls, Ebor Falls, the 1,500 feet twin falls of Wollomombi and Chandler, Metz and Hillgrove Gorges, Big Hill (a 2,250 feet descent in seven miles on the Armidale-Kempsey Road), New England National Park, with its rain forest and Point Lookout, Oaky River Hydro-electric Scheme, the old mining settlement of Hillgrove. Armidale's Tourist Bureau is in Rusden Street.

Glen Innes is famous for its gardens, particularly for its dahlias and roses. Its Rose Festival is held around October—November each year. **Stonehenge,** an unusual rock formation, is seven miles south. There is a Visitors Information Centre in Grey Street.

Inverell is on the Macintyre River, inland from the New England Highway, with pleasant parks along the river. Its annual Floral Week is in October. At **Yaralla,** a private property 19 miles west, visitors are welcome to see the extensive garden with lily ponds, fernery, rock gardens, glasshouse and museum with over ,1000 geological specimens and rare shells. Preferred days are Wednesdays, Thursdays, weekends.

Uralla's appeal for visitors lies mainly in its connection with bushranger Thunderbolt. **Thunderbolt's Rock** is near Uralla, Thunderbolt's grave in Uralla Cemetery.

Tenterfield, near the Queensland border, is credited with being the birthplace of Australian Federation. It was at Tenterfield School of Arts, on 24 October 1889, that Australian statesman Sir Henry Parkes made the speech that gave impetus to the Federation movement. The building has been preserved as a library.

Other centres in New England include Guyra, Walcha, Bingara and Urbenville.

CENTRAL WESTERN NEW SOUTH WALES

THE RIVERINA

Colourful region of early Australian pioneering, gold rushes and bushrangers, the region immediately west of the Blue Mountains, calling itself the Golden West, is today a land that symbolises not only the vastness but the richness and plenty of the inland; with green stands of lucerne and other improved pastures, fields of ripening wheat, sheep and cattle grazing in well grassed paddocks, wide open spaces merging in the distance into blue hills.

Dotted through the Golden West are bustling, well planned communities. Bathurst, Australia's first inland settlement, on the Macquarie River, is rich in history and tradition. Orange, its sister city, 34 miles further west, is famous as the Cherry Blossom City. Other centres include Dubbo, Parkes, Forbes, Molong, Gulgong (the town on the Australian $10 note), Grenfell (birthplace of great Australian short story writer and poet Henry Lawson). Cowra, Wellington, Young and Mudgee.

Northwards, the Golden West gives way to the North West, where the plains are occasionally broken by majestic mountain ranges: the Warrumbungles (between Coonabarabran and Coonamble) and the Nandewars (east of Narrabri). Also in the region are the Macquarie Marshes, noted as a natural breeding ground for birds and the Pilliga Scrub, one of Australia's largest softwood forests.

At Moree, the North West meets the Great Artesian Basin, the enormous store of underground water that makes much of inland Australia productive. 'Bore water' is used for two health pools there.

Amateur 'prospectors' still take the trail to **Lightning Ridge** to try their luck in the opal fields there, and sometimes come up with a worthwhile find as they 'puddle' through old tailings.

Tamworth is the gateway to the North West. Its annual festival, held in October—November, is called the Festival of Light in memory of the somewhat irrelevent fact that Tamworth in 1888 became the first Australian town to have its streets lit with electricity.

Other centres in the North West include Coonabarabran, Nundle, Barraba, Narrabri, Manilla, Quirindi, Gilgandra, Coonamble, Gunnedah, Wee Waa and Walgett (a suitable base for those who want to explore the opal fields at Lightning Ridge but find the accommodation there a little primitive).

The Great Western Plains sweep across New South Wales beyond the fertile areas to the Darling River. This is where visitors can hope to see free running kangaroos and emus. They were once here in great numbers, but the encroachment of civilisation, the activities of commercial hunters and 'sportsmen' have reduced the numbers, particularly of kangaroos, to levels which seriously concern naturalists and conservationists.

Birdlife is also plentiful here. The long-legged silver grey brolgas can sometimes be seen performing their stately dances, whilst the ibis is often seen wading in creek beds and billabongs. Caution, patience and a degree of luck are necessary to see them at close quarters or get them on film. More frequently seen are the noisy, pink breasted galahs, which delight in perching in their hundreds on tree branches, or wheeling in formation close to the roadway.

Main centres on the Great Western Plains are Bourke, Brewarrina, Cobar and Nyngan.

Sheep station holidays, during which visitors watch or take part in mustering, shearing and all the year round activities of a working sheep run, are available in western New South Wales. These may be for an extended period, or one day flying visits from Sydney. Details from New South Wales Government Bureau.

The Riverina, in the south-west of New South Wales, is a rich pastoral and agricultural region through which roll the Murray, Murrumbidgee and Lachlan Rivers. It is a region of wide open plains, sheep and cattle pastures, irrigation schemes, wheatfields, vineyards and (in its south-east quarter) forest and mountain country.

The two main centres of the Riverina, both of them garden cities with many scenic attractions, are Wagga Wagga, on the Murrumbidgee, and Albury, on the Murray. Important towns include Deniliquin, Hay, Cootamundra, Gundagai, Tumut, Temora and West Wyalong. Towns within the Murrumbidgee Irrigation Area, part of the Riverina, include Griffith, Leeton and Narrandera.

For a motoring holiday, the Riverina offers pleasant driving through the sheep and cattle pastures and the wheatfields of the Riverina proper, or the scenic valleys and uplands of the eastern Riverina. For the active holidaymaker, it offers boating, sailing, water ski-ing, swimming and fishing (for Murray cod, perch, catfish and trout) in the dams, rivers and mountain streams. Golf, bowls and tennis facilities are widely available.

Wagga Wagga, 'capital' of the Riverina, is on the Murrumbidgee, about halfway along the main Sydney-Melbourne rail link, and at the junction of the Sturt and Olympic Highways. A Red Arrow tour enables visiting motorists to get a balanced impression of the city.

Albury, largest city in the Riverina, is on the Murray, the river that divides New South Wales from the neighbouring state of Victoria. Lake Hume, a vast water storage known for its aquatic sport, is only eight miles away. Albury is a good base from which to explore the Murray Valley, the Upper Murray region and the nearby Victorian snowfields.

Murrumbidgee Irrigation Area:

Here 500 square miles of orchards, vineyards, cotton and rice fields occupy land that was almost useless semi-desert until irrigation transformed it into a luxuriant garden. Poplars and willows line the canal, adding to the beauty of the region. Inspections are invited at most of the wineries and fruit and vegetable canneries throughout the MIA.

Gateway to the MIA, Narrandera is at the junction of the Murrumbidgee River and the main irrigation canal. It has pleasant parks at Sturt's Beach, around Lake Talbot and at Narrandera Park.

Griffith, largest centre in the MIA, was laid out by Walter Burley Griffin, designer of Canberra. Scenic spots close to the town are Scenic Hill and Lake Wyangan, popular venue for water sports. The town straddles the main irrigation canal. So too does Leeton, which calls itself the 'Garden of the West', and has the biggest cannery in the Southern Hemisphere.

Because of the variety of crops, it's nearly always harvest time in the MIA, so there's always something interesting to see.

Local information services in the Riverina: Wagga Wagga Tourist Bureau, Bayles Street. Albury Tourist Bureau, Dean Street, Murrumbidgee Irrigation Area Tourist Information Centre, East Street, Narrandera.

BROKEN HILL AND THE OUTBACK

No part of New South Wales is more forbidding than the shimmering aridity of the Outback, the vast, sunbaked area that sits astride the Darling River.

Even its unproclaimed capital, Broken Hill, fourth largest city in the State, has a beleaguered look about it, notwithstanding its comparatively recent connection with the outside world by good roads, modern aircraft, and transcontinental trains. But it does make a satisfactory base for exploring the far west.

Broken Hill owes its existence to the biggest silver-lead-zinc deposits in the world, deep in the earth beneath the city streets. Since discovered in 1883 by a German boundary-rider, Charles Rasp, they have given up over a hundred million tons of ore.

Underground inspections of mines are usually not available to visitors, but the surface workings of the Zinc Corporation's mine may be inspected each weekday except Thursday at 2 p.m. On Thursday, the New Broken Hill's surface workings are open for inspection.

Other attractions of Broken Hill itself include the Royal Flying Doctor Service, the School of the Air, Umberumberka Reservoir, Twin Lakes, the regeneration areas where planted trees keep the desert at bay and the city surprisingly green.

WITHIN EASY REACH OF BROKEN HILL AREA

Menindee Lakes, built for water storage, but doing excellent duty as Broken Hill's aquatic playground, with plenty of space in their 40,000 acres for speedboating, water ski-ing, sailing, swimming and fishing. Kinchega National Park takes in part of Menindee Lakes. On the Darling River, 70 miles east of Broken Hill.

Mootwingee, a sacred aboriginal tribal ground dating back 2,000—3,000 years, rich in rock carvings, drawings, etchings, stencils and cave paintings of kangaroos, lizards, emus, dingo tracks, men armed with spears and boomerangs. In the Snake Cave there is a painting of a 28 ft long snake. Birdlife, fauna and vegetation are also interesting. 82 miles north east of Broken Hill. A worthwhile stop on the way is at Yanco Glen Hotel, 19 miles from Broken Hill, to see the collection of Aboriginal artifacts, rubbing stones, message sticks, etc.

Silver City Highway. This runs north from Broken Hill to the Queensland border, south of the Victoria border. Northwards it goes to the remains of Milparinka, once a thriving gold town, the cairn on Mount Poole station where explorer Sturt's second-in-command died; Sturt's depot at Fort Grey; the ruins of the old mining town of Mount Browne; Tibooburra, the most north-westerly town in New South Wales; the dingo proof fence along the Queensland border; and 389 miles away from Broken Hill, across the border, the famous 'Dig Tree' of the ill-starred Burke and Wills expedition. South of Broken Hill, the Silver City Highway goes to Wentworth, on the Darling River, and connects with the Victorian road system at Mildura, on the Murray River.

Wentworth, situated near the junction of the Murray and Darling Rivers, two of the largest and most important in Australia, is one of the oldest towns on the Murray, and in the days of the riverboats was an important port. Local points of interest include the riverboat Ruby, the old gaol, folk museum, lock on the Murray River, Sturt's Tree, old Court House. Wentworth to Broken Hill is 166 miles.

White Cliffs, an old opal mining settlement, worked again since 1964 when two prospectors stumbled on some rich opals only inches beneath ground quit 50 years before. Tourists and amateur prospectors occasionally report worthwhile finds from 'noodling' piles of old opal dirt.

Tourist information about Broken Hill and the West Darling Region is available from the Broken Hill Visitors' Information Centre, Palace Hotel Building, corner of Argent and Sulphide Streets, Broken Hill, 2880. Tours throughout the area are operated by West Darling Tours Pty Ltd., Argent Street, Broken Hill.

NATIONAL PARKS

More than twenty-five areas have been designated National Parks, State Parks, Historic Sites and Nature Reserves under the control of the National Parks and Wildlife Service of New South Wales. A pamphlet giving information about all parks is available from The Director, National Parks and Wildlife Service, ADC Building, 189 Kent Street, Sydney. Phone 27 9711. Many parks have rangers on the spot with literature and information.

NEAR SYDNEY

Royal National Park Heath covered sandstone plateau separating the surf along its eastern boundary from sub-tropical vegetation bordering the Hacking River. 20 miles south, off Princes Highway.

Ku-ring-gai Chase National Park Sandstone plateau with many vista points, falling steeply to flooded valleys of Cowan Water and Pittwater. Wildflowers July to November. Aboriginal engravings. 15 miles north, between Pacific Highway and Pittwater.

Brisbane Water National Park Panoramic vistas spread from the 300 foot sandstone cliffs which rise vertically from the flooded valley of the Hawkesbury River. Waratah and Christmas Bells November to December. 40 miles north near Gosford.

Dharug National Park Aboriginal rock engravings possibly 8,000 years old. 46 miles north, on northern side of Hawkesbury River, near Wiseman's Ferry.

Heathcote State Park Heath covered sandstone country with steep forested gullies. Wildflowers. Birds. 20 miles south, on western side of Princes Highway.

Bouddi State Park Native trails lead to panoramas of coast, vegetation ranging from coastal heath to sub-tropical rain forest. Birds. Small marsupials. 65 miles north, along Scenic Highway from Gosford.

Historic sites near Sydney: **Vaucluse House** (6 miles), fine example of mediaeval gothic architecture built by William Charles Wentworth in 1829; **Captain Cook's Landing Place** (25 miles) Kurnell; **La Perouse Monuments** (9 miles) where the French navigator anchored in 1788, two days after the arrival of the First Fleet; **Bare Island**, off La Perouse, where a fort was built in 1885 to repel a possible attack by the Russian Pacific Fleet.

MOUNTAIN PARKS

Blue Mountains National Park Spectacular mountain scenery resulting from erosion of the Grose River through 2,500 feet of colourful sandstones, shales and coal measures. 40 miles west of Sydney, off Great Western Highway.

Morton National Park A great gulf in the sandstone plateau with Fitzroy Falls at its head. 100 miles south of Sydney on Moss Vale-Nowra Road.

Kosciusko State Park Largest in New South Wales, includes Australia's highest mountain and vast winter snowfields, which give way to massed displays of alpine wildflowers in spring and summer. Good accommodation available within the park. Southern Alps, 300 miles south of Sydney.

New England National Park Eastern escarpment of New England Plateau. Wilderness vegetation from snow gums to sub-tropical rain forest and red cedar. 45 miles east of Armidale, 320 miles north of Sydney.

Barrington Tops National Parks A mountain knoll rising 3,000 feet, with tracks through rain forest, remnant antarctic beech forest, snow-gum plain. 60 miles north-west of Newcastle, 170 miles from Sydney. Access from Gloucester and Scone.

Gibraltar Range National Park Granite mountain mass. Birds. Platypus. Midway between Glen Innes and Grafton on Gwydir Highway, 450 miles from Sydney.

Mount Kaputar National Park Peak on receding crater edge of a once large volcano, 4,000 feet above surrounding plain. 30 miles north-west of Narrabri, 346 miles from Sydney.

Warrumbungle National Park Spectacular scenery resulting from erosion of ancient volcanoes, such as the 300 ft towering spire of the Breadknife, only a few feet thick. 20 miles west of Coonabarabran, 300 miles from Sydney.

Kanangra-Boyd National Park Massive cliffs, deep canyon, under-developed limestone caves, crystal clear streams, magnificent waterfalls. 15 miles from Jenolan Caves, 130 miles from Sydney.

Bundanoon State Park Deeply entrenched gorge of Bundanoon Creek. East of Bundanoon. 100 miles from Sydney.

Barongary State Park At Belmore Falls, Burawong Creek drops from sandstone tops into gorge. Views of Kangaroo Valley. 6 miles south of Robertson, 91 miles from Sydney.

Dorrigo State Park Sub-tropical rain forest on scarp. 2 miles from Dorrigo, 360 miles from Sydney.

Mt Warning State Park Volcanic spire rising from rugged rain forest covered hills. 10 miles from Murwillumbah, 530 miles from Sydney.

OTHER PARKS

Kinchega National Park Grey soil plains and red sand ridges, Darling River and overflow lakes bordered by red gums. Waterfowl. Aboriginal camp sites. 2 miles south-west of Menindee, 75 miles east of Broken Hill, 652 miles from Sydney.

Cocopara National Park Low wooded range overlooking the Murrumbidgee Irrigation Area. Kangaroos. 12 miles north of Griffith, 407 miles from Sydney.

Hill End Historic Site Town where first payable gold in Australia was discovered in 1851. 52 miles north of Bathurst, 180 miles from Sydney.

Mootwingee Historic Site Aboriginal paintings, stencils, rock pickings in caves, overhangs and on rock faces. 80 miles north east of Broken Hill. 760 miles from Sydney.

INFORMATION SERVICES

The New South Wales Government Tourist Bureau has offices at 8 Martin Place, Sydney (2 0136); 345 Little Collins Street, Melbourne (60 1378); 205 Adelaide Street, Brisbane (31 1838). There is a New South Wales Government Travel Centre in the AMP Building, North Terrace, Adelaide (51 7100).

Motorists crossing borders into New South Wales at Albury and Tweed Heads will find Department of Tourism Information Centres beside the highway. Many Regional Tourist Associations maintain information centres in major cities and towns throughout the State. These are listed in this book under the heading for each particular area.

Queensland

A FRONTIER SPIRIT

Queensland evokes a special depth of regional patriotism among it's inhabitants. For them it is 'the Sunshine State' and 'the State of the Future'. Every city and district has its separate slogan promoting the local charms. Great billboards, 'Buy Queensland Made', stand beside the highways.

The Queenslander is warm and out-going, but he can become prickly at a hint of criticism. For in a changing nation and world he sees himself still as the frontiersman, striding toward far horizons of growth and development.

Perhaps his exposure at the northern end of the continent, facing Asia, has bred in him a feeling of insecurity which he must hide under a brave cloak.

Queensland is a State of mighty contrasts and dimensions. It is 670,500 square miles and fewer than two million people; coral islands and blinding tropical downpours; cold, high plains; and a western prairie extending to the horizon.

Queensland has more beef cattle than any other State. Its agriculture is dominated by the sugar industry, earning more than $200 million a year. Coal from central Queensland, bauxite from Weipa, copper, silver, lead and zinc from Mount Isa in the north-west . . . these are providing a bonanza of wealth.

Development in Queensland, particularly of secondary industry, has always lagged a little behind that of southern States. Partly this is because of the distance from Australia's greatest centres of wealth and population; a kind of 'Brisbane Line' mentality among the financiers of Melbourne and Sydney.

Now the barriers are down and the Queenslander can expect to gain not only prosperity but also a greater measure of self-confidence.

The State extends north for nearly 2,000 miles to the Torres Strait and almost to Papua-New Guinea. East is the Pacific, incomparably clear and blue; and the isles and vari-coloured corals of the Great Barrier Reef. North-west is the Gulf of Carpentaria, fed by wide, slow rivers, where trawlers of a score of nations come each year after prawns.

Links with the Pacific islands and Asia go back almost to the beginnings of settlement in Queensland. Melanesian labourers helped build the early sugar plantations. Thousands of Chinese joined the gold rushes last century. The first moves to annex Papua came from Queensland.

The breath of adventure, the sense of a last frontier cling to the northern State, along with the ghosts of drovers and cane-cutters, of fine pearls and tall ships.

Thus Queensland and Queenslanders retain a very special place in the consciousness of all Australians.

CANE FIELD NEAR CAIRNS, NORTH QUEENSLAND

BRISBANE – THE 'DIFFERENT' CAPITAL

Brisbane is the most 'different' of the Australian State capitals. It is built on a cluster of hills and these, together with the Brisbane River winding through the heart of the city, give the place a distinctive style.

The difference is apparent in the people also. Hats may be out of fashion elsewhere, yet still hosts of Brisbane men would consider themselves incompletely dressed without one. This can give to the crowds surging down Queen or George streets a curiously old-fashioned appearance.

If the pace of life seems slower than in Sydney or Melbourne, perhaps it is because there is more room to move about in. Greater Brisbane extends over 375 square miles, making it one of the world's largest cities in area.

The population has grown from 330,000 in 1939 to 816,987 in 1971. Many of the old timber homes, set on stilts, with wide verandahs and maybe a tennis court in the backyard, have given way to apartment blocks. Yet most families retain the ideal of owning a house with a garden in the traditional Australian pattern.

Unlike NSW or Victoria, more Queenslanders live away from their capital city than in it. Brisbane is the State's leading port but the bulk of exports—mainly sugar and minerals—go through smaller centres to the north.

Industrialisation has lagged behind that of other capitals, perhaps because a smaller proportion of the post-war migrants have settled in Queensland.

Some major industries in Brisbane such as meat processing, sugar refining and fruit canning are related to the products of the hinterland. But the availability of a large work-force and a growing market in the city itself have encouraged newer industries to develop on the outskirts.

These include food processing, manufacture of agriculture machinery and electrical goods, car assembly; an entire range of factories with their attendant new suburbs. So development spreads, gobbling up farmland and threatening now to engulf the sister city of Ipswich 24 miles away.

Brisbane is a place of spacious parks and river views, pools and tennis courts, palm trees and sun-drenched days. Some of the world's finest beaches are within an hour's drive and for yachtsmen there is Moreton Bay with its scattering of islands.

The people of Brisbane seem to fit better than most Australians the lean, outdoors image borrowed from the outback.

The old Observatory on Wickham Terrace, a former treadmill, is a reminder of convict origins. But the ghosts cast no shadow on a city which is expanding dynamically, with its ambitions set firmly in the future.

BRISBANE CITY SCENE

BRISBANE TOWN HALL

FABULOUS GOLD COAST

The Gold Coast, stretching for 20 miles from Southport to Coolangatta and the NSW border, is a city built entirely for pleasure. It is garish, gaudy, loud, hectic, and pure fun.

The Strip, the ribbon of intensive development, follows the shoreline, for the visitors who swarm here from all over the world are attracted primarily by the beaches, and the sunshine which prevails for an average of 290 days each year.

From out of the Pacific come a procession of blue rollers, sweeping to shore with their human cargo of surfers and board-riders.

On carnival days the surfboats come curving down the face of the breakers, presenting perhaps the most spectacular moment of any sport anywhere . . . while on the beach the dense phalanxes of lifesavers march under their standards. Big, bronzed men these, who give their time and occasionally their lives in a spirit of voluntary service which is peculiarly Australian.

The Gold Coast is a series of beaches flanked by plush hotels, motels, soaring apartment blocks. It is Southport, Surfers Paradise, Broadbeach, Burleigh Heads, Currumbin, Kirra, Coolangatta and many other resorts, gathered together as a city of 66,000 residents catering to many times that number of visitors.

The Gold Coast is hamburger joints and fine restaurants, blue jeans and boutiques. It is beer gardens and sophisticated nightspots with renowned artists. It is leisure and pleasure, and women of rare shape and beauty.

The Gold Coast is a centre for international conventions and for every sport imaginable. It is flamboyant businessmen and entrepreneurs, golden meter maids; zoos and museums, art galleries and great acquariums; the blaring rhythm of a discotheque; the gathering of parrots and finches at feeding-time in the Currumbin bird sanctuary.

GOLD COAST METER MAID
FEEDING PARROTS, CURRUMBIN SANCTUARY ON THE GOLD COAST

Back from the coast is the very different world of the Macpherson Ranges. Here are slopes of tall timber gashed by ravines and sudden, boiling streams and waterfalls. Quiet bush walks wind about Tamborine Mountain and through the Lamington National Park.

High up the Nerang River is the Numinbah Valley, groves of Antarctic beeches and the Natural Arch, a bridge of rock across a stream with, close by, a cascade of water pouring through a cave lit by glow-worms.

Climb the great hills and a panorama spreads east to the ocean and, on a clear day, north for a hundred miles to the Glasshouse Mountains.

By night the Gold Coast appears as a blaze of neon proclaiming the city where life is for enjoyment, against the background of a summer that never ends.

SURFERS PARADISE SPARKLES AT NIGHT

CANAL HOUSING DEVELOPMENT, GOLD COAST

THE GOLD COAST IS FAMOUS FOR ITS SURF—AND GIRLS

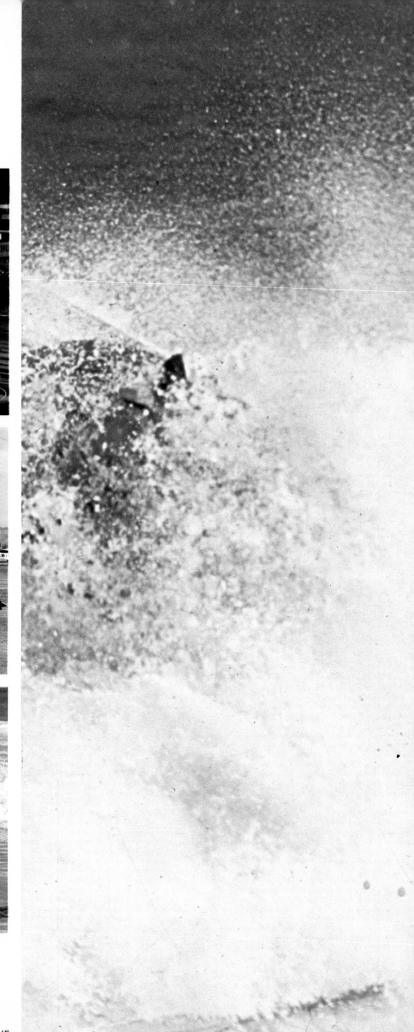
A SURFBOAT CRASHES A WAVE

HINTERLAND STREAM
THE NATURAL ARCH, GOLD COAST HINTERLAND

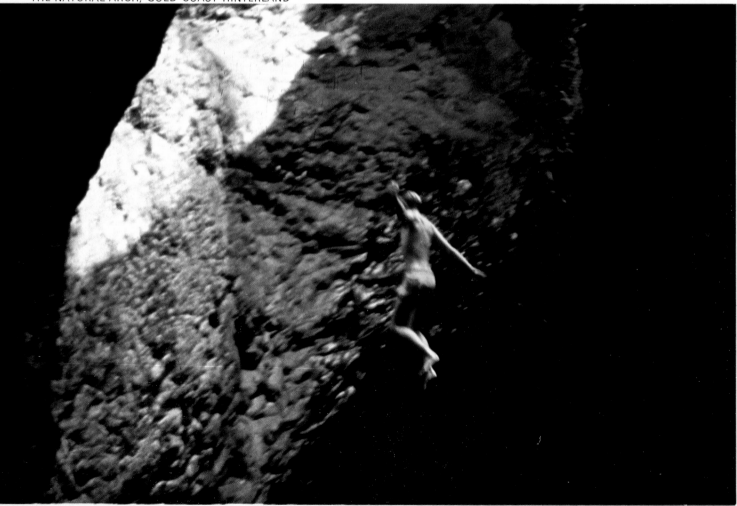

SUNSHINE COAST – *Pure Queensland*

The Gold Coast is international, but the Sunshine Coast north of Brisbane is pure Queensland. It has beaches fully the equal of Surfers Paradise and Coolangatta, but the tempo of life seems less frenzied. Perhaps the holiday crowds are not so sophisticated, but they are more relaxed.

The Sunshine Coast begins at Caloundra, 60 road miles north of Brisbane, and extends northward through Landsborough, Maroochy and Noosa shires. Along the shore are the golden beaches, given over to holiday-making; while in the hinterland are rich sugar cane and pineapple plantations, dairy farms, and fields of grain, fruits and vegetables.

Just south of the town of Landsborough are the Glasshouse Mountains, nine mighty pillars of trachyte rising sheer from the Plain. Peaks like Mount Beerwah (1,760 feet), Tibrogargan (1,160 feet) and Crookneck (1,239 feet) stand as geological works of art, relics of some mighty upheaval long ago. From out at sea, as Captain Cook saw them during his voyage of discovery in 1770, their smooth rock faces can reflect the sun, as though they were monoliths made of glass.

The holiday resorts of the Sunshine Coast include Caloundra, Mooloolaba, Maroochydore, Coolum, Peregian, Noosa Heads and other beaches extending north to Double Island Point and the famous coloured sands of Teewah rising like rainbows for 600 feet above the waves.

Among towns of the hinterland are Nambour, Buderim with the only ginger processing factory in Australia, Woombye, Yandina, Eumundi, Pomona, Maleny, Montville and Kenilworth. The permanent residents of the district, numbering about 40,000, reap the golden harvest of tourism, but it does not dominate their lives in the manner of the Gold Coast.

They have time to spare for fishing, and for enjoying the quiet rivers where the reflections in the water are so clear it is difficult to tell where reality begins and ends.

In Kondalilla National Park on the crest of the Blackall Range a waterfall cascades 250 feet down into a valley of palms and rain forest. North from Tewantin are the Noosa lakes, Weyba, Doonella, Cooroibah, Cootharaba, Figtree and Como, and the freshwater lake, Cooloola, all with their communities of black swans, ducks and other wildfowl.

Nature is very beautiful on the Sunshine Coast, and man has added his own handiwork. On display at Tewantin's unique House of Bottles is a great slab of ambergris, reminder of a time when this was a younger, less crowded place, and whales still sounded offshore on their journeys up the coast.

GLASSHOUSE MOUNTAINS, SUNSHINE COAST HINTERLAND

THE EXOTIC NORTH

The impression made by Queensland's tropical coast is overwhelmingly one of colour and an exotic lushness of growth. The sea, dappled green in the shallows, turns further out to a blue as deep as indigo.

Great fish, including marlin of record proportions, move in waters that are utterly clear, attracting game fishermen from all over the world.

The shore is golden sand, broken occasionally by the mouths of rivers with their spreading mangrove flats. At intervals along the coast are beaches, secluded and often exquisitely beautiful, each with its fringe of palms and the dense green of the rain forest pressing close around.

The coastal strip north of the tropic produces 80 per cent of Australia's sugar on soils which can vary in the same field from black to brown to almost-yellow.

Beyond the plain the mountains rise as walls of greenery, slashed white by waterfalls and rushing streams.

The climate has the drama of the Asian tropics. Winter is the dry season, with bright, clear days.

The wet is a time of steamy humidity, with sudden downpours which can bring 60 to 100 inches of rain and more within the few months from December to the end of March.

The people of the Far North are subtly different from other Queenslanders. They have the traditional friendliness and helpfulness of country-dwellers, and also a Mediterranean exuberance. The latter may come from the preponderance of Italians who helped build the sugar industry, then spread to all levels of society.

The coastal cities like Mackay, Bowen, Ayr, Ingham, Innisfail and Cairns have achieved prosperity on a blend of agriculture and a burgeoning tourist industry.

Townsville, the greatest city in tropical Australia, is the outlet for the produce of the north-west, including the vast mineral output of Mt Isa. Its population, already more than 68,000, is expected to reach 100,000 this century.

The northernmost of Queensland's cities—and some say the most beautiful—is Cairns, 1,162 road miles from Brisbane. North again, Cape York Peninsula extends for a further 700 miles to the Torres Strait and the fading pearling port of Thursday Island.

Traditionally the Peninsula has been the land of Aboriginals and crocodile hunters and hard-bitten cattlemen; but great changes are coming.

Developments in recent years include agriculture at Lakeland Downs, bauxite mining at Weipa, and the prawning rush to the Gulf of Carpentaria. Together these make the beginnings of a boom which could transform the lonely country.

NORTH QUEENSLAND SEASCAPE

MAIN ROAD, CAPE YORK
COOKTOWN, FAR NORTH QUEENSLAND

ABORIGINAL MISSION, CAPE YORK
THE TIP OF AUSTRALIA

SUGAR CANE TRAIN, NORTH QUEENSLAND
THE BLACK MARLIN FISHING GROUNDS OFF CAIRNS RIVAL THE WORLD'S BEST

NORTH QUEENSLAND RAINFOREST

AN ABUNDANCE OF PASTURE

The Darling Downs is spread over $3\frac{1}{2}$ million acres of the richest agricultural land in the State. It is an expanse of rare beauty, studded with areas of national park, with waterfalls and strange rock formations; and mountains which sweep down majestically to a bountiful plain.

The explorer Allan Cunningham discovered the Darling Downs on June 5, 1827, when he 'descended into a beautiful and well-watered valley, affording abundance of the richest pasturage and bounded on each side by a bold, elevated range'.

The district has a population of more than 150,000, producing the bulk of Queensland's wheat crop, also fine wools and fat lambs, dairy produce, and the widest variety of grains, vegetables and fruits.

The largest centre is Toowoomba, with 60,000 people, set 80 miles west of Brisbane on the rim of the Great Dividing Range, 2,000 feet above sea level. It is a clean, uncluttered city of parks and gardens, and the Carnival of Flowers held during the last week in September attracts more than 40,000 visitors annually.

The plains spreading out from Toowoomba have nurtured some of Queensland's finest athletes and Rugby League footballers; as well as mighty racehorses including Bernborough and Rainbird.

South toward the New South Wales border is Stanthorpe, centre of the Granite Belt 3,000 feet above sea level, where the climate has a crisp coolness which is ideal for growing apples and other stone fruits.

Warwick, 55 miles south of Toowoomba, is the second city of the Downs, with a population around 10,000. The three original sheep stations of the district, South Toolburra, Canning Downs and Rosenthal, founded about 1840, are still in existence; the area is renowned for its stud cattle and thoroughbred horses.

An old gum tree near Rosenthal homestead carries the mark of the explorer Ludwig Leichhardt, who set out from the Darling Downs in 1848 on his last expedition.

He stayed at Jimbour House, near Dalby in the north of the Downs, then headed west on his attempt to cross the continent. The interior swallowed him up with all his men in the greatest continuing mystery of Australian exploration.

Thirty miles north-east of Dalby are the Bunya Mountains in what once was the country of the Waka Waka. Long ago in the ripening season Aborigines would come from as far away as the coast to feed on the nuts of the bunya pine. Now the tribes are gone but the forests remain as a national park.

DARLING DOWNS CATTLE

HIGHWAY NEAR TOOWOOMBA, DARLING DOWNS
BULL'S HEAD INN, DRAYTON, DARLING DOWNS

BOUNTEOUS TABLELAND

The ascent to the Atherton Tableland begins only a few miles west of the Coral Sea coast between Innisfail and Cairns. Roads wind up mountainsides and through jungle-clad gullies to emerge on a plateau 2,500 feet above sea level and extending across 3,000 square miles of what many consider the most beautiful countryside in Queensland.

The Atherton Tableland is a profusion of lakes, waterfalls and rushing streams, backed by broad farmlands. Facing the coast is the deep green of rain forest broken by the crimson flash of flame trees and occasionally the splendour of flowering orchids.

Around the crater lakes in the jungle the visitor at dawn may hear the gobble of bush turkeys and the boom-boom of a cassowary, the great flightless bird of the rain forest. Moving in the treetops are flying opossums similar to those of New Guinea; and on the ground, marsupials, mighty pythons, and, farther north where men go more seldom, dingoes coloured dark to blend with the shadows.

Much of the tableland is cleared for dairying, and cultivation of tobacco, maize, peanuts and other crops. The main towns, Mareeba (population 5,000) and Atherton (population 2888), are bustling, cosmopolitan centres where Italian is a second language.

Each year tourists flock through to enjoy the rain forest and photograph the many beautiful waterfalls including the Barron, Millaa Millaa, Malanda, Millstream and Tully falls and the hosts of other pools and rock cascades.

Tinaroo Dam holds back a lake with 130 miles of shoreline and two-thirds the surface area of Sydney Harbour, providing irrigation for 1,100 farms and a playground for sailing and water ski-ing.

The tableland once was volcanic and the craters remain as lakes, each set within its cup of jungle-covered slopes, with the water collected in the middle, cold and limpid-clear. Lakes Barrine, 360 feet deep and covering 256 acres, and Eacham, 226 feet and 130 acres, are said to be linked by subterranean channels.

Another geological masterpiece is Mount Hypipamee crater, 480 feet deep, about which the original tribes had some grim legends.

The first inhabitants of the tableland were shy, and small in stature. Some anthropoligists believed them a separate race who pre-dated the arrival in Australia of the Aborigines.

Their dispossession by successive waves of miners, timber-getters and farmers was mainly peaceful and many of the descendants live around Kuranda, the sleepy township atop the Macalister Range less than half an hour's drive from Cairns.

KURANDA RAILWAY STATION

ATHERTON TABLELANDS FARM
LAKE BARRINE

AGRICULTURE STILL LEADS

Queensland continues to depend for prosperity on primary production—to a greater extent, perhaps, than other States. It has nearly seven million cattle, 38 per cent of the Australian total, plus huge numbers of dairy cattle, sheep and pigs.

Queensland farmers produce rich harvests of grains and fruits in a climate which varies from the northern tropics to the cold, high plains of the Granite Belt along the NSW border.

Pre-eminent among the crops is sugar which earns more than $200 million annually and has contributed much to the unique character of the State. Sugar-growing extended northward, reaching Cairns about 1880 and bringing with it the establishment of the coastal cities which are Queensland's pride.

Mechanical harvesting has done away with the colourful force of seasonal workers, the cane-cutters. But as with the drover, their influence seems still to pervade the Queensland consciousness.

Primary production earned more than $713 million during 1969–70 but the future has uncertainties. The faltering of the wool industry has caused a decline in population in some western districts. Prospects for sugar are clouded after 1974, when current agreements with Britain expire.

Much emphasis has moved toward mining, which has been a part of Queensland's development since the gold-rush era, but is now undergoing its greatest bonanza.

This was the first State to strike payable oil and natural gas. Mount Isa with its copper, silver lead and zinc is one of the world's great mining fields. Bauxite from Cape York peninsula and coal from central Queensland contribute to an annual mineral production which doubled within four years to reach $277,675,000 in 1969–70.

Queensland has a scattering of ghost towns from last century as evidence of the impermanence of mining booms. But the State has such a variety of resources in the land and in the rich prawning and fishing grounds offshore that any setbacks seem likely to be temporary.

Secondary industry has achieved a breadth and maturity which has rendered increasingly hollow the old jibe that Brisbane is 'a branch managers' town'—the head offices being in Melbourne or Sydney or abroad.

'Buy Queensland Made' slogans are up everywhere. They reflect the prickly local pride of the northerners, and also a realisation of the need for employment avenues in an expanding population.

Tourism is an industry with almost unlimited possibilities for development. The glittering 'fun strip' of the Gold Coast is the fastest-growing population centre in Queensland. And in the Great Barrier Reef the State has a tourist attraction second to none in the world.

BAUXITE GOING TO STOCKPILE, CAPE YORK
FIRING SUGAR CANE CROP

ATHERTON TABLELAND TOBACCO CROP
KING PRAWN CATCH AT KARUMBA, GULF OF CARPENTARIA

BARRIER REEF –
A Natural Wonder

The Great Barrier Reef is the mightiest structure ever built by living creatures. It stretches for 1,250 miles from the Gulf of Papua along almost the entire coast of Queensland.

A maze of reefs extends across more than 80,000 square miles of ocean, dotted with hundreds of islands which vary from majestic wooded peaks to sand cays perhaps no larger than somebody's backyard. The ocean roundabout is a deep blue, utterly clear; merging into emerald green in the shallows.

The corals, formed by the minute, living polyps, are endlessly varied. There are staghorns coming up like great antlers. Some branching species are slender and delicate, others solid and heavy like miniature trees.

The Great Barrier Reef has more than 350 species of corals. They can be soft pinks and greens, black and crimson, purples, blues and fawns, yellows and browns. Some are shaped like fans, or broad leaves, or plates, or the delicate stems of plants.

The diver swims into and among a kaleidoscope of moving, living beauty. All around and above and below, the water stirs with life.

The coral, already a mass of brilliant colours, is a backdrop for such creatures as the electric-blue damsel fish; the humbug with its black and white stripes; the venomous but lovely butterfly cod.

There are turtles and sea snakes, giant rays, octopus, sharks, marlin, gropers, parrot fish, coral trout, sweetlip, mackerel, trevally, chinaman; the maori wrasse or humptyhead growing over 100 lbs.; the delectable red emperor, the barramundi cod; big schools of barracuda, bonito, sea mullet, gar and tuna.

The coral polyp, which gives the reef its existence and its beauty, is an animal about one to eight millimetres in diameter and related to the sea anemone.

During its life the creature is pushed gradually outward as secretions of lime enlarge its skeleton.

Thus the reef grows. The beautifully coloured surface is composed of layer on layer of living polyps. Below and supporting this outer 'skin' is the mass of limestone formed from the skeletons of uncounted previous generations.

Like other mighty and seemingly-imperishable works of nature, the Great Barrier Reef has lately come under threat from pollution, and also from a plague of polyp-eating Crown of Thorns starfish.

Governments and scientists are moving—perhaps too slowly—to counter the dangers. For as well as being a living wonder of the world, the Great Barrier Reef is a valuable part of Queensland's economy, attracting hundreds of thousands of visitors annually to its chain of island resorts.

WHITSUNDAY PASSAGE VIEW, FROM LINDEMAN ISLAND

REEF CORAL, WITH GIANT CLAM AT BOTTOM LEFT

BUTTERFLY COD
CRESTED TERN COLONY, MICHEALMAS CAY

GREEN ISLAND
THE SWIMMING POOL, DAYDREAM ISLAND

SOUTH MOLLE ISLAND JETTY

WESTERN QUEENSLAND – OLD AUSTRALIA

Western Queensland is the storied Australia, a land of wide plains stretching away to the horizon, broken occasionally by rock hills and fissured by rivers that might run once or twice in a good year.

Here are the great mobs of sheep and cattle, herded by the stockman of legend with his wide-brimmed hat, his horse and retinue of blue heeler dogs. It is the land of the red kangaroo and the emu, of dust and heat and flies, and of the hardihood and stoical humour which have contributed so much to the national character.

Even the names of the towns have the breath of the outback in them . . . Augathella, Thargomindah, Windorah, Barcaldine, Boulia, Hughenden, Julia Creek. . . .

Beyond Betoota in the farthest south-west corner of Queensland, is Birdsville, head of the Birdsville Track where many travellers have perished of thirst. West again is the waste of dunes extending to the Simpson Desert.

To east and north is the Channel Country, dirt plains patterned by a network of parched watercourses which, after the rare heavy rain, can spread is a brown tide across hundreds of miles of grazing land.

Western Queensland stretches north through broad belts of pastoral country to the Gulf of Carpentaria with its lonely coastline and wide, slow rivers. Offshore a fleet of trawlers nets for prawns in waters that once were empty except for a few crocodile hunters and barramundi fishermen.

Greatest city of the north-west is Mt Isa, with more than 20,000 people of 40 nationalities, and a huge income from copper, silver-lead and zinc. But more typical of the empty land would be Winton with a shire of 20,780 square miles and a population of fewer than 3,000 humans, along with $1\frac{1}{2}$ million sheep and 61,000 beef cattle.

Qantas, the international airline, began in the outback during 1920 and had its first registered office in Winton. Not far away on Dagworth station, in 1895, the poet A. B. 'Banjo' Paterson wrote the national song, 'Waltzing Matilda'.

Great changes have come to the west since then. The swagmen have gone. Wheeled transport has brought the passing of the drover, the hero figure of the old outback.

Yet some things are unaltered. For this still is the country of wide horizons, tinged red and purple at sunset. . . . Of horsemen who might be white, black, or any shade between, but have in common that they face life with courage, leavened by a humor as dry as the land itself.

THE DINGO FENCE ON THE QUEENSLAND, N.S.W. BORDER

WESTERN QUEENSLAND PUB, CROYDON
STOCKMEN ENJOY AN IMPROMPTU RACE

THOMSON RIVER, MID-WEST QUEENSLAND

A BRIEF HISTORY OF QUEENSLAND

The first white men known to have seen and landed on the east coast of Queensland were Captain James Cook and his crew of HMS *Endeavour* in 1770. However this was 164 years after the Dutch vessel *Duyfken* had sailed along the western coast of Cape York peninsula, and early Portuguese and Spanish navigators may also have touched on the Queensland shore.

Cook charted the east coast, naming many capes and bays. He lived ashore for six weeks near present-day Cooktown while repairing his ship and it was there he named the kangaroo.

The British established their penal colony in NSW during 1788 but Queensland remained unvisited for years afterward. Lieutenant Matthew Flinders explored Moreton Bay in 1799 and in 1823 John Oxley discovered the Brisbane River and named it after the then Governor of NSW.

A convict settlement was established in 1824 at Redcliffe, now a popular beach resort, and removed in the following year to the Brisbane River—the site of the present capital of Queensland. The outpost had a grim early history of cruelty and oppression until in 1839 the penal colony was abandoned and free settlers flooded in.

Pastoralists pushed over the Great Divide to the Darling Downs and beyond. A settlement was established at Gladstone and explorers penetrated north and west to find new grazing and farming lands. On June 6, 1859, Queen Victoria signed Letters Patent creating a new colony, and the monarch herself expressed preference for the name, 'Queensland'.

During 1860 the first Legislative Council was appointed and the first elected Parliament, the Legislative Assembly, met in Brisbane. The population of Queensland then was 23,520, a quarter of whom lived in the capital.

In the 1870s and afterward the discovery of gold at Gympie and Charters Towers, and later at the Palmer River on Cape York peninsula, drew large populations to areas that previously were empty. But the story of settlement along the northern seaboard is primarily the story of the sugar industry.

Sugar cane was grown in the Botanic Gardens, Brisbane, in 1850. By 1863 Captain Louis Hope had a flourishing plantation of 20 acres 20 miles from the capital. The industry spread rapidly and most of the northern coastal cities which are Queensland's—and Australia's—greatest example of decentralisation, owed their origin to sugar.

During 1863 Captain Robert Towns brought in 67 Pacific islanders, then called kanakas, to grow cotton. The sugar industry took up the idea and from then until 1901 more than 60,000 Melanesians were recruited to work under indenture in Queensland. This was the notorious 'blackbirding' trade which, in the worst of its excesses, came close to slavery, and it ended after Federation with the repatriation of all remaining kanakas.

In 1901 the colony of Queensland, with a population of nearly 500,000, became a State in the new Australian Federation.

Through two world wars and the great depression of the 1930s, Queensland has remained basically an exporter of primary produce and minerals. But secondary industry also has expanded spectacularly to serve a population swelled by waves of immigration during the 1950s and 1960s.

In recent years the huge State, covering near a quarter of the continent, has reached out in every direction to develop its potential. The Mt Isa field, discovered in 1923, has become one of the world's great producers of copper, silver lead and zinc. Other mineral discoveries included uranium at Mary Kathleen and bauxite at Weipa.

Heavy earth-moving equipment has carved new farming areas from the brigalow scrub of the central-north. Prawning grounds discovered in the Gulf of Carpentaria have attracted trawlers from all over the world.

The Moonie–Brisbane oil pipeline, opened in 1964, inaugurated the first significant commercial oil production in Australia, helping to begin a new era of self-sufficiency.

PHYSICAL FEATURES AND CLIMATE

Queensland has an area of 670,500 square miles, falling into three main physical regions—the tropical maritime coast, the central lowlands and the eastern highlands. The tropical maritime coast extends, geographically, from south of Brisbane, north for more than 1,200 miles to Cape York peninsula, beyond Cooktown.

It is a strip, seldom more than 60 miles wide, but usually with a heavy rainfall which falls mainly in summer. This comes from the trade winds meeting the steep escarpments of the eastern highlands and precipitating their moisture.

In the far north, monsoons and occasional cyclonic depressions bring tropical downpours in the early months of the year. Tully, with an average rainfall of 175 inches, is the wettest town in Australia.

Queensland's greatest rivers in terms of flow are east of the Great Dividing Range and these, allied with the reliable rainfall, form the basis of a flourishing agriculture.

The vegetation of the tropical maritime coast varies from eucalyptus scrub to pockets of dense rain forest, particularly in the Far North where some species of trees and climbing plants are similar to those of South-East Asia.

Temperatures vary from warm temperate in the south to tropical in the north. (The Tropic of Capricorn passes just south of Rockhampton.) Cairns' coldest month—July, with an average of 69·9 degrees (F)—is warmer than Melbourne's hottest month, February, with its average of 68·3 degrees.

The eastern highlands often is more plateau-like than mountainous. It has an average height of 3,000 feet though several peaks in the Bellenden Ker range south of Cairns rise above 5,000 feet. The eastern highlands forms a divide between the rivers flowing east and those flowing west, but it is a series of undulations rather than any single range.

In central Queensland the mountains generally are no more than 2,000 feet high but in places they extend inland for more than 500 miles. In the Darling Downs, just north of the NSW border, and the Atherton Tablelands, inland from Innisfail and Cairns in the Far North, the eastern highlands forms plateaus which are rich agricultural, dairying and cattle-fattening regions.

Queensland has no active volcanoes but in comparatively recent geological times great lava flows covered the Atherton Tablelands, the area north of Charters Towers and the Burnett River valley inland from Maryborough. The resulting basalts have weathered into fertile soils.

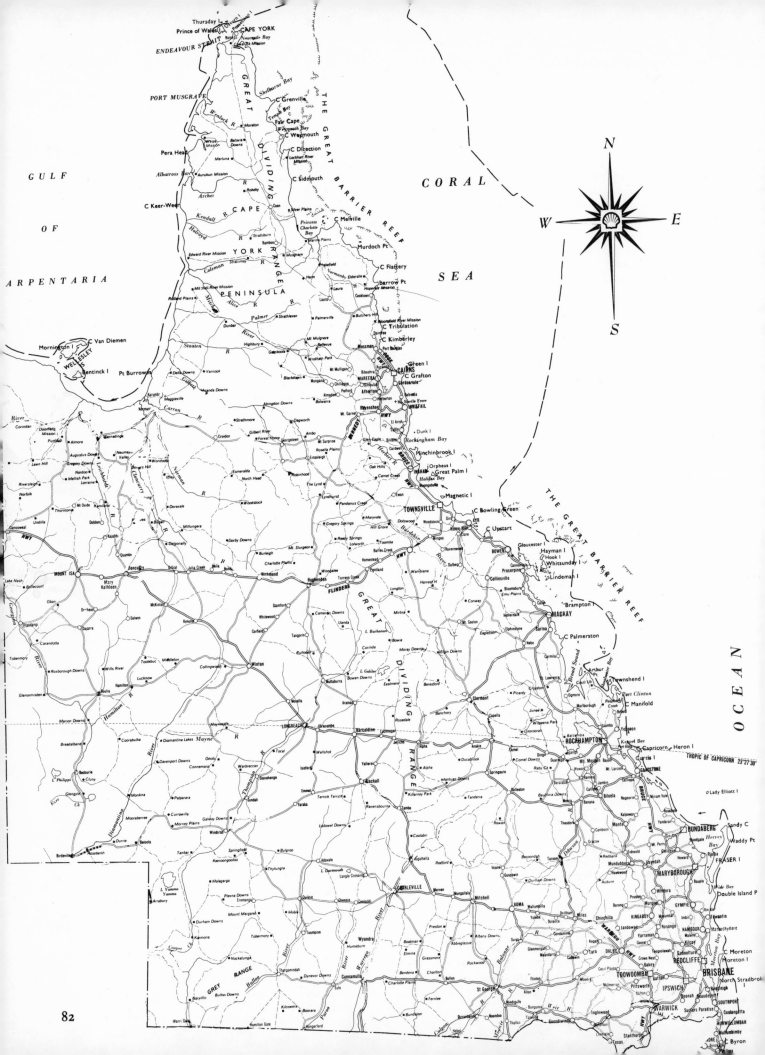

The Glasshouse mountains near Landsborough on the Sunshine Coast of southern Queensland are the eroded remains of volcanoes.

West of the eastern highlands, or Great Dividing Range, is the central lowlands, extending from the Gulf of Carpentaria to the borders of the Northern Territory, South Australia and New South Wales.

The rainfall through most of the inland is light and variable, ranging to below 10 inches annually in the south-west corner, some of which is a true desert of sand dunes. However the Great Artesian Basin covering much of the interior has proved an asset to the pastoral industry with more than 2,000 bores producing a daily flow of 192,000 gallons of water. The deepest source of underground water is 7,000 feet at Blackall, Queensland.

The central lowlands includes the Channel Country, a plain of silt with an intricate system of inter-connected channels. Streams such as the Cooper, Georgina and Diamantina once were large rivers flowing into an inland sea or giant lake, the remnants of which remain as saltpans around Lake Eyre.

Through the ages the climate became dryer, until eventually the deltas of silt brought down by the rivers were left high and dry. Most of the time now the western streams are dry except for a string of waterholes. But after heavy rain, perhaps once in several years, they spread their waters through a maze of channels across the plain, forming what has been described as one of the most perfect examples of natural irrigation in the world.

POPULATION AND INDUSTRY

Queensland's population is a little under two million, of whom 816,987 live in Brisbane. This means that more than half of Queenslanders live outside the metropolis, which is a better example of decentralisation than NSW or Victoria. However 90 per cent of the State's population are concentrated on the coastal strip extending from the NSW border to Cairns.

Queensland is Australia's greatest producer of beef cattle, with herds totalling more than seven million, 38 per cent of the nation's total. The State also has 16,446,000 sheep, 707,000 dairy cattle and 480,000 pigs.

The most lucrative crop is sugar which earns more than $200 million annually.

Queensland farmers also grow wheat, maize and other grains, vegetables, and fruits ranging from tropical varieties to the stone fruits of the Granite Belt on the Darling Downs. They grow cotton in the Dawson, Callide and Burnett valleys.

The State produces 60 per cent of Australia's tobacco, mostly on the Atherton Tablelands and along the Burdekin River valley.

During the year 1969–70 Queensland earned $713 million from primary production.

The State has shared in the mining bonanza which has helped to compensate for the decline in the Australian wool industry. Mt Isa in the north-west is one of the world's great fields of copper, silver lead and zinc. The coastal sands yield rutile. Australia's first commercial oil well was at Moonie in southern Queensland.

Coal is mined on a huge scale in central Queensland.

The output of alumina, produced from bauxite mined at Weipa on Cape York peninsula, passed three million tons in 1969–70, compared with 500,000 tons in 1966.

Mineral production in the State during the 12 months to June 30 1970, totalled $277,675,000—double the figure of four years earlier.

Golden beaches and the unique attraction of the Great Barrier Reef have made tourism one of Queensland's most lucrative industries, which may one day rival sugar. Discovery of rich new prawning grounds in the Gulf of Carpentaria has helped expand fishing to a production of more than $6 million annually, an increase of 200 per cent in a decade.

The rate of development of secondary industry has lagged behind that of NSW, Victoria, and South Australia. However factory production reached $657,900,000 in 1969–70.

Some enterprises such as meat processing, sugar refining and fruit canning are tied to the primary industries of the hinterland. But Queensland also assembles motor vehicles, makes electrical equipment, has chemical and fertiliser plants, refines bauxite and other minerals, and builds heavy engineering equipment, railway rolling-stock and ships.

The influx of migrants makes the provision of new employment avenues through secondary industry a continuing concern of the Queensland Government.

QUEENSLAND'S NATIONAL PARKS

Queensland, and particularly the tropical north-east, is a naturalist's paradise. Some animal species are found nowhere else on the continent. These include the tree kangaroo, the musk-rat kangaroo and a variety of possums including the Herbert River ringtail and the striped ringtail.

The State has about 400 of the more-than-700 species of birds in Australia. Thirty-two of the species occur only in Queensland. One of them is the cassowary, the giant flightless bird of the tropical rain forest.

Queensland has the largest snake in Australia and one of the largest in the world—the scrub python which frequently grows to 15 feet and has been known to reach 28 feet. Saltwater and freshwater crocodiles live in the northern rivers, though commercial hunting has drastically reduced their numbers and there is no national park where they are safe.

Of the 50 major vegetation types in Australia, 37 occur in Queensland.

Offshore is the marine treasure-house of the Great Barrier Reef, which is unique among coral reefs for its size and the variety of life-forms it supports.

National parks are the means by which the community seeks to preserve its unique fauna and flora for future generations. Treat these parks with reverence for they will grow more precious with the passing years.

Four points to remember: No gathering of flora; no hunting of animals; no shooting at birds; no collecting of gem-stones or minerals.

Queensland's national parks are administered by the Department of Forestry (head office 388–400 Ann Street, Brisbane). The department has built graded tracks and set aside picnic areas with shelter sheds, toilets, tables and fireplaces.

A permit is necessary to camp on a national park and it can be obtained without fee from the secretary, Department of Forestry, 388–400 Ann Street, Brisbane, or from the resident overseer on the park.

Camping is permitted on week-days only. On weekends and public holidays the grounds are reserved for day visitors.

Nearly two million acres of Queensland has been reserved for national parks.

The main national parks of the State are:

NORTHERN MAINLAND PARKS

Mount Windsor Tableland (Mossman Gorge)   133,000 acres

Chillagoe and Mungana Caves	4,732 acres
Barron Falls National Park	7,000 acres
Millstream Falls	—
Tully Falls	1,240 acres
Ringrose National Park (Mount Hypipamee—	
The Crater)	900 acres
Lake Barrine	1,200 acres
Lake Eacham	1,200 acres
Bellenden Ker	80,104 acres
Palmerston	6,315 acres

CENTRAL REGION

Carnarvon National Park	66,480 acres
Robinson Gorge	22,000 acres
Salvator Rose Park	64,920 acres
Eungella	122,600 acres

SOUTH-EAST REGION

Bunya Mountains National Park	22,000 acres
Maiala National Park (Mount Glorious)	2,380 acres
Glasshouse Mountains (There are four parks— Mount Beerwah, Mount Coonowrin, Mount Tibrogargan and Mount Ngungun. Another three peaks of the Glasshouse Mountains rise in State forests.)	
Ravensbourne National Park	247 acres
Kondalilla National Park	185 acres
Noosa National Park	930 acres
Queen Mary Falls and Blackfellow's Knob	327 acres
Girraween National Park	12,605 acres
Tamborine Mountains	a number of small parks
Burleigh Heads	about 2 acres
Mount Barney	12,980 acres
Mount Lindesay	600 acres
Mounts Maroon and May	3,630 acres
Cunningham's Gap	7,470 acres
Natural Bridge	491 acres
Springbrook (two parks)	2,858 acres
Lamington	48,510 acres

SOUTH-WEST REGION

The Simpson Desert	1,248,000 acres

ISLAND PARKS

(These are the island parks off the east coast of Queensland, taking in the Great Barrier Reef also. In some island groups only some of the islands are wholly or partly reserves.)
Bunker–Capricorn Islands (including Heron Island)
Keppel Islands
Northumberland Islands
Cumberland Islands (including Brampton and Lindeman)
Whitsunday Islands (including South Molle and Long islands)
Magnetic Island (of which 6,260 acres has been set aside)
Palm Islands (including Orpheus)
Hinchinbrook Island
Dunk Island (area set aside is 1,805 acres)
Green Island
Flinders Islands.

FISHING REGULATIONS

Professional fishing is controlled by a number of regulations, copies of which are available through the Department of Harbors and Marine or at the office of any Patrol Officer or Harbor Master throughout the State.

The notes below are prepared exclusively for amateur fishermen. No licence is required for angling in either salt or fresh water, provided the fish are not offered for sale. Fishing is permitted in any Queensland waters other than areas which have been declared sanctuaries.

All sanctuaries are marked clearly with signs. In tidal waters they include sections of the Coomera River, Coombabah Lake (Southport district); Swan Bay (near Jumpinpin); Barron and Burnett rivers.

Inland streams with sections declared sanctuaries are the Barwon (at Mungindi weir), Macintyre (Goondiwindi), Dumaresq (at Bonshaw and Cunningham), Balonne (St George), Dogwood Creek (Miles), Macintyre Brook (Ben Dor weir and Whetstone), Condamine (Dalby), Severn (Queen Mine water-hole four miles west of Ballandean). Fishing is restricted in lakes Somerset, Kurwongbah and Manchester.

Habitat reserves are set aside in parts of Moreton Bay where destruction of mangroves, digging of worms and other disturbance of the habitat is prohibited.

Legal minimum sizes are set for the various species of fish and details are available from the Department of Harbors and Marine. Size limits are imposed to protect immature fish and thus ensure good catches for present and future generations of fishermen.

The taking of female crabs is prohibited in Queensland waters.

Apart from licensed commercial fishermen, the use of nets is prohibited other than the bait net, the cast (or umbrella) net and a small scoop net.

Collection of shells is prohibited on the reefs at Green Island (off Cairns) and at Heron Island and Wistari reef in the Capricorn group. The taking of triton shells (Charonia tritonis) is prohibited throughout Queensland waters. These rules are imposed to protect the Great Barrier Reef.

Further information may be obtained from the Department of Harbors and Marine, Brisbane, or from Patrol Officers or Harbor Masters at Southport, Tewantin, Maryborough, Bundaberg, Gladstone, Rockhampton, Mackay, Bowen, Townsville, Innisfail and Cairns.

HUNTING

Inquiries should be made to the Department of Primary Industries or the Department of Forestry for up-to-date information on shooting regulations in Queensland. As this is written, legislation is pending to protect various species including the wedge-tail eagle.

The species of fauna are not distributed generally throughout the State, so the authorities have divided Queensland into six fauna districts. Thus conditions such as 'open seasons' for hunters can be applied to particular parts of the State as the situation warrants.

Fauna are divided, for legislative purposes, into (a) permanently-protected fauna; (b) protected fauna (which may be hunted during specified seasons); and (c) pest fauna (open to shooting or trapping at any time).

Legislation also provides for sanctuaries, areas in which all birds and animals except declared pests are totally protected at all times. These include all Queensland islands, all national parks, State forest reserves, and many other areas and private properties. Sanctuary notices are displayed and unauthorised removal of these is an offence.

Pest fauna include wild pigs, water buffaloes, dingoes, foxes, hares, rabbits, wedge-tail eagles, cormorants, eastern swamp hen, white cockatoo, silvereye, crow, pied currawong, grey currawong, sparrow, starling, turtle-dove, galah.

No species of crocodile is protected in Queensland.

Open season fauna (open season from January 1 to December 31, except in sanctuaries) include: Grey kangaroo, red kangaroo, eastern or dusky wallaroo, North Queensland wallaroo, red-necked, scrub or eastern brush wallaby, black-striped wallaby, whiptail, grey-face or pretty-face wallaby, sandy wallaby, red-legged pademelon, water rat, black-tailed or swamp wallaby.

The open season is January 1 to December 31 in districts 4, 5 and 6 (map showing fauna districts attached below) for grey duck (black duck), maned goose (wood duck), quail (all species).

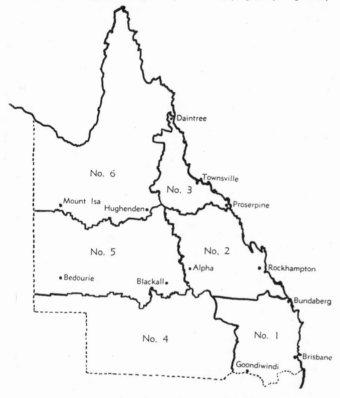

Sketch Map Showing the Approximate Boundaries of the Various Fauna Districts.

In districts 1, 2 and 3, covering areas back from the coast from the NSW border north to Daintree, an open season for wild duck and quail is declared from time to time by an Order-in-Council.

Queensland has an open season from November 14 to March 15 for Australian snipe, pint-tailed snipe, knot, great knot, sandpiper, stint, tattler, whimbrel.

Hunting and shooting regulations do not cover marine mammals, mice, rats (other than water rats), brumbies, and domestic cats gone wild.

The koala, platypus and echidna are permanently protected fauna, which means they are protected in perpetuity. Penalties for destroying them are higher than those provided in other sections of the legislation.

Other creatures not mentioned in the regulations are protected fauna, for which a close season exists throughout the year. Unlike the specified 'permanently protected fauna', however, an open season may be declared on protected fauna from time to time. This could occur in cases of damage to crops, livestock or other property, or a risk in the vicinity of an aerodrome, or if numbers of a particular species reach pest levels.

Detailed regulations control the trapping of wild birds for sale or other purposes, and information should be sought from the State Department of Primary Industries.

HINTS FOR ROAD TRAVELLERS

Queensland is a State of great distances and the traveller away from the coast faces many long stretches of dirt roads. In remote areas garages and spare parts may be rare or non-existent, so care is advisable. Some sections like the Birdsville Track leading from the town of that name in south-west Queensland to Marree in South Australia are best avoided by tourists.

For the outback motorist generally, rain, mechanical failure, or shortage of cash for emergencies can present problems which do not exist in more settled areas. However, with care, travelling in the outback can be a rewarding experience for those who enjoy going off the beaten track—a phrase which, in Queensland, means 'off the bitumen'.

Observance of some simple rules may save you much inconvenience and even danger. At every township you pass, check the state of the road ahead. Never gamble with the weather unless the locals advise it, since a downpour may reduce a dirt road within hours to an impassable bog.

In northern Queensland the wet season from December through to the end of March brings floods which can disrupt traffic for days at a time even on bitumen highways. Outside the 'wet season' belt the temperatures during these months are extremely high. In western Queensland summer temperatures of up to 120 degrees in the shade are common and ground temperatures may exceed 140 degrees. So the months from April to September are best for any outback motoring holiday in Queensland.

Do not leave yourself short of money. Petrol and other supplies cost more in the outback. Also, a reserve is needed in case of mechanical breakdown which, in isolated centres, may mean a long wait for spare parts.

Before setting out make sure your car is in first-class mechanical condition. Take a complete tool kit for minor repairs, a shovel and tomahawk, and a tow-rope. A few pieces of wire may be handy. Take two spare wheels.

Stones may damage the undercarriage of your car. Check brake cables and hoses en route. Broken windscreens and lost mufflers are fairly common.

Carry with you a top radiator hose, bottom radiator hose, fan belt, coil, condenser, set of ignition points, spare distributor cap, quart of engine oil, first-aid kit, box fuses, spare spark plug, tube repair outfit (including patches and clamp), or tubeless repair kit, roll of vinyl tape, two rear lamp globes, two tubes, some spare bolts including engine mounts. You will of of course need a jack, preferably hydraulic, a tyre pump, wheel brace and tyre levers.

You could take along an extra jack with suitable base plate to prevent it from sinking into sand or mud. Take care when using plastic containers for reserve petrol. Preferably use metal jerrycans, but remember these can build up static electricity. When pouring the contents into your tank it is a good idea to touch the lip of the jerrycan against the filter mouth of the petrol tank, thus earthing any spark which may prove disastrous.

Some motoring hints: When driving in bull-dust—a fine dust, concealing potholes—close all windows. On all dirt roads potholes and large stones are hazards. Always drive slowly on winding bush tracks where visibility is restricted. A sharp turn may expose you to a sudden dip in the road, a steep creek crossing, or some other hazard.

Watch out for animals, since these greatly outnumber people in the outback. Collision with a bullock or a large kangaroo means damage to your vehicle and possibly serious personal injury.

When water is across a dirt surface, keep to the centre of the road, which is likely to be the hardest.

Travelling long distances is tiring. Immediately you feel a tendency to drowsiness, pull off the road and rest. Many accidents are caused by drivers falling asleep at the wheel.

If your vehicle becomes bogged in sand, try deflating the tyres to about half normal pressure. This increases the effective gripping surface and may get you clear. If this fails, raise the vehicle with a jack and lodge some hard material under the wheels to give the tyres something on which to grip. You may use grass, leaves, twigs, sticks, stones, small logs, even ant beds.

The same techniques apply when you are bogged in mud. Do not forget to re-inflate the tyres afterward.

Sand mats can be improvised from old sections of matting, hessian or similar material. When the vehicle stalls in sandy country the mats are forced under the front and back wheels and then out in front of the vehicle. At least 30 feet of mat is necessary for the vehicle to gain traction over a loose surface.

Always take with you a good supply of water. If you break down in isolated country, stay with the vehicle. It will be found more easily than a solitary human being. In the high summer temperatures, stay in the shade and move about as little as possible. Use water sparingly since you do not know how long you may have to wait. If your cans of water run out there is always an extra supply available by draining the radiator.

Do not panic. Patience is an indispensable quality for the motorist in such circumstances, as it is for any facet of life in the outback.

When travelling in very remote areas make sure some reliable person in each settlement—preferably the policeman—knows where you are going, when you expect to arrive there and when you expect to return.

You will enjoy outback motoring more if you know something about the area you are travelling through. Take along guide-books and maps. If you carry a camera, keep it out of the sun and cover the lens when the camera is not in use. Beware of the effects which extreme ranges of temperature may have on your film.

For the driver who is prepared to take advice, Australia's motorist organisations have the maps and other information you need for your journey in the outback.

TRANSPORT SERVICES

AIR
The international airport at Brisbane connects with overseas services to London via Singapore and across the Pacific via San Francisco and New York. Some flights call at Tahiti, Honolulu, Manila and Hong Kong, and connections are available to other points in Asia and the Pacific. There are regular services between Brisbane and New Zealand and Brisbane and Papua-New Guinea.

TAA and Ansett Airlines cover Queensland with an extensive network reaching remote townships, missions and pastoral stations in the Gulf and channel country. Regular scheduled flights go to the tourist islands of the Great Barrier Reef.

In the Far North, Bush Pilots Airways have scheduled services linking Cairns, Cooktown and Townsville with isolated centres in the Gulf of Carpentaria and Cape York peninsula regions; also across to Mount Isa and Central Australia; and down in to the channel country of south-west Queensland. Bush Pilots Airways also fly charter services.

RAIL SERVICE
An extensive rail service covers most of Queensland and all the main centres of population. Modern passenger trains carry people north from Brisbane to Cairns, and westward from Townsville to Mount Isa. Regional railway lines extend from the coastal cities to many centres of the inland.

BUS SERVICE
Buses operate between the major country cities and towns, and also cater for travellers to remote areas. Tourist services go as far north as Cooktown and west through Mount Isa to the Northern Territory.

HIRE-DRIVE VEHICLES
Cars, and in some areas four-wheel-drive vehicles, are available for hire at most of the main centres throughout Queensland.

QUEENSLAND DELICACIES

Queenslanders, of course, eat basically the same foods as other Australians. They are the biggest meat-eaters in the nation, reflecting their position as residents of the premier beef-producing State.

Queensland grows a range of delightful tropical fruits, including pineapples, bananas, water melons, custard apples, pawpaws and avocados. Some, like the delicious mango, which ripens during summer, are seldom seen south of Brisbane because they have little 'keeping' quality and are difficult to transport for long distances without deterioration.

The Far North has coconuts, including Australia's only commercial coconut plantation near Innisfail. Another speciality of the State is that favourite of small boys, the macadamia, known locally as the Queensland nut.

Queensland offers a variety of sea foods which few States or nations could better. It has long been famous for prawns which are netted along the eastern coast and also, in more recent years, around Cape York peninsula and in the Gulf of Carpentaria.

The Queensland mud crab is renowned as one of the finest sea delicacies in the world.

The Great Barrier Reef is the home of the red emperor, coral trout, coral cod, maori wrasse and a host of other tropical fish. The coastal waters and estuaries of the Far North have the delectable barramundi, which the American gourmet Maurice Dreicer has pronounced 'one of the great fishes of the world'.

Turtles and dugongs can be fine eating but in recent years they have been protected from white fishermen. Only aboriginals and Torres Strait islanders are now permitted to catch and eat these creatures.

LICENSING REGULATIONS
Hotels throughout Queensland are open from 10 am to 10 pm on six days a week, Monday to Saturday, with an additional 15 minutes after closing time to finish drinks ordered before 10 pm.

Hotels are permitted to open on Sundays for two two-hour sessions, 11 am to 1 pm and 4 pm to 6 pm. Districts may apply to vary these hours. Through most of North Queensland the evening session is 5 pm to 7 pm. However 4 pm to 6 pm applies generally in other areas, including the Gold Coast and Brisbane.

BRISBANE AND ENVIRONS

Brisbane is built on the hills unfolding from the Taylor Range to the banks of the Brisbane River, which winds through the heart of the city on its way seaward. Three fine bridges—the Victoria Bridge, William Jolly Bridge and Story Bridge—add to the character of Brisbane, which is the most 'different' of the State capitals.

The population in 1971 was 816,987, spread over a Greater Brisbane Area of 375 square miles. Port facilities and wharves extend along the river banks. Brisbane has container handling facilities and is a major port for interstate and overseas vessels.

Within a 60-mile radius of the city the visitor can find some of Australia's finest surfing beaches, and also magnificent ranges and fertile valleys. Attractions of the Brisbane area include:

1. BEACHES

The surfing resorts along the Gold Coast to the south, of which Surfers Paradise is the most famous; and the Sunshine Coast to the north, including Caloundra, Mooloolaba, Maroochydore and Noosa. The nearest beaches to the city are the sheltered still-water coves of Moreton Bay. Redcliffe, 20 miles from Brisbane, and nearby Sandgate are protected from the surf by Stradbroke, Moreton and Bribie islands and are popular for family outings and fishing excursions.

2. MOUNTAINS

The D'Aguilar Range, 28 miles north-west of Brisbane along a scenic highway, has magnificent views from Mt Glorious (2,070 ft.) and Mt Nebo (1,900 ft.). The Darlington Range and Mt Tamborine are 45 miles south of Brisbane. Mt Coot-tha (745 ft.) in the Taylor Range a few miles west of the city, gives a view of Brisbane and Moreton Bay extending on clear days to the Glasshouse Mountains in the north, and south to the Lamington Plateau.

3. REDCLIFFE

Redcliffe, on Moreton Bay 20 miles from Brisbane, was the site of the original convict settlement, moved up-river soon afterward following an outbreak of fever. Redcliffe now has 32,200 people and attracts tourists with its safe beaches, broken by rocky headlands jutting into the bay.

4. HISTORIC BUILDINGS AROUND BRISBANE

Parliament House, opposite the Botanic Gardens on the corner of George and Alice streets, was opened in 1868 and is a fine example of French Renaissance architecture.

The Windmill (Observatory) on Wickham Terrace was built by convicts in 1829 to grind maize for the penal settlement; but the sails would not function and it was converted to a treadmill worked by 26 convicts. Two aboriginal murderers were hanged from the windmill in 1841. It has since been used as a signal station, a Fire Brigade lookout, and in 1934 for research into radio and television. It is preserved as a tourist attraction.

Old Government Stores in Queen's Wharf Road leading to the northern end of Victoria Bridge is one of Brisbane's oldest buildings. Below the gable is a plaque on which is engraved a crown with the letters 'G.R.' and the date '1829'.

Government House, in Fernberg Road, Rosalie, built in 1865, is the State Governor's official residence.

The Treasury Building, of Italian Renaissance architecture, occupies a site of 1½ acres at the southern end of Queen Street. It was begun in 1885 but not completed until 1928.

The Deanery, next to St John's Cathedral in Ann Street, was built in 1853 and was the temporary residence of the first Governor, Sir George Ferguson Bowen. From its balcony the Proclamation was read in 1859 to announce Queensland as a separate colony.

The Institute of Technology, at the Botanic Gardens end of George Street, was the official residence of Queensland's first Governor. It is preserved as part of a busy educational complex.

The City Hall, completed in 1930 at the then impressive cost of $2 million, is considered by many to be the most imposing civic centre in any State capital. It is in King George Square near the site of the original pond which was the reservoir for the first settlers.

The G.P.O. at 261-285 Queen Street is of colonial architecture with 19th century Civic, Italian Renaissance and other influences. John Petrie erected the original wing in 1872.

Newstead House in Newstead Park near Breakfast Creek Bridge, was built in 1846 as a town house for Patrick Leslie, the first settler on the Darling Downs. It is open to the public as a museum.

5. BOTANICAL GARDENS

The Botanical Gardens, five blocks from Queen Street via George or Edward streets, covers 50 acres beside the Brisbane River, with thousands of native and exotic tropical and sub-tropical plants. The municipal orchestral shell is the centre for regular free concerts.

6. NEW FARM PARK

New Farm Park, on a bend of the river at New Farm is famous for its 22,000 rose bushes which are at their best in February. Avenues of jacarandas bloom in October and November and the spreading poinciana trees in November and December.

7. MORETON BAY ISLANDS

Day cruises go to Moreton, Stradbroke and Bribie islands and Bribie also is connected with the mainland at Toorbul Point by a toll bridge. These large islands have surf beaches on the ocean side and, on the sheltered side, calm waters for water ski-ing, fishing and boating. Moreton Bay has 365 islands, making it a boat-owners' paradise.

8. THE KOALA SANCTUARY

The Koala sanctuary at Lone Pine on the Brisbane River is only eight miles from the city centre and is accessible by road or by regular launch trips.

9. THE UNIVERSITY OF QUEENSLAND

The University of Queensland has a beautiful riverside setting at St Lucia, enhanced by flowering shrubs and avenues of trees.

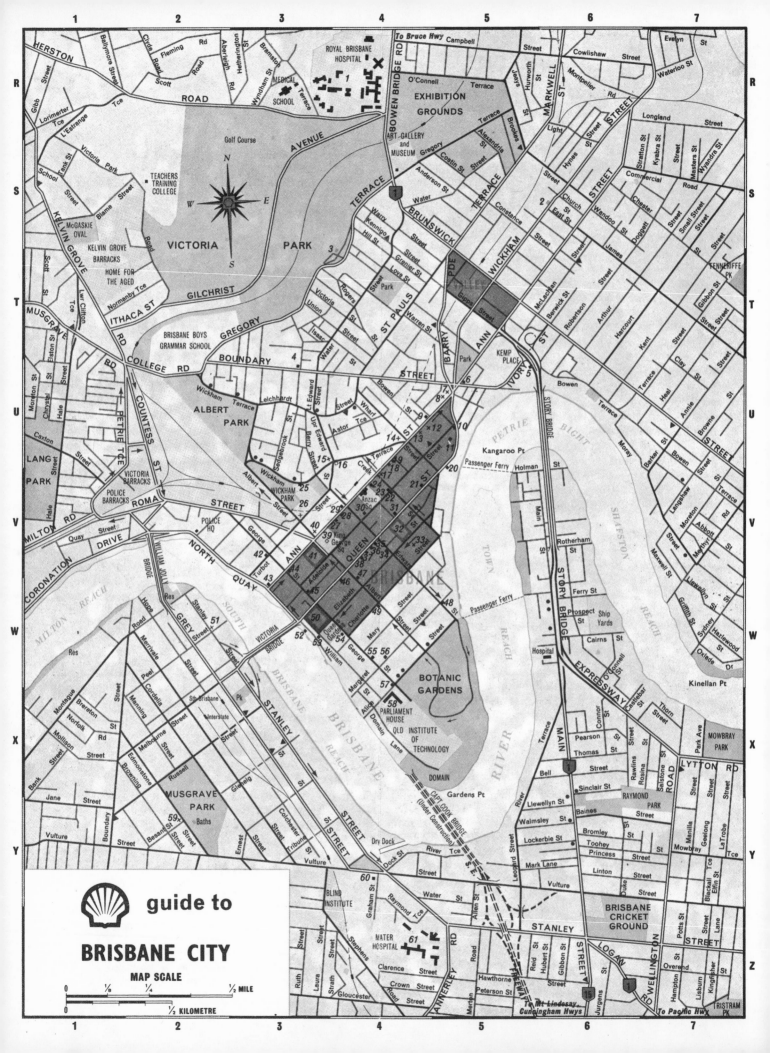

guide to
BRISBANE CITY

MAP SCALE

10. THE OASIS

The Oasis in Station Road, Sunnybank, has a variety of attractions for visitors including three swimming pools, seven acres of gardens and a miniature zoo with collections of butterflies and rare shells.

11. TOWNS OF THE BRISBANE REGION

Beenleigh, 23 miles south of Brisbane, has a population of 1,375. It is best known for its rum distillery and as a centre for dairying and the cultivation of sugar cane and arrowroot.

Ipswich, 24 miles west of Brisbane on the Bremer River, is an industrial centre with a population of more than 56,000. It was one of Queensland's earliest settlements, established during the late 1820s as a camp for convicts quarrying limestone.

Caboolture is a small rural township at the junction of the Bruce and D'Aguilar highways. Branching from here is the road leading to Toorbul Point and Bribie Island.

12. BRISBANE METROPOLITAN CARAVAN PARKS

Newmarket Gardens Caravan Park, 199 Ashgrove Avenue, Ashgrove.

Aspley Gardens Caravan Park, Bruce Highway, Aspley.

Northern Star Caravan Park, 43 Albany Creek Road, Aspley.

Belmont Caravan Park, Belmont Road, Belmont.

Carina Caravan Park, Creek Road, Carina.

San Mateo, Pacific Highway, Eight-Mile Plains.

Brisbane Caravan Park, Scott Street, Hawthorne (near ferry landing).

Morgan's Tourist Waterfront Caravan Park, Lytton Road, Hemmant.

Pacific Caravan Park, 2059 Pacific Highway, Mount Gravatt.

Monte Carlo Caravan Park, 1189 Wynnum Road, Murarrie.

Wynnum Road Caravan Park, 105 Wynnum Road, Tingalpa.

Belcara Caravan Park, 97 Wynnum Road, Wynnum West.

Maps by the courtesy of the Shell Company of Australia.

Full colour maps featuring tourist areas are available from Shell Service Stations.

SHELL DEALERS Shown thus........▲

BRISBANE CITY

GUIDE TO SYMBOLS

Car Parks (covered) .... □
Churches .... +
General Features .... ■
Hospitals .... +
Swimming Pools .... ■
Motels (not indexed) .... ■

No	Feature	Ref
■ 9	Ambulance H.Q. (Q.A.T.B.)	U4
■ 43	Ansett Airlines	W3
+ 15	Baptist Church	U3
■ 57	Bellevue Hotel	W4
+ 14	Bethlehem Lutheran Church	U4
■ 11	Blood Bank	U5
■ 29	Canberra Hotel	V4
■ 46	Carlton Hotel	W4
■ 46	Carlton Theatrette	W4
■ 3	Centenary Swimming Pool	S4
+ 8	Church of Christ	U5
+ 7	City Congregational Church	U5

■ 41	City Hall	V3
■ 24	Commonwealth Offices	V4
■ 60	Conservatorium of Music	Y4
■ 45	Criterion Hotel	W3
■ 20	Customs House	U5
+26	Dental Hospital	V3
■ 54	Executive Building	W4
■ 49	Festival Hall	W4
■ 32	G.P.O.	V4
+59	Greek Orthodox Church	Y2
■ 22	Gresham Hotel	V4
■ 48	Harbours & Marine Dept.	W5
■ 52	Hayles Cruises	W3
■ 36	Her Majesty's Theatre	V4
■ 55	Hotel Cecil	W4
■ 44	Lennons Hotel	V4
■ 4	Main Roads Dept.	U3
■ 42	Majestic Hotel	V3
■ 19	Masonic Temple	U4
+ 61	Mater Hospital	Z4
+ 40	Methodist Church	V4
■ 47	Metro Theatre	V4
□ 39	Municipal Car Park	V4
□ 16	Municipal Car Park	U4
■ 10	National Hotel	U5

■ 25	Observatory	V3
■ 37	Odeon Theatre	V4
■ 58	Parliament House	X4
■ 28	Peoples Palace	V4
■ 53	Public Library	W3
■ 31	Qantas House	V4
■ 30	QLD. Govt. Tourist Bureau	V4
■ 6	R.A.C.Q. Head Office	U5
■ 34	R.A.C.Q. Travel Service	V4
■ 38	Regent Theatre	V4
+ 1	Royal Brisbane Hospital	R4
■ 5	Royal QLD. Yacht Club	T5
■ 18	SHELL HOUSE	U4
+ 17	St. Andrews Presb. Church	V4
■ 51	St. Helens Hospital	W2
+ 12	St. Johns Cathedral (Angl.)	U4
+ 13	St. Martins Hospital	U4
+ 33	St. Stephens Cathedral (R.C.)	V4
■ 27	Salvation Army H.Q.	V4
■ 21	Stock Exchange	V4
■ 56	Synagogue	W4
■ 23	T.A.A. Head Office	V4
■ 50	Treasury Building	W3
■ 2	Valley Baths	S6
■ 35	Wintergarden Theatre	V4

THE GOLD COAST

The Gold Coast, Queensland's fun strip for holiday-makers, begins at Southport, 47 miles south of Brisbane, and extends along 20 miles of golden beaches to Coolangatta on the NSW border. The area is classified as a single city rather than a string of towns and the permanent population, now 66,000, is the fastest-growing in Queensland.

The business of the Gold Coast is tourism. Accommodation is varied to suit every budget, with penthouse suites, hotels and motels of varying quality and tariff, guest houses, apartments, flats, caravan parks and camping grounds.

The boutiques, cosmopolitan bars, discotheques and restaurants, cabarets and night-clubs are of international standard. Sports available to tourists include water-skiing, motor-racing, cycling, trotting, coursing, boating, fishing, shooting, golf, tennis, squash, croquet, bowls, basketball, cricket, archery and horse racing.

Of course the main attractions to visitors are the ocean and abundant sunshine. The surfing beaches south from Southport include the famous Surfers Paradise, Broadbeach, Mermaid Beach, Nobby's Beach, Miami, Burleigh, Pacific Beach, Palm Beach, Currumbin, Tugun, Bilinga, Kirra and Coolangatta.

PLACES OF INTEREST FOR VISITORS TO THE GOLD COAST AND DISTRICT INCLUDE

1. **Natureland Zoo,** Coolangatta. Porpoise pool and aquarium.

2. **Auto Museum,** Kirra, a collection of early model motor vehicles.

3. **Bird Sanctuary,** Currumbin, where wild birds, mostly brightly coloured lorrikeets, fly down from the bush to be hand-fed. Nearby **Santa-Land** is a parkland of life-size fun and fantasy, in cartoon style, for children and adults.

4. **Burleigh Heads National Park,** with graded walks along which the lucky visitor may see koalas, wallabies and other animals.

5. **Fauna reserve** at West Burleigh, where koalas and platypus are fed each afternoon.

6. **Chair-lift** at Nobby's Beach takes visitors from beside the Gold Coast Highway for 1,100 feet up to Sky Terrace lookout. Also at Nobby's Beach, at the shopping centre, is **Traintasia,** a miniature railway track 450 feet long, with stations, bridges, lights, signals, tunnels and, of course, scale-model trains.

7. **Cascades Park and Gardens,** between Broadbeach and Surfers Paradise, is a riverside park.

8. At **Surfers Paradise** are the **Barrier Reef Aquarium, London's Wax Museum,** and **Australian Pioneers Museum.**

9. **Marineland of Australia,** Southport, with underwater feeding of sharks, gropers, stingrays and other marine creatures. Southport also has the **South Pacific Trade Fair,** featuring displays of Australian products and industries, an aboriginal museum, a collection of dolls, and a show of interesting firearms and other weapons. **Ski-land of Australia,** at Southport, has its own water ballet and facilities for water ski-ing and ski-jumping.

PLACES OF INTEREST IN THE HINTERLAND INCLUDE

Pioneer House, Advance Town, Numinbah Valley Road,

seven miles from Nerang. An original pioneer house at the foot of Springbrook Range.

Boomerang Factory at Mudgeeraba on Springbrook Road, where visitors may buy boomerangs and watch displays of boomerang throwing.

Alpine Panorama, at the end of Springbrook Road is a spectacular view of the Queensland–NSW border country and seascape.

Thunderbird Park at Cedar Creek on Tamborine Mountain 27 miles from Southport is a resort for gem fossickers.

Jasper Farm at Wonga Wallen, Upper Coomera, a private property where fossickers may seek jaspers on payment of a nominal fee. Prospecting tools on hire.

RECREATION FACILITIES ON THE GOLD COAST INCLUDE

Golf 18-hole courses at Southport, Burleigh Heads, Coolangatta and Broadbeach.

Squash Southport, Surfers Paradise, Burleigh Heads, Coolangatta.

Tennis Southport, Surfers Paradise, Burleigh Heads, Coolangatta, Miami.

Fishing Motor or rowing boats for hire at Tweed Heads, Tallebudgera Creek, Surfers Paradise, The Spit, Labrador, Angler's Paradise, Hollywell, Paradise Point, Coombabah.

Pedal-boats For hire at Currumbin Inlet.

Horse racing Southport on Saturdays and public holidays.

Shooting Rifle clubs at Southport and Currumbin.

Night trotting Southport on Saturdays and public holidays.

Greyhound coursing Border Park raceway, Tweed Heads, Coolangatta's 'twin town' just across the NSW border.

Roller skating Coolangatta, Miami, Southport.

Riding stables Nerang, Ingleside.

Cruises Launches go from Southport to South Stradbroke Island and along the Nerang River.

CULTURAL ACTIVITIES AND NIGHT LIFE

Southport and Surfers Paradise have a number of art galleries. Theatre groups at Surfers Paradise and Coolangatta are active. Night life centres around the many night clubs, restaurants and luxury hotels, which feature top international entertainers.

THE SUNSHINE COAST

The Sunshine Coast begins at Caloundra, 60 road miles north of Brisbane. It extends north for a further 40 miles to Noosa Heads and Tewantin and inland to include the towns of Buderim, Nambour, Woombye, Yandina, Eumundi, Pomona, Maleny, Montville and Kenilworth. The Sunshine Coast has a total population of about 40,000 living in three shires, Landsborough, Maroochy and Noosa.

Tourism is the major industry along the coast but the hinterland produces sugar cane, tropical and citrus fruits, ginger and vegetables and is also fine dairying and beef-cattle fattening country.

Surfing beaches include Caloundra, King's Beach, Moffat Beach, Dicky Beach, Buddina Beach, Mooloolaba, Alexandra Headland, Maroochydore, Ninderry, Mudjimba, Marcoola, Yaroomba, Coolum Beach, Peregian, Sunshine Beach, Noosa Heads. Caloundra has the still-water swimming areas of Bulcock Beach and Golden Beach.

Accommodation for visitors is plentiful, including motels, hotels, guest houses, caravan parks and camping grounds. Many flats and houses are available for holiday letting.

LARGER TOWNS ON THE SUNSHINE COAST INCLUDE

Buderim, a few miles inland from Mooloolaba. Buderim has the only ginger factory in the southern hemisphere.

Caloundra, 60 road miles north of Brisbane and the southernmost resort of the Sunshine Coast. It is at the end of Pumicestone Channel which separates Bribie Island from the mainland. In Caloundra Harbor and Pumicestone Passage are 50 square miles of waterways with facilities for motor cruisers, yachts, fishing trawlers and dinghies. There is excellent reef fishing a few miles offshore.

Mooloolaba and Alexandra Headland, adjoining resorts at the mouth of the Mooloolah River. The Government spent $1,900,000 here on construction of a safe harbour for small craft. The new Government pilot station for the Port of Brisbane is at Mooloolaba. Activities for visitors include surf and river swimming, fishing, board-riding, yachting and open-sea trimaran and catamaran racing. Charter boats for cruising and deep-sea fishing leave from the public jetty.

Maroochydore, at the mouth of the picturesque Maroochy River which has flocks of black swans and pelicans. There is a magnificent surfing beach and also a safe river beach for children. Scenic flights operate from Maroochydore airport.

Noosa Heads, at the mouth of the Noosa River, is a surfing, fishing and sailing resort. A few miles up-river is **Tewantin,** a base for trips to the chain of lakes which extend northward for 48 miles with a varied wildlife of black swans, ducks, cranes and herons. Organised motor trips and cruises go from Tewantin and nearby Noosaville to view the famous coloured sands of Teewah and Rainbow Beach which rise 600 feet above sea level. Attractions at Tewantin include the House of Bottles.

Nambour, on the Bruce Highway, the main highway heading north. Nambour is the commercial centre of the Sunshine Coast and is surrounded by rich farmlands.

POINTS OF INTEREST ON THE SUNSHINE COAST HINTERLAND

Kondalilla National Park, north of the township of Maleny, covers 185 acres on the crest of the Blackall Range. There are picnic amenities.

Noosa National Park, near Noosa Heads, has an area of 825 acres and borders the Pacific Ocean. Walkways enable visitors to explore this sanctuary for bird and animal life.

Mary Cairncross Park, south-east of Maleny, is 100 acres of rain forest with walking tracks and picnic amenities.

Picnic spots There are dozens of established sites for picnicking and camping on all the main roads between the beach areas and the Blackall Range; on top of the range and beyond; and at all national parks.

Double Island Point lighthouse is on the Ocean Beach north of Tewantin, from which it is separated by the Forty-Mile Beach, including the coloured sands of Teewah.

Recreation facilities on the Sunshine Coast include tennis and squash courts; golf and mini-golf courses; skating rinks; and facilities for bowls, croquet, fishing, hiking, sailing and water ski-ing.

WILDFLOWERS

Kawana, south of Mooloolaba, and Peregian, south of Sunshine Beach and Noosa Heads, have beautiful displays of wildflowers during the winter and of Christmas bells in December. During the second half of August each year the Caloundra branch of the Wildlife Preservation Society holds an eight-day Wildflower Show, with native plants on sale.

BIRDS

The Sunshine Coast is rich in bird life including waders on the shores of ocean and estuaries; birds of open bush and rain forest species; Bell Miners in colonies from Kenilworth to Borumba Dam; waterfowl on lakes, dams and swamps. Brolgas, jabirus and emus are sometimes seen.

Pelagic species include Australian Gannets, migrants from New Zealand during winter; and mutton birds on their return flight from the eastern Pacific to their breeding ground in Bass Strait. Winter migrant birds from south and west come for the banksia and paperbark blossoming, when itinerant beekeepers also arrive.

Visitors are welcome at meetings of the Caloundra branch of the Wildlife Preservation Society held on the third Wednesday each month at 8 pm at 16 Orvieto Terrace, Caloundra. The list of birds of south-east Queensland is available from the society.

THE GREAT BARRIER REEF

The Great Barrier Reef, about 1,250 miles long and spread across 80,000 square miles of ocean, varies from 10 to 150 miles in its distance from the Queensland coast. Its islands and colourful coral reefs form a tourist attraction unique in the world.

Modern tourist resorts have been established on some of the islands. Attractions include swimming in crystal-clear lagoons; incomparable game and reef fishing; and viewing of the beautiful corals either from glass-bottomed boats or free-diving with scuba gear.

THE MAIN RESORTS OF THE GREAT BARRIER REEF INCLUDE

Fraser Island, off the coast about 30 miles north of Maryborough. At the north-east tip is Orchid Beach Island Village with accommodation in self-contained units. The island has 90 miles of ocean beaches and more than 40 freshwater lakes. Island Airways has a service between the island and Hervey Bay and Maryborough.

Heron Island, 45 miles north-east of Gladstone. This is a haven for birds and for giant turtles which lay their eggs ashore. Charter launches operate between Heron Island and Gladstone Tuesdays and Saturdays. A helicopter service on Saturdays, Mondays and Tuesdays makes multiple direct flights to and from Gladstone. Accommodation includes luxury units, motel-type units and cabins.

Quoin Island, near Gladstone. It covers 87 acres and launches operate any day to suit guests. Motel-type accommodation.

Great Keppel Island, 30 miles north-east of Rockhampton. Daily launch service to and from Emu Park and Rosslyn Bay. Coral Air Service flies twice daily between Rockhampton and the island. Accommodation includes self-contained lodges; and cabins with communal toilet.

Brampton Island, 18 miles north of Mackay Harbor. It covers four square miles and is the southernmost of the 70-island Cumberland Group which stretches through Whitsunday Passage. Day cruises leave Mackay Harbor for Brampton Wednesdays, Fridays and Sundays. TAA flies daily between Mackay and the island. Accommodation is self-contained units.

Lindeman Island, at the southern end of Whitsunday Passage, 42 miles north of Mackay. It is a mountainous island of four square miles, fringed with coral reefs. Daily air service from Mackay. Self-contained suites to accommodate 72 guests.

Long Island, in the Whitsunday Islands group. It is a national park of 2,066 acres with dense rain forest. Happy Bay resort has single, double and family-unit accommodation. Launch operates from Shute Harbor, near Proserpine, Tuesdays, Fridays and Sundays.

Hook Island, in Whitsunday Passage. This has the world's largest underwater observatory for viewing a living coral reef with its wealth of marine activity. Launch daily from Shute Harbor.

South Molle Island, in Whitsunday Passage. It covers more than 1,000 acres, with fine views of the Whitsunday Islands. Launches leave Shute Harbor daily. Accommodation in units or budget-priced cabins.

Daydream Island, one of the Molle group adjacent to the Whitsunday archipelago. It covers 28 acres. Helicopter service from Proserpine Sundays, Tuesdays and Fridays. Launch service from Shute Harbor as required. Accommodation is in a modern two-storey building with double and single units.

Hayman Island, 18 miles from the mainland at the northern end of Whitsunday Passage. It covers 850 acres. Launches leave daily from Shute Harbor and twice daily on Fridays and Sundays. A helicopter operates on various days from Proserpine and Mackay. A modern fully-licensed hotel offers single and double units and lodges also are available.

Magnetic Island, five miles from Townsville. It covers 20 square miles, has 25 miles of coastline and 23 beautiful beaches with fringing reefs. Marine Gardens Coral Observatory contains living coral and reef fish. Accommodation includes first-class hotels, motels, guest houses, flats, units and cottages. Launch service from Townsville five times daily. A vehicular ferry operates three times a week, and makes extra trips in the peak holiday season.

Orpheus Island, in the Palm Islands group 50 miles north of Townsville. The island is about seven miles long and varies in width between a quarter-mile and $1\frac{1}{2}$ miles, and it is 14 miles from the Outer Barrier Reef. The Lodge is on a long, sandy bay on the sheltered side of the island and accommodates 23 in cabins, and bungalows. There also are economy cabins with communal amenities. Bush Pilots Airways flies between Townsville and Palm Island on Fridays. The flight connects at Palm Island with the launch, *Moana*, which cruises for $1\frac{1}{4}$ hours through sheltered waters to Orpheus. Launch service direct from Townsville on Tuesdays.

Bedarra Island, four miles from the Hull River mouth, with Tully 15 miles further inland. It is a picturesque island with dense jungle. Launch service from Hull River as required. Air services from Tully, Innisfail or Townsville. Accommodation for 10 persons in twin-bed cottages with own amenities.

Dunk Island, three miles from the coast, near Tully, 60 miles south of Cairns. It has 14 miles of shore-line including $3\frac{1}{2}$ miles of sandy beaches. Dunk rises to 890 feet and has many miles of graded tracks and jungle walks with magnificent views of the coast and nearby islands. Air charter service from Townsville, Cairns, Innisfail and Tully. Launch leaves Clump Point Jetty at Mission Beach on Saturdays, Sundays, Tuesdays and Wednesdays. Chalet accommodation for 74 guests. Single rooms also available.

Green Island, 17 miles north-east of Cairns. It covers 32 acres, a low-lying cay built up from the reef with accumulations of sand and coral debris, covered with thick vegetation. An underwater observatory and aquarium provides splendid viewing of marine life. Glass-bottomed boats cruise over surrounding coral reefs. Launch service between Cairns and Green Island daily. Fully-licensed hotel on the island with cabin accommodation.

Barrier Reef cruises operate from major towns along the coast between Gladstone and Cairns. Further inquiries about this and other aspects of holiday-making on the Great Barrier Reef should be made to any office of the Queensland State Tourist Bureau.

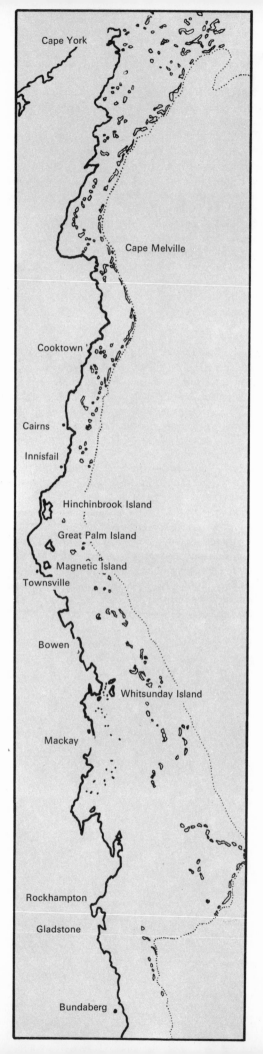

NORTHERN QUEENSLAND

WESTERN QUEENSLAND

For the purposes of this guide North Queensland is the coastal plain extending from Mackay, 675 miles from Brisbane, to Cooktown 700 miles further north. Tourism is one of the area's chief money-earners and accommodation is plentiful and geared to the industry.

The highway from Brisbane to Cairns is bitumen throughout. Attractions of the many resort towns and their environs include the rain forest and its unique wildlife; fine beaches for swimming; and the isles and coral outcrops of the Great Barrier Reef offshore.

Full details on a district level may be obtained from any office of the Queensland Government Tourist Bureau or from one of the many travel agencies established in all main centres.

CITIES AND TOWNS OF THE REGION INCLUDE

Mackay, with about 30,000 people, 675 road miles from Brisbane. It is a major tourist and commercial centre, with one of the most scenic harbours on the Queensland coast. It has the world's largest bulk sugar loading terminal.

Proserpine, 756 miles from Brisbane. A mile north of the town is the turnoff to Shute Harbor, from which launches cruise to the Great Barrier Reef islands.

Bowen, on the shores of Port Denison, a farming and meat-works centre and the northern gateway to the Whitsunday Islands.

Ayr and **Home Hill,** twin sugar towns on either side of the Burdekin River about 60 miles south of Townsville.

Townsville, 931 miles from Brisbane. This is Australia's largest tropical city with a population of 68,000, the site of the James Cook University of North Queensland, and also of huge meatworks and other industries and a growing military base.

Ingham, 72 miles north of Townsville, is supported by sugar cane-growing, timber and tourism. Thirty-two miles westward is Wallaman Falls with a drop of 984 feet, making it the highest waterfall in Australia.

Tully, another agricultural and tourist centre. To the east, ranging to the coast is a tropical rain forest and the ocean beaches of Mission Beach and Bingil Bay.

Innisfail, 1,107 miles north of Brisbane, is the largest centre between Townsville and Cairns, with a population of 7,430. The surrounding district produces sugar, tropical fruits, tea, timber and fat beef and dairy cattle.

Cairns, with 32,000 people, is on Trinity Bay 1,162 miles north of Brisbane. Bitumen highways lead to the Atherton Tableland and connect with the dirt roads of Cape York peninsula which extends for a further 700 miles to the Torres Strait. Cairns is a port for sugar, beef, timber, and other products, and also one of the leading tourist centres in Queensland. North from Cairns, the **Cook Highway** follows the coast for 26 of the 47 miles to Mossman, and is one of the most spectacular drives in Queensland. Nine miles south of Mossman and three miles off the highway is **Port Douglas,** which claims 'the best beach in the world'.

Cooktown, 208 miles north of Cairns via the Atherton Table-land, was an early goldfields boom town and has an excellent museum. The road is dirt-surfaced and is impassable in wet weather. In dry weather it is trafficable for any make of car, but during the wet season travellers should check the conditions ahead at every stop on the way.

Western Queensland is an area too vast for any detailed visitors' guide to be given here. It is cattle and sheep and mining country with vast pastoral holdings and scattered townships, and dry plains which turn to a morass in the infrequent periods of heavy rain.

The great majority of roads are dirt-surfaced and subject to weather.

Easily the largest centre is **Mount Isa,** 1,187 miles from Brisbane and 630 miles west of Townsville. It has more than 20,000 people, supported mainly by one of the great copper, silver lead and zinc mining fields of the world. More than 15,000 tourists are shown through Mount Isa Mines each year.

Hotel and motel accommodation and service station facilities vary in quality throughout western Queensland and before any outback motoring trip full information should be sought from the Queensland Government Tourist Bureau and from the Royal Automobile Club of Queensland, corner Ann and Boundary streets, Brisbane.

SOME CENTRES OF INTEREST TO TOURISTS

Burketown, Normanton and **Croydon** in the Gulf Country reflect a distinct frontier atmosphere. **Karumba Lodge** at the mouth of the Norman River is a tourist fishing and hunting centre.

Winton, 860 miles from Brisbane, is a commercial centre of the Channel Country, a great beef cattle-raising area. **Opalton,** one of the earliest opal fields in Queensland, is 78 miles to the south-west. Dagworth station near Winton is where A. B. ('Banjo') Paterson wrote the national song, 'Waltzing Matilda'.

Longreach, 768 miles from Brisbane, is the principal town of the great wool-producing area of the central-west.

Mitchell, 350 miles west of Brisbane, has ample motel and hotel accommodation. There is a caravan park on the Warrego Highway opposite Carnarvon National Park.

Roma, 53 miles east of Mitchell on the Warrego Highway, was the centre of Australia's earliest oil search. Campbell Park has natural gas barbecues for boiling the billy or grilling steak.

In the southern border districts of western Queensland the largest towns include **Goondiwindi, Mungindi, Dirranbandi** and **Cunnamulla** and, in the far west, **Thargomindah.**

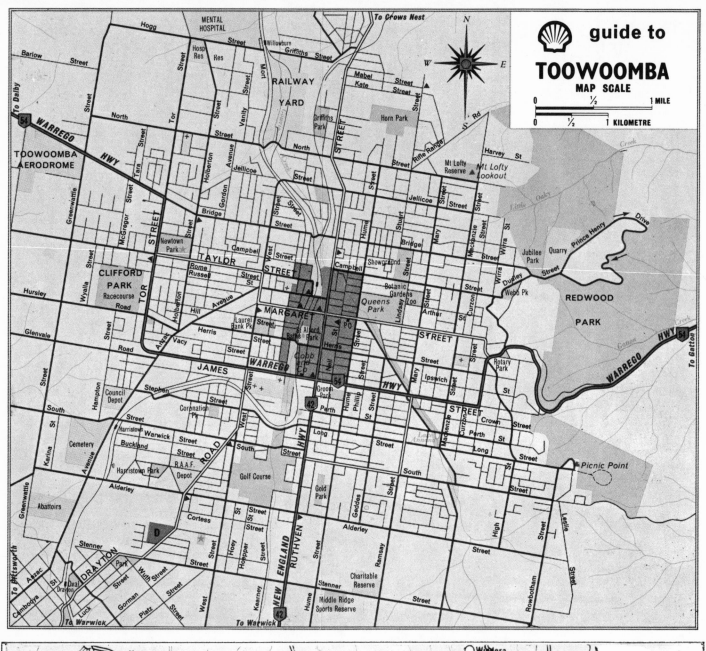

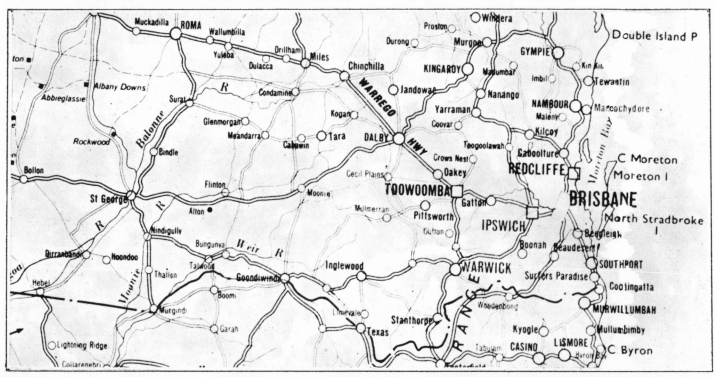

DARLING DOWNS

The Darling Downs in south-east Queensland covers 3½ million acres and produces wheat and other grains, wool, fat lambs, beef, fruits, dairy produce and fodder.

The commercial and industrial centre, **Toowoomba,** is 80 miles from Brisbane along the Warrego Highway and has a population of 60,000. The agricultural wealth of the Darling Downs passes through Toowoomba. Its industries include manufacture of agricultural machinery and implements, and diesel engines; timber and planing mills; furniture factories and brickworks; flour mills; a yeast factory; two breweries; cattle and poultry abattoirs; bacon, cheese, and butter factories.

SOME OTHER CENTRES OF INTEREST ON THE DARLING DOWNS

Warwick, 55 miles south of Toowoomba on the banks of the Condamine River is the second-largest city on the Downs, with 10,000 people. The area is noted for its stud cattle and thoroughbred horses.

Stanthorpe, in mountain country 23 miles from the NSW border and about 150 miles south-west of Brisbane, has 8,500 people. It is 3,000 feet above sea level and is the centre of the Granite Belt which produces apples, pears and stone fruits.

Dalby is on the northern edge of the Darling Downs, just over 50 miles north-west of Toowoomba. Around it is one of the richest wheat-growing areas in Queensland.

About 30 miles north-east of Dalby is the **Bunya Mountains National Park,** covering more than 24,000 acres and renowned for its Bunya pine forests.

Accommodation and service station facilities throughout the Darling Downs area are excellent.

Maps by the courtesy of the Shell Company of Australia.

Full colour maps featuring tourist areas are available from Shell Service Stations.

guide to

THE BUNYA MOUNTAINS

MAP SCALE

Walking Track

HEIGHTS

| -2400' | 2400'-3000' | 3000'-3400' | +3400' |

ATHERTON TABLELAND

CENTRAL COAST (to Rockhampton)

The Atherton Tableland covers 3,000 square miles and has about 23,500 people. The crops include tobacco, peanuts, maize and vegetables and this is one of the few dairying areas within the northern tropics.

Rain forest and volcanic lakes attract large numbers of tourists and accommodation and other facilities for travellers are excellent.

The Tableland is about 2,500 feet above sea level. Roads from the coast are fully sealed. Access is from Innisfail along the Palmerston Highway; from Gordonvale along the Gillies Highway; and from Cairns via Kuranda.

THE PRINCIPAL TOWNS ARE

Mareeba, population 5,000, about 43 miles west of Cairns. Centre of tobacco farming and also the railway junction serving the pastoral lands west toward the Gulf of Carpentaria.
Atherton, the commercial centre of the Tableland, 21 miles south of Mareeba.

Good roads go from Atherton to a number of small townships:—
Yungaburra, 10 miles east of Atherton, is near the crater lakes, Barrine (2,400 feet above sea level, 256 acres water surface, up to 360 feet deep) and Eacham (2,478 feet, 130 acres, 226 feet), which are surrounded by national parks.
Malanda, nine miles south of Yungaburra, is a dairying centre. The Malanda Falls are nearby.
Millaa Millaa, 20 miles south of Malanda, is a centre for dairying and timber production. There are a number of waterfalls nearby to attract tourists.
Ravenshoe, an old mining town 32 miles south of Atherton, gives access to Millstream Falls, Tully Gorge, Koombooloomba Dam and Little Millstream Falls.
Herberton, 12 miles south-west of Atherton, is another old mining town.
Mount Hypipamee Crater and **Dinner Creek Falls** are a short distance off the main Atherton–Ravenshoe road. The crater, 3,250 feet above sea level, is 480 feet deep. It is a geological oddity of uncertain origin for with its granite sides it is certainly not a volanic crater.

From **Tolga,** just north of Atherton, a road connects with Tinaroo Dam, an irrigation reservoir holding a capacity of 330,000 acre feet of water. The dam is a tourist attraction with facilities for swimming and boating, and a motel and a caravan park.

The winter climate on the Tableland is mild, but it is advisable to take warm clothing. During the wet season, between December and early April, access routes to the coast are sometimes cut by heavy rain.

Leaving the Sunshine Coast, the Bruce Highway runs north through **Gympie** (population 11,500) on the banks of the Mary River. This is a former gold-rush town, now a centre for dairying, cattle fattening, tropical fruit-growing and timber production.

Thirty-three miles east, on the coast, is **Tin Can Bay,** a prawning and fishing port and a favourite resort of amateur fishermen.

The Central Coast stretching north to the Tropic of Capricorn and Rockhampton is the outlet for the cattle country. It is a region of coal mines and industrial enterprise as well as pastoral and agricultural production.

NORTH FROM GYMPIE, THE MAIN CENTRES ARE

Maryborough, 178 miles north of Brisbane. This city of 20,000 produces ships and railway locomotives. On the coast 22 miles away is Hervey Bay with its seaside resorts of Pialba, Scarness, Torquay and Urangan. Hervey Bay is one of the finest fishing grounds on the Queensland coast.
Bundaberg, at the mouth of the Burnett River, 33 miles east of the Bruce Highway. It has 25,000 people and is the main centre of Queensland's southern sugar belt and for the 3,000 square miles of the Central Burnett agricultural district. It has a bulk sugar terminal and is the home of Bundaberg Rum. Tourists come for the deep-sea fishing.
Gladstone, 135 miles from Bundaberg and 360 miles north of Brisbane, on Port Curtis. This is now the busiest port in Queensland outside Brisbane, with exports of coal, beef, dairy products, sea-foods, fruits, tobacco and peanuts. It is an ocean oil terminal and the site of a multi-million-dollar alumina plant, processing bauxite from Cape York peninsula. Gladstone (population 13,000) has been selected as the wheat port for central Queensland. Tannum Sands, 22 miles south, is an ocean beach resort. Gladstone is the terminal of the annual Brisbane–Gladstone yacht race at Easter, and the centre from which air and launch services operate to Heron Island.
Rockhampton (population 46,000), just north of the Tropic of Capricorn, 429 miles north of Brisbane. The population of the immediate Rockhampton district is more than 100,000. This is the commercial capital of central Queensland, serving the hinterland industries of beef cattle raising, agriculture and mining. The city's Botanical Gardens are famous for their displays of tropical blooms and ferns. Olsen's Caves 16 miles north of Rockhampton have impressive limestone formations. Twenty-six miles from Rockhampton is the coastal resort of **Yeppoon,** which is connected with another beach tourist centre, **Emu Park,** by 12 miles of coastal scenic road.

The Northern Territory

AN IMMENSE SCALE

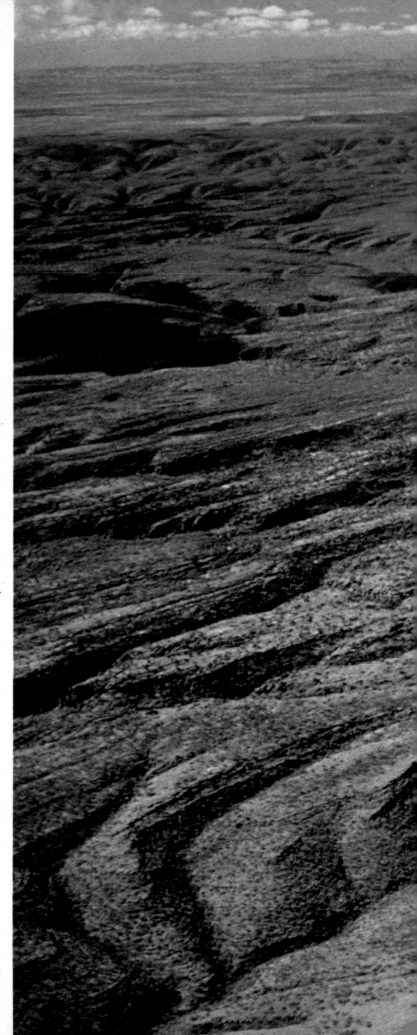

The Northern Territory is acquiring a face and a future. The long-held picture of a useless and desolate frontier land is being replaced by an understanding of its potential, and of its great diversity of scenery, climate, vegetation and animal life.

The Territory's own development is forcing recognition. The value of mining has increased fourfold in five years, the cattle industry is becoming regularised and important, tourism is growing rapidly and there is a new future seen in fisheries, forestry and agricultural production. The big towns of Darwin and Alice Springs are modern, thriving centres, and roads and communications are expanding into areas that were once little more than wilderness.

It is no land of milk and honey. There are great tracts of desert and funeral scrublands, undeveloped and hostile regions which are testing to man's endurance and ingenuity. There are, beside the hard-won comfort of the whites, the squalid shanties of the slowly emerging aboriginal population. There are staggering problems of climate and distance.

But for territorians it is a land, too, of enchantment. They have sunshine and space and they can live at their own pace, growing with the land and taking a pioneer's pride in their efforts. They have, among the parched plains and forest lands, some of the world's most spectacular landforms and an abundance of animal and bird life.

DRY WATERCOURSES AND COLOURFUL HILLS IN THE McDONNEL RANGES AREA OF CENTRAL AUSTRALIA

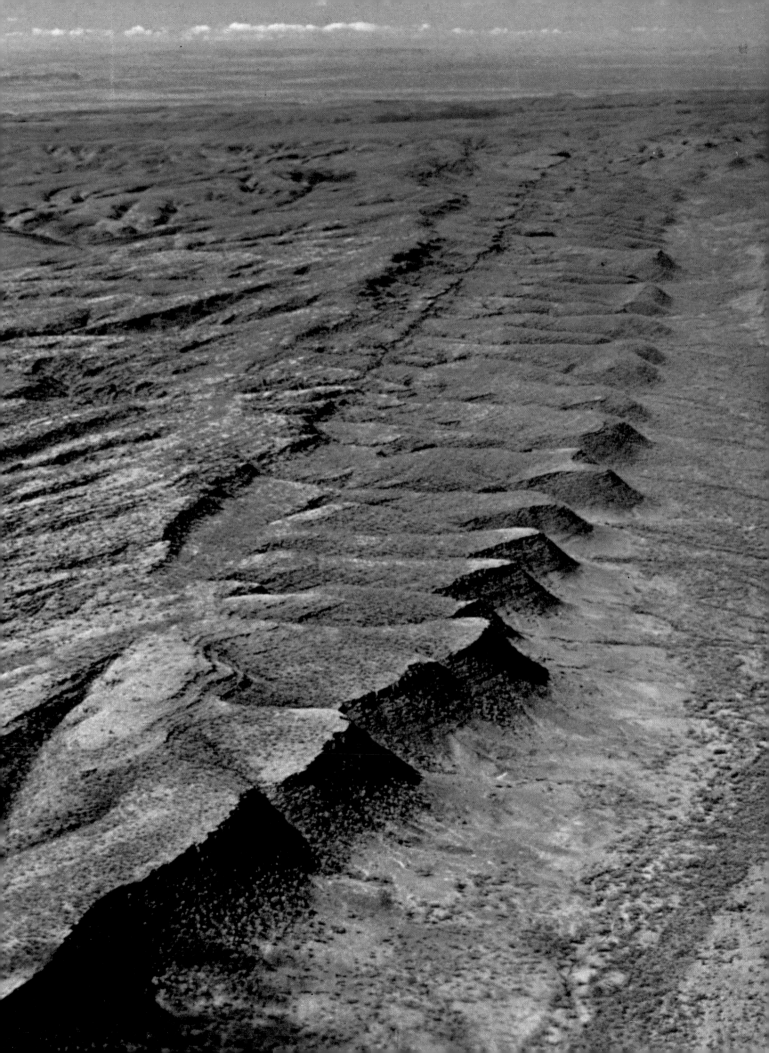

ALICE – *Heart of the Centre*

Alice Springs began in 1870 as a little depot town for the Overland Telegraph It was known originally as Stuart, after the explorer of the centre, John McDouall Stuart, but the post office and telegraph station at a waterhole two miles away was named Alice Springs. When the post office was moved to the town the name Alice Springs went with it.

The tranquil waterhole, with the restored Old Telegraph Station, is one of the sights of the town, along with the John Flynn Memorial Church, the Flying Doctor Base and the School of the Air, the grave of Albert Namatjira, Rex Battarbee's T'mara-Mara art gallery, displaying the works of Namatjira and other aboriginal painters, and the delightful Pitchi Ritchi, a bird and flower sanctuary where William Ricketts' symbolic sculptures of aborigines are set in pleasant bushland.

Alice Springs is the magnet, the focus of attention, for the traveller to the red centre. It remains one of the most beautiful towns in Australia, unaffected or perhaps en-hanced by the creeping rash of plastic and chrome, timber finishes, neon signs and pot plants that have come with its growth as a tourist destination.

The new "Alice" has lost its pot-holed streets, and its shanty dwellings have given way to modern homes and buildings—motels, restaurants, art galleries, gift shops, tourist cabins and, of course, camera shops. They do not seem to overwhelm the town. They cannot, after all, compete with the red and purple waves of color that move at dusk on the hills of the MacDonnell Ranges. Or with the greenery of its gardens and the splendid ghost gums that line its streets.

Despite the attractions of "The Alice" it is doomed to play second fiddle to the country surrounding it. It is this incomparable series of chasms, glens, gaps, rocks, valleys and mountains that brings the tourists flocking to the town in tens of thousands every year—particularly in the warm, clear winter months.

VIEW OF ALICE SPRINGS

▲ FIRST OVERLAND TELEGRAPH STATION, ALICE SPRINGS   ▼ DRY BED OF THE TODD RIVER

SCENIC WONDERS OF THE CENTRE

Ayers Rock crouches lion-like on a wide sandy plain of spinifex and desert oak—timeless, enigmatic and of an awesome immensity. The red rock is five and a half miles in circumference and 1,143 feet high. Its astonished discoverer W. C. Gosse called it "an immense pebble rising abruptly from the plain—certainly the most wonderful natural feature I have seen."

The Rock is the supreme tourist attraction in Central Australia. Despite its remoteness—270 miles from Alice Springs—over 25,000 visitors a year come to see it

Twenty miles away to the west are The Olgas, a cluster of rounded, massive rocks with an equal air of alien mystery. They are as dramatic and vividly colored as Ayers Rock and lack only the majesty of its great bulk. The tallest of the Olgas, Mt. Olga itself, is 1,790 feet above the oasis-like Valley of the Winds that runs through the rock system.

Ernest Giles, who first saw Mt. Olga and named it for the Queen of Spain, described the rocks as "minarets, giant cupolas and monstrous domes . . . huge memorials to the ancient times of earth."

The MacDonnell Range system of Central Australia marches in long and eerily symmetrical lines across the land. Hidden within the stark chains of rock are places which, although overshadowed by the magnificence of Ayers Rock and The Olgas, have their own fantastic beauty of shape, color and texture.

The best of the scenery lies west of Alice Springs, where the Finke and other rivers have cut chasms and gorges into the mountains. Closest to the town are Heavitree Gap, Simpson's Gap and Standley Chasm, where cliffs 200 to 250 feet high and only 12 to 18 feet apart leap into colorful life as the sun reaches into them near midday.

Further out are the Ellery, Serpentine, Glen Helen and Ormiston Gorges. Ormiston is the greatest of them, its cliffs rising hundreds of feet from the clear still waters of Ormiston Creek. Near Glen Helen, where the Finke River passes through the range are Stonehenge, Window Rock and the vertical strata known as the Organ Pipes. The backdrop to this region is Mt. Sonder, rising 4,400 feet and the most distintive and beautiful of the central mountains.

The Finke River course runs down past the Hermannsburg Aboriginal mission and a monument to Albert Namatjira, and into Palm Valley, an oasis in a deepwalled gully with many beautiful waterholes. Within the valley are the tall, graceful *Livistona mariae* palms and a cicle of rocks—Sundial, Cathedral, Battleship, Corroboree —that make up the Amphitheatre.

THE OLGAS

HAAST BLUFF, CENTRAL AUSTRALIA

AYERS ROCK CHANGES COLOUR WITH THE TIME OF DAY

PEOPLE OF THE TERRITORY

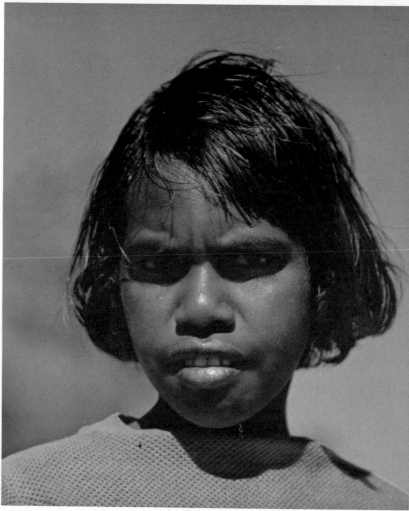

ABORIGINAL SCHOOLGIRL, BANKA BANKA

While the Northern Territory is acquiring a surface veneer of civilisation—growing towns, modern houses, better roads, communications and services—it is still an empty and often dangerous frontier land.

It gives its people a hard life—testing them with its harshness of climate, danger, isolation and tough outdoor work. It hones them still into the fundamental man of the Australian bush—solitary, self reliant, resourceful and still trading in the now devalued currency of friendship, hospitality and yarn-spinning conversation.

Even in the towns, civilised as they are to the point of sophistication, there is an easy-going atmosphere combined with community pride and a frontier spirit. Among the people are many of the zestful and eccentric "characters" who put down their shallow roots in such isolated places.

The territory was built on the hardships, endurance and vision of its pioneers. It has its heroes and its legendary characters. The best known is the Rev. John Flynn—Flynn of the Inland—who did much to end the danger and handicaps of isolation. He founded his "mantle of safety" with the Flying Doctor Service, which brings swift medical attention to the most remote regions.

Its best loved character was Bill Harney, the Keeper of Ayers Rock and author, raconteur and bush cook extraordinary. When he died in 1962 he left behind thousands of friends across Australia, many poems and eight books which are a treasure house of simple wisdom and of understanding of aborigines and the bush.

Other names are remembered—the late and tragic Albert Namatjira, whose paintings capture the strange colors and shapes and the spirit of the Central Australian mountains; Harold Bell Lasseter, who searched for a great reef of gold; Bob Buck, who found Lasseter's body; Peter Allen, the bounty hunter who has spent 50 years trapping dingoes; Stuart, Gosse, Giles and others who blazed the first trails into the centre; Mrs Aeneas Gunn, who wrote *We of the Never Never*—just the beginning of a roll-call of strong people who "took on" the Territory.

BUSHMAN, ALICE SPRINGS

SAFARIS AT THE 'TOP END'

East of Darwin are the blacksoil plains of Marrakai, the spectacular waterfalls of the Jim Jim Creek region and the wild, dense country of the South Alligator and East Alligator Rivers.

This is Safari territory, rich in Australia's nearest approach to big game—buffaloes, crocodiles, kangaroos and wild pigs—and also in taipans, pythons and king brown snakes.

The tough professional hunters who worked the hostile country alone in the days of unrestricted shooting have now been joined by sportsmen on shoots organised by safari operators from Darwin.

But most safari travellers are not shooters. They want only to look at the scenery, observe and photograph birds and animals and chase buffaloes across the plains in wild-riding four-wheel-drive vehicles.

They see some fascinating sights: billabongs covered with water lilies and teeming with bird life, herds of buffaloes on the plains or standing contentedly neck deep in water holes, clouds of geese wheeling above the trees, crocodiles sunning themselves on waterside rocks or mud patches, rows of pillar-like anthills, aboriginal cave paintings and spectacular rock and cliff features.

The Northern Territory administration has decided that part of this region, 1,000 square miles adjoining the western boundary of the Arnhem Land aboriginal reserve should be developed as a major national park.

Safari trips range from one-day bus tours to full scale hunting and photographic safaris with guides. There are also safari camps in the Jim Jim Creek region, comfortable bases for hunting shooting and photographic trips in the surrounding country. Prices range from $12 to $20 for a day safari tour to $100 a day for a single hunter on safari.

NOURLANGIE ROCK, IN ONE OF THE RICHEST GAME AREAS IN ARNHEM LAND

▲ HUNTER IN ARNHEM LAND FISHES FOR BARRAMUNDI ▼ HUNTING SALTWATER CROCODILES BRINGS TRAVELLERS TO SAFARI CAMP

UNIQUE WILDLIFE

Water buffalo, introduced from Asia last century, lumber across the grasslands of the Top End. Dangerous saltwater crocodiles are plentiful in the coastal rivers and estuaries, and the timid, fish-eating "freshies" in the inland rivers and billabongs.

These are the glamour animals of the Top End, an area of abundant and fascinating wildlife which, because the natural environment is largely unaltered, has developed with little interference.

Sanctuaries close to Darwin and near main roads allow visitors to see many varieties of animals and birds easily. A popular viewing area is the Marrakai Plain, where the buffalo roam with wallabies, wallaroos and the red kangaroo.

The reptiles of the north include the deadly taipan, the large and strikingly colored non-venemous python, the frilled lizard and the giant perentie goanna lizard, which can grow to a length of six feet.

Abundant water birds include the stately jabiru storks and brolgas, magpie geese and burdekin ducks, tiny grebes and the decorative lotus bird, which travels on large fragile feet across the lily pads of the lagoons. Some land birds peculiar to the north are the rock pigeon, the sandstone thrush, the grass wren and the pretty fairy wren, which carries a patch of lilac on its crown. Finches, emus and the unique plains turkey or bustard inhabit the marginal scrub and grasslands further south.

A different set of animals and birds live in the drier areas of the centre. A group of small mammals, mainly of the rat kangaroo variety, find havens among the rocky outcrops and sheltered ravines. Birds are chiefly wrens of various genera and other species, such as wagtails, that can live on practically nothing. Three distinctive birds are the beautiful Alexandra parrot, the curious night parrot and the gibber bird.

Roaming through the territory grasslands are a number of wild introduced animals—donkeys, brumbies, goats, pigs, foxes, camels, dingoes and rabbits.

BEARDED DRAGON

▲ AUSTRALIAN BLACK SWAN

▲ SPANGLED DRONGO

▲ FEMALE KOEL CUCKOO

▲ AUSTRALIAN PELICAN

FINCHES OF CENTRAL AUSTRALIA ▶

TRIBESMEN OF PAST & PRESENT

"Cultural transition" is the official expression for the situation of the Northern Territory's aborigines—half-in and half-out of white society culturally, socially and economically estranged from its goals.

The aboriginal population is now increasing steadily after many years of decline. They are the descendants of the great tribes of the past—the Arandas, the Pintjantjarra, the Loritjas, Pintubis, Gurindji and others that roamed the land, their harsh lives enriched only by their intricate and highly developed culture and mythology.

Of the 21,000 aborigines in the territory most, about 13,500, live on Government settlements like the Roper River settlement or Maningrida in the Arnhem Land aboriginal reserve, or on mission stations, like Hermannsburg Mission in the south. Here they live a form of tribal life under an umberella of health, education and welfare services.

About 4,500 live on cattle stations. Strict laws guarantee the colored stockman a wage and support for their families, They are expert riders, horse breakers and cattle workers and they play the part to the full with their cowboy hats and elastic-sided boots.

About 3,000 live in or near the towns—technically assimilated but finding that most white people have little time to spare for them. The aboriginal townspeople demonstrate most dramatically the ends of the scale in the assimilation problem. Some live in squalid camps, jobless, lethargic and often alcoholic. Others catch on to the community philosophy and find jobs, good living conditions and a future.

Their example is a hopeful sign, but the final hurdle for future generations may be to win the trust and acceptance of disparaging or cruelly indifferent whites.

Government policy is to assist in the social, economic and educational advancement of aborigines. It provides health services, education and vocational training, housing and employment opportunities. It also has a scheme to give financial and technical assistance for aboriginal owned and run businesses.

ABORIGINES, CENTRAL AUSTRALIA

ABORIGINAL ART AT NOURLANGIE ROCK

PINTUKI CORROBOREE DANCERS, HAAST BLUFF

GATEWAY OF THE NORTH

Darwin, built on a peninsula on the eastern shores of Port Darwin, a deep inlet of Clarence Strait between Bathhurst and Melville Islands and the mainland, is no longer the rough, ramshackle town of wartime memory.

In its growth as the administrative centre of the Northern Territory, the service centre for a large and developing pastoral and mining area, and as an all-seasons holiday resort it has become a modern city of character and colour.

The city is young, with over half of the 33,000 population under 24, and restless. Motels, hotels, office buildings, stores and public buildings have sprung up. Port installations are being greatly expanded. Suburbs of attractive homes and gardens are spreading rapidly, and the attractive layouts of street plantations, reserves and public gardens add to the air of well being.

It is a cosmopolitan place, proud of its fame as the nation's most racially mixed and tolerant city. The rip-roaring wildness of its early days has been broken down by civilisation, but it is a place of free and friendly spirit, attractive to itinerant adventures and those who like an open community life.

The big increase in tourism is not surprising. The winter climate is delightful and the city is surrounded by warm, lazy water abundant with fish and lapping onto some excellent beaches. Close at hand are delightful inland fishing and swimming spots, and places to see the fascinating wildlife of the north.

Captain John Stokes on H. M. S. *Beagle* discovered the port in 1839 and named it after Charles Darwin, the pioneer of evolution, who had been on the ship. A small settlement established on the spot in 1864 was named Palmerston after the then prime minister of Great Britain but when the territory came under Federal Government control in 1911 its named was changed back to Darwin.

Darwin suffered the first enemy attack on Australian soil in 1942 when 243 people were killed by Japanese bombs. Relics of the attack may still be seen around the city.

THE BEACH AT FANNIE BAY ▼   PALM SHADED HOTEL COURTYARD WELCOMES TOURISTS ▶

MODERN HOMES AT DARWIN ARE SUITED TO THE TROPICS

NORTHERN TERRITORY

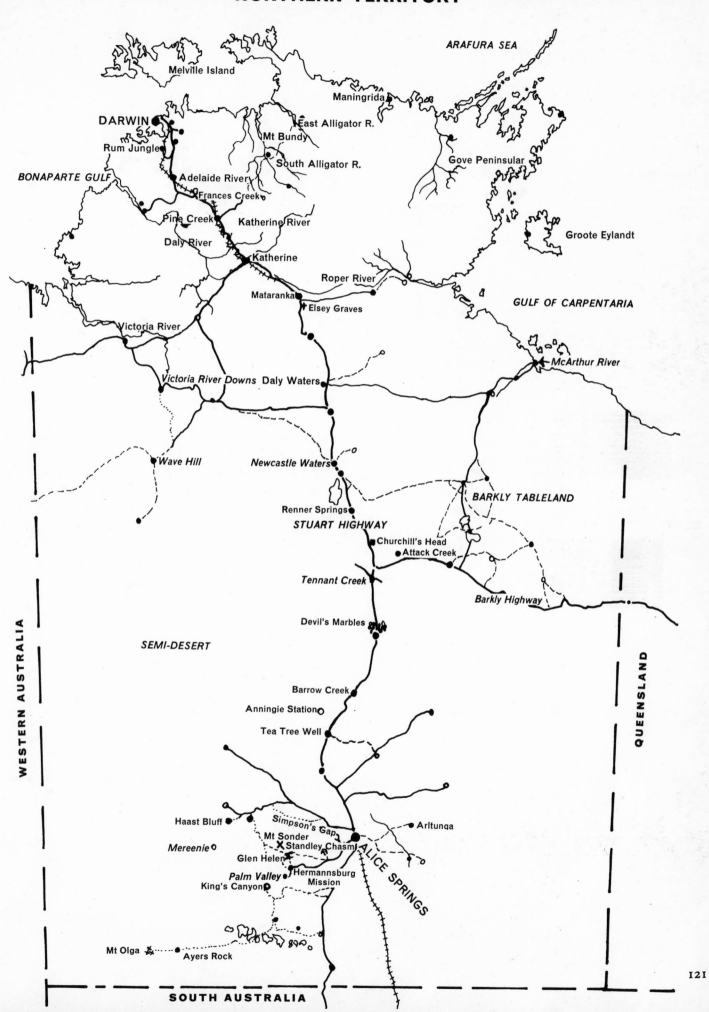

ARAFURA SEA

Melville Island

Maningrida

DARWIN

East Alligator R.

Mt Bundy

Rum Jungle

Gove Peninsular

BONAPARTE GULF

Adelaide Rivery

South Alligator R.

Frances Creek

Groote Eylandt

Pine Creek

Katherine River

Daly River

Katherine

Roper River

GULF OF CARPENTARIA

Mataranka

Elsey Graves

Victoria River

McArthur River

WESTERN AUSTRALIA

Victoria River Downs Daly Waters

Wave Hill

Newcastle Waters

BARKLY TABLELAND

Renner Springs

STUART HIGHWAY

Churchill's Head

Attack Creek

Tennant Creek

Barkly Highway

Devil's Marbles

SEMI-DESERT

Barrow Creek

QUEENSLAND

Anningie Station

Tea Tree Well

Haast Bluff

Simpson's Gap

Arltunga

Mt Sonder

Standley Chasm

Mereenie

Glen Helen

ALICE SPRINGS

Palm Valley

Hermannsburg
Mission

King's Canyon

Mt Olga

Ayers Rock

SOUTH AUSTRALIA

NORTHERN TERRITORY TOURIST GUIDE

SETTLEMENT

SETTLEMENT Dutch navigators are believed to have been aware of the northern coast of Australia as early as 1623. They were followed by Abel Tasman in 1644. Matthew Flinders chartered part of the coastline during his circumnavigation of the continent in 1802-1803, but the actual annexation of northern Australia was initiated by Sir Stamford Raffles who advocated the need for a strategic port for trade in the Malay archipeligo after the loss of Java in 1815.

Raffles briefed Lieutenant Phillip Parker King who made a survey of the coast in 1817. King discovered and named Raffles Bay, Port Essington, the Alligator River and Melville and Batman islands. King recommended these places as trading centres though his estimate was later shown to be ill-founded.

A settlement at Port Essington was founded in 1824 by Captain J. G. Bremer who landed with a party of convicts in the *Tamar*. Bremer took possession of the northern coast between 129 deg. East and 135 deg. East, but lack of fresh water at Port Essington led to the settlement being moved to Melville Island. After further setbacks the settlement was moved again, to Raffles Bay. It was abandoned in 1829.

Fear of colonization by the French lead to a new colony on Port Essington under Capt. Bremer being established in 1838. It was called Victoria and lasted till 1849. Ten years earlier Wickham and Stokes on H.M.S. *Beagle* had discovered and named Port Darwin and the Victoria River.

Inland discovery was opened up by Ludwig Leichhardt, who travelled overland from Queensland to Port Essington in 1845, and A. C. Gregory who explored the Victoria River and then followed Leichhardt's trail from Roper River to Queensland in 1855-56. However it was not until John McDouall Stuart crossed the continent from south to north in 1860-1862 that the South Australian Government began to show much real interest in the northern territory. In 1863 it was placed under the control of South Australia and in 1869 a survey of Port Darwin by George Goyder led to the establishment of a settlement there named Palmerston.

In 1872 The Overland Telegraph Line was erected under the direction of Charles Todd and a submarine cable was laid to Java connecting Australia to the rest of the world.

Further significant journeys of exploration were made during the 1870's by W. E. Giles, P. E. Warburton and John Forrest, while the first railway from present day Darwin to Pine Creek was built in 1889. In 1911 the Northern Territory was taken over by the Federal Government and the town of Palmerston was re-named Darwin.

PHYSICAL

PHYSICAL The Northern Territory covers an area of 523,620 square miles and has a coastline of more than 1,000 miles. In area it represents more than one-sixth of the entire Australian continent.

Roughly one third of this is undeveloped unsettled desert, where the annual rainfall averages less than 15 inches. Four-fifths of the Northern Territory lies within the tropics, yet with the exception of the northern belt the rainfall is light and insufficient for other than specialised agriculture. Darwin receives an average of 58 inches of rain during the wet season and only 2 inches throughout the rest of the year.

Physically, the territory is a giant tableland whose main rivers, the Victoria, Daly, Roper South and East Alligator, flow north into the ocean while other seasonal rivers flow inland. The land rises towards Central Australia, the main mountain ranges being the MacDonnells, whose highest peak is 4,955 ft above sea level, and the Musgrave Ranges.

Apart from the tropical growth in the north, the vegetation generally consists of saltbush and spinifex with hardy eucalypts. Transportation is by road or rail and, increasingly, by air. The bitumenised Barkly Highway runs to Mt Isa in Queensland, while the major artery, the Stuart Highway, extends to Alice Springs. The railway from Darwin southwards ends at Larrimah, while the railway north from Port Augusta stops at Alice Springs, leaving a gap of 600 miles. Freight from Adelaide to Darwin is hauled by a rail-road combination.

In recent years much money has been spent on 'beef roads' constructed to speed the delivery of stock from pastoral properties to railheads. Mail, medical services, and other supplies are carried by air and light planes play an important part of communications in the territory which has more than 100 aerodromes.

The main pastoral industry of the Territory is beef. The annual sale is about 230,000 head, worth almost $21 million. More than one quarter of these cattle are slaughtered in the territory for export. Other primary industries are Forestry (in the far north); prawning which produces exports worth nearly $5 million a year to Japan; commercial grain sorghum (still in the development stage) and buffalo raising for meat.

But the most spectacular industrial development in recent years has been the growth of mining—now the Territory's biggest single industry and biggest money-earner. Mineral production in 1975 is expected to be in excess of $140 million. By this time production of bauxite and alumina at Gove should reach $60 million and production of manganese ore at Groote Elyandt about $20 million. At Tennant Creek, production of copper, gold and bismuth should be worth about $25 million and at Frances Creek, production of iron ore could be in excess of $8 million. The significance of these figures is clear when it is realised that in 1964 the Territory's annual value of production of minerals was less than $11 million. Meanwhile the total expenditure on offshore exploration for oil is currently running at the rate of $20 million a year. A promising discovery of natural gas was made by the Petrel No. 1 offshore well in August 1969. On land, evaluation of the Mereenie oil and gas field has indicated reserves of 300 million barrels of oil, and a million million cubic feet of gas. An important natural gas find at Palm Valley, near Alice Springs, has been confirmed, and indications are that a major field exists.

ABORIGINES

ABORIGINES Although the aboriginal population of approximately 21,000 people accounts for less than a third of the Northern Territory's population, it is increasing rapidly. Most aborigines live on remote Government settlements or on those conducted by religious missionary organisations. Approximately 60 million square miles of the Northern Territory is reserved for the aborigines. About 13,500 aborigines live on settlements; another 4,500 live on cattle stations and more than 3,000 live in or near the main towns and centres. The Commonwealth Government organises programmes for the social, economic and educational advancement of the aborigines and in recent years has provided financial and technical assistance for the development of aboriginal-owned and-run business enterprises. Much of this aid comes from sources such as the Aboriginal Benefits Trust Fund which receives roylties from mineral and timber exploitation on reserves. With the increasing mining developments at Gove Peninsular and Groote Eylandt the Trust will have received $5 million by 1975.

ADMINISTRATION

ADMINISTRATION Since 1947 The Northern Territory has been administered by a Legislative Council, together with an Administrator based at Darwin assisted by a District Officer at Alice Springs. The Legislative Council comprises six Government members, and eleven elected members. The administrator is appointed by the Government. The present Administrator is Mr F. C. Chaney. The official members hold office for as long as the Governor General pleases and the elected members for not more than three years. All ordinances passed by the council must be presented to the Administrator for assent, and within six months after the Administrator's assent the Governor General may disallow the ordinance in part or in whole or recommend changes. Moves are being made to expand the role of the elected members.

WHEN TROUBLE STRIKES

The Northern Territory climate, especially in the Centre, can sometimes be a dangerous hazard to the uninitiated. Its effects are most often realised when a traveller is faced with vehicle breakdown. When this happens, remember the following:

1. Stay with your vehicle

2. Conserve water supplies and food.

3. Don't walk about or exert yourself unnecessarily—particularly in the heat of the day.

4. Use all available shade. If natural shade is insufficient, rig up a shelter—using a tent fly, leafy boughs or anything that will give shade—against the side of your vehicle in lean-to fashion. Wear a hat or other head covering.

5. In the cool of the night, dig a hole under your vehicle to keep water and provisions cool by day. If you cannot provide shade for yourself any other way, make the hole large enough to accommodate yourself.

6. If your water situation becomes really desperate dew can be sopped up from leaves or stones just before sunrise, using a sponge or a piece of cloth or tissue. In some cases, drops can be shaken off tree leaves or flowers and caught in a container. A little water is better than none at all.

Another method of beating thirst requires some plants, a plastic sheet and a container—and a little time and patience. In the daytime, dig a square hole one yard by 18 inches deep. Insert fairly flat container to catch water. Heap newly-picked leaves (mulga, saltbush, acacia) or roots about the container. Completely cover hole with plastic sheet roughened on the underside with sand. Hold firmly in place at corners with stones. Put small stone at centre on top of sheet so plastic will sag over mouth of container. The amount of water you will get from condensation due to daytime heat and fall of air temperature overnight will depend on wetness of the soil and succulence of leaves, but overnight in reasonable conditions, enough water should be produced to keep you alive.

7. If you are for any sound reason compelled to leave the vehicle for any time—e.g. to go to a visible nearby waterhole—leave a note on the steering wheel, and "blaze" your track—i.e. shave or bruise tree trunks, snap and leave hanging small branches, saplings and tall grass, and make your footprints as clear as you can, so that you can find your way back. The big waterhole or windmill might be easily seen from where the vehicle is—but the comparatively small vehicle may be completely invisible to you when you turn to come back to it.

8. Recognised distress signals are: 3 shouts, or 3 shots, in quick succession: 3 fires or 3 smoke columns in a row (use green leaves for denser smoke); 3 flashes from a torch, mirror, or similar article.

9. If an aircraft or helicopter approaches, do all you can to attract the attention: e.g. with smoke signals (burning green leaves), mirror flashes, the waving of large, conspicuously coloured pieces of cloth, or by signs marked out on the ground.

NATIONAL PARKS & RESERVES

A selection of some of the major national parks and reserves of the Northern Territory are listed below and indicated on the accompanying map. For further information write to The Northern Territory Reserves Board, Gap Road, Alice Springs 5750; The Tourist Bureau, Darwin or Alice Springs; the Chief Inspector of Wildlife, Animal Industry and Agriculture, Northern Territory Administration, Darwin 5790.

1. Cobourg Peninsular Sanctuary (505,600 acres). Accessible by air or sea only. The site of the Victoria settlement and later an aboriginal reserve until 1961, this is now a reserve for wildlife in a tropical monsoon climate.

2. Woolwonga Wildlife Sanctuary (193,680 acres). This area of swamps and lagoons at the conjunction of the South Alligator River and Jim Jim and Death Adder creeks, is a sanctuary for waterfowl. Access from Darwin, via Humpty Doo and Mt Bundy is difficult. Accomodation at Jim Jim.

3. Berry Springs Recreation Reserve (628 acres). Only 40 miles south of Darwin, this small reserve offers camping, swimming and interesting bushwalking.

4. Daly River Recreation Reserve (148 acres). On the Daly River crossing and reached by an access road leaving the Stuart Highway about 90 miles south of Darwin. Camping and swimming.

5. Edith Falls National Park (402 acres). Reached by leaving the Stuart Highway about 35 miles north of Katherine, this is a series of small waterfalls and clear deep pools containing freshwater crocodiles. Features aboriginal paintings, sightseeing, picknicking and swimming.

6. Sixteen Mile Caves (640 acres). The caves contain a large colony of Orange Horseshoe Bats. The access road from the Stuart Highway is very poor and visitors are advised to enquire from the park rangers at Katherine, since the gate may be locked.

7. Katherine Gorge National Park (56,069 acres). On the Katherine River, 22 miles east of the township. A majestic canyon with steep walls and deep water. Wildlife includes crocodiles, wallabies and bower birds. There is a caravan-camping area at the mouth of the gorge and further accomodation at Katherine. Guided tours of the gorge by boat and horse riding.

8. Mataranka Pool Reserve (10 acres). Reached by a turnoff on the west, one mile south of Mataranka. Thermal springs in a lush tropical setting at blood temperature all year round. Beside the springs is a shady area for caravans. Homestead is licensed and accomodation available.

9. Attack Creek Memorial Reserve. This small reserve of less than an acre contains a monument to John McDouall Stuart on the left hand side of the creek's southern bank. Here, illness and hostile natives forced Stuart and his two companions to turn back on 25 June, 1860.

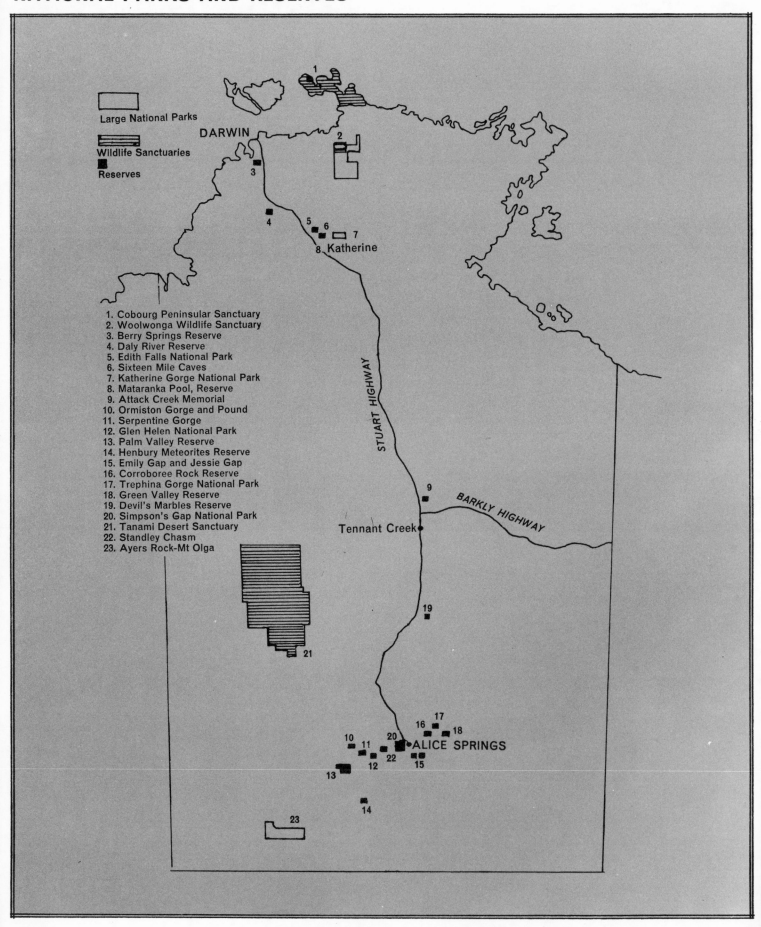

Large National Parks

Wildlife Sanctuaries

Reserves

DARWIN

3

4

5 6

7

8 Katherine

STUART HIGHWAY

1. Cobourg Peninsular Sanctuary
2. Woolwonga Wildlife Sanctuary
3. Berry Springs Reserve
4. Daly River Reserve
5. Edith Falls National Park
6. Sixteen Mile Caves
7. Katherine Gorge National Park
8. Mataranka Pool, Reserve
9. Attack Creek Memorial
10. Ormiston Gorge and Pound
11. Serpentine Gorge
12. Glen Helen National Park
13. Palm Valley Reserve
14. Henbury Meteorites Reserve
15. Emily Gap and Jessie Gap
16. Corroboree Rock Reserve
17. Trephina Gorge National Park
18. Green Valley Reserve
19. Devil's Marbles Reserve
20. Simpson's Gap National Park
21. Tanami Desert Sanctuary
22. Standley Chasm
23. Ayers Rock-Mt Olga

9

BARKLY HIGHWAY

Tennant Creek

19

21

17

16

18

10

20

11

ALICE SPRINGS

22

12

15

13

14

23

10. Ormiston Gorge and Pound National Park (19,520 acres). A spectacular canyon on a tributary of the Finke River near Mt Sonder, 72 miles west of Alice Springs. Through the gorge is the Pound, surrounded by rocky cliffs. Camping area below gorge has few facilities.

11. Serpentine Gorge National Park (2,400 acres). This is a small Gorge about 60 miles west of Alice Springs. Ideal for photography. There may be a pool, depending on the winter rains.

12. Glen Helen National Park (954 acres). Situated in the West MacDonnell Ranges, it is reached by a dirt road 81 miles from Alice Springs on the Finke River. This river gorge offers magnificent scenery. No accomodation.

13. Palm Valley Flora and Fauna Reserve (113,000 acres). Discovered in 1872 by the explorer Ernest Giles, west of Alice Springs via Hermannsburg and named after its *Livistona* palms. Contains some of the oldest plant forms on earth. Regular bus tours there.

14. Henbury Meteorites Reserve (40 acres). Three large meteorite craters and ten smaller craters may be seen.

15. Emily Gap and Jessie Gap Scenic Reserves (1,718 acres). These two gorges are about seven miles from Alice Springs, Emily Gap being the nearer of the two. No tourist facilities but scenic attractions and Aboriginal paintings.

16. Corroboree Rock Scenic Reserve (18 acres). A ridge of dolerite beds which has been raised by past earth movements so that it stands on edge, broken into great blocks. Named because it is believed to have been an important aboriginal site.

17. Trephina Gorge National Park (4,378 acres). In the East MacDonnell Ranges 46 miles from Alice Springs, this large gorge was cut by a tributary of the Todd River. Dark red cliffs with large Eucalypts long the bed of the river. Sightseeing but no tourist facilities.

18. Green Valley Scenic Reserve (1,293 acres). In the East MacDonnell Ranges 54 miles from Alice Springs. A wide gorge with rugged ranges. Some tourist accomodation in cabins at nearby Ross River.

19. Devil's Marbles Scenic Reserve (4,519 acres). On the Stuart Highway about 60 miles south of Tennant Creek. These are giant rounded granite boulders piled on top of each other and with huge caverns underneath. Nearest accomodation at Tennant Creek.

20. Simpson's Gap National Park (640 acres). A gap in the rocky ridges of the West MacDonnell Ranges, 14 miles west of Alice Springs. Permanent waterhole, Ghost Gums and flowering plants. Nearest accomodation Alice Springs.

21. Tanami Desert Wildlife Sanctuary (9,300,000 acres). A vast desert reserve 200 miles north-west of Alice Springs. Mainly flat, spinifex-covered country set aside for the conservation of Central Australian wildlife. Contains many marsupials, birds and reptiles. Visitors should make enquiries at Alice Springs before setting out.

22. Standley Chasm (2,400 acres). Deep crevice with 200-ft high walls, 32 miles west of Alice Springs, where the sun penetrates for only a short time each day. Picnicking, scenic site.

23. Ayers Rock-Mt Olga National Park (311,680 acres). Situated 276 miles south-west of Alice Springs and reachable only by very rough road impassable after even moderate rain, this reserve surrounds the two great geological features. Close to Ayers Rock is a hotel-motel, motel, chalets and a caravan-camping area. Rangers are on duty.

ALONG THE HIGHWAY

SOME OF THE INTERESTING STOPPING POINTS ALONG THE STUART HIGHWAY FROM ALICE SPRINGS NORTHWARDS ARE:

Old Telegraph Station (2 miles). Part of the Overland Telegraph line, the station was built in the early 1870's beside springs in an almost dry river. The river was later named the Todd after Sir Charles Todd, Postmaster-General of South Australia. The Springs were named Alice Springs, after his wife. Both the Telegraph Station and the original springs now form part of a reserve controlled by the Northern Territory Reserves Board.

Tea Tree Well (132 miles). About 13 miles to the north of this spot, a cairn has been built to commemorate the fact that on 22 April, 1860, the explorer John McDouall Stuart reached Australia's geographical heart. Stuart named the spot Mount Sturt, after his close friend Captain Charles Sturt, leader of an exploratory expedition in 1844-45. Later the spot was renamed Central Mount Stuart.

Barrow Creek (176 miles). The victims of one of the earliest tragedies in the Territory are buried beside the highway here. They were a postmaster and lineman, James Stapleton and John Franks, murdered by tribesmen at a repeater station for the Overland Telegraph Line in 1874. Stapleton, who had four spears in his body, lived long enough to exchange telegraph messages with his wife in Adelaide. The whites extracted a terrible revenge for the deaths, shooting at least 70 aborigines, men women and children.

The Devil's Marbles (250 miles). These are two groups of giant granite boulders which cover several square miles in this area. The rounded boulders vary in size from a foot to 20 feet in diameter and some weigh thousands of tons. Several are almost perfectly round, others form house-size caverns beneath them. Many aboriginal legends are associated with the Marbles.

Tennant Creek (315 miles). This is one of the oldest mining areas in the Territory, beginning as a goldfield in the 1930's and now a centre for the mining of several other important minerals. In the 1870's a repeater station in the Overland Telegraph Line was built at Tennant Creek. The station's massive stone walls are still standing as part of a pastoral station on the banks of the creek itself, seven miles away from the present town.

The Barkly Highway (330 miles). The Territory's second major route joins the Stuart Highway from Mt Isa in Queensland. Nearby is the imposing memorial to John Flynn, founder of the Flying Doctor Service. Part of the inscription on the plaque reads: "He brought to lonely places a spiritual ministry and spread a mantle of safety over them by medicine aviation and radio."

Attack Creek (359 miles). Here, on 25 June, 1860, the explorer John McDouall Stuart, who was attempting to cross the continent from the south, turned back for Adelaide after a large group of aborigines attacked his party at a creek which now is named after the incident. There is a monument to Stuart where the creek crosses the road.

Churchill's Head (368 miles). On the right hand side of the road is a rock formation which has earned its name from its resemblance to the profile of Britain's war time leader.

Renner Springs (414 miles). From this point northwards, the arid zone of the Northern Territory gives way to greener vegetation. Lubra's Lookout, a huge rock, is regarded by Territorians as the marker peg for the boundary in climatic zones. The rock may be climbed to get a view of Renner Springs Plain and its freshwater springs.

Newcastle Waters (487 miles). This is the half-way point between Alice Springs and Darwin. It is also the junction of two stock routes that bisect the Northern Territory. At one time, a hundred thousand cattle on the hoof passed the Newcastle pub every droving season on their way to fattening lands in the east, but now huge road trains using the new beef roads have superseded overland droving. Newcastle Waters also marks the edge of the lush Barkly Tablelands extending to Queensland.

Daly Waters (565 miles). Once a vital link in the chain of airfields stretching between the northern and southern extremities of the continent. Today jet airliners pass over the small township at 500 m.p.h. and 30,000 feet.

Elsey Graves (658 miles). A rock cairn and graveyard at this spot marks the site of Elsey station homestead, made famous through Mrs Aeneas Gunn's classic, *We of the Never Never*. In the graveyard are buried several of the characters of the book, among them the "Fizzer", Henry Ventilia Peckham, who rode hundreds of miles in a year delivering mail to Outback stations in the years when the cattle industry was the backbone of the Territory's economy.

Mataranka (670 miles). A swimming pool at the present Mataranka Homestead is fed by a warm spring that gushes hundreds of thousands of gallons of water a day which eventually flows underground into the Waterhouse River. The spring is surrounded by palms and paperbarks and visitors are accomodated at the homestead.

Katherine (734 miles). The township is built on a limestone belt that extends for 30 miles, honeycombed with subterranean caverns. In one cave system 16 miles south of the township, ancient stalactites and stalagmites and an underground stream may be seen. Katherine Gorge, 20 miles away, has walls 200 feet high, through which the river flows.

Pine Creek (799 miles). Once one of the Northern Territory's earliest goldfields, Pine Creek had a population of 1,000. At that time, before the turn of the century, reef gold was assayed at up to 800 ounces to the ton.

Adelaide River (882). Five hundred servicemen are buried here at the only war memorial cemetery on the Australian mainland. A special memorial commemorates 287 servicemen who have no known graves. Darwin suffered heavily in the first raids on Australian soil in February 1942, and military installations between Darwin and Katherine were bombed more than 50 times.

Rum Jungle (894 miles). Site of the Rum Jungle uranium mine. Production of uranium oxide is expected to cease during 1971 as the supply or ore which can be treated economically will be exhausted when the present stockpile has been used up. However, conducted tours of the treatment plant and works are made every Tuesday afternoon during the Dry Season.

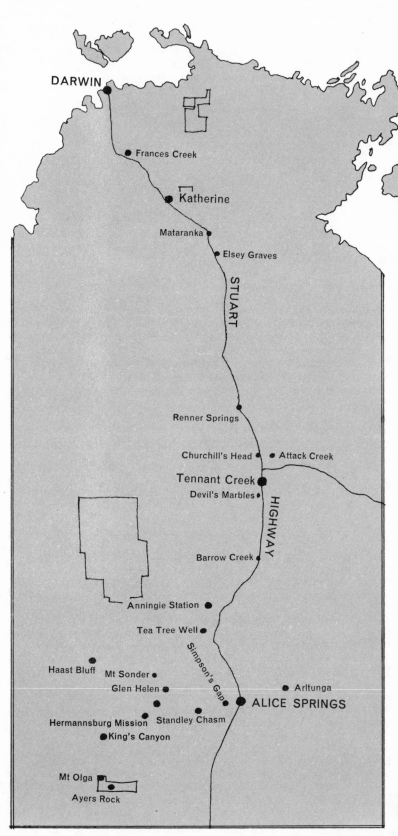

HINTS FOR DRIVERS

Road conditions vary from bitumen to bush track. In the northern part of the Territory, check before leaving the bitumen in the Rainy season (November to April).

NARROW BRIDGES: Many bridges on main highways are wide enough for only one vehicle at a time. On approaching a bridge, slow down, check if another vehicle is approaching—and always be prepared to give way.

ROAD TRAINS: Always give way to road trains; do not try to exert your rights.

HIGHWAY FATIGUE: If you feel even slightly drowsy, pull over, stop, and have a sleep before continuing.

ROVING ANIMALS: Most highways pass through pastoral properties, so watch out for cattle, donkeys, horses and buffalo.

STREAM CROSSINGS: In the Rainy season, stream crossings in the northern part of the Territory may be flooded. Always cross slowly; if in doubt about the depth of the water, stop and check this before proceeding.

DRIVING IN THE BUSH: Before driving in remote areas away from the bitumen, adequate preparation is essential.
1. Have your vehicle thoroughly checked at a reliable garage. Most important, make sure your tyres and battery are in first class condition.
2. Carry the following items:
— extra supplies of water, food, petrol and oil. Do not rely solely on canvas waterbags mounted outside the vehicle; they may be damaged. Carry a stout can of water inside the vehicle. Carry petrol only in approved containers.
— a reliable jack, preferably with a base plate to prevent it from sinking into mud or sand. If your jack has no base plate, take along a house brick.
— a pump and tyre-repair kit, fan belt, radiator hoses.
— a good set of tools, a coil of rope or wire.
— a torch and spare battery.
It is also useful to carry an axe to cut bushes and timber, a shovel to shift mud or sand.
Two lengths of coir matting, 18 inches by 20 feet long, make excellent sand mats for use in debogging. (Only required in remote outback touring.)
Tubeless tyres not recommended. Preferable to fit tubes and carry an extra spare.
3. Fitting a kangaroo bar and mesh insect screen could prove useful (though not essential) protection for your radiator; a screen can be fitted to protect your windscreen from flying stones.
4. Obtain reliable maps and enquire about condition of roads from a reliable authority—e.g. area police station, Automobile Association of Northern Territory.
5. Finally, and most importantly, before setting out on little-used bush tracks, tell some reliable person of your intended schedule so that if you become overdue, a search party will know where to start looking.

SHOOTING & FISHING

Shooting in the Territory is strictly controlled and regulated. Although few Territory animals have yet been threatened with outright extinction, some species have been seriously depleted by uncontrolled destruction.

Nevertheless, sporting shooters who learn and obey the regulations can enjoy a fairly rewarding stay in the Top End. Here is an outline of these regulations:

● All firearms brought into the Territory must be licensed or registered by the N. T. Police Force. Visitors entering the Northern Territory with firearms of any description are obliged to report to a Police Station within two days of their entry, and attend to the licensing or registration of those firearms.

● A licence for a high-powered firearm will be granted only if the owner can show he has "a substantial reason for requiring such a weapon". Courts have upheld a ruling that sporting purposes or holiday shooting do not constitute a "substantial reason".

● Wildlife Sanctuaries: It is an offence to enter a Wildlife Sanctuary without first obtaining a permit from the Chief Inspector of Wildlife.

● Protected Areas: May be entered at will, but it is an offence to bring a firearm or trap into a protected area. Note: Maps showing all sanctuaries and protected areas are available for inspection at all N. T. Police Stations and the N. T. Tourist Bureau.

● It is an offence to discharge a firearm without reasonable cause anywhere in the Greater Darwin area (extending approximately 11 miles south of the city), within 10 miles of the Tennant Creek Post Office, or within 2 miles of the post offices at Batchelor, Adelaide River, Pine Creek, Katherine, Mataranka, Larrimah and Alice Springs, or within 2 miles of the police station at Elliott.

● Persons shooting on property without the owner's consent are liable to prosecution. Note that almost all areas in the Territory that tourists are likely to visit or drive through are pastoral property; station owners are generally opposed to shooting because of danger and disturbance to stock.

● It is an offence to discharge a firearm into, or to explode any explosive substance or device in, a freshwater lake, lagoon or billabong for the purpose of taking or killing fish. It is forbidden to have any explosive substance in a boat without lawful excuse, or to be in possession of any river fish killed, stunned or stupefied by any of these methods.

SPECIES UNDER PROTECTION

Freshwater Crocodiles: fully protected, all year round—no permits are issued under any circumstances.

Buffalo, Saltwater Crocodile and Red Kangaroo: Partly protected all year round—may be taken or killed only under a licence issued by the Chief Inspector of Wildlife.
Game birds (Limited Bag)—Ducks and geese of all kinds except magpie geese, burdekin ducks and pygmy geese are open for season each year during the period 1st July to 31st October.
Magpie geese are open for season from August 1 to December 31.
Burdekin ducks and pygmy geese are now fully protected all year round.
Partly protected birds: The following birds are partly protected; i.e. they may be taken or killed only under a licence issued by the Chief Inspector of Wildlife:
Parrots & Cockatoos   Finches

Red-collared lorikeet	Zebra finch
Varied lorikeet	Banded finch
Red-tailed black cockatoo	Black-ringed finch
White cockatoo	Chestnut-breasted finch
Pink cockatoo	Yellow-tailed finch
Galah	Pictorella finch
Corella	Star finch
Little Corella	Crimson finch
Cockatiel	Long-tailed finch
Red-winged parrot	Black-tailed finch
Port Lincoln parrot	Masked finch
Mulga Parrot	Gouldian finch
Bourke parrot	Budgerigar

Penalties for infringements of shooting regulations are heavy. For example for shooting partly protected animals such as buffalo without a licence, there is a maximum penalty of $400 fine or 6 months imprisonment.

For further information contact the Chief Inspector of Wildlife, Animal Industry Branch, Mitchell Street, Darwin.

PESTS

The following species only are classed as pests within the areas described, and may be destroyed year round within those areas-but not elsewhere.

wild rabbits	Northern Territory
wild donkeys	,, ,,
wild pigs	,, ,,
wild camels	,, ,,
wild goats	,, ,,
Foxes	,, ,,
Dingoes & wild dogs	,, ,,
Black rat	,, ,,
Norway rat	,, ,,
House mouse	,, ,,
Little reddish fruit bat	,, ,,
Gould's fruit bat	,, ,,
Snakes of all species	,, ,,
Wedge-tailed eagles	Alice Springs pastoral district
Agile Wallaby	All that part of the Northern Territory north of the 15th parallel of south latitude, excluding the Arnhem Land Aboriginal Reserve.

All other animals are fully protected—no permits are issued under any circumstances.

FISHING

ANGLING: No licences are required. NETTING: On the coast, amateurs are restricted to a beach seine net of a maximum length of 150 feet and a mesh of not more than 2½ inches. Inland, all netting is prohibited without a permit.

SPEAR FISHING: On the coast, no restrictions. Inland, only a straight long-handled aboriginal-type spear held in the hand may be used. Further information will be gladly provided by Mr Puffet, Officer-in-charge of Northern Territories Fishing Section, N. T. Administration, Darwin (Tel. 489).

ALICE SPRINGS GUIDE

Nestling in the heart of the picturesque MacDonnell Ranges, close to the geographical centre of Australia, Alice Springs is a modern, thriving town with a unique and delightful personality. It has four first-class hotels, eight motels, three guest houses and five caravan parks, and is steadily expanding and improving its accommodation facilities.

Served by frequent rail, road and air services, Alice offers all the comforts of the coastal cities with the added colourful attractions of the outback. It serves as a departure point for tours to Ayers Rock and the Olgas, as well as to a number of dramatic gorges and valleys, tourist camps and aboriginal missions near to the town.

TRAVELLING TO AND FROM THE ALICE

PRIVATE CAR: The highway from Port Augusta to Alice Springs is unsealed; many people like to travel this stretch by rail, with their car conveyed aboard the same train.

The Stuart highway from Alice Springs to Darwin is sealed bitumen.

The Barkly highway from Cloncurry to Three Ways (16 miles north of Tennant Creek) is sealed bitumen.

AIR: There are daily air services by Ansett and T.A.A. between the interstate capitals and Alice Springs. Connellan Airways and S.A.A.T.A.S. Air Charters operate scheduled services over a wide network, connecting Alice Springs with all major ports and stations in the Northern Territory, the north-west of Western Australia and Mt Isa in Queensland.

RAIL: Comfortable air-conditioned trains operate twice weekly between Alice Springs and Adelaide via Port Augusta.

COACH: Redline Coaches operate scheduled twice-weekly express services between Darwin, Alice Springs and Ayers Rock and the capital cities of all other States. In addition, campout tours and scenic tours operate weekly throughout the year. Camping gear may be obtained from Redline, or passengers can use their own equipment.

Ansett-Pioneer: Scheduled weekly services operate between Alice Springs and Ayers Rock with three express services and a three-day accomodation tour between Darwin and Alice Springs (April to September). Other services include the "Northlander" to Darwin via Tanami Desert and Kununurra, and the "Overlander", Alice Springs to Cairns. Three weekly express services operate between Alice Springs and Adelaide.

C.A.T.A. operates scheduled twice weekly services between Alice Springs and Ayers Rock. Additional package tours, including Coach/Air/Accommodation operate from all Capital cities, in association with T.A.A. (Timetables and further details may be obtained from the Northern Territory Bureaux or from the Coach companies concerned.)

CLIMATE

In the winter holiday season (April to October) days are sunny and nights are cool. In the summer, days are hot, but the nights are cool and comfortable. The average temperature and rainfall are very similar to those of Phoenix, Arizona.

ALICE SPRINGS

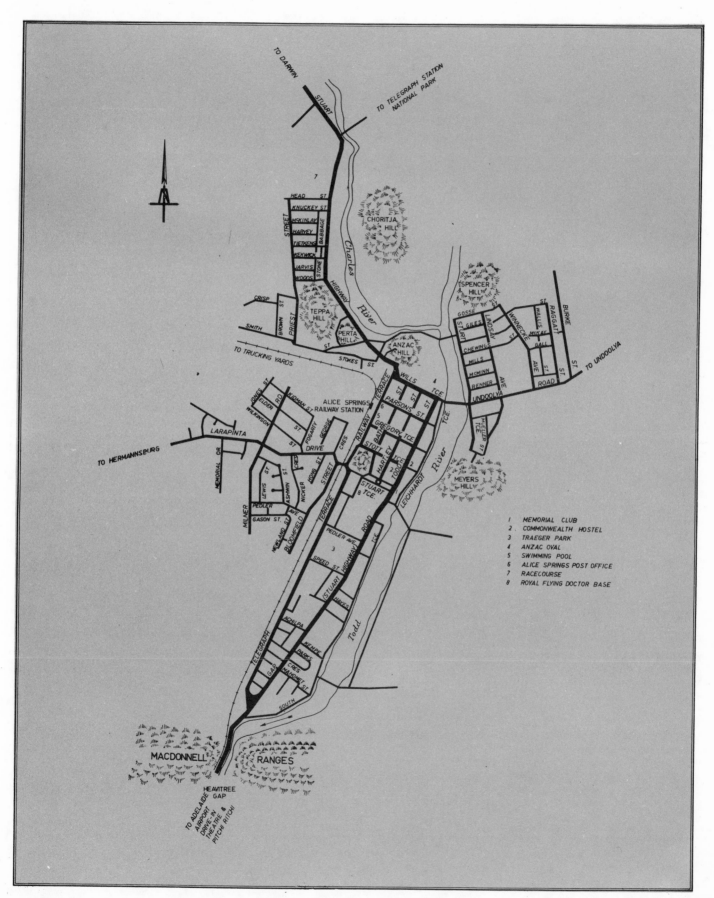

WHAT TO WEAR

For men: For everyday business wear and informal evenings, short-sleeved shirts with or without tie, shorts, long socks and shoes. Long slacks, shirts and tie are required dining attire at some hotels. In the winter jackets and sweaters will be needed at night.

For women: Light cotton frocks with shoes or sandals for business wear and informal evenings. For semi-formal functions, smart after-five dress or cocktail frock. In the winter cardigans or warm jackets will be necessary at night.

Formal wear (Fully formal occasions): Men—long-sleeved white shirt, black bow tie, long black trousers, black shoes and socks; cummerbund usually worn with Tuxedo jacket. Women—short or long evening frock, gloves optional. Stoles and jackets, including furs, often worn during winter evenings.

WHERE TO DINE

HOTEL RESAURANTS:
Hotel Alice Springs; Mt Gillen Hotel-Motel; Riverside Hotel Stuart Arms Hotel.

MOTEL RESTAURANTS (Licensed):
Midland; Oasis; Zdena.

CITY RESTAURANTS & CAFES:
Centre Restaurant (Licensed); Sorrento Cafe (Licensed); Tuckerbox Cafe; Tiki Cafeteria; Heavitree Gap Restaurant; Papa Luigi's Bistro (Licensed); Lizzie's.

WHAT TO SEE

OLD TELEGRAPH STATION AND ORIGINAL ALICE SPRINGS: Two miles north of town (off Stuart Highway). In 1870, the South Australian Government decided to construct a telegraph line from Port Augusta to Port Darwin. In 1872 a telegraph office and ancillary buildings were built beside springs in an almost dry river: the river was named after Sir Charles Todd, Superintendent of Telegraphs, and the springs after his wife, Alice. This picturesque area is now under the control of the N.T. Reserves Board, which is restoring the old station. An entry fee of 10c is payable to the Curator.

VIEW OF TOWN: Anzac Hill at northern end of town, and Billy Goat Hill at southern end give panoramic view.

JOHN FLYNN MEMORIAL CHURCH: Todd Street. Completed in 1956 as memorial to founder of Royal Flying Doctor Service of Australia. Used by United Church in North Australia (union of Presbyterian, Methodist and Congregational). Open every day 9.00 a.m. to 5.00 p.m. Visitors should be sure to see the Museum behind the organ wall. For a donation, booklets giving details of points of interest in the church are available from the table next to the organ.

FLYING DOCTOR BASE: Located between the hospital and goal. Best time for a visit is at 2.00 p.m. and 4.00 p.m. when medical and traffic radio sessions are held. Easy walking distance of town centre.

SCHOOL OF THE AIR: Situated at the Royal Flying Doctor Base—easy walking distance from the town centre. The first known school of its kind; voluntary broadcasts by Alice Springs teachers supplement correspondence lessons for children of the Outback. Sessions at 10 a.m. and 2.45 p.m., Monday to Friday (school and public holidays excepted).

NAMATJIRA'S GRAVE: Two miles west of the town, in Alice Springs cemetery in the third roadway on the left through the gate. Some say Albert Namatjira's problems have been over-romanticised, but his fame in Australia and overseas as a full blood aborigine painting in western style is undeniable.

REX BATTERBEE'S TMARA-MARA ART GALLERY: 6 Sturt Terrace (on the east side across the bridge and turn right). Collection of paintings by Albert Namatjira and other aborigines who paint in western style.

Paintings and prints for sale.
Hours: Monday to Friday, 10.00 a.m.—12 noon, 2.00 p.m.—5.00 p.m.
Saturday: 10.00 a.m.—12 noon

MRS JENKINS' OPAL DISPLAY: Parsons Street, opposite Post Office. Open any time of day. Please telephone 2 1814 for night appointment.

PITCHI RITCHI SANCTUARY: Approximately 2 miles from town, along the south road through Heavitree Gap, then over the cement causeway on the left. A native bird and flower sanctuary with remarkable sculptures of aborigines carved by Victorian, William Ricketts.

ALICE SPRINGS ART GALLERY: 76 Todd Street (Tel. 2 2058, A.H. 2 1532).

GUTH ART STUDIO: 65 Hartley Street (Tel. 2 2013).

DATE GARDEN: The only commercial date farm in Australia, a quarter of a mile across Heavitree Gap Causeway, adjacent to Pitchi Ritchi Sanctuary, and opposite the Heavitree Gap Caravan Park.

A.I.M. OLDTIMERS' HOME: Three miles south of town. A unique community for old bushmen and aged bush ladies.

OLD TRAIN: Located in Railway Station yard.

OLD GRAVEYARD: At back of Railway Station are graves of early settlers.

AMOONGUNA ABORIGINAL SETTLEMENT: 8 miles south-east of town, May be visited only if permission is obtained from Welfare Department, Hartley Street (Tel. 2 1411).

GEM CAVE: Todd Street, 9-5.30 p.m. Unique display of fossils and gems.

WALLACE AVIARIES: 3 miles from town on Emily Gap Road. A colourful variety of some 500 Australian birds, also many species of cactus. Week days. Ring 2 1962 for appointment.

SIMPSON'S GAP. 14 miles west of Alice. This colourful picnic spot has a permanent waterhole. Call in on your way to Standley Chasm.

JOHN FLYNN'S GRAVE. On the road to Simpson's Gap. The headstone for the founder of the Royal Flying Doctor Service is one of the gigantic boulders known as The Devil's Marbles, transported from 250 miles north, on the Stuart Highway.

KING'S CANYON. In the George Gill range, 140 miles west of Alice Springs. Massive, many-hued walls rear over 900 feet high. Four-wheel-drive vehicles only. Chalet accoomdation at Wallara Lodge, or camping.

PALM VALLEY: About 90 miles west of Alice Springs. Huge rock canyon with groves of tall palms said to be many centuries old. Four-wheel-drive vehicles only. Chalet accommodation or camping.

HERMANNSBURG ABORIGINAL MISSION: About 83 miles west of Alice Springs, on the Finke River. This is Central Australia's earliest mission and a working cattle station (founded 1877). A donation of 50 cents is expected of visitors. Allow a full day.

ROSS RIVER RESORT: About 48 miles east of Alice Springs. A "dude ranch" atmosphere, with horseback riding tours, walks, photography and Central Australian hospitality. An overnight stay is recommended.

Many other interesting places well worth a visit are Emily and Jessie Gaps, Trephina Gorge and Corroboree Rock, Valley of Eagles and Arltunga (the ghost gold-mining town) all in the east; Santa Teresa Mission on the fringe of the Simpson Desert, Serpentine and Ellery Gorges (on the way to Ormiston) and Glen of Palms (for four-wheel-drive vehicles). Further information from Northern Territory Tourist Bureaux or tour operators.

GENERAL SERVICES

AIRLINES (Local): Connellan Airways, 51 Todd St (Tel. 2 1755); S.A.A.T.A.S. Air Charter, 78 Todd St (Tel. 2 1847). (Interstate): Ansett-ANA, Todd Street, (Tel. 2 1777); T.A.A, Todd Street, (Tel. 2 1688).

BANKS: The following Banks are represented in Alice Springs: A.N.Z. Todd Street (Tel. 2 1144); Commonwealth Parsons Street (Tel. 2 1072); National Todd Street (Tel. 2 1993); N.S.W. Todd Street (Tel. 2 1243).

CAR AGENTS: Hastings Deering P/L, Stuart Highway (Tel. 2 1888), Ford; Kittle Bros Ltd, cnr Todd St & Wills Terrace (Tel. 2 1155), Holden; Lackman Agencies, 33 Railway Terrace (Tel. 2 1004), Landrover, Rambler, Rover, Peugeot, Volkswagon, Toyota, Chrysler, Fiat; Oasis Service Station, Gap Road (Tel. 2 1866); Ramsay Motors P/L, Brown Street (Tel. 2 1213); Sutton Motors, Smith Street (Tel. 2 1334), B.M.C.; Todd Driveway, cnr Todd St & Wills Terrace (Tel. 2 1676), Datsun.

CHURCHES:
Catholic, Hartley Street (Tel. 2 1049); Church of England, Bath Street (Tel. 2 1056); United Church, Todd Street (Tel. 2 1006); Lutheran Church, Gap Road (Tel. 2 2330); Salvation Army, 58 Hartley Street (Tel. 2 1960).

DRIVE YOURSELF CARS: Avis Rent-A-Car, 78 Todd Street (Tel. 2 1375); D.J. Auto Rentals, Todd Street (Tel. 2 1320); Drive Yorself Land-rovers Pty Ltd, Todd Street (Tel. 2 1320); Kays Rent-A-Car, Todd Street (Tel. 2 1676).

ELECTRIC LIGHT AND POWER: 240 v. A.C.

GAS: Portagas available from Harris & Leunig, Todd Street (Tel. 2 1266); Elder Smith Goldsborough Mort, Todd St (Tel. 2 1655).

ICE: Self Service machine on footpath outside Egars, Gregory Terrace; Caltex Service Station, Todd Street; B.P. Gap Service Station, Gap Road; Alice Springs Supermarket; Racecourse area.

LIBRARY: Hartley Street (Tel. 2 2303)

LIQUOR HOURS: 10 a.m. to 10 p.m., Monday to Saturday. Late Nights with cabaret (to 11.30 p.m.)

MOTOR CYCLE SALES: Murray Neck, Todd Street (Tel. 2 1031).

NEWSPAPER: The local newspaper, *Centralian Advocate* published weekly on Thursday. Interstate newspapers imported daily by air.

POST OFFICE: Corner of Railway Terrace and Parsons St (Tel. 2 1020). Hours: 9.00 a.m.—5.00 p.m. Monday to Friday; 9.00 a.m.—11 a.m. Saturday.

ROAD FREIGHT AGENTS: (for baggage) Commonwealth Railways (Tel. 2 1011); Richard Mitchell & Co P/L, 14 Stuart Highway (Tel. 2 1796); Wridgway Bros, Todd Street (Tel. 2 1680); John Dring Ltd (Tel. 2 1399); Ansett Freight (Tel. 2 1761).

ROAD INFORMATION: Oasis Garage, Gap Road. Official Automobile Association of N.T. garage; or Northern Territory Tourist Bureau.

AUTOMOBILE ASSOCIATION OF N.T. Members of inter state automobile associations visiting the Territory assume the same rights to the A.A.N.T. services as do regular members. Since this is a young organisation, services are largely restricted to road service, maps and road information. There is at present no office in Alice Springs, but the official garage is: Oasis Service Station, Gap Road (Tel. 2 1866) Contact this garage for road service up to 8 miles from town centre and for road information and maps. The other A.A. garages "up the track" are: Tennant Creek (Tel. 41); Katherine (Tel. 44); Adelaide River (Tel. 6); Darwin (Tel. 3983).

SHOPS: 9.00 a.m.—5.30 p.m. Monday to Friday; 9.00 a.m.—11.30 p.m. Saturday.

DARWIN GUIDE

Built on the shores of a fine harbour with 150 miles of golden coast-line, Darwin is rapidly outgrowing the small peninsula on which it stands. Around the coastline and to the south-east, new self-contained suburbs are steadily extending from the inner city area.

About 33,000 people live in Darwin today; an annual increase of 11 per cent makes this the fastest-growing city in Australia. Amenities and services are expanding also.

The architecture of Darwin's modern houses, hotels, motels and offices takes full advantage of the climate and results in comfortable living. Most buildings are airconditioned or fan-cooled.

Active and spectator sports cater for all interests. There are excellent beaches and inland swimming and picnic spots within easy driving distance. Fishing is good from beach, rocks or boat, or at inland lagoons, especially for barramundi and saratoga.

TRAVELLING TO AND FROM DARWIN

PRIVATE CAR: The highway from Port Augusta to Alice Springs is unsealed; many people like to travel this stretch by rail with their car conveyed aboard the same train. The Stuart Highway from Alice Springs to Darwin is sealed bitumen. The Barkly Highway from Three Ways (16 miles north of Tennant Creek) to Mt Isa is sealed bitumen.

AIR: International: Qantas Airways and BOAC scheduled daily service passing through Darwin. Details from Qantas Airways, 74 Mitchell Street, Darwin (Tel. 3350); N.T. Tourist Bureau, 40 Smith Street, Darwin (Tel. 6611); Ferguson's Travel, Smith Street, Darwin; Anthony's Travel, Smith Street, Darwin.

Pan American Airways. Scheduled north and southbound flights pass through Darwin each week. PanAm agents in Darwin: Ansett Airlines, Mitchell Street (Tel. 6763). Overseas Airlines Bookings also at N.T. Tourist Bureau, Anthony's, or Ferguson Travel.

Interstate: Daily services by T.A.A. and Ansett Airlines between the southern capitals and Darwin. Connellan Airways operate scheduled services over a wide network, connecting Darwin with all major ports and stations in the Northern Territory, the north-west of Western Australia and Mt Isa in Queensland. Regular services are also operated by M.M.A. between Perth/Darwin and Gove, Groote Eylandt.

RAIL: Trains operate twice weekly between Alice Springs and Adelaide, via Port Augusta.

COACH: Redline Coaches operate scheduled weekly services between Darwin, Alice Springs, Ayers Rock and the capital cities of the southern and eastern states. In addition, safari tours and accommodation tours operate weekly throughout the year. Camping gear may be obtained from Redline, or passengers can use their own equipment.

Ansett-Pioneer: Three weekly express services operate between Brisbane, Darwin, Alice Springs, Ayers Rock. A three-day accommodation tour operates (April to September) between Darwin and Alice Springs. Other services include the "Northlander" to Darwin via Tanami Desert and Kununurra, and the "Overlander" Alice Springs to Cairns.

A bi-weekly express service operates between Darwin and Alice Springs, throughout the year connecting with the rail service Alice Springs/Adelaide.

C.A.T.A. operates scheduled weekly services between Alice Springs and Ayers Rock. Additional package tours including coach/air/ accommodation operate from all capital cities in association with

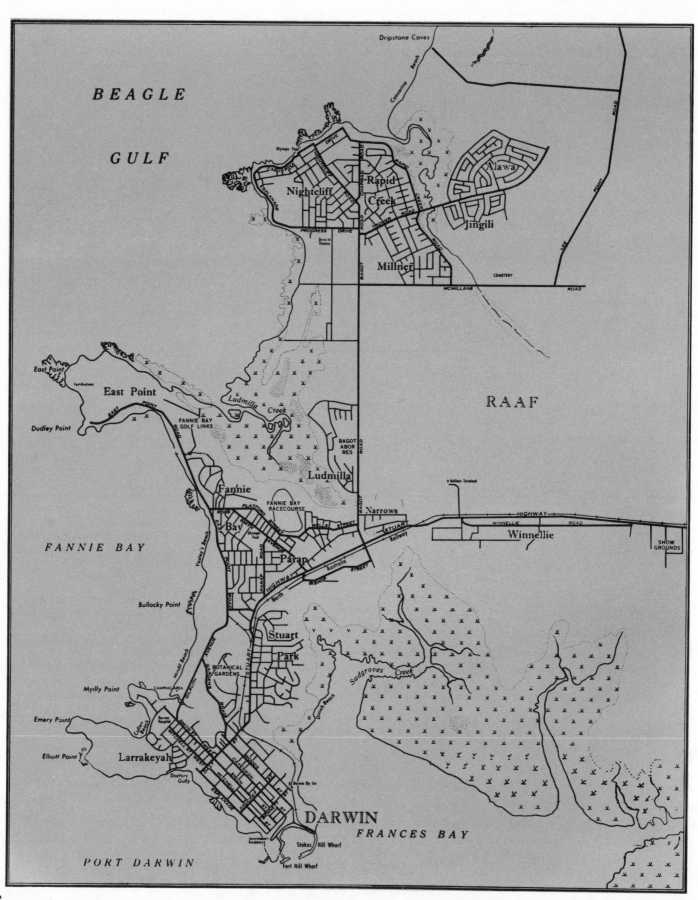

T.A.A./Murray Valley Coaches. (Timetables and further details may be obtained from the Northern Territory Tourist Bureau, or from the coach companies concerned.)

SHIPPING: Interstate passenger vessels: State Shipping Service (Tel. 2901) operate regular voyages between Fremantle and Darwin. Round-Australia voyages (Fremantle-Darwin-Sydney-Melbourne-Fremantle) operate approximately every 2 months; bookings may be made through N.T. Tourist Bureau.

Overseas passenger vessels. Cruise ships are now calling regularly at Darwin. Passengers may now join these cruises at Darwin. Bookings and further information from N.T. Tourist Bureaux or Burns, Philp & Co. Ltd.

CLIMATE: The temperature in coastal Darwin rarely exceeds 98 degrees and the overall average throughout the year is 82.4 degrees. In the Dry Season (April to November) days are warm and humidity low, with constant sunshine and no rain. During the Rainy Season (November to April) the humidity rises and there are tropical downpours and thunderstorms.

WHAT TO SEE

HARBOUR AND BEACHES—cruises by arrangement.

CHINESE TEMPLE AND JOSS HOUSE, Lichfield Street, off Woods Street at rear of Don Motor Hotel. Darwin has a steadily increasing population of approximately 500 Chinese, many of whom are members of the temple. They worship individually, at any time, and visitors are always welcome.

CHURCHES, old and new. To take only three examples, the dramatically modern architecture of the United Church and the Roman Catholic Cathedral in Smith Street contrasts with the delightful old stone Anglican church in upper Smith Street, erected in 1903.

OLD TOWN HALL, upper Smith Street. Built in 1883, recently served as Darwin's Motor Registry Office; in late 1967 became temporary building for newly formed Museums Board (see "General Service Information").

THE OLD COURTHOUSE-CUM-POLICE STATION in the Esplanade, between Smith and Mitchell Street, overlooking the Harbour. Built in the early 1880s from local shale; now Naval Headquarters.

MODERN LAWCOURTS and Government Buildings, upper Mitchell Street.

BOTANICAL GARDENS. Approximately 1½ miles from the city. Cool shade and relaxation among lush tropical plants and trees. Historic Holtze Cottage, built by the first curator, and a group of carved and painted grave-posts traditional to the Tiwi tribe are of further interest. Tea room and well equipped children's playing area under shady trees. Modern ampitheatre where evening concerts and band recitals may be enjoyed by the public.

FANNIE BAY GAOL, built around 1882-3. Architect was J. G. Knight, later Government Resident in the Northern Territory, who designed most of the fine old stone buildings erected in Darwin in the 1870s and 1880s. In the early days there were no surrounding walls, for the lack of transportation and roads made it unlikely that escapees would get far away before recapture.

MONUMENT commemorating exact spot at which Keith and Ross Smith crossed the coastline on their epic 1919 flight from London to Australia—opposite Fannie Bay Gaol.

REMAINS OF DARWIN DEFENCES: Fast Point Reserve.

REGULAR DAY TOURS by Ansett/Pioneer and Darwin Tourist Services. Bookings may be made with the operators or with N.T. Tourist Bureau, Smith Street, Darwin.

SOUTH OF DARWIN

Thirteen miles south of Darwin, just off the Stuart Highway on the left, is YARRAWONGA PARK—a zoological garden in which crocodiles, buffalo, brolgas, emus, dingoes and snakes of the Territory may be viewed and photographed at close range in complete safety. Proprietor,

Dr McKenzie. Admission: Adults 30 cents, children 10 cents (Tel. 4 5531).

Sixteen miles south of Darwin, on the left, is the turn-off to HOWARD SPRINGS RECREATION RESERVE along four miles of sealed road. Developed and controlled by the Reserves Board, this is a very popular camping and picnic spot, with toilet facilities, fireplaces and a fully stocked kiosk. Firewood and water are provided free of charge. A large freshwater pool is formed by a concrete wall holding back the spring waters, surrounded by tropical trees and shrubs; the area is floodlit at night. Admission: 10 cents per person. A caravan park is established. No shooting or fishing is permitted on the Reserve.

Twenty-two miles south of Darwin is the turn-off to the left for 18 miles of sealed road leading to the CSIRO experimental rice project, HUMPTY DOO. Nearby is the FOGG DAM BIRD SANCTUARY, under the control of the Chief Inspector of Wild Life. On a large expanse of water covered in water lilies, many species of waterfowl, at times in their thousands, can be seen. On the open plains, buffalo graze in the distance. Remember it is an offence to bring a firearm into a wild life protected area.

Thirty miles south of Darwin is the turn-off on the right for BERRY SPRINGS. Nine miles of unsealed, graded road lead to a popular swimming and picnic spot. Two constantly flowing natural pools are linked by a narrow stream and shaded with overhanging trees and pandanus palms. There are dressing sheds and toilets. A small mobile kiosk operates on Saturdays, Sundays, Mondays and Public Holidays. Under Reserves Board control: Admission 10 cents per person.

MANTON DAM, the picturesque source of Darwin's water supply, lies 42 miles south of Darwin. Take the sealed turn-off to the right just before the Manton River crossing. A wide expanse of river can be viewed from a railed footwalk atop the dam itself; the scene is especially attractive from late December to mid-March when the rains cause the catchment waters to spill steadily over the dam. Bird life is plentiful—no shooting.

SPECIAL TOURS

TO ABORIGINAL RESERVES: First Sunday of each month from July to October, the N.T. Tourist Bureau operates full day conducted tours of Bathurst Island Catholic Mission. Permits arranged, lunch provided. *Note:* Permits to enter aboriginal reserves are granted only to people who can substantiate a genuine scientific and anthropological interest. The people of the Territory do not regard the aborigines as tourist curiosities, and the effective daily operation of welfare settlements and mission stations is of paramount importance. Conducted tours arranged by the N.T. Tourist Bureau therefore offer an exceptional opportunity to the visitor.

KUNUNURRA (Ord River Scheme): Flights from Darwin by M.M.A. or Connellan Airways, or special charter. Details from N.T. Tourist Bureau operator.

PORTUGUESE TIMOR: T.A.A. operates regular weekly flights throughout the year. Return fare Darwin/Bacau $57.40; Darwin/Dili $67.40.

WILDLIFE "SAFARIS"

Regions where wildlife can be observed close to the highway include Fogg Dam, and the Adelaide River area. There are other places further afield from Darwin where wildlife is still more abundant. These include the relatively unspoiled Marrakai Plains, Daly River area and Jim Jim Creek regions, where kangaroos, wallabies, buffalo, crocodiles, various reptiles large and small, and teeming bird life may be viewed and photographed. Trips to these area are known as "safari tours".

CARS: There are two alternate roads leading through the Marrakai Plains to the Jim Jim Creek: New Mt Bundy route (supersedes the old Marrakai road): turn east off the Stuart Highway at the 22-mile mark. Proceed along the newly-made bitumen road for 35 miles, then take the dirt road branching off to the left, across the Mary River Plains. From here on, the road is unsealed. Mileage, Darwin-Jim Jim: 145 miles. Pine Creek road: proceed through the township of Pine Creek and take the dirt road to the right, which is unsealed along its entire length. Mileage Darwin-Jim Jim: 250 miles. *Note:* Drivers are strongly advised to consult road information authorities to learn which road is currently in the better condition. In the Rainy Season, the roads are often impassable, even to 4-wheel-drive vehicles.

COACH OPERATORS: Ansett-Pioneer: 5-day coach tours to Jim Jim Safari Lodge depart Darwin each Monday. "Arnhemlander" tours depart Darwin Friday night and return Sunday night. Darwin Tourist Services: 10-hour, 4-wheel-drive coach tours to Marrakai Plains region depart Darwin Tuesdays, Thursdays and Saturdays at 9 a.m. No shooting permitted. Peter Thomsen's Safaris: Land, water, or combined land-water safaris by arrangement. 4-wheel-drive vehicle. One-day safari tour operates with a minimum of two persons. Fishing and shooting available under permit.

AIR CHARTER: Charter flights may be arranged with Arnhem Air Charters or S.A.A.T.A.S. to any of the safari camp operators listed below. S.A.A.T.A.S. operate one-day to five-day tours to Patonga—bookings at S.A.A.T.A.S. or the N.T. Tourist Bureau.

SAFARI CAMPS: For those who wish to spend a little longer among the wildlife, 3 "safari" camps are operated in the Jim Jim Creek region. Nourlangie Safari Camp—Situated in a wildlife protected area. Billabongs nearby. Hunting permit required. Accommodation: $12 per person per day, in 2-bed rooms. Jeep Trips: 25 cents per mile per person. Hunting Safaris: $20 per person per day all inclusive. 6-Day Photographic and Sightseeing Tour—$80 all inclusive. Depart Monday 10 a.m. Boat: Rates on application. Telegrams: Nourlangie O.P.R. Patonga Safari Lodge—Modern comfortable bedrooms, spacious recreation room. Large billabong nearby. Hunting Safaris (with guide): 1 hunter $100 per day; 2 hunters $75 per day, 3 hunters $60 per day each; 1 hunter and wife $120 per day; Group of 4 or 5 hunters $50 per day each; Larger hunting parties, prices on request. Scenic Photograpic Safari $20 per day per person. Deposit of 25 per cent required on each booking. Firearms and fishing gear supplied at no extra cost. Permit for shooting required. Telegrams: Patonga O.P.R. Darwin. Mail: Box 623 P.O. Darwin.

MOTEL JIM JIM AND COOINDA STORE: On the banks of Jim Jim Creek. General Store; liquor licence. Petrol available. Tourist accommodation available. Telegrams: Cooinda O.P.R. Darwin. Mail: Box 1090, P.O. Darwin. Regular "Arnhemlander" Coach Tours Departing Darwin Monday and Friday. Bookings from Ansett-Pioneer and N.T. Tourist Bureau.

WOOLIANA: Fishing and camping ground on banks of Daly River. Tourist accommodation available. Telegrams: Wooliana O.P.R. Darwin.

GENERAL SERVICE INFORMATION

AIRLINES: Arnhem Air Charters, Wells Street, Fannie Bay (Tel. 3330); Connellan Airways, Daly Street (Tel. 6431); S.A.A.T.A.S., Foyer, Hotel Darwin (Tel. 2684); Ansett Airlines, Herbert Street (Tel. 2957); T.A.A., Bennet Street (Tel. 2941); M.M.A., Cavanagh Street (Tel. 6551).

AUTOMOBILE ASSOCIATION: Members of interstate automobile associations visiting the Territory assume the same rights to the A.A.N.T. services as do regular members. Head Office, 71 Smith Street (Tel. 3837).

BUSES: Local terminal at Smith Street East. Interstate: Ansett-Pioneer, Herbert Street (Tel. 2957); Redline, Bennett Street (Tel. 6226).

DRIVE YOURSELF CARS: Avis Rent-A-Car, 62 Stuart Highway (Tel. 6495); B.M. Auto Sales, 49 Stuart Highway (Tel. 2656); City Car Rentals, Smith Street (Tel. 6036); Darwin Rent-A-Car Edmund Street (Tel. 6086); Economy Car Rentals, Mitchell Street (Tel. 6505); Hertz Rent-A-Car, Highway Service Station, Daly Street (Tel. 2976); Hunter's Drive Yourself (Mini Mokes only), 75 Smith Street (Tel. 6070); Kay's Rent-A-Car, Darwin Tourist Services, Cavanagh Street (Tel. 3693); U Drive, Cavenagh Street (Tel. 6621).

134

GUIDE TO KATHERINE

Katherine stands at the junction of the Stuart Highway and the road from Western Australia. It is 220 miles south of Darwin—a leisurely day's drive. The two major interstate airlines operate to its airport, and it is also a terminal for Connellan Airways.

A flourishing township of 2,000 people, Katherine is a "must" for any visitor to the Northern Territory. Scenic attractions include the low-level river frontage recreation area, three miles north of town—a delightful swimming and picnic spot with facilities for campers and caravanners; the limestone caves 16 miles south of town; and of course, most importantly, the mighty Katherine Gorge, 20 miles to the east. Katherine's large meat abattoirs may also be inspected by arrangement. Experimental farms in the area are researching problems of tropical agriculture: inspection may be arranged with the Officer-in-Charge, CSIRO Experimental Farm (Tel. 190).

KATHERINE GORGE

KATHERINE GORGE: The 20-mile road to the gorge varies in condition, but is easily passable to the average motorist, provided care is taken in some of the more rugged creek crossings.

The Katherine River is the first permanent waterway encountered as one journeys north from the South Australian border. Over the ages, this great river has cut through rock formations to create one of the world's most majestic gorges. Katherine Gorge must stand with Ayers Rock as one of the two major tourist attractions of the Northern Territory. The Gorge is a photographer's delight at any hour of the day, but the early morning tours are especially recommended to those who wish to view or photograph the breathtaking reflections before the first breezes mar them—or to see freshwater crocodiles basking in the morning sun.

The Gorge area is under the control of the Northern Territory Reserves Board, which has provided showers, toilets, fireplaces and tables for visitors. An entry fee of 10 cents is charged to all visitors to the Gorge to help defray the Board's expenses. There is a caravan park and camping ground with all amenities.

During the Dry Season (April to October) two organisations operate boat tours of the Gorge: Corroboree Tours (Tel. 208), March Motors (Tel. 44).

Coach tours and bus services to the Katherine Gorge run daily. Inquiries at Katherine Motel.

SIXTEEN-MILE LIMESTONE CAVES

SIXTEEN-MILE LIMESTONE CAVES: The caves are situated 16 miles south of Katherine, one mile off the western side of the Stuart Highway. Caverns are of great size with magnificent limestone formations, including imposing stalagmites and stalactites. The caves are under the control of the Reserves Board, which has in turn leased them to March Motors for development. White and coloured lighting and stairs have been installed, and other work has been carried out to makes the caves accessible to the average visitor without discomfort.

A guide is constantly in attendance, and tours leave the Caves entrance each hour on the hour. Tour fee is $1, with tickets available at March Motors or at the Caves themselves. Katherine Tourist Centre (Tel. 170).

AYERS ROCK AND THE OLGAS

Ayers Rock, a massive single rock monolith 270 road miles south-west of Alice Springs, is acknowledged as one of the tourist wonders of the world. More than 2 miles long, 1½ miles wide and 1,100 feet high, this phenomenon was aptly described by its astonished discoverer as "an immense pebble rising abruptly from the plains."

Twenty miles west of Ayers Rock are the Olgas, a group of huge rocky domes 4½ miles long and 3 miles wide which many visitors find of even greater interest than Ayers Rock.

Here are some important points for intending visitors to the Ayers Rock-Mount Olga Reserve.

1. "Scare" stories about the state of the unsealed road from Alice Springs to the Rock should be ignored. Consult the Tourist Bureau at Alice Springs for up-to-date, accurate information about the current state of the road, which is rarely impassable to conventional vehicles.

2. Allow one full day for travelling down, one day at Ayers Rock, one day at The Olgas, and a full day to return. At Mt Ebenezer, Victory Downs and Curtin Springs, stores, meals and accommodation are available to travellers to and from the Rock.

3. Hours for entry to the Reserve are 7 a.m. to 10 p.m.

4. On entering the Reserve, a permit fee of $1 is payable to the Curator at his Lodge. This helps to offset the considerable costs incurred by the Reserves Board in maintaining and preserving this vast Reserve for future generations.

5. Good drinking water and hot and cold showers are available at the Rock.

6. There is no firewood available at the Rock. It is suggested that travellers bring either a portable gas stove or their own firewood.

7. Should you intend to climb Ayers Rock and explore the great domes of The Olgas—no visit is complete unless you do—bring strong rubber footwear. Long trousers are also advisable to guard against the prickly spinifex of The Olgas.

8. Photography: The Curator will advise you of some of the best times and places at which to photograph the Rock. A wide-angle lens is useful, though not essential, to photograph The Olgas.

ONCE AT THE RESERVE VISITORS ARE ASKED TO:

Don't throw litter from your vehicle; large litter pits are provided in the camping area.

Drivers should keep strictly to the established roads. Remember that the region suffers from inadequate rainfall. If tourists were permitted to make their own tracks over the light undergrowth, the whole area would quickly become denuded of flora. Future generations would then be visiting a vast dustbowl, instead of the relatively lush and verdant region that is the Reserve today.

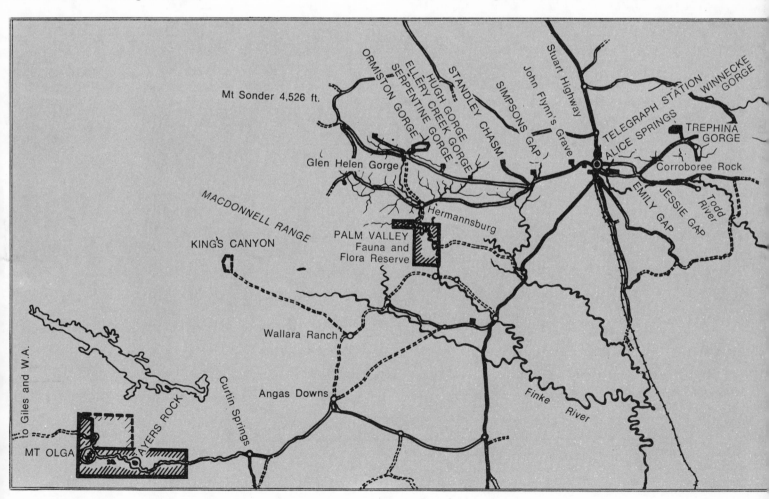

Tasmania

CHURCH RUIN AT PORT ARTHUR'S OLD PENAL SETTLEMENT

THE GREEN AND MELLOW STATE

The very isolation that Tasmania, as the island State and the smallest State, has suffered has brought it, in this golden age of tourism, to the forefront of the travel experiences Australia offers.

A Tasmanian holiday has become the new capsule experience—enriched even at the beginning by the casting off of ties from the mainland for the crossing of Bass Strait, and sustained by the traveller's ability to 'see all' within the water defined boundaries of the State.

But Tasmania's tourist industry would not prosper for long if it was built on the basis of novelty, or the over statement of promises that plague the modern traveller.

Its solid foundation is that Tasmania holds a richness of atmosphere, a diversity of pastime, scenery and historic association that is unsurpassed by any other Australian region.

Its west coast is a wild sweep of nature—jagged mountains, lakes, rushing rivers and dense rainforest—containing one of the world's few remaining unexplored regions; its east coast is a peaceful region of delightful coastal scenery; its north coast and midlands country is more gentle and European in aspect that any other Australian countryside; its Great Central Plateau is the spectacular cradle of its snowfields and the fountain of its abundant water supply and its hydro-electric power; its peninsulas and islands each have some new aspect or association to delight the eye or the senses.

Throughout the island there are particular places of fascination: Port Arthur, Lake Pedder, Battery Point, Cataract Gorge, Ross Bridge, The Oatlands Mill, Richmond, Maria Island, Lake St Clair National Park, Queenstown, The Salmon Ponds, The Great Western Tiers, The Savage River—the list is as long as it is varied.

The Tasmanians, progressing on many fronts through their long established pastoral, timber and manufacturing industries, and through new mining and industrial development, are particularly engrossed and keen to play their part in the field of tourism. For they are proud of their State, and pleased to play host to the visitors who come to discover it.

▼ MT FREYCINET AND HAZARDS BEACH, FREYCINET PENINSULA   THE DERWENT RIVER, MACQUARIE PLAINS

HISTORY PRESERVED

Tasmania was founded as a British settlement in an age of gentlemanly privilege and Georgian elegance of architecture and manners. Its settlers, as they established their lands and a more ordered life in the towns, sought to emulate something of the surroundings and social trappings of their distant homeland.

On their country holdings they built handsome homesteads in park like grounds, and workman's cottages, stables and farm buildings as picturesque and enduring as those of the estates of England. The material was usually the solid plentiful and manageable freestone from quarries of the district or from individual properties.

As Hobart grew, simple but imposing warehouses were built to hold the traffic of the busy port, and fine churches, public buildings and residences which had the same elegance and severity notable in English and Italian architectural style of the early 19th century.

In the villages of the country tranquility and nobility of design were happily combined in the stone public houses, barracks, courthouse, churches and in the leafy groves of introduced English trees.

The soft climate, gentle landscape and the grandeur of the early colonial architecture gives much of today's Tasmania a mellowness and a richness of historic association which, because it is confined in a small, waterbound land has more impact than any of the historic regions of mainland Australia.

It is this atmosphere of history, the evocation of the past, as much as the fascinating old buildings themselves, that makes their study absorbing to the traveller in Tasmania.

The historic buildings and sites are too many to enumerate here (see guide section) but among the 'musts' for the visitor are a leisurely trip through the historic old midlands towns like Longford, Ross, Richmond and Oatlands, a visit to Franklin and Entally Houses near Launceston, to Battery Point, Sullivan's Cove and Salamanca Place in Hobart, to Port Arthur and the old west coast mining towns.

▼ FRANKLIN HOUSE, LAUNCESTON, 1838

▲ THE GRANGE, CAMPBELL TOWN, 1848–89   ▼ ST JOHN'S CHURCH OF ENGLAND, CAMPBELL TOWN, 1869

ROSS BRIDGE OVER MACQUARIE RIVER

THE RIVAL CITIES

Hobart's 125,000 inhabitants have, happily, managed to escape the rush and bustle that has infected the mainland capitals of eastern Australia.

The Tasmanian capital is a rapidly developing and vital city with modern office blocks, hotels and stores springing up, and a gambling casino in the offing, but its people can still live at a pace which allows them to enjoy the beauty around them—the broad sweep of the Derwent Estuary and the backdrop of forest clad Mt. Wellington, which is snow capped in winter. There is no doubt that Hobart is the most picturesquely sited of all the State capitals.

It is also the most solid and dignified—a veritable showcase of Colonial architecture.

Around its fine deepwater port, where the Empress of *Tasmania* and many ships of commerce tie up, and where the famous Sydney-Hobart yacht race ends each New Year, there is still something of the air of an old 19th century seaport town. The old freestone bondstores and warehouses still cluster in picturesque Salamanca Place, a reminder of the roaring days where the seamen drank in tough waterfront taverns. The Georgian houses and cottages of the merchants and workers that the port sustained are at nearby Battery Point.

Launceston is the 'capital' of northern Tasmania, and its citizens like to conduct a running battle with the city of the south, Hobart. Launceston is a small city of provincial atmosphere, but it is an important one—the pivot of a network of highways that serve the rich coastal lands to east and west, and an important link for transport services and communications between Tasmania and the mainland.

The city lies 40 miles from the coast at the junction of the North Esk, South Esk and Tamar Rivers. It is a peaceful place, spread over attractive, hilly countryside and supporting a population of 61,000. Its greatest natural attraction is the Cataract Gorge, a few miles from the centre of the city. The South Esk River has cut a deep canyon through the hills, and its rapids are spectacular after heavy rain. A pathway along the gorge leads to Cliff Grounds Park, where both English and native trees flourish and where picnic grounds and a swimming pool are reached by a suspension bridge.

Launceston is deservedly proud of its parks and private gardens. European trees, particularly oaks and elms, thrive in its mild, moist climate, and their mixture with the native flora makes a pleasant botanic confluence in the city's ample garden areas.

BOTANIC GARDENS, LAUNCESTON

THE CASINO AT WREST POINT, HOBART

▲ CONSTITUTION DOCK, HOBART ▼ LAUNCESTON FROM GORGE BRIDGE ▼ FOUNTAIN IN PRINCE'S SQUARE

GREAT BUSHLAND RESERVES

Tasmania, with its dense forest lands and spectacular peaks, high altitude lakes, rushing rivers and streams and rugged, indented coast, has the natural beauty and richness of flora and fauna to make it a paradise for nature lovers and bush walkers.

Many national parks have been established, most of them in the mountain country of the centre and west. The biggest and best known of them is the Cradle Mountain—Lake St. Clair National Park, which covers an area of 525 square miles. The many walking tracks are well marked and huts are spaced one day's walk from each other. The biggest of these is the picturesque Waldheim Chalet, built in the Tyrolean style, and the main track is from here to Cynthia Bay on Lake St. Clair, 60 miles south. The 20 square mile lake lies at an altitude of 2,418 ft. The bush area around is the home of the Bennett's and Rufous wallabies, both unique Tasmanian varieties.

Cradle Mountain, in the north of the park is 5,069 ft high and holds the beautiful Crater Lake in its rocky embrace. There are many other notable mountains in the park, some of them eroded into fantastic shapes.

Further south is the Frenchman's Cap park, now isolated and recommended for experienced bush walkers only. It is dominated by the white ice-cut cliff face which gives it its name.

In the South-West National Park is Lake Pedder, a glacial lake encircled by towering mountains and with a magnificent beach of white quartz. It is threatened now by plans for the development of a hydro-electric scheme on the Serpentine River.

The Hartz Mountain Park is in rugged south-western country, with access from the Huon Valley. The peaks, a magnet for climbers, are snow capped for most of the year, and their lower slopes are clad in magnificent rain forests. Best known are Mt. Picton, the Arthur Range and Federation Peak.

The Mt. Field Park, the third biggest reserve in the State, is the main ski area. It is the most accessible of the reserves, being only 25 miles from New Norfolk in the Derwent Valley. It is an area of glacial lakes and superb waterfalls, the best known being the Russell Falls, a beautiful series of cascades dropping into a gorge of rainforest and tree ferns. The forests here contain stands of deciduous beech and the streams and lakes abound in mountain shrimps (*aspanades Tasmaniae*).

Other winter sports areas are in the Ben Lomond and Mt. Barrow Parks, which also contain spectacular forest and mountain scenery.

The biggest of the coastal reserves is the east coast Freycinet National Park flanking Coles Bay. Its magnificent coastal scenery includes the impressive red granite backbone known as 'The Hazards', secluded bays and inlets and many varieties of ground orchids in the unspoiled bushland. Smaller coastal reserves are on Bruny Island, Schouten Island, at Rocky Cape in the north and on the Tasman Peninsula.

LAKE PEDDER

▲ CRADLE LAKE

▼ FRENCHMAN'S CAP RANGE

RUSSELL FALLS ▶

PORT ARTHUR – A Grim Relic

The grimness and meaning of Port Arthur has been softened and blurred by time. But it is still possible, if the weather and the imagination are at work, for the stone ruins to strike a claustrophobic dread into the heart.

Whether the ruins of the infamous penal establishment are considered by visitors to be horrifying or merely picturesque, there is no doubt that they are the greatest single tourist attraction in Tasmania.

They are on the Tasman Peninsula, which extends from the Forestier Peninsula to the east and south of Hobart and screens Pittwater and the Derwent Esturay from the Tasman Sea.

The whole area of both peninsulas is magnificently scenic, with sweeping pasture and timber lands and a seaward coastline of sheltered bays and towering cliffs and capes. Many secondary roads and tracks and a host of secluded beauty spots make it a bush walkers paradise.

Eaglehawk Neck is on the isthmus between the two peninsulas. In the days of the penal colony hounds were tethered in a tight line across the neck to prevent escapes. The line was continually patrolled and guard posts were established in the nearby hills. No prisoner ever pierced the fearful barrier, although some swam to freedom. Near Eaglehawk Neck are four fascinating formations of coastal rock—Tasman's Arch, Devil's Kitchen, the Blowhole and the Tesselated Pavement.

The Port Arthur Ruins have been preserved or in part restored. Those still standing include the church, said to have been designed by the convict James Blackburn; the Model Prison, which followed the design of Pentonville England and was wheel shaped so that a warder standing in the centre could look into all the cells; The Exile Cottage, originally a hospital and then the home of the exiled Irish rebel, William Smith O'Brien, and the guard house.

Complete buildings are the Lunatic Asylum (now the Tasman Council Chambers) and the Commandant's residence (now privately owned).

The prison was established by Governor Arthur in 1830 and 30,000 prisoners passed through there. Although transportation ceased in 1853 the prison was not abandoned until 1877. Many buildings were demolished by contractors and others were badly damaged by a bushfire which swept through the peninsula in 1897.

In the middle of Port Arthur Bay stands the Isle of the Dead, with its 1,646 graves. Only 180, those of prison staff or the military, record names of the dead.

Other historic convict establishments on the peninsulas include the coal mines settlement at Slopen Main, the Saltwater Creek agricultural centre, and the timber mills at Predmaydena and Koonya on the shores of Norfolk Bay.

PENITENTIARY RUINS

RICH NORTH COAST

The north coast contains the richest agricultural land in Tasmania and is the most densely settled region. Apart from Launceston thriving towns like Burnie, Devonport, Wynyard, Ulverstone, Smithton and Stanley are busy centres of commerce and industry.

The narrow 190 mile long strip of coastal plain between the island's central mountains and Bass Strait is linked in the west by the coastal Bass Highway and railway from Launceston to Smithton and in the less settled east by the Tasman Highway and rail to Derby.

The farms, orchards and pastures of the north are green all the year round, watered by the short, fast rivers which drain the high country to the south, and by an average annual rainfall which exceeds 30 inches.

The beauty of the region is one of gentle pastoral landscape, creased by many small, clear streams and with distant vistas of mountain peaks and ranges. The great amount of introduced European trees and hedge plants gives an air faintly reminiscent of the English countryside.

The northern coastline is not generally spectacular and lacks the chains of beaches which are a feature of the mainland coast. There is more variety of coastal scenery in the lonely north east and in the extreme west, past Wynyard, where austerely impressive headlands jut into the sea.

It is worth extending any journey to explore the interesting north-west coast between Table Cape and Circular Head and to the Arthur River Region at the end of the Bass Highway. The river cuts a deep gorge through typically wild west coast country.

The larger towns on the Bass Highway are convenient bases for exploration of the gentle lowland country and the magnificent mountains, which can be reached in an hours driving from the coast.

The Tasman Highway, which connects Launceston with Hobart via the east coast, cuts through fine farming country around Scottsdale and the old tin mining town of Derby. It is attractive country, but the traveller with time can further enhance the journey by taking the northern loop road to the coast, through the beautiful valley town of Lilydale and its surrounding lavender farms, and to the secluded seaside town of Bridport.

▼ THE 'NUT' AT STANLEY

▲ THE INDUSTRIAL TOWN OF BURNIE
▼ MT ROLAND, SHEFFIELD

THE HOLIDAY COAST

The east coast is more like mainland Australia than any other part of Tasmania. Its scenery is varied but, on the whole, less spectacular than the rest of the State. It has an equable climate for most of the year and its picturesque seaside resorts are popular with Tasmanian holiday-makers. Most are on sheltered inlets, but within easy reach of surfing and fishing grounds.

The region, long reliant on its agricultural and pastoral industry and fishing as its economic basis, is now becoming oriented to tourism as mainlanders take the 266 mile Tasman Highway drive from Hobart to Launceston as a stage of their island holiday.

First stop from Hobart is the century-old former coaching village of Buckland, in the Prosser Valley. The old stone church is noted for its magnificent 14th century stained glass window, brought out from England. At the mouth of the Prosser River is Orford, a popular resort surrounded by mountains and the seaward bulk of Maria Island, a former convict settlement. Also opposite Maria Island is Triabunna, a flourishing fishing town on Spring Bay which once held the Maria Island garrison and a big whaling base in the 1830's.

Further north is Swansea on Oyster Bay, centre for Glamorgan, the oldest rural community in Tasmania and renowned for its lake and river fishing. The annual Tasmanian angling championships are held here. Coles Bay is the focus of the east coast, a region of snowy beaches, great cliffs, ocean pools and bush paths lined with wildflowers in the Spring. The charm of the secluded coves is expressed in their names—Sleepy Bay, Wineglass Bay, the Fisheries, Friendly Beaches and Honeymoon Bay. Moulting Lagoon may not sound so inviting, but is in fact a peaceful haven for black swans. A small wonder of Coles Bay is The Hazards, thousand feet high hills of red granite from which the facings of many Hobart buildings have been quarried.

The Hazards are in the Freycinet National Park, a 16,000 acre reserve and wildlife sanctuary. Bird life is prolific in the unspoiled bush and 60 varieties of ground orchid have been identified here.

On through Bicheno, where the whalers once kept a lookout for waterspouts from Peggy Point, through Seymour, down St. Mary's Pass, a long winding descent to sea level, to Scamander and St. Helens, where the highway turns west towards inland Scottsdale and Launceston, across the rich pastures and wooded hill country of the north east. The east coast has left a feeling of peace and unspoiled tranquility.

▼ FISHING BOATS AT TRIABUNNA

OYSTER BAY ST COLUMBA'S FALLS, 17 MILES WEST OF ST HELENS

Y. A. SHIRREFS

BOYER

▼ EDDYSTONE POINT FROM LIGHTHOUSE

UNIQUE WEST COAST

The west coast of Tasmania is a stretch of country unique to Australia. It is lonely and sparsely populated, clothed for the most part by dense, rain soaked forests, cleft by mountains of savage magnificence and ravines carrying turbulent rivers to the coast.

Many parts of the south-west have not been traversed by man, as progress is made virtually impossible by the 'horizontal' (*anedo-petalum*) plant which grows so densely that a path has to be hacked through it with an axe. In the more open country to the north flowering heaths and shrubs flourish, and many species of ferns grow in the deep moist valleys.

The forest land is the haunt of the almost legendery Tasmanian tiger (thylacine), a marsupial wolf with a brown pelt, marked across the hindquarters with darker brown and black stripes, and the Tasmanian devil (sarcophiles).

The hills and gorges of the west are rich in metal minerals, but because of difficulty of access it was left to the 'loners' to skim the cream. Until 1932, when a road was pushed through to Queenstown, the mining towns' only connection with the world was through small boats which braved the difficult entrances of Macquarie and Trial Harbours.

Now modern roads also link the west with the Bass Highway to the north. The fascinating mining towns like Zeehan, Gormanston, Rosebery and Waratah, and the big scale mining complexes which are developing around them, are now within easy reach of the traveller. In boom times at the turn of the century Zeehan had a population of 10,000 as the miners tried their luck in the silver and lead workings. Queenstown, the main town of the west, is surrounded by spectacular, bare mountains, tinged with rainbow colours. The slopes have been denuded by the sulphur fumes of early mining and leached away by heavy rains.

The little town of Strahan, in Macquarie Harbour, is the only developed port on the rugged west coast, and is also the west coasters' holiday resort. Launch trips are made from here up the Gordon River, which cuts into spectacular mountain country. There is excellent fishing in the inlet here, and also in the Arthur, Savage and Pieman River headwaters.

The grandeur of the upper west coast mountain and forest scenery makes a trip along the road circuit an unforgettable experience, the only drawback being that the area is plagued by exceptionally heavy rainfall which knows no seasons. The south-west remains virtually unexplored, with only one trafficable road into its heart, from the Derwent Valley to a point north of Lake Pedder and the Serpentine River.

▼ THE 'GATES OF HELL' ENTRANCE TO MACQUARIE HARBOUR
LAKES IN THE WESTERN ARTHURS ▶

HUON VALLEY'S SOFT BEAUTY

The Huon Valley, to the south-west of Hobart and flanking the D'Entrecasteaux Channel in the east and the Huon River Estuary in the west, is the heart of Tasmania's apple country.

In Spring blossom time it is a region of soft and magical beauty, of mountain glade and water scenery that merges with the rich orchard and pasture lands. Many of the magnificent orchards—some of them damaged in the terrible bushfires of 1967—are more than a century old. Lady Franklin, wife of Sir John Franklin, Tasmanian Governor from 1837–43, is said to have encouraged apple growing when she established an orchard at Franklin on the western shores of the Huon Estuary.

Gradually the swampy and densely timbered country was cleared and cultivated for apple growing, and shipments of fruit to British and European countries began in 1864. The region had previously been known by English ship builders for its supplies of the highly prized Huon Pine, which began as early as 1829.

A popular journey from Hobart, taking in mountain, river, orchard and coastal scenery, is a 90 mile round tour of the peninsula, through the main town of Huonville, where a deepwater port on the estuary services fruit and timber ships and the A.P.P.M. wood pulp mill, and on through small and beautiful coastal towns like Cygnet, Gordon, Woodbridge, Kettering, Snug, Margate, Kingston and Taroona.

At Kettering a ferry service runs across the D'Entrecasteaux Channel to Bruny Island, a long, irregular land mass which shelters the Huon River Estuary. It was first discovered by Tobias Furneaux, second in command in James Cook's second voyage in 1773. Cook himself landed there in 1777. It is said the first apple trees in Tasmania were planted by Robert Brown, the botanist with William Bligh's expedition, at Adventure Bay, on the island, in 1788.

The island supports a small number of fruit growers and mixed farmers. It is mountainous in the south, well wooded and picturesque, with a ragged eastern coastline where bold headlands thrust into the channel. There are many enclosed bays which offer safe anchorage for small craft.

The west side of the Huon Estuary is less frequented by travellers, but rewarding to those who like to leave the beaten track. The road crosses the estuary at Huonville and runs through Geeveston to Dover, a small fishing port on the shores of Port Esperence.

Nearby is Adamson's Peak (4,017 feet) which has been likened to Mt Fujiyama because of its snow clad, conical symmetry.

Further south are thermal pools and Hastings Caves, near the towns of Hastings and Southport. The largest, Newdgate Cave, is a spectacular cavern, illuminated and open for inspection daily.

▲ APPLE TREES IN BLOSSOM

▲ HUON VALLEY   ▼ 'THE SLEEPING BEAUTY' FROM LONGLEY

TOURIST GUIDE

DISCOVERY AND EARLY SETTLEMENT

Several European nations showed an interest in the island of Tasmania before it was finally settled by the British in 1803. The initial discovery was made by the Dutchman, Abel Tasman in 1642. Tasman named the land Van Diemen's Land, in honour of the Governor who had sent him out. He did not know that he had discovered an island, but thought of it as the southern part of the Australian continent.

It was not until 1772 that the island was again visited; this time by the French navigator, Marion du Fresne, who largely followed the route taken by Tasman. Then followed Furneaux, in 1773, who discovered the section of the East coast north of St. Patrick's Head. In 1792, D'Entrecasteaux discovered the channel between the mainland and Bruny Island, which now carries his name, and the Huon River.

A major discovery was made in 1798 and 99, when Bass and Flinders circumnavigated the island, thus discovering the north and west coasts and proving the existence of Bass Strait.

The first settlement took place on 7 September, 1803, when Bowen's party landed at Risdon, near Hobart. In 1804 Lieut. Collins chose the present site of Hobart as the place for a town. With the establishment of a permanent settlement on both the Derwent River in 1803 and the Tamar River in 1804 there quickly followed an extension of exploration into the interior of the island.

It was not until the beginning of the twentieth century that the primary exploration of Tasmania was largely completed. Even today there are still places, particularly in the southwest, which have not been visited by Europeans.

Old Hobart Town, Van Diemen's Land (Tasmania). A peaceful view painted by G. W. Evans. (*National Library, Canberra*)

ABORIGINES

The Aboriginals of Tasmania were different, both physically and culturally, from those of the mainland. Many theories have been formulated about their origin, but very little first-hand information about these Aboriginals has survived. Their tribal life was rapidly disrupted by European settlement and the subsequent disagreements and misunderstandings which led to cruel and systematic slaughter by the whites.

Over the years their numbers gradually dwindled and the remaining few were moved to Oyster Cove. Here, in 1876, Queen Truganini, the last member of the Tasmanian Aboriginals died.

Today, their camp middens may be found in many places, especially along the coastline and the major river systems.

PHYSICAL

The island State of Tasmania is the smallest of the Australian States and is separated from the mainland by 150 miles of Bass Strait. It extends 180 miles north to south and 190 miles east to west, encompassing a total land area about equal in size to Scotland, or slightly less than one-third the area of Victoria.

The island is broken up by a continual succession of hills and mountains, which increase in ruggedness from east to west. The altitude, which rises to over 4,000 ft. on the central plateau, causes a considerable variability of climate. The yearly rainfall varies from an upper limit of 145 in. at Lake Margaret on the west coast to a lower limit of 19 in. in the midlands.

Topography and rainfall result in high altitude lakes and many swift rivers flowing from the central highlands. These waters have been extensively harnessed for the production of hydro-electric energy, which has encouraged the establishment of industries whose development is dependent upon the availability of cheap power.

The Tasmanian landscape is picturesque, with the mountains of the western half of the island, and the bold coastline of the south and south-east particularly spectacular. The vegetation is rich and varied, and the country is characteristically green.

CLIMATE

Tasmania has a cool temperate climate similar to that of New Zealand with a warm summer, mild winter and considerable diurnal range of temperature. The mean annual temperature at Hobart is 54·4 degrees.

February is generally the hottest month, the mean maximum temperature at Hobart being 70·6 degrees, compared with Melbourne 78·6 degrees, Sydney 78·7 degrees, Adelaide 85·7 degrees, Perth 85·1 degrees and Brisbane 84·6 degrees. The annual rainfall at Queenstown (west) averages about 100 in. at Oatlands (midlands) it is about 23 in. and at Swansea (east) it is about 25 in. The average at Hobart is just over 25 in.

Tasmania is substantially free from mist, fog, dust and other air impurities. In winter frosts are common, but these are generally followed by sunny days.

PRIMARY INDUSTRIES

Primary industries have always been important in the Tasmanian economy, and despite the industrial expansion of recent years, the State remains heavily dependent on rural, forest and mining production for its prosperity. The significance of such industries lies not only in their value for local consumption, but in the wealth they bring from exports, and in the provision of raw materials for use in secondary industry, notably newsprint, paper, zinc, copper, confectionary, and fruit and vegetable processing.

The principal crops are apples and pears, followed by potatoes, green peas and other vegetables. Most of Tasmania's apples and pears are shipped to England and the countries of Western Europe, whilst a large proportion of the potato crop is shipped to Sydney.

The valleys of the Huon, Derwent, Tamar and Mersey Rivers, together with the Tasman Peninsula are the source of most of the island's apple and pear production, while the climate of the northern coast and surrounding areas makes it particularly suitable for dairying.

Some 80% of Australia's hop requirements are grown under irrigation in the sheltered river valley of the Derwent.

Tasmania has some of the finest hardwood forests in the world. In general the best eucalypt forests occur where the rainfall is between 30 in. and 60 in. per annum.

Of increasing importance to the Tasmanian economy is the pulp and paper industry and the hardboard industry. Australian Newsprint Mills started production of newsprint at Boyer in the Derwent Valley in 1941 and Associated Pulp and Paper Mills Ltd. started production of fine writing and printing papers at Burnie in 1938.

MANUFACTURING INDUSTRIES

Tasmania is one of the few producers in Australia of sodium alginate, calcium carbide and newsprint. It also has a large paper manufacturing industry and produces the greater percentage of Australian zinc, aluminium and titanium oxide.

Important factors influencing industrial development in Tasmania are the low cost of hydro-electricity, water supplies, availability of essential raw materials, temperate climate, deep water access ports, and factory sites in areas free from industrial congestion.

TRANSPORT AND COMMUNICATIONS

Railways

There are 588 miles of railway in Tasmania, of which 500 are operated by the Tasmanian Government Railways and 88 by the Emu Bay Company.

The main line from Hobart to Launceston is 134 miles long, and the main branch lines extending from it are the Derwent Valley Line from Bridgewater Junction to Kallista [45 miles] and the Fingal Line from Conara Junction to St. Mary's [47 miles]. The Western Line runs from Launceston to Stanley [168 miles] and the North-Eastern Line runs from Launceston to Herrick [85 miles]. The Emu Bay Railway Company's line runs from Burnie to Zeehan.

The best known train is the 'Tasman Limited' which operates daily, except Sunday, and carries passengers between Hobart, Launceston and Wynyard.

Road Transport

Road passenger services operated by the Transport Commission and private companies extend to the majority of the populated areas throughout the State. Additionally, subsidiary road services connect inland towns with the coastal centres.

Sea Transport

A regular sea link between Tasmania and the Australian Mainland is maintained by the vehicular-passenger ferries *Princess of Tasmania* and *Empress of Australia*. The *Princess* operates between Melbourne and Devonport, three crossings each week, and the *Empress* between Sydney and Hobart, Bell Bay and Burnie. These vessels are designed to enable cars to drive on and off at the terminal ports, and passengers are accommodated in one, two and four berth cabins. The *Princess of Tasmania* also has accommodation for sitting up passengers. The *Australian Trader* also operates between Melbourne and Devonport. It is primarily a cargo carrier, but does provide limited facilities for passengers.

Air Transport

Frequent daily services between Tasmania and the Australian mainland are maintained by the two major civil airlines—T.A.A. and ANSETT. Airports are located at Launceston, Wynyard, Devonport and Smithton in the north and Hobart in the south. There are also airfields at Currie on King Island and Whitemark on Flinders Island.

T.A.A. also operates intrastate services to St. Helen's on the east coast, Devonport, Wynyard and Smithton on the north-west coast, and Strachan on the west coast.

NORTH-WEST COAST GUIDE

For many visitors the north-west coast provides the starting point of their Tasmanian holiday. It is rich with a great variety of scenery. The Bass Highway runs parallel to the main railway line, winding around bays and headlands of the Bass Strait coastline, and provides a link between the many busy towns. The visitor has a choice of a seaside holiday at one of the many uncrowded beaches from Port Sorell to Stanley, or in the highlands of the north-west. Well constructed highways go deep into the mountains, making these rugged and beautiful mountain areas accessible to the motorist.

ACCESS

The north-west, only 230 air miles from Melbourne, may be reached direct from the mainland by either sea or air. Both national airlines, ANSETT and T.A.A. operate morning and afternoon services each day. Airports are located at Smithton, Wynyard (Burnie) and Devonport.

The region is served by three passenger-vehicular ships. The *Princess of Tasmania* makes three round trips each week, departing Melbourne each Monday, Wednesday and Friday and returning from Devonport each Tuesday, Thursday and Sunday, while the *Australian Trader* departs from Melbourne each Sunday and from Burnie each Monday.

The *Empress of Australia* makes three round trips each fortnight between Sydney and the Tasmanian ports of Hobart, Bell Bay and Burnie. The ship visits the last named ports in turn, and passengers may elect to embark or disembark at either port.

Daily air, rail and bus services operate between Hobart, Launceston and the north-west coast. Passenger rail services are maintained by the 'Tasman Limited', which runs, Monday to Saturday, between Hobart, Launceston and Wynyard.

The north-west is linked with the west coast of Tasmania by the privately-owned Emu Bay Railway Co., which operates between Burnie and Rosebury, and by the Waratah and Murchison Highways from Somerset to Queenstown.

WHAT TO SEE

Each of the north-west coast towns has something to offer the visitor, however, many of these places can be easily reached from either Burnie or Devonport, the two largest towns.

DEVONPORT

Devonport, by the Mersey River, is one of the four largest population centres in Tasmania and the fastest growing area outside of Hobart and Launceston. It is both an air and sea port for the rich agricultural district and the expanding industries.

It is recognised as an ideal base from which the main attractions of the north-west may be visited.

DEVONPORT DIRECTORY

TOWN BUS SERVICES
Leave corner of Rooke and Stewart Streets regularly for East Devonport, North Devonport via Mersey Bluff and Devonport West.

RIVER FERRY
A passenger ferry (from near the railway station) crosses to East Devonport providing continous service.

HIRE AND DRIVE CARS
Hire and drive cars are readily available and bookings may be made at all Tasmanian Tourist Bureaux. Kay's, Perry's, Tasmanian, Alpha Avis, Bewglass.

CASUAL MEALS
In addition to the hotels, meals may be obtained at a number of cafes and at the Mersey Bluff Kiosk.

RETAIL TRADING HOURS
Monday to Thursday 9 am to 5.30 pm. Fridays 9 am to 9 pm. Shops are closed on Saturday mornings.

SERVICE CLUBS
Apex, Jaycees, Lions, Rotary, Soroptomists.

AIR CHARTER FLIGHTS
An air charter company with modern light aircraft operates throughout Tasmania from Devonport. The planes seat three passengers and may be chartered. Full information may be obtained from the Devonport Government Tourist Bureau.

SWIMMING
There are good sheltered beaches at Mersey Bluff, Coles Beach and East Devonport, also a children's swimming pool at the Mersey Bluff.

GOLF, BOWLING, TENNIS, CROQUET
At 'Woodrising', Spreyton, just four miles from the Post Office, is an excellent 18-hole course. Bowling greens and tennis courts are at Fenton Street, Devonport and Wrights Street, East Devonport, while the croquet green adjoins the tennis court in Fenton Street. Visitors are made welcome.

FISHING
The estuary of the River Mersey at Devonport and its upper reaches, offers great sport for the rod fisherman, and within easy distance are the Forth and Leven Rivers, all well stocked with trout. The coastline abounds with couta, rock cod, flathead and a variety of other fish.

MUNICIPAL LIBRARY
Located in Stewart Street. Hours Monday to Friday, 11 am to 5.30 pm. Friday 7 pm to 9 pm.

MAIN ATTRACTIONS

1. Cradle Mountain This is a day trip travelling via Forth, where the road winds along the banks of the Forth River, through to Wilmot. The road ends at Dove Lake, which commands striking views of the famous Cradle Mountain and the surrounding mountain and lake country.

2. Mole Creek Caves At Mole Creek, 15 miles west of Deloraine, are the limestone King Solomon and Marapooka Caves.

3. Gowrie Park The visitor can inspect the new Mersey—Forth Hydro-Electric Scheme for seven new power stations.

4. Gunn's Plains Caves These caves are about 14 miles from Ulverstone. The road follows the Leven River valley through magnificent rural, mountain and river scenery.

5. Latrobe Situated only five miles from the *Princess of Tasmania* ferry terminal at Devonport, Latrobe was one of the first settled towns on the north-west coast. The Mersey River flows through the town and features Bell's Parade, a notable scenic and picnic site. Short drives can be made on sealed roads to the beach resorts of Port Sorell and Hawley. There is good fishing, both freshwater and salt, and field shooting.

6. Port Sorell Only 12 miles from Latrobe, this town is sited on the Rubicon River. The Watch House, a place of historical interest in the centre of the town, was the site of the first magistrate's court and goal on the north-west coast. The gaol dates back to 1834.

BURNIE

With a population of 18,000, Burnie is the third largest town in Tasmania and a major industrial centre. Its development is firmly based on the industrial giant, Associated Pulp and Paper Mills Ltd. which, with its two subsidaries, has over 2,400 employees. In addition, Australian Titan Products Pty. Ltd. at Heybridge, and the Tasmanian Plywood Mills Ltd., Somerset, help to broaden the base of Burnie's economy.

BURNIE DIRECTORY

HIRE AND DRIVE CARS
Available from: Alpha Car Rentals, Tasmanian Car Rentals, Perry's Car Rental Service, Avis Rent-a-car.

SERVICE CLUBS
Those represented in Burnie include: Jaycees, Apex Club, Lions' Club, Rotary Club, Rostrum Clubs, Chamber of Commerce, Burnie Arts Council, Soroptimists's Club.

SPORTING FACILITIES
Burnie War Memorial Olympic Pool, comprising an eight-lane swimming pool of Olympic standard, diving pool and tower and learner's and toddlers' pools, complete with kiosk, dressing rooms and parking facilities in a garden setting.

The town's main sports oval and cycle track is located at West Park.

In addition to a number of other sports grounds for football, cricket, soccer, rugby and hockey, there are tennis courts, two bowling greens, two golf courses and a big indoor sports centre at Upper Burnie for basketball and table tennis. Bowling clubs are located at South Burnie and Parklands. Golf courses are located at Burnie, Seabrook and Wynyard. Tennis at Parklands. Gun Club, at Burnie.

THEATRES
Star Picture Theatre, Mount Street.
Drive in Theatre Somerset.
Burnie Theatre, Alexander Street.

PUBLIC LIBRARY
Catley Street.

GOVERNMENT TOURIST BUREAU
Mount Street.

There is much to offer the tourist both within Burnie and extending out from the town.

1. Round Hill This hill, 4 miles from the town and 800 ft. above sea level, gives a panoramic view of the town and surrounding countryside. On a clear day there is a view 80 miles along the coast to the Tamar Heads, as well as to the mountainous area inland.

2. Burnie Folk Museum This collection, established in 1942, consists of many thousands of relics of the early days of Tasmania, antiques, manuscripts, works of art, many thousands of photographs and a large natural history collection. The museum is situated in Alexander St., near the Wilmot St. Junction.

3. Underground River East from Natone, in the Blyth Valley, this spot will be of interest to many tourists. This trip has a special attraction to the angler, as midway between Upper Natone and Hampshire is Lake Kara. It has been stocked with trout, and there are picnic facilities in a bush setting.

4. Wynyard and Table Cape A drive to Wynyard and Table Cape, then along Tollymore Road is a delight because of the sweep of rugged coastline. Table Cape rises hundreds of feet above Bass Strait and dominates the coastline. Further west and off the highway is Boat Harbour. This increasingly popular holiday resort has extensive accommodation. Sisters Beach, some 12 miles from Wynyard, leads to aboriginal caves which contain centuries-old native middens.

5. Hellyer Gorge Hellyer Gorge is about 30 miles from Burnie on the Murchison Highway. A lunch break can be made at this popular picnic and fishing ground en route to Rosebery and Queenstown.

6. Stanley Stanley, nestling at the foot of The Mut, an amazing formation that rises abruptly from the ocean to nearly 500 ft., became the first settlement in north-west Tasmania. The Van Diemen's Land Company made its headquarters here in 1826. Many of the original buildings still remain.

AERIAL TOURS

a Tours from Devonport Airport by Air Charter Services Pty. Ltd.
—to Cradle Mountain, Lake Pedder, Frenchman's Cap, Queenstown, returning via Black Bluff. Cost per person, $29.00.
—to Cradle Mountain, including Dove and Crater Lakes. Cost per person, $10.00.
—the Holiday Coast, from Devonport to Stanley and return. Cost per person, $10.00.
—to Queenstown and return, via Cradle Mountain. Cost per person, $17.50.
—to Great Lakes Area and Poatina and Great Lake Hydro Power Scheme. Cost per preson, $11.65.
The aircraft used on these tours is a Cessna 182G, four-passenger executive aircraft. Minimum charge, three persons per tour.

b Tours from Smithton by North West Air Charters Pty. Ltd.
—to Woolnorth, Hunter Island, Three Hummock Island, Robbins Island, Cost for two persons, $17.00, three persons, $25.00
—to King Island, Hunter Island, Three Hummock Island, Robbins Island. Cost for two persons $40.00, three persons, $60.00
—To Pieman Heads, Corinna, Savage River, Port Latta. Cost for two persons, $27.00, three persons, $40.50
—to Savage River, Queenstown, Strachan, Lake Pedder, Cradle Mountain. Cost for two persons, $54.00, three persons, $81.00

ACCOMMODATION GUIDE

Hotels and Motels
1. Devonport Devonport Travel Lodge, Tarleton St., 278872.
Elimatta Hotel, 15 Victoria Pde., 242271.
Four Seasons Motor-Hotel, 12 Thomas St., 278441.
Gateway Motor Inn, 14 Fenton St., 244922.
Sunrise Motel, 140 Fenton St., 241631.
2. Burnie Beach Hotel, 1 Wilson St., 312333.
Burnie Motor Lodge, 36 Queen St., 311088.
Emu Hotel, Wivenhoe, 312466.
Seabrook Motel, Somerset, 351209.
Top of the Town Hotel-Motel, 195 Mount St., 314444.
Four Seasons Town House, 139 Wilson St. 314455.

CAMPING CARAVAN PARKS

DEVONPORT Terminal Caravan Park, Mersey Bluff.
ULVERSTONE Ulverstone Caravan Park, Picnic Point Caravan Ground, Turner's Beach Camping Ground, Buttons Creek Caravan Park.

WYNYARD Walker's Caravan Park, East Wynyard Caravan Park.
BOAT HARBOUR Boat Harbour Beach Caravan Park.
STANLEY Henry Hellyer Park.
SHEFFIELD Caravan Park, High St.
PORT SORELL Port Sorell Reserve, Hawley Beach, Moomba Caravan Park.
LATROBE Bell's Parade.
DELORAINE Apex Club Caravan Park.

Holiday Cottages and Flats

BURNIE Ocean View Motel Apartments
DEVONPORT Kawana Holiday Flats, Koolewong Holiday Flats, Hometel Holiday Flats, Spreyton, Seakist Holiday Flats, Coles Beach.

PORTAGAS FILLING AVAILABLE:
Burnie; Burnie plumbing Supplies, Mount St.
Devonport; Phoenix Shipbuilding and Engineering Co. Pty. Ltd., Terminal Traders, Stephen St., East Devonport. Also at Smithton, Ulverstone, Wynyard.

AUTOMATIC LAUNDERIES
Automatic coin operated laundries are located in Devonport and Burnie.

FOUNTAIN IN PRINCE'S SQUARE LAUNCESTON

LAUNCESTON GUIDE

Launceston, with a population of over 60,000 is Tasmania's second city and commercial centre for the rich northern half of the State. The city is located at the head of the Tamar River, at the junction of the North and South Esk Rivers.

ACCESS

Launceston is served daily by both national airlines through the airport at Western Junction.

The passenger vehicle ferry, *Empress of Australia* links Launceston with Sydney through the ferry terminal at Bell Bay, 40 miles downstream.

Regular bus and rail services connect Launceston with the *Princess of Tasmania* ferry terminal at Devonport, 65 miles to the west and with Hobart to the south.

WHAT TO SEE

1. City Park The park, ten acres of lawns and flower gardens, provides a small zoo in addition to the John Hart Conservatory with its fine displays of begonias and cyclamens.

2. Cataract Gorge and Cliff Grounds The Gorge, a few minutes from the centre of the city, provides a pleasant outing in naturally rugged and beautiful surroundings. The Cliff Grounds have been carefully laid out with native flora and English trees and offer the facilities of a tea house in the gardens and an Olympic-sized swimming pool.

3. Trevallyn Dam This is a storage dam built by the Hydro-Electric Commission to supply the Trevallyn power station. The surrounding area makes a delightful spot for a picnic. The grounds are open daily until 5 p.m.

4. Entally House Situated 8 miles from Launceston at Hadspen, this is an early colonial home furnished with prized antiques. (see HISTORY PRESERVED)

5. Franklin House This fine old Georgian house has been restored by the National Trust. It is located on the Midlands Highway, 4 miles south of Launceston. (see HISTORY PRESERVED)

6. Wildlife Sanctuary The Sanctuary, located south of the city along Punch Bowl Road, has an interesting collection of native animals, snakes and birds living in their natural environment.

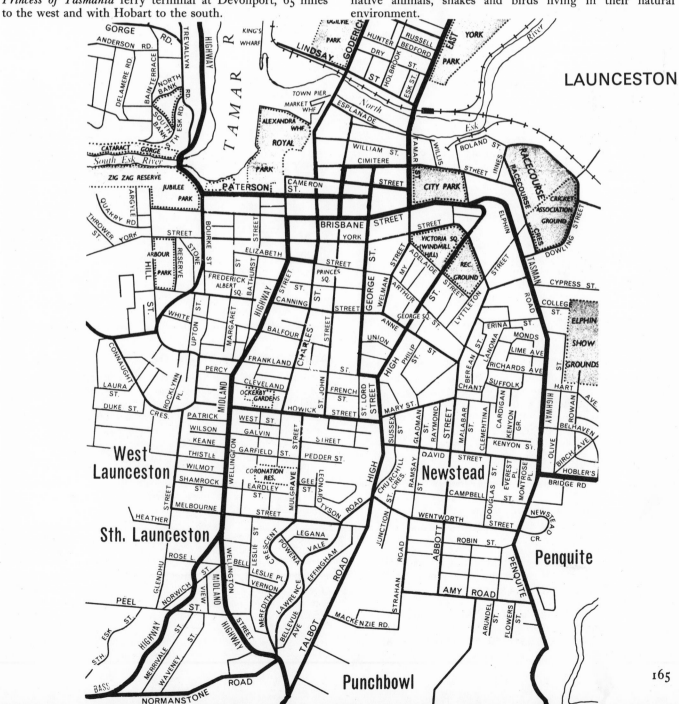

7. Lilydale Falls and Lavender Farm A 46 mile journey to Lilydale, north-east of Launceston, takes in a visit to the beautiful Falls, plus a visit to the Lavender Farm on the return trip.

8. West Tamar Round Trip By following the West Tamar Highway (skirting the Tamar River) to Beauty Point, this trip offers superb river and orchard views and crosses the spectacular new Batman Bridge. A 1½ hour launch trip is available, subject to a minimum number of bookings.

9. Poatina—Great Lake From Launceston, following the Bass Highway to Deloraine, the tourist soon reaches the Golden Valley and from there can travel to the Great Lake. It is possible to drive around the Lake and down to the Poatina power station which is more than 2000 ft. below ground level.

10. Bridport The popular beach resort of Bridport may be reached by travelling to the east of Launceston, via the Tasman Highway, through rich farmland to Scottsdale and then to the destination.

LAUNCESTON DIRECTORY

Tasmanian Government Tourist Bureau, Cnr. Paterson and St. John Streets.
General Post Office, Cnr. Cameron and St. John Streets.
Queen Victoria Museum and Art Gallery, Wellington Street.
Public Library, Cnr. Cameron and St. John Streets
Town Hall, St. John Street.
Railway Station, Invermay Road.
Examiner Office, 71 Paterson Street.
Masonic Hall, 39 Brisbane Street.
T.A.A. Terminal Office; Cnr. Brisbane and George Streets.
Ansett/A.N.A. Terminal Office, Cnr. Brisbane and George Streets.
Albert Hall, Tamar Street.
Police Headquarters, Cameron Street.
Royal Automobile Club Office, 113 George Street.
CLUBS
C.T.A., 78 Charles Street.
Launceston Club, 61 Tamar Street.
Masonic Club, Cnr. George and Cimitiere Streets.
Working Men's Club, 53 Elizabeth Street.
Northern Club, 61 Cameron Street.
Tattersall's Club, Quadrant.
R.S.S.A.I.L.A. Club, Anzac Hostel, Paterson Street.
Australian Italian Club, 65 George Street.
CHURCHES
St. John's Church of England, 155 St. John Street.
Holy Trinity, Church of England, Cameron Street.
St. Pauls Church of England, Cleveland Street.
Church of the Apostles (R.C.), Margaret Street.
St. Andrew's Pres. Church, Cnr. St John and Patersons Streets.
Chalmer's Pres. Church, Frederick Street.
Memorial Baptist Church, Wellington Street.
Baptist Church, 45 Brisbane Street.
Paterson Street Methodist, Paterson Street.
Margaret Street Methodist, Margaret Street.
Christ Church Congregational, Frederick Street.
Church of Christ, Margaret Street.
Salvation Army Citadel, Elizabeth Street.
Christadelphians, 69 Balfour Street.
Theosophical Society, 54 Elizabeth Street.
Seventh Day Adventist, Cnr. Percy and Maitland Streets.
First Church of Christ Scientist, 109 York Street.
Launceston City Mission, 48 Frederick Street.
Jewish Synagogue, St. John Street.
British and Foreign Bible Society, 44 Brisbane Street.
Gospel Hall, Elizabeth Street.
Reformed Church, Cnr. Bathurst and Frederick Streets.
St. Thomas Moores (R.C.) Cnr. Abbott and Campbell Streets.

St. Aidens Church of England, Arthur Street.
St. Marks Church of England, Cnr. Hobart and Normanstone Roads.
St. Oswalds Church of England, Bain Terrace, Trevallyn.
Seventh Day Adventist Church, Talbot Road, near Six Ways.
Bethlehem Lutheran Church, Cnr. Frankland and St. John's Streets.
THEATRES (CINEMA)
Princess, Brisbane Street.
Majestic, Brisbane Street.
Tatler, off St. John Street.
Star, Invermay Road.
Village Drive-In, Mowbray.
THEATRES (LEGITIMATE)
National, Cnr. Charles and Paterson Streets.
Little Theatre, Tamar Street.
PUBLIC GARDENS AND PARKS
City Park and Conservatory, Tamar Street.
Princes Square, City.
Albert Square, Margaret Street.
Royal Park, Paterson Street.
Windmill Hill Gardens, High Street.
Ockerby Gardens, Cleveland Street.
Kings Park, Paterson Street.
Punch Bowl Reserve and Rhododendron Gardens Punch Bowl.

AERIAL TOURS

Tours From Launceston Airport by Charter Pty. Ltd.
Local scenic flights in the latest Cessna and Piper aircraft from $2.00 per person.
—to Great Lake, Western Tiers, Tamar Valley and the City of Launceston. $25.00 (three passengers), $35.00 (six passengers).
—to St. Helen's via the coast to Half Moon Bay and return via Ben Lomond National Park. Full day trips, including lunch at St. Helen's $42.00 (three passengers), $65.00 (six passengers).
—to Cradle Mountain, Mt., Ossa, Lake St. Clair, Lake King William, Miena and the Hydro-Electric Works. Half day trips only. $48.00 (three passengers), $70.00 (six passengers).
—to Lake Pedder, Port Davey, then via the coast to Strachan, Queenstown or Zeehan, Mt. Ossa and the Lakes Country and on to the Hydro-Electric Works. Half day trips, $84.00 (three passengers), $130.00 (six passengers).

The type of aircraft used on the above tours are Cessna 172 (three passengers) and Cherokee 140 (six passengers).

ACCOMMODATION GUIDE

HOTELS Centennial Motor Hotel, 110 Balfour St., 31 4957.
Cornwall Motor Hotel, 39 Cameron St., 2 2421.
Hotel Tasmania, 191 Charles St., 2 5934.
Launceston Hotel, 107 Brisbane St., 2 2206.
Town House Motor Hotel, 3 Brisbane St., 312055.
St. James Hotel, 122 York St., 2 2097.
MOTELS Commodore Motel, 13 Brisbane St., 314666.
Travel Lodge Motel, 303 Hobart Rd., 469881.
Motel Maldon, 32 Brisbane St., 313979.
Parklane Motel, 9 Brisbane St., 314233.
Village Motor Inn, Westbury Rd., 442541.
C.T.A. Motel, 78 Charles St., 312177.
HOLIDAY COTTAGES Rubina Joy Flats.
CAMPING GROUNDS Glen Dhu Caravan Park, Launceston; Georgetown Caravan Park; Lilydale Falls Reserve; Bridport Foreshore Camping Reserve; North-East Park, Scottsdale.
PORTAGAS FILLING AVAILABLE AT: Launceston, Bessants Fairway Service, 103 Hobart Rd, C.H. Smith & Co., 16 Charles St.
AUTOMATIC LAUNDRIES A coin-operated automatic laundry is located in Launceston.
CARAVAN HIRE SERVICE Ron Carter Caravans, Tasmanian Mobile Motels.

EAST (RESORT) COAST GUIDE

The journey from Launceston to Hobart via the east coast covers approximately 266 miles and can generally be comfortably completed in two days. Any of the numerous seaside resort towns will provide a convenient over-night stop.

The east coast offers a variety of interesting resorts. During the summer months it provides splendid beaches for swimming and surfing. In any season, the tourist may indulge in the excellent angling, harbour and ocean fishing, or bush walking and mountain-climbing.

St. Helens Situated on George Bay, St. Helens is perfect for swimming, sailing, fishing and bush walking. An interesting spot, 16 miles into the forest country, is St. Columba Falls.

Binalong Bay This is a fishing village located on the rugged ocean front, 8 miles from St. Helens.

Scamander This fishing village on the Scamander River has become a very popular resort. Bream fishing in the river is popular and there are fine surf beaches.

St. Mary's This town is sited on the headwaters of the South Esk River, and beneath the Mt. Nicholas Range. The road from St. Helens passes through the spectacular St. Mary's Pass, a long, winding descent of 1000 ft. through dense rain-forest country to the coastal belt.

Falmouth Noted for its fishing and duck-shooting, Falmouth is a sporting-man's holiday resort only 8 miles from St. Mary's.

Bicheno A former whaling station, Bicheno is now perhaps the best known holiday resort on the east coast. It is still largely a fishing village and it is often possible to arrange trips with the local fishermen. However, there are other interesting scenic spots to visit. These include a low-tide walk across the sand-bar to Diamond Island to visit the penguins. Another interesting walk takes the visitor from Red Bill Point to the Gulch, then on to the Blowhole and Rice Beach. At the Blowhole a spectacle is the Rocking Rock, an 80 ton granite boulder which has been rocking gently with every wave for hundreds of years. There are the ten miles of beautiful clean, white, sandy beaches.

Coles Bay Coles Bay 17 miles from the main highway, offers a wide variety of impressive scenery. 'The Hazards', 1500 ft. hills of solid red granite are a fantastic sight. In addition, the visitor can wander overland to the peaceful Sleepy Bay, or across the peninsula to Wineglass Bay or to Hazards Beach.

Swansea A picturesque resort set on Oyster Bay, Swansea is an ideal spot for fishermen. Bream fishing is excellent in the Swan River as is rock fishing along the coast. There are excellent facilities for swimming and picnicing.

Orford This is a popular seaside and fishing resort at the mouth of the Prosser River. An interesting trip is the 13 mile ocean journey to Maria Island, a former convict settlement.

Buckland A very old village, 35 miles from Hobart, Buckland deserves a stop because of its very old stone church. The church is noted for its magnificent stained-glass window, said to date from the fourteenth century. It was given to Dean Cox, just rector of Buckland, by his friend Lord Robert Cecil the secretary of State for the Colonies.

TASMAN PENINSULA—THE PRISON PENINSULA

Eaglehawk Neck

But for this narrow strip of land Tasman Peninsula would be an island, and thus the peninsula was ideally suited for use as a penal colony. To escape from Port Arthur it would have been necessary to cross this narrow strip of land, difficult enough with normal guarding arrangements, but when the unique guard system was instituted escape became virtually impossible.

From shore to shore across the Neck a line of hounds was tethered on short chains, so that there was only six inches of space between each. The line was continually patrolled by soldiers and constables, with watching posts on the hills, and so effective was this system that no prisoner was ever known to have escaped.

Within two or three miles of Eaglehawk Neck are four coastal features of special interest: Tasman's Arch, the Devils' Kitchen, the Blowhole and the Tesselated Pavement. On rough days the sea pounding into the Kitchen and the Blowhole forms a magnificent spectacle. The Tesselated Pavement is a geological curiosity which, at first sight, appears to be the work of masons.

Port Arthur

Port Arthur was selected in 1830 by Governor Arthur as the centre where the convict settlements at Macquarie Harbour and Maria Island could be consolidated. By 1854 about 9,000 people lived on Tasman's Peninsula at various out-stations with Port Arthur as the punishment centre. As the transportation system slackened and convicts were rehabilitated elsewhere, Port Arthur declined, and in 1878 the Penal Colony was abandoned. After years of neglect Port Arthur has become a tourist centre.

Port Arthur during occupation 1860. (*Beattie Collection, National Library, Canberra*)

Points of Interest.

1. Model Prison now being restored. Actually called the Separate Treatment Prison, based on the solitary confinement principle, the Model Prison was used to house those convicts who did not respond to treatment.

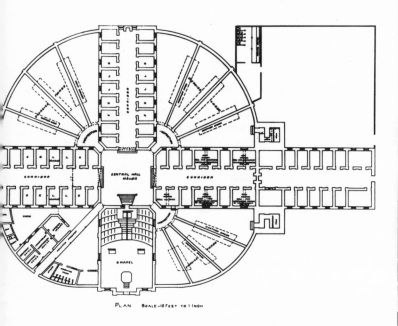

Plan of Model Prison, Port Arthur. (*Beattie Collection, National Library, Canberra*)

2. The Hospital Built in 1842, and now in a poor state of repair, the existence of the Hospital indicates the care taken to keep the convicts fit and productive.

3. Penitentiary Also built in 1842, this four-storied building housed 657 men.

4. Watch Tower and Powder Magazine In the base of the Watch Tower, built in 1835, were cells for condemned prisoners awaiting transportation to Hobart for hanging. No hangings were performed at Port Arthur.

5. Church The church was designed by a convict architect, and erected in 1836. However, it was never consecrated because it was used by different denominations.

6. Point Puer Situated across the bay from Port Arthur, Point Puer was an establishment where juveniles could be educated and taught a trade. The baking ovens are all that remains as ruins.

7. Dead Island Lying off Point Puer, this was the cemetery of Port Arthur where nearly 2,000 people were buried; 200 of them were free settlers.

8. Safety Cove This was an area which was developed as a convict farm. A beautiful peaceful beach adjoined the property. An intriguing feature, Remarkable Cave, lies over the hill from the beach to the south.

9. Other Subsidiary Establishments The ruins of these still remain to be seen and are all worth a visit. They include the Coal Mines settlement at Slopen Main, the Saltwater Creek Agricultural Centre and the timber mills at Premaydena and Koonya.

GUIDED TOURS AT PORT ARTHUR

Guided tours at the Port Arthur Settlement commence at the following times: 9.30 am, 11.00 am, 11.30 am, 1.00 pm, 1.45 pm, 2.30 pm, 4 pm, (September to May inclusive); 9.30 am, 11.00 am, 1.30 pm, 3.00 pm, (June, July and August).

All tours include a visit to the model prison which houses a display of authentic Port Arthur relics, and a description of the most interesting buildings and of facts associated with the penal settlement is given during the tour. Admission to museum, 50c adults, 25c children (6-15 years).

Port Arthur Church and Port Arthur during occupation 1859. (*Beattie Collection, National Library, Canberra*)

ACCOMMODATION GUIDE

Hotels and Motels
ST. HELENS Nautilus Motel, St. Helens Hotel-Motel.
SCAMANDER Scamander River Motor-Hotel, Surfside Motel.
BICHENO Silver Sands Motor-Hotel, Midway Motel.
SWANSEA Swansea Motor Inn.
ORFORD Blue Waters Hotel-Motel, Island View Motel.
EAGLEHAWK NECK, Lufra Hotel, Motel Penzance.
PORT ARTHUR Four Seasons Hotel-Motel.

Holiday Cottages
ST. HELENS Akaroa Holiday Cottages, Parkside Holiday Cottages, Ningle Nook Corraleau Holiday Homes.
SCAMANDER Green-Acres Holiday Flats Pelican Sands.
FALMOUTH Iluka Caravan and Camping Park.
BICHENO 'The Galleon', Ova-night and Holiday Cabins, Holiday Units.
SWANSEA Central Holiday Units, Kenmore Car Park.
ORFORD El-siesta Holiday Units, Orford Holiday Flats, Seabreeze Flats.

Caravan and Camping Areas
ST. HELENS Parkside Caravan Park, Binalong Bay Camping Area, King's Park, Hill Crest Caravan Inn.
SCAMANDER Kookaburra Caravan and Camping Park.
BICHENO Bicheno Caravan Park.
COLES BAY Scenery and preservation Board Camping Ground.
SWANSEA Swan Haven Park, Kenmore Caravan Park.
ORFORD Caravan Park, situated on the banks of the Prosser River.
TRIABUNNA Triabunna Caravan Park.
PORT ARTHUR Scenery Preservation Board Camping Ground.

HOBART GUIDE

Hobart, the capital city of Tasmania, is sited between the foot of Mt. Wellington and the shore of the Derwent River. The city was founded in 1803 and since has grown into a thriving city of 124,000 citizens. The early residents built well of solid freestone, and many of these beautiful Georgian buildings still stand today.

The Port of Hobart is one of the world's finest natural deep water harbours and the 12 mile approach along the Derwent presents a scene that may not be matched anywhere in the world. The port is busiest from February to May, when large overseas ships call to take away the annual crop of apples and pears.

The suburban area of Hobart is expanding rapidly, particularly on the eastern shore, served by the impressive new Tasman Bridge. It links the city with the Tasman Highway, the main road to Hobart Airport, the east coast and Tasman Peninsula.

ACCESS
The Port of Hobart is the southern terminal for the Sydney-Tasmania vehicular ferry *Empress of Australia* which makes fortnightly calls to the city and berths alongside Battery Point.

Air services are operated by each of the national airlines, between Melbourne, Hobart and Launceston, three times daily in the morning, afternoon and evening.

The city and suburbs are well served by motor and electric trolley buses controlled by the Metropolitan Transport Trust.

WHAT TO SEE
In and Around Hobart
1. Mount Wellington The 12 mile trip to the pinnacle of Mt. Wellington is probably the most popular of all. At the summit, the visitor finds himself 4,166 ft. above sea level with magnificent panoramic views extending in all directions.

2. City Sights and Mt. Nelson Another short scenic drive is to the Signal Station on Mt. Nelson. The drive provides a view of the city and its suburbs which sprawl out along the shores of the Derwent River. These views are perhaps prettiest in the evening.

3. Parliament House This is one of the oldest buildings in Hobart, dating back to 1840. It is at the lower end of Murray St., opposite the wharves, and is fronted by spacious parks and gardens.

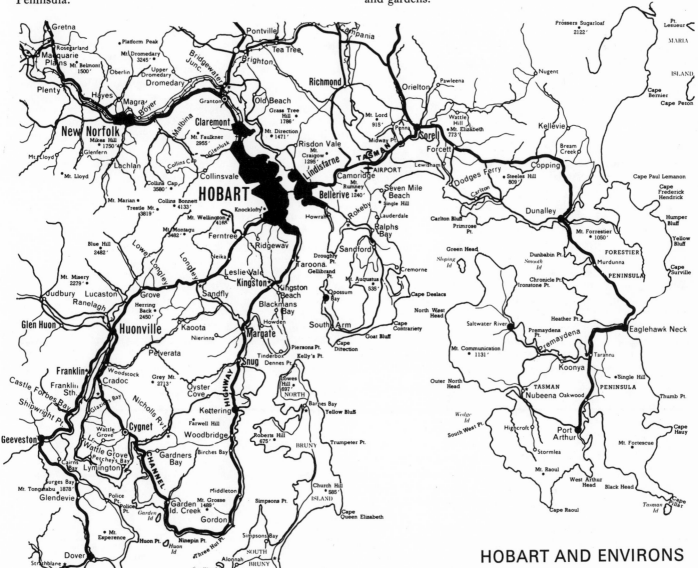

HOBART AND ENVIRONS

4. Tasmanian Museum and Art Gallery Located at 5 Argyle St., the Museum and Art Gallery houses a fine collection of historical exhibits, with the emphasis on Tasmanian aborigines and early colonial activities. It is open daily, except for Christmas Day, Anzac Day and Good Friday.

5. Botanical Gardens In the Domain, near Government House, the Gardens are open daily throughout the year. Tea rooms, serving light refreshments, are within the Gardens.

6. Cat and Fiddle Arcade In the heart of the shopping block. The arcade features smart shops and eating places and opens onto Cat and Fiddle Square. Here, in a setting of trees and a fountain, the animated mural enacts the old nursery rhyme every hour, on the hour.

7. Battery Point This is a small suburb of Hobart close to the wharves where the visitor will find numerous beautiful old buildings and relics dating back to the founding of the city.

8. Constitution Dock Here, at New Year period, the yachts are moored after the Sydney-Hobart race.

9. The Shot Tower, Taroona The Shot Tower, on the Channel Highway just beyond Taroona, is historically interesting and offers magnificent views of the Derwent Estuary. The Tower is open for inspection and a small admission is charged.

10. The Van Diemen's Land Folk Museum This museum is located at Narryna, 103 Hampden Road, Battery Point. It features exhibits of the life and times of the Tasmanian pioneers. A small admission is charged.

11. Cadbury's Factory, Claremont A visit to this famous chocolate factory is an interesting diversion. It is necessary to make an appointment for an inspection of the factory. These are conducted on Tuesday and Thursday at 9 am and 2 pm and include refreshments.

Out of Hobart

1. Port Arthur and Eaglehawk Neck For the tourist based in Hobart, this trip can be very easily completed in one day. [SEE EAST COAST]

2. The Huon Valley this journey is particularly beautiful in the spring when the apple and pear trees are in bloom, and again in autumn, when the rich colours of the mature fruit and the changing colours of the leaves provide a beautiful spectacle.

An interesting route for the round trip to Huonville, the centre of the fruit growing district, is via the shoulder of Mt. Wellington (Ferntree) overland to Huonville. The return is via Cygnet and the D'Entrecasteaux Channel, which offers spectacular views of the coastline.

3. Hastings Caves and Thermal Pool These limestone caves are located 70 miles from Hobart, following a long and winding road. The thermal swimming pool at Hastings is situated in a fern glade less then 100 yards from the road. The temperature of the water is usually about 80 degrees. At the end of the road a short and easy track leads to Newdegate Cave. Inspections of the caves may be made at 10.15 am, 11.15 am, (12.15 pm October to April), 1.15 pm, 2.15 pm, 3.15 pm., and 4.15 pm, daily throughout the year. Admission, 60c adults and 30c children under 16 years.

4. Bruny Island An irregular-shaped island, south of Hobart, it was named after Admiral Bruni D'Entrecasteaux, who surveyed the channel lying between the island and the mainland of Tasmania in 1793. There is a regular ferry service between Kettering, 23 miles south of Hobart, and Barnes Bay. The ferry will carry approximately 40 cars and the fare for car and driver is based on the horsepower rating. Cars up to 11 h.p. pay 80c. and over 11 h.p. the fare is $1.00. Passengers travel free.

The eastern shores of the island are rugged, with several bold headlands including Cape Queen Elizabeth, Fluted Cape and Cape Connella. An interesting memorial museum has been built at Adventure Bay, commemorating the discovery and early history of Bruny Island. This museum is privately owned, and is open daily except Wednesday, between 1.30 pm. and 3.00 pm. A guide is in attendance, and admission is 25c.

5. The Derwent Valley The road from Hobart into the heart of the Derwent Valley clings to the shores of the river, and offers much pretty scenery. At New Norfolk, the main town in the valley, the early settlers built well of native stone. Today many of their buildings remain to add the charm of history to the beauty of the countryside. Outstanding among the town's early buildings are the historic Bush Hotel, established in 1815, the Old Colony Inn and St. Matthew's Church of England.

Rural produce is the Valley's main industry, the most important crop being hops. Most of the hops used by brewers throughout Australia come from this Valley and the fields of tall vines are dominated by the conical roofs of the coast houses. This very 'English' part of Tasmania is particularly beautiful in autumn when all the orchards, and the poplars which border the hopfields, are at their most colourful.

6. The Plenty Salmon Ponds The Salmon Ponds are seven miles from New Norfolk, along the lower road to Bushy Park. Here the first Brown and Rainbow Trout in the Southern Hemisphere were successfully raised in 1864, an event which led to the stocking of streams and lakes in Australia and New Zealand.

A tea room and kiosk is available, and spacious lawns make a delightful spot for a picnic. A new museum has been established, and here are displayed the life cycle of the trout, other fresh-water fish, and some of the aquatic oddities that are found in Tasmanian waters.

Nearly a thousand tame trout, ranging in size from fingerlings to mature specimens of four or five pounds, live in the large outdoor ponds. Admission is 20c for adults and 10c for children under 14 years.

7. Russell Falls Tumbling 120 ft. in two sheer drops, this spectacular waterfall has attracted visitors from all over the world. It is within the National Park, which can be reached by following the road from the Salmon Ponds, through Glenora and Westbury. Inside the Park, the Falls can be reached after only a few minutes walk from the entrance.

8. Gordon River Road This is a magnificent scenic road open to the public by permit only obtainable from the Hydro-Electric Commission. The road extends 53 miles past Maydena in the Derwent Valley into some of Tasmania's most rugged and spectacular country.

Derwent River Cruises (Summer months only)
By Cabin Cruiser—
New Norfolk Day Trip (10 am Sunday and Wednesday). $4.00.
D'Entrecasteaux Channel Day Trip (10 am Saturday). $4.00.
Harbour Cruise (10 am, 2.30 pm, Monday, Tuesday. Thursday and Friday). $2.
Lunch available on day trips, $1.50.
By Ferry—
New Norfolk Day Trip (10 am Monday, Thursday and Saturday). $2.50.
D'Entrecasteaux Channel Day Trip (10 am Tuesday). $3.25.
Harbour Cruise (10 am Wednesday; 2.30 pm Wednesday and Friday; 8 pm Sunday). $1.50.
Lunch available on day trips, $1.

AERIAL TOURS

TOURS FROM HOBART BY TASAIR PTY. LTD.
Minimum two passengers.
Lake Pedder, via Derwent and Huon Valleys. $16.00 per person.

Lake Pedder, Bathurst Harbour, and Precipitous Bluff. $27.00 per person.

Tasman Peninsula, Derwent Estuary. $11.50 per person.

Hobart and Derwent Estuary. $6.00 per person.

Lake St Clair, Du Cane Ranges, and HEC Schemes. $22.50. per person

Tasman Peninsula, Maria Island, Coles Bay. $16.75 per person.

Derwent Estuary, Bruny Island, and Huon Valley. $12.50 per person.

Derwent Estuary, Tasman Peninsula, and Freycinet Peninsula. $22.00 per person.

The type of aircraft used on the above tours are three and five seater air-conditioned Cessnas. All costs to be shared between persons on tour.

HOBART DIRECTORY

Tasmanian Government Tourist and Immigration Department Cnr Macquarie and Murray Streets.
General Post Office, Cnr Elizabeth and Macquarie Streets.
Museum and Art Gallery, Cnr Argyle and Macquarie Streets.
State Library, Cnr Murray and Bathurst Streets.
Town Hall, Cnr Macquarie and Elizabeth Streets.
City Hall, 59 Macquarie Street.
Parliament House, Murray Street.
Railway Station, Liverpool Street.
Masonic Hall, Harrington Street.
Police Headquarters, Liverpool Street.
Royal Hobart Hospital, Liverpool Street.
'Narryna' Folk Museum, 103 Hampden Road, Battery Point.
YMCA, Cnr Argyle and Liverpool Streets.
ANSETT Terminal Office, 178 Liverpool Street.
T.A.A. Terminal Office, 4 Liverpool Street.

CLUBS
Airforce Club of Tasmania, 61 Davey Street.
Athenaeum Club, 29 Davey Street.
Civic Club, 138–140 Macquarie Street.
C.T.A., 121–123 Collins Street.
R.S.S.A.I.L.A., A.P.A. Buildings, 121 Macquarie Street.
Motor Yacht Club of Tasmania, 6 Victoria Street.
Naval Memorial House Club, 63 Davey Street.
Naval Military and Air Force Club of Tasmania, 31 Davey Street.
Queen Mary (Ladies) Club, 143 Macquarie Street.
Royal Automobile Club of Tasmania, 172 Macquarie Street.
Royal Yacht Club of Tasmania, Maryville Esplanade, Sandy Bay.
Tasmanian Club, 132 Macquarie Street.
Working Men's Club, 213 Liverpool Street.
Nurses' Bureau and Club, 180 Macquarie Street.
The Flying Angel Mission to Seamen, Hunter Street.
Masonic Club, Cnr Barrack and Macquarie Streets.

CHURCHES
St David's Cathedral (C. of E.), Cnr Macquarie and Murray Streets.
Holy Trinity Church of England, 50 Warwick Street.
St George's Church of England, Cromwell Street, Battery Point.
St John's Church of England, 120 Goulburn Street.
All Saints Church of England, 339 Macquarie Street.
St Mary's Cathedral, (R.C.), Cnr Harrington and Patrick Streets.
St Joseph's R.C. Church, Cnr Harrington and Macquarie Streets.
Church of St Francis Xavier (R.C.), Adelaide Street, South Hobart.
Hobart Baptist Church, 286 Elizabeth Street.
Scots' Church (Pres.), 27 Bathurst Street.
St John's Pres. Church, 188 Macquarie Street.

Wesley Methodist Church, Melville Street.
Davey Street Congregational Church, opposite St David's Park.
Memorial Congregational Church, Cnr Brisbane and Elizabeth Streets.
Methodist Church, 207 Davey Street.
Church of Christ, 181 Collins Street.
First Church of Christ Scientist, 69–71 Brisbane Street.
Salvation Army Citadel, Liverpool Street.
Seventh Day Adventist, Cnr Warwick and Watkins Avenue.
Jewish Synogogue, Argyle Street.
Theosophical Society, Phone 2 6529.
Society of Friends, Meeting House, 393 Argyle Street.
St John's Church of England, St John's Avenue, New Town.

THEATRES (CINEMA)
Avalon Theatre, 52 Melville Street.
Odeon Theatre, 163 Liverpool Street.
Prince of Wales Theatre, 83–85 Macquarie Street.
State Theatre, 375 Elizabeth Street, North Hobart.
Tatler Newsreel Theatrette, 86 Murray Street.
Elwick Drive-In Theatre, Elwick Road, Glenorchy.
Eastside Drive-In Theatre, Flagstaff Gully Road, Warrane.

THEATRES (LEGITIMATE)
Theatre Royal, 29 Campbell Street.
Playhouse, Bathurst Street.

BANKS
A. & N.Z. Bank, Cnr Elizabeth and Collins Streets and 154 Liverpool Street.
Bank of New South Wales, 28 Elizabeth Street.
Commercial Bank of Australia Ltd., Cnr Elizabeth and Collins Streets and 110 Liverpool Street.
Commercial Bank of Sydney Ltd, 56 Elizabeth Street.
Commonwealth Bank of Australia, Cnr Elizabeth and Liverpool Streets.
Hobart Savings Bank, Cnr Elizabeth and Liverpool Streets and 26 Murray Street.
National Bank of Australia Ltd, Cnr Elizabeth and Liverpool Streets and 170a Macquarie Street.

PUBLIC GARDENS AND PARKS
Botanical Gardens and Conservatory, Domain.
Franklin Square, Macquarie and Elizabeth Streets.
St David's Park, Davey Street.
Fitzroy Gardens, Fitzroy Place.
Parliament Square, Morrison Street.
Princes Park, Castray Esplanade.

SPORTS GROUNDS AND RACECOURSES
Tasmanian Cricket Association Ground, Domain.
North Hobart Recreation Ground, Argyle and Ryde Streets.
Queenborough Recreation Ground, Sandy Bay.
King George V Oval, Glenorchy.
New Town Sports Ground, Clare Street.
South Hobart and West Hobart Recreation Grounds.
Elwick Racecourse, Elwick Road, Glenorchy
Elwick Showground, Glenorchy.
Croquet Lawns at Sandy Bay and New Town.

ACCOMMODATION GUIDE

Hotels

Prince of Wales, 55 Hampden Rd. 237452
Wrest Point Riviera, Sandy Bay, 251021
Waratah Motor-Hotel, 272 Murray St., 343685
Town House, 167 Macquarie St., 344422
Hotel St. Ives, 86 Sandy Bay Rd., 235679
Hadleys Orient, 34 Murray St., 237521
Beach House, Beach Road, 251161
Black Prince, 145 Elizabeth St., 343501
Brisbane Hotel, 3 Brisbane St., 344920
Claremont Motor Hotel, 71 363
Shoreline Hotel, Howrah 479504

Motels

Blue Hills Motel, 96A Sandy Bay Rd., 232861
City Motel, Argyle St., 342658
Village Motel, Berriedale, 726721
Four Seasons Motel, Sandy Bay Rd., 252511
Marquis of Hastings, West Hobart, 343541
Motel Jason, Lindisfarne, 438666
Motel Panorama, Montagu Bay, 442411
TraveLodge, Park St., 342911
Motel Sunny Side, 300 Park St., 284520
Motel Mayfair, 17 Cavell St., 341670

Holiday Cottages

Aloha Holiday Flats, Sandy Bay.
Baal-Yandho, Sandy Bay.
Elstree Court Flats, Sandy Bay.
Furnished Flat, Argyle St., Hobart.
Furnished House, Melville St., Hobart.
Graham Court Flats, New Town.
Holiday Flat, Dunnyrne.
Sandy Bay Court Flats, Sandy Bay.
Sharavogue, South Hobart.

Caravan and Camping Areas

HOBART Peel St., Caravan Park, Nelson Road.
BRUNY IS. Adventure Bay, Gordon Camping and Caravan Grounds.
CYGNET Cygnet Caravan Park.
GLENORCHY Elwick Caravan Park, Berriedale Camping Area.
NEW NORFOLK Caravan Park.
PORTAGAS AVAILABLE FROM R. M. Cannon & Co. Pty. Ltd. Campbell St.
Ampol Service Station, Argyle St.
A. H. Gifford Pty. Ltd. Elizabeth St.
B.P. Service Station, Sandy Bay.
Ampol Service Station, Bellerive.
Beltana Service Station, Lindisfarne.
Golden Fleece Service Station, 2 Sandy Bay.

Automatic Laundries

Coin-operated laundries are located in Hobart itself, and in the suburbs of Moonah, Glenorchy, Sandy Bay and Bellerive.

WEST COAST GUIDE

One of Tasmania's most spectacular regions is its west coast, a country of wild mountain ranges, lonely valleys and dense rain-forest bestrewn with lakes and tarns. The road winds through bushlands still free of tracks and past abandoned huts and settlements which once were the homes of trappers and prospectors or booming mining townships.

Few other places on earth could match the variety of minerals that are won from Tasmania's west coast.

The most prolific minerals are copper, lead, zinc, tin and iron, with lesser traces of silver and gold. Sulphur in the form of pyrites is also common and its use in the manufacture of Sulphuric acid is increasing with the demand for artificial fertilizers.

Many rarer minerals are present. These include osmiridium, tungsten, cadmium and manganese, although some of these are only won in payable quantities at places outside the west coast area.

A list of mines now producing on the west coast is not as great as in the past, but modern techniques enable the economical use of deposits considered worked out by the early operators. Although the small deposits of high grade ores are now gone, the enormous extent of the lesser grade deposits ensures the prosperity of the west coast for many years to come.

Several west coast mines are worked as open cuts and provide spectacular sights as enormous earth moving machinery bites into cliffs of ore. Huge dump trucks carry away many tons of material in each load, and at the treatment plants, as much ore is processed in a day as might have been processed in a year by the early methods used on these fields.

At Queenstown, and Savage River it is possible to view the mine workings. Prior arrangement is advisable either with the mine management or the Tourist Bureau.

1. Savage River

The town of Savage River lies beside the turbulent river of the same name, to the west of Waratah. It is the site of Tasmania's newest mineral bonanza—iron ore. The iron deposits have been known for many years, but only recently has the pelletising process made its exploitation economical.

Savage River is set in rugged country, where rivers flow swift and deep. The Savage itself is a tributary of the Pieman River which is noted as one of the outstanding fishing streams on the west coast. Good roads now give quick access to the Savage River township, either north from Queenstown or south from Burnie.

Inspections of the concentrating mill are available Tuesday to Saturday inclusive. (Ladies should wear slacks and low-heeled shoes to view the mill.)

2. Rosebery

Rosebery is a thriving town of over 2,000 inhabitants situated in the Pieman River Valley at the base of Mt. Murchison (4,183 ft.). Here the Electrolytic Zinc Company conducts mining and milling operations together with an additional plant at Williamsford, 5 miles away. Visitors to Rosebery may travel by road from Zeehan, or by rail from Burnie.

3. Strahan

From Queenstown, Strahan may be reached by road. The trip brings the tourist to the lip of the King River Valley where there is a magnificent view of the virgin bush extending 2,000 ft. below the roadside. Strahan on Macquarie Harbour is the port town of the west coast, a quiet place today, still retaining the flavour of the copper boom. The town is the starting point for the famous Gordon River Trip, by motor launch. This day-long cruise traverses the length of Macquarie Harbour then passes some 20 miles up the Gordon River. The launch leaves Strahan at 9.00 am on most days between November and April, and returns about 4.15 pm.

Another interesting trip from Strahan is to Ocean Beach, four miles from the town. The beach is 25 miles long and has an enormous surf sweeping up to the high sand dunes. From there the lonely forlorn lighthouse on Cape Sorell can be seen on the other side of Macquarie Harbour.

4. Queenstown

The final 2 miles into Queenstown via the Lyell Highway are undoubtedly the most spectacular on any highway in Australia. Bordering the steep eroded gullies which plunge into the town, it skirts the slopes, winding narrowly down Mt. Owen. On all sides the tourist sees the radiant colours of the bare rock slopes. Even the heavy rains of 100 in. to 200 in. fail to quench the brilliance of the colourings.

Inspections of features of interest in the Mt. Lyell workings can be arranged. The Mt. Lyell Co. is entirely responsible for the existence of Queenstown. Today, almost all of the 4,500 inhabitants are connected directly or indirectly with the Company.

5. Zeehan

During the silver-lead boom at the turn of the century, Zeehan boasted 10,000 inhabitants. Until recently, barely 600 people lived there.

Now new prosperity is coming to Zeehan, through enlargements to the nearby Renison Bell tin mine. The mine management is building 250 new houses in Zeehan to accommodate the workers needed to staff the new extensions.

An interesting place to visit while in Zeehan is the West Coast Pioneers Memorial Museum which has a fine collection of mineral samples from all over the world.

ACCOMMODATION GUIDE

Hotels and Motels
QUEENSTOWN Four Seasons Motor-Hotel, phone 5
Four Seasons Motor-Hotel, phone 550
Silver Hills Motel, phone 148, 349 and 350
SAVAGE RIVER Savage River Motor Inn, phone 39 1201

Camping and Caravan Parks
QUEENSTOWN Preston St. Reserve Caravan Park.
NATIONAL PARK National Park Caravan and Camping Area.
LAKE ST. CLAIR Scenery Preservation Board Camping Area.
WAYATINAH H.E.C. Caravan and Camping Area.
ROSEBERY Rosebery Caravan Park.
TARRALEAH H.E.C. Caravan and Camping Area.
STRAHAN Ocean Beach, 4 miles from Strahan, Recreation Reserve, West Strahan Beach, People's Park, Strahan.

Holiday Cottages and Flats
STRAHAN Sharonlee Holiday Units.
NATIONAL PARK Park Lodge Cottages.
PORTAGAS FILLING AVAILABLE at Queenstown and Zeehan.

HISTORY PRESERVED

Tasmania, the second of the Australian States to be settled, now has a treasury of old houses and other excellent examples of colonial architecture. Of the many examples to be seen most are privately owned and thus not open to the public. Several others have been restored and are now open for public inspection.
Among these are:

1. **Narryna** Also known as the 'Van Diemen's Land Folk Museum', it is situated in the Hobart suburb of Battery Point. Narryna is opened daily except Monday, from 10.00 am to 12 noon and 2.00 pm to 5.00 pm.

2. **Runnymede** This is a National Trust property located at 61 Bay Road, New Town, near Hobart. It was built in 1844 and has been preserved as a home of the 1860's. The house is open daily from 2.00 to 5.00 pm. except on Monday.

3. **Richmond** An example of an old world village, situated on the Coal River 15 miles from Hobart. Here can be found numerous interesting historic features including the old freestone bridge, the old gaol, built in 1825, St. John's Church (1835), the oldest Roman Catholic Church in Australia, and St. Luke's Church of England built in 1834. In addition to these features there are many other interesting restored relics in this town founded over 135 years ago.

4. **The Ross Bridge** Another very old bridge crossing the Macquarie River at Ross on the Midland Highway. It was constructed by convict labour in 1836.

5. **The Grange** This house, located at Campbell Town on the Midland Highway, was built in 1848–49. It is now leased by the National Trust to the Adult Education Board. The interior is not open to the public, but the outside may be inspected.

6. **The 'Disappearing' House** An interesting old home, located at Conara Junction, again on the Midland Highway. Because of terrain this house seems to disappear and then reappear as the traveller approaches the house from the highway.

7. **Clarendon House** at Evandale, south of Launceston. This majestic home, built in the late 1830's, has been restored by the National Trust. It is open for inspection at regular intervals. Enquiries should be made at Franklin House.

8. **Pleasant Banks** This a privately-owned home, built in 1854 and located at Evandale. It is open for inspection.

9. **Franklin House** Another National Trust house, built in 1838, Franklin House is situated only 4 miles from Launceston on the main highway to Hobart. It is open for inspection daily 9.30 am to 12.30 pm, and 1.30 pm to 5.00 pm, except Good Friday, Anzac Day and Christmas Day.

10. **Staffordshire House** Built in 1833, this is probably the only existing example of a merchant's combined business premises and dwelling house. It is located in Charles St. Launceston, the heart of the city. Only the exterior may be inspected.

11. **Entally House** Another beautifully sited period house, restored and preserved as an early settler's home by the Tasmanian Scenery Preservation Board. The home is located at the village of Hadspen, on the Bass Highway, 8 miles from Launceston. Entally is open every day from 10.30 am to 5.00 pm, except Christmas Day and Good Friday, and in the month of July.

Along the main highways, for example the Midland, Bass and the Esk highways there are many old buildings which the visitor may be interested to view from the road as they are passing by.

NATIONAL PARKS AND RESERVES

With a view to ensuring the preservation of much of Tasmania's natural scenery, large areas of the State have been proclaimed scenic reserves by Act of Parliament. These areas are principally located in spectacular mountain country.

1. Rocky Cape National Park (4,000 acres) This park in the north-west of Tasmania, can be reached via the Bass Highway through Wynyard, Boat Harbour and Rocky Cape. It is an area of impressive coastal scenery including old sea caves, 60–70 ft. above existing sea-level, containing aboriginal middens and cave paintings.

Caravan and camping facilities are available, plus a motel and some apartments.

2. Mt. Barrow National Park (1,134 acres) Another National Park located in northern Tasmania, with access via the Tasman Highway, Mt. Barrow provides panoramic views of the North Esk and St. Patrick River Valleys. In addition, it is an important skiing area in winter.

Accommodation available at Launceston.

3. Ben Lomond National Park (39,615 acres) Situated in the north-east between Launceston and St. Mary's, Ben Lomond is a winter sports playground as well as providing a wide variety of wonderful views in any season.

Accommodation available at Launceston.

4. Freycinet Peninsula National Park (18,420 acres) This National Park, on the east coast of Tasmania, is an area of spectacular coastal scenery which include Sleepy Bay, Hazard's Beach, Wineglass Bay and the rugged peaks of the 'Hazards'.

Accommodation is available at Coles Bay.

5. Schouten Island Coastal Reserve (8,500 acres) Also found on the east coast, this Reserve is accessible only by boat. The Island is a valuable wildlife sanctuary.

6. Port Arthur and Tasman Peninsula Reserves (1,440 acres) This reserve, in the extreme south-east of Tasmania, provides numerous points of interest. These include the ruins of the prison buildings at Port Arthur, the convict coal mine at Saltwater Creek. Natural features worthy of note are Tasman Arch, the Blowhole, Waterfall Bay, Fossil Island, the Tessellated Pavement and Remarkable Cave.

Accommodation is available at several caravan and camping parks in addition to several motels and holiday flats.

7. Hartz Mountains National Park (21,300 acres) This is an area in the south which provides its own magnificent mountain scenery as well as views of the rugged, inhospitable south-west. The peaks are snow-covered for most of the year.

No amenities or supplies are available at the park, accommodation is obtainable at Huonville and Geeveston.

8. Fluted Cape—Cloudy Bay Coastal Reserve (600 acres) This small reserve on Bruny Island near Adventure Bay was visited by the early explorers including Furneaux, (1773), Cook (1777), Bligh (1788), and D'Entrecasteaux (1792–3). The Reserve commands magnificent coastal views.

Accommodation is available in camping and caravan areas and one hotel.

9. South-West National Park (473,000 acres) In a primitive wilderness area the South-West National Park is a paradise for experienced bush walkers and mountaineers. A particular point of interest is the large glacial lake, Lake Pedder, with its magnificent white quartz beach, circled by towering mountain ranges.

There is no ranger in attendance at this Park.

10. Mt. Field National Park (40,058 acres) This is a popular winter sports region (July–October) with ski huts and a ski tow available. It is an area of superb views, waterfalls and glacial lakes, being the site of the well-known Russell Falls.

Camping and caravan sites are available in the Park.

11. Frenchman's Cap National Park (25,240 acres) The ice-cut cliff face on the 4,739 ft. peak of the Frenchman's Cap is the most spectacular feature here. It is an uninhabited region, ideal for experienced bush walkers and mountaineers.

There is no accommodation nor facilities in or near the park.

12. Cradle Mountain—Lake St. Clair National Park (338,496 acres) Another area of most spectacular mountain scenery, containing many of Tasmania's highest peaks—Cradle Mt. (5,069 ft.), Barn Bluff (5,114 ft.), Mt. Ossa (5,305 ft.) as well as the picturesque mountain lakes—Lake St. Clair, Lake Dove and Crater Lake. Lake St. Clair is accessible by road, or by the overland track which takes 5 days in easy stages. The Lake provides marvellous mountain scenery and good fishing. Accommodation is available in the Chalet and cabins at Waldheim, with cabins, caravan and camping areas at Lake St. Clair. There are huts on the overland track with rangers at Waldheim and Lake St. Clair.

13. Gordon River Reserve (6,200 acres) This is another wilderness area offering magnificent scenery. At the mouth of the River, at Macquarie Harbour, are the ruins of the former convict settlement.

Accommodation, including caravan and camping parks, is available at Strahan.

14. Pieman River Reserve (8,125 acres) A densely forested area of rugged and impressive mountain scenery, located in the north-west of Tasmania.

Accommodation is available at Waratah and Savage River.

15. Cave Reserves

Hastings Caves (131 acres) found in the south.

Maracoopa Caves (146 acres), King Solomon Caves (500 acres) and Baldock Caves (105 acres) all found at Mole Creek, inland from Devonport in northern Tasmania.

Gunn's Plains Caves (24 acres) are located near Ulverstone in the north.

BUSH WALKING—ADVICE TO BUSH WALKERS

1. Consult the Park Ranger before setting out. Tell him your plans and seek his advice on tracks and local weather conditions.
2. Walkers should be adequately equipped and be prepared to camp in unattended huts.
3. In planning a walk, it is advisable to allow for delays by bad weather.
4. Careful attention to food and equipment will save trouble and discomfort.
5. ESSENTIAL DETAILS:
● wear stout, waterproof boots or strong shoes.
● wear thick slacks or long trousers, not shorts, which give no protection from the vegetation, rocky slopes, snakes or climate.
● carry ample food, light in weight but nourishing. Appetites may increase due to altitude and exercise.
● carry down sleeping bags, waterproof cape or coat, change of clothing, spare socks, woollen sweater.
● carry first-aid materials, matches, light hiking tent and a light axe.
6. drain car radiators before leaving them.

FISHING IN TASMANIA

Licences

Angling Licences are available at the Tasmanian Government Tourist Bureaux and most sports stores and police stations.

Fishing Season

Estuary waters open for fishing on the first Saturday in August. Most other rivers and lakes open on the first Saturday in September and close on the last Sunday in April. The exceptions being Great Lake, Lake Leake, Dee Lagoon and Lagoon of Islands which open on the last Saturday in October and close on the last Sunday in May.

Anglers are strongly advised to purchase flies of local pattern in Launceston or Hobart, since much of the Tasmanian fly-life is unique and standard and overseas patterns are often unsatisfactory.

The North-West Coast

Chiefly river fishing, Rebecca Lagoon and Waratah Dams being the only lake fishing of any consequence. For example the Mersey River at Latrobe or the Moina area and the Arthur River in the far north-west.

Northern

River fishing abounds and good roads lead to numerous lakes and lagoons. The best river fishing in the north is centred at Launceston. Between October to November, during the mayfly hatch, dry fly fishing is ideal in the South Esk River system. This often comes on again in April. Good river fishing is available on the Meander, South and North Esk and St. Patrick's Rivers.

The Highlands

The great number of lakes and waterways now covering the Central Plateau provides a great variety of wet and dry fly fishing.

From December to March the climate on the highlands (average lake level 3,000 to 3,400 ft.) is mildest and good on-the-spot accommodation is available at Miena, Tarraleah, Bronte Park and Derwent Bridge.

Southern

Stream fishing is difficult because most of the southern streams flow through mountainous and rugged country. The Huon River is noted for its large fish. The river is best fished from a boat anywhere between Huonville to Raneleagh.

The Mountain River and Nicholas Rivulat are relatively easily fished during the white bait run. Other good spots are the Denison, Esperance and Lune Rivers.

The Derwent River supports a large fishing population, but the river is not easily fished. Glenora and Plenty are perhaps the most worthwhile and rewarding spots. The Ouse River is one of the best dry fly rivers in the south, as too is the Shannon River. Other rivers, eg. the Coal, Plenty, Styx and Russell Rivers all provide good fishing.

Saltwater Fishing

The saltwater fisherman may follow his sport anywhere around the coast of Tasmania. The varieties of fish to be caught are many.

Piers and jetties provide comfortable fishing spots, while the rugged coastline and broad sandy beaches are ideal for rock and surf fishermen.

SKIN-DIVING AND SPEAR FISHING

The main varieties sought for are carp, trumpeter and various species of parrot fish. The most popular spots for spear fishing are St. Helens, Bicheno, Swansea and Orford on the East Coast and Bruny Island in the south. There are restrictions placed on the number of crayfish and abalone bagged.

GAME FISHING

The coastal waters of the east and south-east coasts are an ideal location. The principal bases for game fishing are Eaglehawk Neck on the Tasman Peninsula, Dunally and Triabunna.

Various types of game fish and sharks frequent the waters and are generally more prevalent during the months between November and August.

Principal among the game fish in Tasmanian waters is the Bluefin Tuna, which may be sighted in schools from late spring, through summer and autumn, to the onset of the following winter.

The warmer months see an abundance of shark in Tasmanian waters, and large numbers have been sighted during the summer and autumn seasons.

The Mako (or Blue Pointer) is one of the many species which never fail to provide a challenge to game anglers. The dreaded White Death Shark is also found around these waters.

Enquiries regarding game fishing in Tasmania will be welcomed by the Secretary of the Tuna Club of Tasmania, who will endeavour to arrange for boats and gear. He may be contacted through the Tasmanian Government Tourist Bureau.

The charges for a boat vary according to the type of boat preferred and also the season.

Gear in limited quantities is available from the Association, but the experienced angler will no doubt prefer to bring his own equipment.

TYPES OF FISH AND WHERE THEY ARE FOUND

Brown Trout Waters
With very few exceptions all rivers and lakes in Tasmania are stocked with brown trout.

Rainbow Trout Waters
Great Lake, Lake Leake, Lake St. Clair, Lake King William, Dee Lagoon, Lagoon of Islands and Blackman's Lagoon.

Blackfish
All slow-flowing sections of northern and north-western rivers and Huon River.

Redfin
Lake Echo, Lake Dulverton, Dee Lagoon and Bradys Lagoon, Coal, Tamar, Jordon, Meander and Macquarie Rivers.

Freshwater Lobster
Northern and western rivers and Lake Pedder.

Australian Salmon
Arthur, Pieman, Black, Tamar, Mussel Roe, Carlton, Derwent and Huon Rivers and King Island.

Trumpeter
Off-shore kelp beds and estuary waters.

Perch (sea)
Off-shore banks and large river estuaries.

Trevally
Off-shore kelp beds and large river estuaries.

Flounder
Shallow sandy bays and river estuaries.

Whiting
Derwent and Tamar Rivers.

Sea Crayfish
Off-shore kelp beds and rocky coasts.

Flathead
Off-shore sandy areas and river estuaries.

Rock Cod
Rocky coasts and estuaries.

Tuna (Yellowfin, Southern Bluefin, Albacore)
Sport fishing centred on Eaglehawk Neck and Fortesque Bay.

Black Bream
Estuaries and coastal lagoons from Tamar River in the north, via the east coast to the rivers in the south.

BOATING—SAFETY TIPS

● When you anchor, keep well out of the channel and be sure that you have ample room to swing in all directions.
● Drop the anchor overboard hand over hand. Never throw it. If you, or anyone on board, gets caught in the line, real danger may result.
● When fending off with a boat-hook, never brace it against your body. A sudden surge may cause internal injuries. Hold a pole or bar to one side of the body.
● Always watch the sky for a change of weather. Plan your trips after you have checked the local weather forecast.
● Be on the alert for danger signals, such as sudden changes in wind or rapidly gathering clouds. In a small boat, head for port as quickly as possible.
● If you carry pets aboard, keep a harness on them. If they fall overboard they can be hauled in with a boat-hook.
● As soon as bad weather threatens, have all passengers on deck don life jackets. Wearing a life jacket in stormy weather is the mark of a good seaman.
● Have the engine well warmed up before leaving the mooring, slip or dock. Tight quarters, such as these, often require split-second manoeuvering, with quick bursts of speed that can stall a cold motor.
● If you have trouble backing a single-screw powerboat, try shifting to neutral and then giving a short, sharp burst forward with full right or left rudder. The effect will be to impel the stern to port or starboard, without imparting much forward motion to the boat.
● Always watch the wake when passing near other boats or in a crowded harbour. Remember that you are legally responsible for any damage done by your wake.
● Extra gasoline should be carried only in an approved container and stowed in a safe location.
● Motor must be turned off when fuel is being taken aboard.
● Don't jump into your boat. When boarding from a dock, step gently into the centre, steadying yourself on the dock.
● Ski hitches, in attaching the line to the boat, should hold the line above the motor, or attach them to the transom so that a slack line will not dip into the water and foul either the motor or the propeller.
● Never keep paints and thinners on board during the season. Bottles break, cans rust and, in general, fire hazards are greatly multiplied by these highly inflammable liquids.

BOATING REGULATIONS

The following regulations apply to the owners of power boats.
● All boats with an engine(s) are required to be registered in Tasmania with a Tasmanian Marine Board or Harbour Trust.
● A licence is required to take charge of the navigation of any registered boat.
● A boat that does eight knots has to be registered.
● Applicant for the licence must be at least 17 years of age and required to pass an eyesight test and satisfy the examiner that he is competent to operate and navigate such a vessel.
● A speed limit of five knots applies to all motor boats within close proximity of the shore, wharves, persons bathing, or other vessels or buoys, unless towing water skiers in defined areas.
● Water ski-ing is only permitted during daylight hours. Should it be carried out after daylight hours written permission must be obtained from the Harbour Master. Also no motor boat shall tow more than three water-skiers at one time.
● No motor launch shall tow an aquaplaner or water-skier unless in addition to the person in charge of such motor launch there is carried at least one other person over the age of 10 years who shall act as observer.
● No person shall drive a motor launch or ride upon any aquaplane, water-ski, or similar device at a speed or in a manner dangerous to any person or likely to cause damage by its wash or otherwise to any property or vessel (including a rowing boat) or in any manner likely to cause a nuisance or annoyance to any other person.
● A copy of the complete regulations can be obtained from a Tasmanian Marine Board or Harbour Trust.

AUSTRALIA'S WESTERN THIRD

This vast territory, the State of Western Australia in the Commonwealth of Australia, is a paradox. Much of it is flat, harsh and featureless—the eroded top of a great plateau which tilts imperceptibly from west to east—yet to the perceptive eye it is beautiful in an infinite range of colours and forms. It is arid for most of the year yet grows more than a quarter of the nation's wheat crop. Most of its rivers flow inland and underground, losing themselves beneath the sand; but those streams which reach the sea and are fed by cyclonic and monsoonal rains discharge for a brief season more water than the great Mississippi.

For the most part its vegetation is sparse, yet where the big trees grow they spread their canopies 300 feet above the forest floor. A shower of rain can transform in a matter of days a glaring ocean of sandhills into a gargantuan garden of wildflowers. . .

The caprice of the West, the riotous inconsistency of its climate and topography, have challenged and tantalised land-taking Australians for nearly 150 years. Successive generations have struggled to tame its wilderness, to tap its mineral wealth and realise its agricultural and pastoral potential. But until recent years the success they achieved was at best partial and precarious and confined mainly to temperate regions near the sea. Now, however, a new breed of frontiersmen armed with the weapons of modern science and technology have joined the battle against environment. Within a decade they have made more advances, with more permanence, than their forbears did in a century.

Today Western Australia is attracting new settlers and developmental capital at an unprecedented rate. Its production of raw materials, notably base metals, is rocketing. Heavy industries are firmly established near its capital, Perth. New towns are springing up in its deserts—served by new roads and railways and airfields and ports.

KWINANA FREEWAY AND NARROWS BRIDGE

PERTH, SPLENDID IN ISOLATION

Western Australia's capital, Perth, must in the geographical sense be accounted as one of the 'loneliest' cities on earth. Its nearest metropolitan neighbour in Australia is Adelaide, 1,400 miles away to the east across the Great Victoria Desert. To the north the cities of Java are nearly 2,000 miles distant, and 4,000 miles of ocean separate it from South Africa to the west. The icy wastes of Antarctica lie 2,000 miles to the south.

Despite this formidable isolation, Perth is a gracious, pleasant and prosperous place to live. The climate is mild and sunny for most of the year—extremes of heat occurring in brief spells between December and March. Its situation, on land rising from a broad tidal 'pool' some 12 miles from the estuary of the Swan River, is superb.

While it may be true that Perth cannot claim to be a city of architectural distinction, it has individuality and charm. Its skyline is not yet dominated by the multi-storey glasshouses which now overshadow the inner areas of the eastern capitals and a number of historic buildings in the Georgian and Victorian styles have been preserved.

Heavy industries have not been permitted to establish themselves near commercial and residential areas. They have been dispersed on the coast south of the port of Fremantle at the river's mouth and as a consequence Perth itself has no smog problem and the river itself is relatively unpolluted by industrial waste.

King's Park, a 1,000 acre bushland reserve and one of the most beautiful public recreation areas in Australia, is only a few minutes walk away from the heart of the city. It contains a representative selection of West Australian trees and in the wildflower season blazes with colour. Its highest point, Mount Eliza, commands a magnificent panorama of the river and its foreshores.

Perth is also fortunate in its nearness to many beauty spots in the Darling Ranges—including the Canning and Serpentine Dams and Mundaring Weir, from which water is pumped through a 300 mile pipeline to the eastern gold-fields. These hill resorts, and a number of fine ocean and river beaches, are all within an hour's drive of the city.

Rottnest Island—so named by early Dutch navigators who mistook its population of quokka wallabies for giant rats—is another favourite playground for Perth's citizens. It is only 12 miles from Fremantle and is reached by ferry or plane from Perth airport.

▼ UNIVERSITY OF WESTERN AUSTRALIA   ▶ PERTH FROM KING'S PARK

FASCINATING FLORA & FAUNA

Botanists have listed more than 6,500 kinds of flowering plants, about 50 ferns and over 400 marine algae in Western Australia—half the world's flora. Many of the species are entirely endemic—they have evolved from ancient forms which flourished when Antarctica was covered by dense forests and they have not spread to other parts of the world.

The wildflowers of the West, seen at their best in September, October and November, attract thousands of visitors to the State every year, particularly to the south-west where the vivid blue leschenaultia, the delicately fashioned kangaroo paw and the banksias and heaths make breathtaking displays of colour and the brown boronia perfumes the air.

Rainfall on the desert instantly stimulates the germination of countless small annuals which cover the sandhills and flats with glowing colour. Among the most spectacular are Sturt's Desert Pea, Desert Pride and the pink, yellow or white everlastings which may at times carpet hundreds of square miles.

Although large areas of Western Australia have been reduced to virtual wasteland by pastoral mismanagement and the natural habitat of many unique species of birds and animals destroyed, the relative sparsity of settlement in the semi-arid interior has enabled the more robust fauna to survive more easily than in the eastern States. In the back country one still sees large herds of kangaroos and emus

Endemism is less marked among West Australian animals than among plants. Probably the best known of the 'exclusives' is the short-tailed wallaby or quokka (*Setonix bracyurus*) which abounds on Rottnest Island near Perth and is a great tourist attraction. In all 22 species of kangaroos and wallabies have been listed west of the South Australian and Northern Territory borders, but notably absent from the ranks of the marsupials are koalas and wombats

Among the monotremes, echidnas are fairly common in the temperate zone but platypuses have never been found. Excepting the dingo, who is thought to have been brought in by the aborigines about 25,000 years ago and can therefore fairly claim to be classed as a native—and a few species of phalangers or bats—placental mammals are mainly marine species.

Where the surface water occurs bird life is enormously prolific. Streams and permanent waterholes support myriad populations of pigeons, doves, wrens, finches, honey-eaters and parrots—although fewer varieties of the latter family are listed than elsewhere in Australia. Among the tropical notabilities are brolgas, two species of bower birds and the 'wild turkey' or Australian bustard

Eighteen species of ducks and swans have been observed on coastal lagoons and river reaches—including the famed black swan which so intrigued early explorers and has been taken as the State's emblem.

MORRISON (VERTICORDIA NITENS), MID WEST COAST

▲ SPLENDID WREN
▼ AGILE WALLABY, KIMBERLEY RANGES

HONEY POSSUM

RED CAPPED PARROT ▶

DESOLATE FASCINATING DESERT LAND

Ninety per cent of Western Australia receives an average yearly rainfall of less than 14 inches and about 35 per cent less than eight inches. The driest areas, where the annual mean is less than six inches are in the Gibson and Great Victoria Deserts and a long, narrow corridor of drought extending westward to the shores of Shark Bay.

This is grim, indescribably harsh country—a seemingly limitless expanse of red sandhills, glittering gibber plains and extensive 'clayplans', the beds of ancient lakes which hold water only after heavy storms and are usually coated with gypsum or salt crystals precipitated when the rainwater evaporates. Here and there low, table-topped hills, often of brightly banded jasper, rise above the shimmering ground mirage.

To the uninitiated the vistas of the eastern deserts are almost hypnotically repetitive. Silence and loneliness brood over desolation. But to those who, for one reason or another, have accustomed themselves to travelling and living in such an environment, the region is fascinating for its subtleties and inconsistencies. The adjusted eye perceives the wide spectrum of life supported where it would seem illogical to expect that any could exist—plants, animals and reptiles adapted to survive total drought which may last for years, and a diurnial temperature range which sometimes exceeds 100° F.

In such a geographical context any tiny oasis by a freshwater soak, a procession of gnarled trees tracing the meanderings of a stream deep beneath the sand, rock pools replenished by the heavy dews of the desert night—all these are the richly exciting discoveries of travel.

There is no surface water of any account. All but the most torrential rain is immediately soaked up by the sand and finds its way by an uncharted drainage system into storages in the bedrock of the Great Plateau. Most of the water flows inland, but on the northern margin of the Nullarbor Plain the bedrock slopes towards the sea and the underground streams have carved out labyrinthine caverns in the overlying limestone. In some areas the roofs of these caves have collapsed, creating great blowholes which give access to subterranean waterfalls and pools.

This vast cave system is still unexplored, but its secret rivers eventually find their way into the Southern Ocean. Far out to sea, off Israelite Bay, submarine springs of fresh water occur—so copious that the whaling ships of a century ago were able to replenish their butts by lowering them overside.

LIMESTONE PINNACLES, NAMBUNG NATIONAL PARK

▲ SAND DUNES AT EUCLA   ▼ ACROSS LAKE MOORE FROM MT SINGLETON

SOUTH WEST - *The Gentle Heart*

The south-western segment of Western Australia is topographically and climatically very different from the rest of the State. Lying below the 35th Parallel, bounded on two sides by the Indian Ocean and containing extensive highlands, it receives liberal rainfall and for the most part escapes the fierce summer heat which sears the north and the inland.

It is a region of tall forests, heathlands and fertile valleys watered by numerous small rivers and streams which flow all the year round. In spring it is a wildflower garden and attracts visitors from all over the world who come to explore a perfumed floral labyrinth re-created each year beneath the soaring karri stands and along the mountain ridges.

The karris (*E. diversicolor*) are the kings of the south-western bush. They share with gigantic mountain ash trees of Victoria and Tasmania the distinction of being numbered among the world's tallest trees. Only the redwoods of California attain greater heights—more than 300 feet.

The forests of the South West which contain, besides karri, large tracts of jarrah and other commercially valuable hardwoods, are of great economic importance to the State. They dominate the hinterland and support a thriving timber industry. But on the narrow plains on the seaward side of the Darling escarpment, and in the wider valleys, dairying and mixed farming is well established and the acreage of land under intensive cultivation is steadily increasing.

Although not as highly mineralised as most other divisions of the State, the South West contains bauxite fields and large deposits of sub-bituminous coal which have been mined on the Collie River since the turn of the century and are still important as a source of fuel for thermal power generators.

Bunbury, the provincial capital, has a population of about 20,000 and is a centre of prosperous secondary industry. It is sited on the picturesque Leschenault Estuary, but the natural beauty of the coast has in recent years been marred by beach sand mining for ilmenite, a source of titanium oxide.

Albany, the historic port 140 road miles to the south and east, is still unspoiled by foreshore erosion and unsightly industrial building and is a base from which visitors to the West can explore the best of the wildflower country, the Porongurup and Stirling Ranges, and the fascinating limestone caves along the coast between Busselton and Augusta.

KING GEORGE SOUND AND ALBANY HARBOUR

ORGAN PIPES, AUGUSTA JEWEL CAVE

MAGIC OF THE KIMBERLEYS

When West Australians use the term 'the North West' they generally refer to all State territory north of the 26th Parallel—almost 600,000 square miles of wild, desolate country which, although it enjoys a magnificent winter climate and is in parts savagely beautiful, is difficult to settle and develop because of the extreme heat and violent storms, to which it is subjected in summer.

In the far north the terrain is mountainous and broken. It is drained by large rivers which carry enormous volumes of floodwater in the monsoon season between December and April. Some relatively small areas on the seaward side of the ranges record a 40-50 inch rainfall and have tropical vegetation, but for the most part the highlands receive only about half this amount. They are clothed by open forest and rank native grasses and shrubs which have for almost a century supported an open range cattle industry.

However, as the mean elevation of the land decreases to the south and east precipitation decreases and becomes irregular. The plains are semi-arid and areas of true desert occur in the central eastern sector.

For the dreamers about northern development, the Kimberleys constitute the Promised Land on the other side of the Never Never. The faithful believe implicitly in the potential of the area, that bold enterprise and the tools of modern technology will one day combine to unlock a treasure-house of natural resources.

This conception of 162,000 square miles of inhospitable and climatically trying wilderness is over-romantic. Past generations have cherished similar dreams and worked desperately hard to make them come true. The visually splendid but capricious country has always dispelled illusion in the end.

The only industry in the Kimberleys to support a permanent workforce for any length of time was pearling which was centred on Broome where in 1912 more than 400 luggers were based.

Present interest in the area is based partly in minerals exploration—a large bauxite deposit has been discovered near Admiralty Gulf—but mainly on the $100 million Ord irrigation project which, when completed in the mid-1970s, will bring dry-season water to 170,000 acres of black-soil plain suitable for tropical agriculture.

WINDJANA GORGE, KIMBERLEY RANGES

▲ MAIN STREET, BROOME

▼ ORD RIVER IRRIGATION SCHEME IN REMOTE KIMBERLEYS

SPINIFEX COVERED RIDGES, PILBARA REGION

A PEOPLE APART

Development in physical isolation from the rest of the Commonwealth has created in Western Australia a complex of political and social attitudes which differ subtly from those of the eastern states. This difference is historically based.

Fifteen hundred free settlers from the United Kingdom were farming land in the Swan Valley and had built a village on the site of Perth in 1830, years before Melbourne, Adelaide and Brisbane were founded. Yet, despite its seniority, the growth of the colony was slow. In 1885 the population was only 35,000, of whom only 15,000 were females

Gold strikes, first in the northern and later in the eastern provinces, gave the West its first big economic boost. Tens of thousands of immigrants, mostly from the Pacific coast which was then suffering a depression, more than doubled the population during the 1890s. Those who failed to strike it lucky on the incredibly rich Coolgardie-Kalgoorlie fields stayed on to farm in the South West or work in the small industries established to serve predominantly rural communities.

Until well into the 20th century Perth remained a large country town which, although it had the status of a capital, existed solely as a commercial and service centre for the gold mining and grazing industries. The tempo of its life was leisured. Its people enjoyed moderate prosperity and unparallelled opportunities to indulge in outdoor recreations and sports in a benign climate. Their social structure derived unmistakably from Victorian England, but they were powerfully influenced by the fact that the outback, with all its legendary demands on human fortitude and endurance, existed in reality only just beyond the city limits.

Thus the 'West Australian type' became fixed—if not rustic then at least neither metropolitan nor cosmopolitan. By tradition the people of the West were conservative but hospitable and easy-going. On the other hand they resented what they considered to be the Federal Government's persistent neglect of their claim to equality in the Commonwealth partnership and, on one occasion in 1933, voted overwhelmingly in favour of secession. However, no action to effect a political separation was taken by the State legislature and as the country recovered from the great depression, West Australians were persuaded that resignation from the Commonwealth was both impractical and undesirable.

Nevertheless a sense of 'separateness' persists to this day, despite the profound changes wrought by the mining boom and explosive industrial development—and by the absorption within the community of large numbers of migrants from other countries.

▼ GOLD MINER, KALGOORLIE   ▼ ABORIGINAL STOCKMAN   THE HAY STREET MALL, PERTH ▶

MINING AND INDUSTRY – *Dramatic Growth*

The 1960s were a decade of dramatic change for the people of Western Australia. The geographical isolation of the State had hitherto retarded full exploitation of its natural resources and for many years its economy had been largely dependent on the slowly declining production of the Kalgoorlie goldfields.

Then, almost overnight, the situation was transformed. The techniques of modern transportation and mechanical engineering were applied to the problems of development in the West. Modern aeroplanes, motor transport and giant cargo vessels overthrew the tyranny of distance and modern earth-moving and freight handling machinery solved the manpower problem in the outback.

The technological revolution revived interest in minerals exploration—and dramatic results were obtained almost immediately. Between 1960 and 1964 enormous deposits of high grade iron ore were located in the Pilbara division of the North West, rich nickel was discovered at Kambalda and elsewhere on the eastern goldfields, oil was found on Barrow Island, natural gas on the mainland, and large-scale projects were launched to mine bauxite, industrial salt, manganese and ilmenite.

At the same time major processing plants mushroomed in the Kwinana area on Cockburn Sound, 30 miles south of Perth. They included the Commonwealth's largest oil refinery, an integrated iron and steel industry to process ore from Koolyanobbing on the edge of the eastern goldfields, an alumina refinery drawing its bauxite from the Darling Ranges, and a refinery for the nickel concentrates produced near Kalgoorlie. Money—and people—flowed into the State even faster than in 1893 when the great goldrush brought the West its first boom. New dormitory cities for industrial workers sprang up near the formerly secluded seaside resort of Rockingham on Cockburn Sound and tens of thousands of construction workers found highly paid employment building the new roads, ports, railways and towns needed to service the mines.

In time, of course, the boom will subside, but the State will enjoy its legacy of immeasurably improved transport and communications—hundreds of miles of sealed highway through districts hitherto regarded as inaccessible, a standard-gauge rail link with the eastern capitals, harbours capable of accommodating the largest ships afloat, and a high-capacity microwave telecommunications system.

Thus the spin-off of high-pressure minerals exploitation will, given wise management, create conditions in which the West will become as industrially important to the Australian Commonwealth as the eastern states and support an equal population.

Premier's Dept., W.A.

MT TOM PRICE, PILBARA REGION

THE MAINSTAY OF AGRICULTURE

Rich mineral discoveries and the establishment of heavy industries near Perth have transformed the economy of Western Australia in recent years but the State's prosperity is still firmly underpinned by its capacity to produce wool, wheat and meat for export.

For a century after the founding of the colony, farming in the west was chiefly confined to the well watered, fertile soils of the Swan River valley and the narrow coastal strip under the lee of the Darling Ranges southward of Geraldton. The area of easily arable land was not, by Australian standards, very large but it grew grain, dairy produce, fruit, vegetables and vines of excellent quality. The enormous tracts of the semi-arid hinterland were given over to grazing.

In time the pastoral lands, particularly in the north, began to deteriorate and the flocks and herds declined. But this loss of production was—from a State if not regional point of view—more than compensated by the success which attended the introduction of modern, scientific methods to the agriculture of the south.

The techniques of correcting soil deficiencies by the use of artificial fertilisers, particularly superphosphate, and the perfection of quick-maturing strains of wheat enabled millions of acres of sandplain, which had no surface water but received fairly dependable winter rain, to be brought under crop.

The wheatlands east of the ranges expanded rapidly after the Second World War and now extend as far as 250 miles inland into country which was once regarded as semi-desert. In a good season the West Australian wheat belt can grow upwards of 80 million bushels—a production figure exceeded in the Commonwealth only by New South Wales.

Comparable improvements were at the same time made in the temperate zone wool and meat industries.

Possibly the most spectacular success of agricultural science, however, was achieved in the Esperance district, 370 miles south-east of Perth, where soil chemists pinpointed copper and zinc deficiencies and evolved corrective treatment which turned some three million acres of heath and low scrub into lush farms. Similar results are being obtained on tracts of scarpland north of Perth.

The wealth of the West is by no means confined to mineral exploitation. If the land is conserved and well managed it will assure West Australians of prosperity long after the mines have been worked out.

CATTLE GRAZING, SOUTH EAST

HOP GROWING, SOUTH EAST

COTTON GROWING ON ORD RIVER

A BRIEF HISTORY OF WESTERN AUSTRALIA

The first Europeans known to have visited the shores of Western Australia were the crew of the tiny Dutch sailing ship *Eendracht* which in the year 1616 explored the mid-western coast in the area now known as Shark Bay. Already the Aborigines had been here for at least 20,000 years, and possibly Indonesian, Malay and Chinese fishermen had touched upon the Kimberley coast during their voyages among the northern islands.

In the years following Dirk Hartog's visit in 1616 Dutch vessels often reached the Western Australian coast en route to the East Indies. Some, such as the *Batavia* in 1629 and the *Vergulden Draeck* in 1656 were wrecked on the western coast of 'New Holland'. The Dutch, however, were not impressed by the continent's arid north-west, or its Aboriginal inhabitants, and made no move to establish a settlement.

Early British navigators examined the south land in greater detail. William Dampier, who reached it in 1688 and again in 1699 formed a poor opinion of the land, and described the natives as 'the miserablest people in the world'. For another hundred years there was little activity along Australia's western coast. Not until the 1820s, after the colonisation of New South Wales, was the western coast extensively charted. The first settlement, a small military outpost, was at King George Sound (the present-day site of Albany) in 1826.

In 1829 Captain Fremantle of H.M.S. *Challenger* took formal possession of the western third of the continent, and a colony was established at the Swan River with Captain Stirling as its first Lieutenant-Governor. This was intended to be a colony for free men only.

Agricultural development was much slower than had been hoped, in spite of the rush of settlers wanting to take up grants of land. Few of the colonists had anticipated the difficulty of carving farms from virgin bush. For several decades the colony stagnated and real progress seemed impossible. As a desperate measure convicts were sent to Western Australia, and between 1850 and 1886 many public buildings (including the Town Hall and many others still standing in Perth), roads, jetties and agricultural works were completed by convict labour.

Progress was more rapid in the 1850s and 1860s. The south-western corner of the State was settled, and the remote northern and inland areas partly explored in a search for better farm lands, timber and minerals. During the 1870s the pastoralists pushed northwards to the De Grey, Gascoyne and Murchison districts.

Gold brought the first really big influx of settlers to the west. First at Halls Creek in the Kimberleys, then at the Yilgarn, Pilbara, Ashburton and Murchison goldfields, and finally the big goldrushes to Kalgoorlie. The population leapt from 35,000 in 1885 to 239,000 in 1904.

Gradually, as surface gold was worked out, people turned to farming. Western Australia came more and more to rely on primary industries, with increasing sheep numbers and growing wheat lands. This made the State's economy particularly vulnerable as world wheat and wool prices fell in the world-wide economic depression of the 1930s. Then followed the Second World War with its disruptive effect on the people and the development of Western Australia.

The years since 1945 have been prosperous ones for Western Australia, with a growing population, soaring wool prices and huge areas of wheat. Oil was found at North West Cape in 1953, then in commercial quantities at Barrow Island in 1966. By 1967 the great iron ore exploitation was well under way. Near Perth bauxite, the raw material of aluminium, had been discovered, and the levelling of the jarrah forests for bauxite open-cut mining is now proceeding. The old Eastern Goldfields region sprang to life in 1967 with the discovery and mining of nickel. The Kwinana industrial complex came into being, with oil, alumina and nickel refining plants. But recently this mineral and industrial boom has to some extent been counterbalanced by a considerable decline in rural prosperity.

THE BARRACKS ARCH, St. George's Terrace Perth, built 1863

THE OLD MILL, South Perth, built 1835

PHYSICAL FEATURES AND CLIMATE

Western Australia can be considered in two major physical regions—a tableland known as the great plateau, and the low-lying coastal strip or coastal plains.

The plateau comprises more than ninety per cent of the State, and varies greatly in elevation, being mostly 1,000 to 2,000 feet above sea level, but reaching 4,000 feet in the north-west. Its surface, for the most part, is gently undulating.

On this plateau the rivers follow two broad patterns: those that flow to the sea, and those that flow to inland drainage basins. The north-western rivers flowing to the sea reach many hundreds of miles in length; but most flow strongly only after heavy rains. Those of the south-west are shorter, and have cut deep valleys down the Darling Scarp to the sea.

The huge region of inland drainage is arid and almost without large rivers. Creeks run from higher parts but soon disappear into sandy flats or empty into the extensive saltlakes or claypans which are dry except after rare good rains. These lakes are usually elongated north-south, and in places are interconnected to form long chains of lakes, probably the remains of ancient river systems which flowed under different climatic conditions. Some vast areas have no surface drainage, for example where the drainage is underground through caverns in the limestone of the Nullarbor, or in the sand-dune deserts.

The great plateau slopes down gradually to the south, broken by the Stirling and Mt Barren ranges which rise suddenly near the south coast. To the west, the plateau drops suddenly to a low coastal plain, forming the Darling Range or Scarp which extends north and south of Perth.

The coastal plains vary in width. The Swan coastal plain, on which Perth is situated, averages about 15 miles in width. A narrow, broken strip of coastal plain extends up the coast to the Kimberleys, and becomes quite wide in places, as near Port Hedland and Exmouth Gulf.

Western Australia has an area of 975,920 square miles, and extends from latitude 13°44′ S to latitude 35° 08′ S, a north-south distance of 1,500 miles. Consequently it has very considerable variations in climate, from tropical summer rainfall in the Kimberleys, through central and interior regions of very low and erratic rainfall, to the southern areas, which have regular winter rains.

The climate of the southern parts is warm-temperate, never extremely cold and only in mid-summer becoming uncomfortably hot at times. This summer heat is dry and less oppressive than tropical humid heat, and is usually relieved by afternoon sea breezes near the coast. Winters are cool, rainy, without snow except an occasional light fall on the peaks of the Stirling Ranges in the far south. Perth is Australia's sunniest capital, with an average of eight hours of sunshine daily. Its mean temperature is 66°F and average rainfall is 35 inches.

Western Australia, though comprising almost one-third of the total area of Australia, contains only about eight per cent of the total population. The Perth metropolitan area is the most densely populated, with almost 700,000 inhabitants, a density of three thousand persons per square mile. Western Australia as a whole has an average population density of only one person per square mile. The population of the State is expected to reach one million during 1971.

Primary Industry

The principal primary industries of Western Australia include forestry, agriculture, grazing, dairying, fishing and mining.

Although the indigenous forests suitable for milling cover only a very small percentage of the State they are of considerable economic importance because of the strength and durability of these hardwoods, particularly the two main economically important species, jarrah and karri. Permanent State forests total 4.5 million acres, with a further 2.5 million acres in timber reserves.

Agricultural products include wheat, oats, barley, hay, pasture seed, cotton, fruit and vegetables. Pastoral products are principally wool, mutton and beef. The pastoral industry utilises the vast semi-arid mulga and spinifex regions of the inland and North West, where over-grazing has caused considerable deterioration in the scrubland environment. Some tropical agriculture has developed on the Gascoyne River at Carnarvon, where bananas are grown, while in the Kimberleys irrigation from the Ord River dam has enabled cotton and some grain sorghum to be grown.

The fishing industry has grown tenfold since the end of the Second World War, and is now Australia's largest in value of production. Rock lobsters or crayfish constitute the most valuable part of the industry, being exported to the United States. Salmon, netted in bays of the southern coast, are another species extensively exploited. With interest being shown in more remote parts of the State it is possible that tuna and prawns along the North West will become increasingly important. Larger amounts of bluefin tuna are being caught off the southern coast. Only the production of pearlshell has declined, being now less than one-quarter of its level of fifty years ago.

The pattern of mineral exploitation has changed greatly in recent years, with iron ore, nickel and bauxite becoming prominent, and gold declining in value. The mineral boom has caused intensive mineral exploration and claim-pegging activity almost throughout the State, but much of the pegging is purely speculative on land often worthless for commercial mineral production. This great rush to exploit Western Australia's minerals has led to concern over land use, particularly over the possibility of mining or quarrying on farmlands, State forests, water catchment areas, and public lands including national parks, nature reserves, Aboriginal reserves and sacred sites, and beaches. Pressure on the Government to apply protective restrictions on mining has led to the establishment of a Ministry of Environmental Protection and an inquiry into the antiquated Mining Act.

Secondary Industry

Situated principally at Kwinana, Fremantle and around Perth, Western Australia's secondary industry has become widely diversified, dealing with metals, machines and implements, sawmilling, paper and printing, chemicals, dyes, paints, clothing, motor vehicle assembly, mine and quarry products, furniture, bricks, glass, food, drinks, tobacco, tyres and other commodities.

In the past ten years the number of factories has increased by 31 per cent to more than five thousand, employing almost seventy thousand people. However, in value of factory output Western Australia exceeds only Tasmania, the Northern Territory and the Australian Capital Territory.

NATIONAL PARKS AND NATURE RESERVES

From small beginnings Western Australia's national parks and nature reserves are gradually growing to quite an impressive total. However in a State of almost a million square miles the parks and nature reserves are yet but a very small percentage of the total area; many more reserves must be established if sufficient samples of our natural environment are to be preserved. The following is a summary of Western Australia's national parks and some of the more important nature reserves at the beginning of 1971. For further details see *Australia's National Parks* by Michael Morcombe (Lansdowne Press) and the Periwinkle series on *Australian National Parks*, particularly the two volumes on western and central Australia, and northern Australia.

Main national parks of Western Australia as at 31 January 1971

Cape Arid	642,000 acres
Cape Le Grande	54,876
Cape Range	33,171
Chichester Range	372,163
Frank Hann	64,480
Geikie Gorge	7,750
Gooseberry Hill	81
Greenmount	127
Hamersley Range	1,485,430
John Forrest	3,903
Kalamunda	919
Kalbarri	365,145
Lesmurdie Falls	86
Moore River	26,030
Neerabup	2,785
Porongorup	5,531
Serpentine	1,571
Sir James Mitchell	2,717
Stirling Range	285,874
Torndirrup	8,905
Walpole-Nornalup	33,007
Watheroo	76,646
Walyunga	4,320
Yalgorup	9,891
Yanchep	6,894
new parks not yet officially named:	
Avon Valley	10,764
west of Marchagee	10,890
west of Coorow	3,441
Porongorups area	150
TOTAL	3,532,528 acres

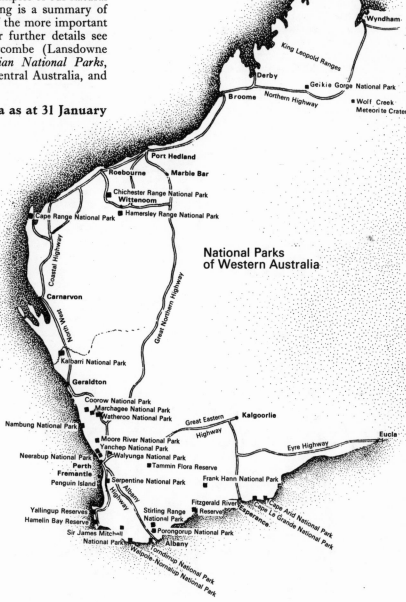

National Parks of Western Australia

Major flora and fauna reserves

Barrow Island	50,000 acres
Bernier and Doore Island	26,000
Dryandra State Forest, an unofficial but very important reserve	
Fitzgerald River	604,000
Houtman Abrolhos Islands	
Lake Magenta	232,000
Tuttanning (east Pingelly)	3,260

Some of these areas, particularly the flora and fauna reserves and the big new national parks of desert and north-west areas are difficult to reach or require four wheel drive in places or at certain times of the year. Anyone intending to visit parks or reserves in the more remote areas should obtain further information from:

The National Parks Board, Matilda Bay Reserve, Hackett Drive, Nedlands;

The Department of Fisheries and Fauna, 108 Adelaide Terrace, Perth.

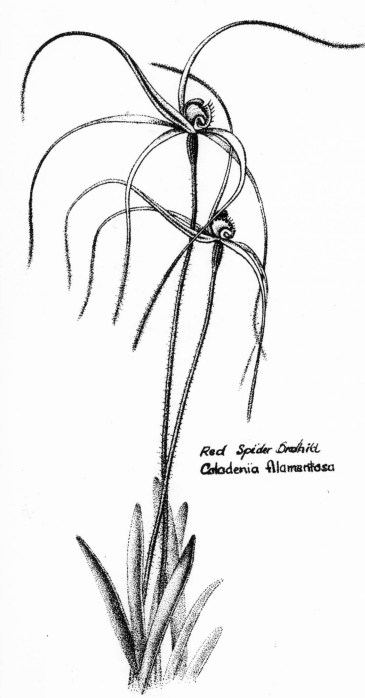

Red Spider Orchid
Caladenia filamentosa

HINTS FOR ROAD TRAVELLERS

Western Australia is the largest and most sparsely populated of the states. Only the south-west corner, perhaps one-eighth of the total area, has a landscape and climate reasonably hospitable and roads suitable for touring at any time of the year.

The road traveller to the North West and Kimberleys must be prepared for dirt tracks (though marked on maps as 'highways'), which are rough, corrugated, with deep potholes and embedded sharp rocks. Creek crossings and stock grids require special care. Trailers and caravans seem particularly vulnerable, and often suffer such mishaps as broken axles after hundreds of miles of rough roads. As help may be far away and spare parts almost unobtainable it is best to travel without towing, or to take a heavily built trailer. Whatever the outfit, travel with extreme caution.

Heavy trucks and road trains present a problem on such roads, stirring up huge clouds of dust that hang in the air for miles behind. To drive blindly into dust, either when overtaking or travelling in the opposite direction to the truck is to risk a head-on collision. This has happened quite a few time with loss of life, not only in the north but also on the dirt section of the Nullarbor.

Places of scenic interest in the North West and far north are widely spaced. Between are hundreds of miles of monotonous mulga scrub (except at end of winter when massed wildflowers appear), saltbush or spinifex, which must be endured along with heat, dust, flies and, in many areas, poor facilities.

Before setting off on really remote or little-used tracks, tell some reliable person of your intended schedule so that if you become overdue enquiries can be made and a search begun if necessary. Have your vehicle in first-class condition, with cooling system, tyres and battery checked for reliability. Certain spares and extra equipment could be useful, and possibly prevent a dangerous situation.

tyre levers and repair kit
a reliable jack, with broad baseplate to prevent sinking in sand
fan belt and radiator hoses
comprehensive set of tools
coil of rope or wire
axe and shovel
torch and batteries
for really outback travel, sand mats or mesh for loose ground
second spare; tyres with tubes preferable
reliable maps.

Enquire about conditions of roads ahead whenever the opportunity arises.

If purchasing a vehicle specifically for travel in the north and outback a four wheel drive will repay its greater cost and fuel consumption by making out-of-the-way places accessible, and will do so with greater safety, reliability, and in general give greater ease of mind whenever tracks are rough, sandy or muddy.

TRANSPORT SERVICES

AIR

The international airport at Perth connects with overseas services via Singapore and South Africa. Perth is the western terminus for interstate flights.

There is an extensive air network within the State, reaching remote towns, missions and stations. Towns with air service include Albany, Derby, Esperance, Geraldton, Kalgoorlie, Kununurra, Learmonth, Mt Tom Price, Onslow, Port Hedland, Roebourne, Rottnest Island, Wittenoom and Wyndham.

BUS SERVICE

Outside the metropolitan area a regular bus service to some country towns is operated by the railway road service.

RAIL SERVICE

Covers only the southern part of the State.

HIRE-DRIVE VEHICLES

Cars, and in a few cases four wheel drives and trucks, are available in the Perth area and the following country towns: Albany, Carnarvon, Dampier, Esperance, Geraldton, Kalgoorlie, Mt Newman, Port Hedland, Wittenoom, Kununurra.

TOURS

Include spring wildflower tours (enquire W.A. Government Tourist Bureau) and 'package' deal tours to the north and North West.

PROTECTION OF NATIVE FAUNA

Fauna reserves and national parks play a major part in the overall plan for conservation of fauna; these are detailed elsewhere.

Outside these reserves, fauna is protected through the Fauna Conservation Act. All native vertebrate terrestrial fauna, except those species declared vermin or otherwise unprotected, are protected against being taken, hunted or confined. In Western Australia the native fauna subject to any degree of human predation are ducks, eagles, kangaroos, emus and the dingo. Red Kangaroos and Hill Kangaroos, or euros, which until now have been killed in huge numbers for the pet food industry, have during 1970 come under controls to ensure conservation of the species and at the same time to provide a stable level of 'harvesting' of kangaroos for the industry. The Grey Kangaroo is now protected, and Red Kangaroos and euros may be taken only by landholders, leaseholders and licensed professional kangaroo shooters and only in the shires of Ashburton, Sandstone, Cue, Carnarvon, Meekatharra, Mt Magnet, Murchison, Roebourne, Tableland, Upper Gascoyne, West Kimberley, Wiluna, Hall's Creek, Kalgoorlie, Laverton, Broome, Leonora, Wyndham, Menzies, Marble Bar, Yalgoo, Nullagine, Port Hedland and Mount Marshall. This control now allows a reasonable level to be set on the number of kangaroos killed, so that they neither become an excessive nuisance on pastoral properties nor on the other hand are in danger of extermination.

Fresh-water crocodiles have been fully protected for some time in Western Australia, but there is still some poaching. Recently there have been some fines and confiscation of boats and other equipment imposed on persons caught. During 1970 salt-water crocodiles were given full protection. Both species occur, in Western Australia, only in the Kimberleys, where they have become rare.

PROTECTION OF NATIVE FLORA

As with fauna, national parks and nature reserves are vital in conservation of flora, while State forests, crown lands, water catchment areas and road verges all play a part. In Western Australia, rather than a list of protected flowers, *all* wildflowers of certain areas are protected:

(a) all Crown lands, State forests, lands reserved for public purposes under the provisions of the Land Act and every road with the South West and Eucla Divisions of the State; and
(b) outside the South West and Eucla Divisions of the State, the land reserved for the protection of indigenous flora or fauna.

But although picking is prohibited, burning of roadsides and small reserves at excessively frequent intervals, ploughing of firebreaks along road verges, and the bulldozing of roadside vegetation by some shires, State and Commonwealth government departments is causing heavier loss of wildflowers than any picking of flowers could do. The commercial picking of a few species, particularly kangaroo-paws of several types, and the golden verticordias, for sale in Perth, makes an alarmingly heavy demand on these plants, although they are supposed to come only from private land with consent of the owner.

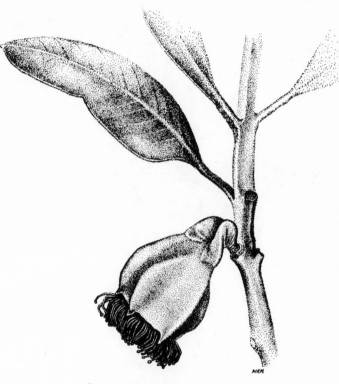

Square-fruited Mallee
Eucalyptus tetraptera

THE ROUND HOUSE, Fremantle, built in 1831 as a gaol.

REGIONAL TOURIST GUIDE

PERTH AND ENVIRONS

The City of Perth, on the northern shores of the wide Swan River, is the centre of a compact region containing more than two-thirds of the State's one million inhabitants. Perth is an isolated city, 1,700 miles across the desert from the nearest eastern Australian city, Adelaide. Yet in recent years it has become something of an international capital with the sudden influx of visitors involved in mining, investment, industry and tourism.

The Perth region includes Western Australia's principal port, Fremantle, situated only twelve miles westward, and Kwinana, twenty miles to the south-west on the shores of Cockburn Sound.

Attractions of the Perth area include:

1 Beaches. The ocean beaches close to Perth are Cottesloe, North Cottesloe, Swanbourne, South Beach, City Beach, Scarborough, North Beach and Sorrento. River beaches include Nedlands, Como, Peppermint Grove, Point Walter and Mosman Bay. The beaches nearest the city, though partly sheltered by Rottnest and Garden islands, offer some surf, while beaches towards Rockingham are more sheltered and popular for small boats, and swimming for children.

2 Darling Ranges, only about twelve miles east of Perth, are forested and form an attractive residential area; from high points extensive views of city and eastern suburbs may be obtained, while the bushland has a great variety of wildflowers in spring.

3 Fremantle, the 'Western Gateway' to Australia, has a population of approximately 26,000, and is situated at the mouth of the Swan, twelve miles west of Perth. The port has container handling facilities, bulk wheat loading, and a modern passenger terminal, this being the first Australian port for most liners from Europe. The town was settled in 1829, and consequently has many historic buildings: the Town Hall (1887); the Round House (1831, oldest building in the State); and many others built in the period 1854 to 1898.

4 Historic buildings around Perth:

The Old Town Hall at the corner of Barrack and Hay Streets in the city was built in 1867-70. Nearby is a plaque in the pavement marking the place of the founding of Perth in 1829.

Government House, built in 1859-64 in Romantic Gothic style, is set in large formal gardens, St George's Terrace. (Not open for inspection.)

Barracks Archway, at the western end of St George's Terrace, is the remains of a much larger brick building completed in 1867. The rest of the building was demolished in 1966 to make way for the Mitchell Freeway.

The Old Mill, at the southern end of the Narrows Bridge, South Perth, has been restored to its original appearance, and houses relics of the pioneering days.

Old Court House, situated in Stirling Gardens was built in 1836 and is now the oldest building in the city. It is of primitive Georgian architecture; it is now used as an industrial court.

Old Gaol and Courthouse, Beaufort Street, now part of the museum and art gallery, was built 1856.

St George's Cathedral, Cathedral Avenue.

St Mary's Cathedral, Victoria Square.

Treasury Building, built 1874, at the corner of St. George's Terrace and Barrack Street.

The Cloisters, St George's Terrace, 1858.

5 John Forrest National Park, 16 miles east along the Great Eastern Highway, preserves some 4,000 acres of bushland on top of the Darling Ranges overlooking the city; good spring wildflowers, river swimming pool.

6 King's Park has a thousand acres of semi-natural bushland overlooking the city, the river and the Narrows Bridge. There are roads and paths through the park, and lookout points commanding superb views. King's Park contains the Botanic Gardens, with thousands of wildflowers, from all parts of the State, in cultivation. Nearby in the park is the Pioneer Women's Memorial Fountain in landscaped surroundings, the War Memorial, and a restaurant.

7 Kwinana, situated on the shores of the sheltered natural harbour of Cockburn Sound, has been planned as a major industrial complex.

First was the B.P. oil refinery, followed by the B.H.P. integrated iron and steel industry (with iron ore coming by rail 250 miles from Koolyanobbing), the Alcoa alumina refinery (bauxite from the Darling Ranges), and the Western Mining Corporation's nickel refinery. Residential areas have been established nearby.

8 Mundaring Weir. Built in 1902 to supply the eastern goldfields through a 350 mile pipeline, this concrete wall dam is 25 miles east of Perth on the Helena River. An old disused pumping station, made redundant by new electric pumps, is now the C. Y. O'Connor (who was the project engineer) historical museum.

9 Rottnest Island, a low sandy island twelve miles west of Fremantle, is a very popular summer resort. It is a public reserve and wildlife sanctuary, admirably suited to water sports such as fishing, skin-diving, swimming and yachting.

10 Serpentine Dam, the newest of Perth's big reservoirs in the hills, is a massive earth-fill wall 171 feet high, a contrast to the concrete walls of the older Canning and Mundaring dams. This man-made lake is set in virgin jarrah forest south of Perth. The immediate vicinity of the wall has been skilfully landscaped with many Western Australian flowering trees, shrubs and smaller wildflowers.

11 The University of Western Australia, near the Swan River at Nedlands, has many fine buildings, a blending of old and modern architecture, set in extensive gardens. Two of the most prominent buildings are Winthrop Hall and the library building.

12 Yanchep National Park, situated near the coast 32 miles north of Perth, has an expanse of natural bushland with many wildflowers in spring, limestone caves richly decorated with stalactites and stalagmites, and several lakes. The ocean beach is quite close. Accommodation in or near the park includes hotel, lodge, guest house, caravan and camping park.

13 Towns of Perth Region:

Armadale, 19 miles south-east on the edge of the forested Darling Range, is a residential outer suburb bordering on extensive State forest country, dairying and orchard country. The *Olde Narrogin Inne,* built in 1856 at the junction of Albany and South-West highways, is still in use.

Rockingham, twenty-eight miles south of Perth, is a seaside resort on the sheltered waters of Cockburn Sound, where yachting and other water sports are popular.

Serpentine, on the South-West Highway, where the falls are the main attraction.

14 Perth Metropolitan Caravan Parks are situated as follows:

Swan Garden Caravan Park, Toodyay Road, Middle Swan. Tel. 74 2420;

Caraglen Caravan Park, Kalamunda Road, Bushmead. Tel. 74 2351;

Forrestfield Caravan Park, Hawtin Road, Forrestfield. Tel. 69 6378;

Perth Caravan Park, Hale Road, Forrestfield. Tel. 69 6111;

Kenlorn Caravan Park, 224 Treasure Road, Queens Park. Tel. 68 2604;

Orange Grove Caravan Park, Lot 19, Kelvin Road, Orange Grove. Tel. 69 6226

Caravan Village, Albany Highway, Gosnells. Tel. 96 2746;

Lakeview Terrace Caravan Park, Lake Road, Kelmscott. Tel. 97 5646;

Como Beach Caravan Park, 4 Ednah Street, Como. Tel. 67 1286;

Franklin Caravan Park, West Coast Highway, Sorrento. Tel. 47 2072.

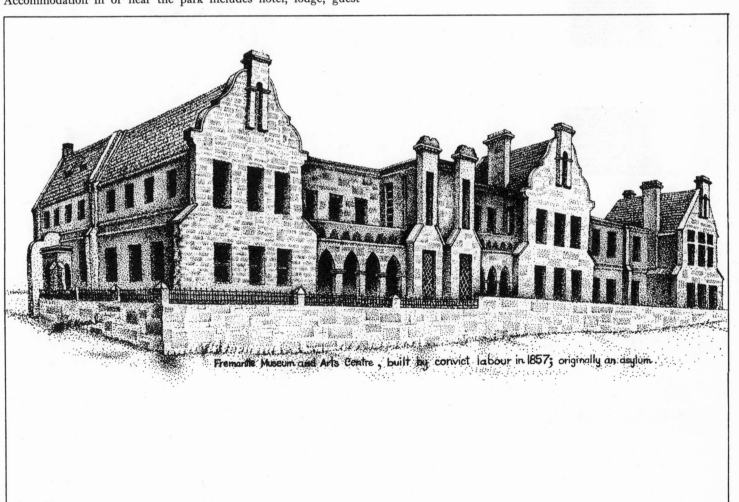

Fremantle Museum and Arts Centre, built by convict labour in 1857; originally an asylum.

THE SOUTH WEST: BUNBURY REGION

The region centred upon the port of Bunbury covers more than eight thousand square miles and supports a population of eighty thousand people. The region is rich in agriculture, timber and minerals, and has adequate power, water supplies and transport.

Bunbury is on the west coast one hundred miles south of Perth. It is the region's centre of transport and industry. The South West is one of the State's main agricultural areas, the centre of dairying and fruit growing. Some areas, particularly the Waroona, Harvey and Collie River districts, are irrigated for more intensive production of milk.

South and south-east from Bunbury are the major forests of Western Australia, with most of the State's 3,000,000 acres of prime jarrah forest and almost all of its 800,000 acres of karri.

Minerals of the region include coal at Collie, tin at Greenbushes and ilmenite at Capel. Bauxite is to be mined in the ranges of the hinterland and refined at Pinjarra and Bunbury.

Most of the natural attractions of the region are in the less developed parts, where there is a rural atmosphere and large tracts of bushland and forests, including majestic karri. Features of interest, in the vicinity of towns of the Bunbury region, include:

Augusta, a small town, one of the oldest settlements in the State, situated at the mouth of the Blackwood River near Cape Leeuwin. Nearby are the magnificent Jewel Caves, where there is a main cavern 95 feet high, 270 feet long and 140 feet wide. Some sections have clear pools of water, while throughout the variety and colour of stalactites, stalagmites and other formations is exceptional. Augusta offers river and ocean beaches, enclosed waters for boating, coastal scenery and natural bushland. There are several caravan and camping areas with all facilities.

Balingup, a small town 150 miles south of Perth; district activities are principally fruit growing, timber, dairy farming, sheep, and cheese manufacture.

Busselton, situated on Geographe Bay, 148 miles south of Perth, is one of the South West's most popular holiday resorts, with good ocean beaches. Local features of interest are:

1 **Historic buildings:** St Mary's Church, built 1843 and the oldest stone church in W.A.; *Cattle Chosen,* homestead of pioneer settler John Garrett Bussell; the Old Flour Mill; Busselton Museum, built 1855.

2 **Ilmenite mining** may be seen at Wonnerup, and on the Bunbury–Busselton road at Capel. This is an opportunity to see the effect of extensive open-cut mining upon the environment.

3 **Yallingup Caves,** situated some 20 miles to the south-west, are richly decorated with stalactites, columns, shawls and other formations. Accommodation at Caves House, caravans parks along coast.

4 **Coastal Scenery.** The coastal stretch from Cape Naturaliste to Cape Leeuwin is in places rugged, with rocky headlands such as Canal Rocks, and in other places has superb beaches with good surf and fishing.

5 **Sports facilities** include golf, tennis, bowling, sailing, fishing.

Collie, 125 miles south of Perth, is best known for its coal, produced by both open cut and deep mining methods; some of the coal is used by the nearby Muja power station which feeds electricity into the State grid. Other local activities include sheep and dairy farming.

Mandurah, a popular holiday resort 47 miles from Perth at the entrance of Peel Inlet, where there is a wide expanse of protected water for boating and fishing. There are several flora and fauna reserves on the shores of the inlet.

Manjimup, one of the State's principal timber milling towns. Other district activities include beef, fat lamb and butter production. There are two historic homesteads, built in 1856. Hotel, motel and caravan park facilities.

Northcliffe, a small town south of Manjimup and Pemberton, in timber and dairy country; from here a road leads south to the beautiful coastline of Point D'Entrecasteaux and Windy Harbour.

Pemberton, town of the 'Kingdom of the Karri', is 211 miles south of Perth. The small sawmilling town is in a valley between hills covered with tall karri trees, some of the best areas having been preserved in Warren National Park, Beedelup National Park, Carey Park, Brockway forest and Big Brook forest. Other attractions close to Pemberton include the Gloucester Tree with a fire lookout room 200 feet above the ground, and Fonty's Pool on the Manjimup road. One building, Warren House, dates back to 1872. Sports available include trout fishing in forest streams, river swimming pool, golf course and tennis courts. Accommodation includes hotel, guest house and caravan-camping grounds, with all facilities, in very attractive karri setting.

THE SOUTH WEST: ALBANY REGION

Albany is the principal town and port for the whole south coastal region; it is situated on the shores of a deep landlocked natural harbour 254 miles from Perth. The town has a history going back to the earliest settlements of the west. The magnificent harbour, surrounded by hills, is in itself a tourist attraction, with panoramic views from the summit of Mt Clarence, overlooking the town.

Albany is a port for the export of wheat and wool. Local industries include whaling, superphosphate manufacture, salmon, fruit and vegetable canning, and woollen mills.

Places of interest around Albany include:

1 **Ocean coastline.** For many miles westwards and east of Albany the coast is hilly, forming, deep bays, high rocky headlands, boulders, cliffs, interspersed with wide bays with magnificent white beaches and clear turquoise-green water, superbly suited to colour photography, fishing, swimming, and general sightseeing. Westwards are The Gap, Jimmy Newell's Harbour, Blowholes and Natural Bridge; east are Mt Gardner and Two People Bay (forming a special reserve for the rare Noisy Scrub Bird), Mt Manypeaks, and Cheyne Beach.

2 **Middleton Beach,** a long sweep of beach in King George Sound (part of Albany Harbour) is Albany's main swimming area.

3 **Emu Point** and **Oyster Harbour,** several miles east of Albany, provide sheltered water for children, and very popular for water-skiing, small boats.

4 **Porongorups Range** and **National Park,** 25 miles north of Albany, has steep granite hills, enormous boulders, bare granite domes, sculptured rocks on summits, karri forest on lower slopes, wildflowers in spring. Walk tracks up to Castle Rock, Devil's Slide, giving extensive views.

5 **Stirling Ranges National Park,** situated 55 miles north of Albany, has magnificent scenery of pointed peaks, cliffs, often cloud-capped. Extensive views far over flat plains from the heights. Rough climbing tracks up Bluff Knoll (3,640 ft) and Toolbrunup (3,450 ft). Outstanding for wildflowers, some of which are unique to this range.

6 **Strawberry Hill Farm,** built in 1834, is the oldest dwelling place in Western Australia; it has been restored and opened for inspection.

7 **Sports facilities:** golf courses, bowling greens, tennis courts, river, harbour and ocean 'big-game' fishing, yachting, water-skiing and water sports.

Accommodation: numerous hotels, motels, guest houses and holiday flats, and several caravan–camping parks.

Towns and local features of interest in the region include:

Cranbrook, about 270 miles south of Perth, is a small town near the western end of the Stirling Ranges, and consequently makes a good base for exploration of the very large national park. Surrounding country is wheat, sheep and cattle farming land.

Denmark, situated on the south coast west of Albany, is 257 miles from Perth via Albany Highway and Mt Barker. The Denmark River and Wilson's Inlet are very suitable for boating, swimming and fishing, making the town a very popular summer holiday resort. Nearby are karri forests and a scenic ocean coastline. Accommodation includes hotel, motel, holiday cottages, flats, guest houses and caravan park.

Mt Barker, on the Albany Highway 223 miles from Perth, still has some relics of its pioneering days, including the old gaol, the Kendenup homestead, and the old ore-crushing battery of Western Australia's early goldmine at Kendenup. Other attractions include Lake Poorarecup for swimming and water skiing, and the nearby

Porongorups and Stirling Ranges. Mt Barker is the principal town of a district which produces beef, fat lambs, apples and dairy products. Accommodation includes hotel, caravan and camping facilities.

Nornalup, a small holiday resort town on the Walpole Inlet; attractions are sightseeing amid a great deal of superb natural scenery including coastal and karri forest, as well as boating, fishing and swimming. Holiday cottages, guest houses.

Walpole, a small settlement close to Nornalup, is almost surrounded by the large Walpole-Nornalup National Park, which has magnificent stands of karri, red tingle, with wildflowers in the undergrowth and coastal sandplains. Activities include sightseeing, fishing, swimming, yachting. Hotel, guesthouse, caravan and camping.

THE SOUTH WEST: WEST COAST HINTERLAND

This region covers much of the 'grain bowl', producing almost seventy per cent of the State's wheat harvest. With an area of 41,000 square miles, and a population of 70,000, this central wheatbelt has more than one-third of Western Australia's cleared land. This region clips more wool than any other part of the West, and also produces mutton, beef cattle, oats and barley.

There are also some secondary industries, including the Wundowie charcoal iron and steel, which produces iron from ore railed from Koolyanobbing, north-east of Southern Cross.

Roads are closely interwoven throughout this region, connecting the many large and small wheatbelt towns, making the whole region easily accessible to the tourist.

Towns with features of interest for tourists include:

Beverley, on the Avon River 98 miles east of Perth, in wheat, sheep and cattle country. An aeronautical exhibition has been built as a memorial to a local aircraft builder; the history of aviation in Western Australia is told in pictures and words, and a plane built by Selby Ford in 1929 is on display.

Hyden, a small town 215 miles east of Perth. Nearby are remarkably shaped and coloured rock formations, the most famous of which is Wave Rock. Other formations in the area are King Rocks, the Humps, Hippo's Yawn, Bate's Cave and Gnamma Holes. Some bushland around the rocks has been retained, and the whole area has a good wildflower display in early spring months. Accommodation: hotel, caravan and camping grounds.

Lancelin, on the west coast about 70 miles north of Perth, is a small fishing and holiday town. Its main attraction is the unique Nambung National Park 40 miles northwards, containing the 'Pinnacles Desert', where wind erosion has exposed tall limestone pillars that rise in hundreds like giant tombstones from the sand dunes. Other parts of the coastal sandplain carry heathland vegetation with many wildflowers in spring. Four wheel drive is very helpful, though, with some walking in final approach, two wheel drive entry is usually possible.

Merredin, 162 miles east of Perth, is a major wheatbelt town on the Great Eastern Highway. Features of interest are roadside wildflowers in spring, swimming pool and other sports facilities, Memorial Library, and in September, an agricultural show which is a major event for farming community.

Narrogin, 128 miles south-east of Perth, is a major town in an important wheat and wool producing region. The major feature of tourist interest in the district is the unique Dryandra State Forest a few miles north-west of the town. As the whole wheatbelt has long been cleared and farmed, areas of entirely natural forest are now extremely rare. The Dryandra forest contains virgin wandoo woodland of the type that once covered much of the wheatbelt. It is an extremely important wildlife sanctuary for the Marsupial Anteater or Numbat, has many birds including the Mallee Fowl, and an arboretum of native flowering trees near the forestry settlement. There are good tracks, suitable for cars, through the forest. Dryandra has in recent years survived attempts to destroy it for farming, and more recently for mining. It is one of the last examples of natural environment of any size through the entire central wheatbelt, and therefore the last home of many animals and wildflowers. Accommodation includes hotel, motel and caravan-camping park.

THE OLD FARM, Strawberry Hill, Albany, completed 1836

Esperance, mid-way along the south coast and 450 miles south-east from Perth, has a past linked with the earliest voyages of discovery around the Australian coast. But only in recent years has this region been developed and the town prospered.

Esperance was named in 1792 when Rear Admiral Antoine D'Entrecasteaux's flagship *L'Recherche* and the escorting frigate *L'Esperance* anchored in the bay. Even earlier, in 1627 the Dutch navigator Pieter Nuyts had sailed into this bay. The first settlement began around 1864 and the town was established in 1893 as a port for the goldfields to the north. Attempts to grow crops on the dry mallee sandplains were largely unsuccessful until recent years when American investors—the Chase Syndicate and the Esperance Land Development Company—succeeded in bringing large tracts of land into production through the addition of chemical elements to the deficient soil. Esperance has now found added importance as the port for shipping nickel ore, salt and wheat.

The Esperance region has much to offer visitors, particularly along the coast.

Cape Le Grande National Park contains magnificent coastal scenery a few miles east of the town. Here will be found high bare granite domes and peaks, some with caves near their summits. Frenchman's Peak in particular has a huge cavern through the top. These hills meet the ocean in rocky headlands, between which are sheltered stretches of white beach. This scenic coast continues eastwards for many miles to beautiful Duke of Orleans Bay, and further again to the big new coastal national park at Cape Arid. The whole area has a good variety of wilflowers.

Archipelago of the Recherche, a maze of small rocky islands off the coast near Cape Le Grande some islands have wildlife not found on the mainland.

Pink Lake, a strange pinkish salt lake near Esperance.

Orleans Farms, where the homestead contains originals by many of Australia's best artists.

Accommodation includes hotels, motel, holiday cottages and a number of caravan and camping parks with good facilities.

Other towns of the Esperance region are:

Eucla, almost on the W.A.-S.A. State border at the head of the Great Australian Bight. Coming from the east, Eucla pass, seven miles inside Western Australia, gives a first glimpse of the ocean. The modern Eucla is on the plateau at the top of the pass. At the edge of the sea across the coastal plain is the old Eucla telegraph repeating station, built in 1877, and now almost covered by the drifting sand dunes. Modern Eucla exists to serve Nullarbor motorists. There is a roadhouse which has also a caravan park, and a hotel with self contained units, service station and some repair services.

Hopetoun, on the south coast west of Esperance, is reached by road via Ravensthorpe. The tiny town is the eastern gateway to the really magnificent coastal scenery of the big Fitzgerald River Flora and Fauna Reserve. Visible westwards from the town are the peaks of East Mt Barren, in the reserve. It is easy to drive to this peak in conventional vehicles, but four wheel drive is essential for many tracks within the reserve. It is also possible to enter from the western side from Albany via Bremer Bay. This reserve has an exceptional number of wilflowers that occur in no other place in the world, but is threatened by open-cut mining claims.

Norseman, at the western end of the Eyre Highway across the Nullarbor, is about 450 miles from Perth. Main activities are wheat and sheep farming, and the mining of gold and pyrites. When travelling from the east to Western Australia Norseman marks the beginning of two routes to Perth: turn north to Kalgoorlie then west to Perth, or go south to Esperance then along the south coast and finally north to Perth.

Ravensthorpe, near the south coast about 330 miles from Perth, is primarily a copper and magnesite mining town, but is also the centre of a pastoral and grain-growing district.

Situated 371 miles east of Perth, Kalgoorlie has been a gold mining centre for more than seventy years. Although the value of gold has in recent years declined the town has been given a new lease of life with the discovery of nickel, 35 miles south at Kambalda, 160 miles to the north-east (Poseidon), and elsewhere. Already the value of nickel is greater than the value of gold produced.

Alluvial gold was discovered at Coolgardie, 25 miles west, in 1892, causing the first gold rush. Then followed the Kalgoorlie strike on the 'Golden Mile', reputedly the richest square mile of rock ever known—to date it has produced gold worth $1,250 million.

Kalgoorlie was linked to Perth by rail in 1892, alleviating some of the hardships of life in the desert, and in 1903 the 346-mile pipeline from Mundaring Weir in the Darling Ranges was completed, bringing to the miners the luxury of abundant water.

Places of interest in an around Kalgoorlie include:

Golden Mile mines, surface workings (inspections can be arranged).

Golden Mile museum and collection of gemstones.

Kambalda model township (35 miles south), built by Western Mining Corporation for nickel miners.

Paddy Hannan's Tree, where Hannan first found gold.

School of Mines.

Accommodation at Kalgoorlie includes about thirty hotels, several

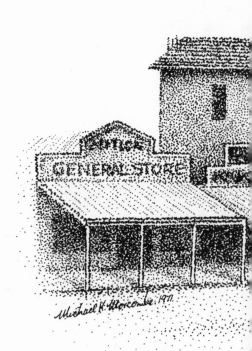

motels, guest houses, caravan and camping park.

Other towns of this region are:

Coolgardie, just 24 miles west of Kalgoorlie, is now almost a ghost town. The impressive old stone buildings that line the main street remain to show the fomer prosperity of the city that once had twenty thousand inhabitants. There are interesting museum-type displays and collections of old mining relics on display in the main street. Accommodation: several hotels, motel, and caravan-camping area.

Southern Cross, 235 miles east of Perth, is the main town of the far eastern wheatbelt. The town had its beginnings in the goldrush days of the Yilgarn field in 1887, but was soon overshadowed by the richer Coolgardie strike further into the desert. Modern developments in wheat farming have made it possible to grow wheat in this rather arid climate. Thirty-five miles away is the small 'model town' of Kool-yanobbing, near the iron ore deposits being mined by B.H.P. Ltd for the Kwinana blast furnaces.

Accommodation: hotels, motels, caravan park.

Small towns of the region: northwards from Kalgoorlie are scattered old mining and pastoral towns, like Menzies, Leonora, Laverton and Wiluna. These have a past linked with the gold-rush days, and have continued as centres for the pastoral industry. Today these outback areas have again become busy with prospecting activity for nickel and other minerals of new importance. Wiluna has abundant supplies of underground water which is now being used to begin extensive irrigation of melons and citrus trees for eastern and overseas markets, with the advantage of the hot desert climate to ripen fruit early.

THE UPPER WEST COAST: THE GERALDTON REGION

Geraldton, Western Australia's largest town north of Perth, is a principal port for the upper west coast and its hinterland, which comprises a very large and important agricultural and mineral region. Grain and wool are the principal products, about one-fifth of Western Australia's grain harvest being shipped out of Geraldton each year. Westwards, in the Indian Ocean, the Abrolhos Islands are the major rock lobster or crayfishing grounds of the State.

Tourist attractions in and near Geraldton are:

Abrolhos Islands, a cluster of many small islands set among coral reefs, where the Dutch ship *Batavia* was wrecked in 1629. Relics of this and other wrecks are still being found by skindivers along the coast. The Abrolhos are superbly suited to underwater exploration, underwater photography, and spearfishing among the coral reefs. The islands themselves are an important fauna reserve, where thousands of sea birds nest in colonies. Launch trips to the islands can be arranged.

Geraldton Sunshine Festival, usually held during the first week of the school holidays at the beginning of September.

Sea-shell museum, on highway near Geraldton.

Sports possibilities include deep-sea, coastal and spear fishing, yachting, swimming, golf, bowls.

Accommodation: numerous hotels, guest houses, motels, flats, cottages for rent, and three caravan–camping parks with all facilities.

, goldmining ghost town , with fine old Government buildings, constructed 1898

Towns of tourist interest in the Geraldton region are:

Coorow and **Carnamah,** 174 miles and 191 miles from Perth respectively, are small towns of sheep and wheat farming districts. The sandplain country in the area has an exceptional display of wildflowers in spring. There are several new national parks for conservation of wildflowers situated on sandplains west of Corow and west of Marchagee (which is just south of Coorow on the highway.)

Kalbarri, a small holiday and fishing township at the mouth of the Murchison River 103 miles north of Geraldton, is almost surrounded by the magnificent big Kalbarri National Park. The park's main scenic feature is the huge gorge of the Murchison River, about 50 miles long and 500 feet deep, cut through multicoloured rock. Most easily accessible are Hawk's Head Lookout, Ross Graham Lookout; best scenery at The Loop, Z-bend, and Double Gorge. Surrounding sandplains are very rich in wildflowers. Accommodation at Kalbarri includes hotel, flats, cottages, several caravan and camping parks. Visit Kalbarri May to September for sightseeing in river gorge, July to November for wildflowers, August to April for swimming.

Northampton, 31 miles north of Geraldton and 343 miles from Perth, is a small sheep and wheat town; there is also some lead mining in the district. For tourists the main attraction of the hilly Northampton area is the variety of spring wildflowers, which are often different to those of more inland and more flat and sandy areas. Accommodation: hotel, caravan park.

Perenjori, south-east of Geraldton and 221 miles from Perth, is a wheat and sheep farming centre whose main attraction is the bush and roadside display of wildflowers in August and September, particularly eastwards in the uncleared mulga country.

Port Gregory, on the coast not far north of Geraldton, is near a stretch of pinkish water known as Hutt Lagoon; nearby are the old ruins of the convict hiring station of Lynton.

Yalgoo, due east of Geraldton and 320 miles from Perth, is in uncleared semi-arid mulga scrub country which, provided that sufficient rain has fallen during the winter, carries massed displays of papery everlastings from July to September. A day's drive out from Geraldton through Mullewa to Yalgoo and perhaps on to Mt Magnet or south to Payne's Find can, in a good season, traverse some of the State's best displays of massed wildflowers.

THE UPPER WEST COAST: CARNARVON REGION

Carnarvon is the principal town and port of a region stretching from Shark Bay to North West Cape, covering an area of 45,000 square miles. This region has always been sparsely populated, being, with an average annual rainfall of less than ten inches, too dry for agriculture. Most of the region, covered with low mulga scrub, is used for grazing sheep.

The town is situated at the mouth of the Gascoyne River, the major river of this part of the coast. Although the river flows only after good rains over its inland catchment area (usually during a summer cyclone) there are abundant supplies of water in the deep sand of the river bed throughout the year. This is pumped out for the irrigation of the banana plantations up-river from the town.

Carnarvon has a warm and mainly dry climate from April to October, making this the best time for a visit; summer months are hot. It has become a very popular winter tourist resort.

Places of interest around Carnarvon are:

Blowholes, on coast on Quobba station 42 miles north of Carnarvon, where coast is rocky and waves spout up through holes; also a good area for fishing, collecting oysters.

Cape Couvier, about 57 miles north of Carnarvon, has multi-coloured, four hundred foot high cliffs.

Carnarvon Space Tracking Station, just east of the town on Brown Range, is part of a world-wide network of American space vehicle tracking stations. Conducted tours can be arranged only through the Carnarvon district tourist bureau.

Miaboolya Beach, six miles north of Carnarvon, off the Quobba road.

Oyster Creek, about five miles south of Carnarvon, is a good place for fishing from small boats.

Rocky Pool, a permanent waterhole and swimming pool on the Gascoyne River 34 miles west of Carnarvon on the Junction road.

Sports: water skiing, swimming, boating, fishing. Big-game fishing can be arranged through tourist bureau. Also tennis, bowling.

Accommodation: numerous hotels, motels, caravan and camping parks.

TOWNS OF THE CARNARVON REGION

Denham (Shark Bay), 567 miles north of Perth, is the only town in the Shark Bay area. It is situated on the west coast of Peron Peninsula in the centre of Shark Bay. Fishing and fish processing are the main local activities. The main tourist season is April to August, when the weather is warm but not too hot. Principal attractions are fishing and water sports. Accommodation includes hotel, caravan parks.

Exmouth is situated on the eastern side of North West Cape, 250 miles north of Carnarvon. The Cape has excellent beach and game fishing, while there is outstanding scenery in Cape Range National Park, where there are deep gorges and high cliffs. Near the tip of the Cape is the American V.L.F. radio transmitting station with towers more than a thousand feet high. Accommodation: hotels, motels, caravan and camping parks.

Gascoyne Junction, 110 miles east of Carnarvon, is the only town in a wide area of pastoral country where sheep stations average 90,000 acres each. The Kennedy Ranges running north from the Junction have creeks, springs and lush vegetation in their gorges, in spite of their barren appearance.

THE NORTHWEST: ASHBURTON REGION

The Ashburton region takes its name from the major local river, and covers approximately the same area as the drainage basin of that river and its tributaries, altogether about 24,000 square miles.

Onslow, 890 miles north of Perth, is the principal town and port of the region. Because the climate is so arid grazing of sheep on large stations is the principal activity, and the population is sparse and scattered; the population of Onslow and its hinterland is only about thirteen thousand. Onslow is the nearest mainland port for the commercial oilfield of Barrow Island. Features of interest around Onslow include:

Ashburton River, a major river which flows strongly only after one of the unpredictable cyclones have brought rain, usually in summer. The road to Onslow crosses the river south of the town. Like other north-western rivers the Ashburton is lined with white-trunked river gums, making it cool, shaded and green after the endless dry mulga and spinifex plains. These riverside trees attract birds, and in favourable seasons thousands of budgerigars, galahs and corellas nest in the hollows of trees along this and other watercourses of the north-west.
Fishing places: Two-mile Creek, Four-mile Creek, and town jetty.
Old Police Station, Onslow.
Accommodation: hotel, caravan park.

THE NORTHWEST: THE PILBARA REGION

The Pilbara covers a huge area of 171,462 square miles, extending from the Indian Ocean to the Northern Territory border, and from the Tropic of Capricorn northwards to the Kimberleys.

In recent years the Pilbara region has been the scene of major developments in iron ore discovery, mining and export. New towns have appeared in the semi-desert north-western interior, harbours have been deepened or constructed, and hundreds of miles of railways have been built in a region which for more than a century has been able to support only pastoral activities and a very sparse population.

Most of iron ore mining activity is in the Hamersley and Ophthalmia Ranges, over an area of about 25,000 square miles, where estimates of ore reserves go as high as twenty thousand million tons or more. The biggest single deposit at present being worked, Mt Whaleback, is believed to contain two thousand million tons, and others could prove to be larger.

Other developments in the Pilbara include solar salt, produced by solar evaporation of seawater on shallow coastal lakes and inlets, and inland salt lakes.

However most visitors to the North West are more interested in the magnificent natural scenery. The rugged red and golden ranges, deep gorges and oasis-like river pools provide some of Australia's most spectacular scenery and a richness of colour that must be seen to be believed.

The Pilbara region is extremely hot from October to April, with the possibility of cyclones and flooding rains. From May to September the days are warm, dry, and nights reasonably cool. While roads in some areas have improved, with the bitumen creeping gradually further north, most roads, even though called 'highways', can often be rough and sometimes dangerous with deep holes, rocks and hundreds of miles of severe corrugations.

Towns of the Pilbara, and their local attractions, are:

Dampier, on the coast 40 miles west of Roebourne, about one thousand miles from Perth, was the first of the large iron ore ports. A huge iron ore pelletizing plant is the main secondary industry, while solar salt is collected nearby. The port's loading facilities are highly mechanized. While the townsite is open to visitors, a permit must be obtained from the operating company for inspection of works and port.

Goldsworthy, first of the new mining towns, located 70 miles east of Port Hedland.

Karratha, a few miles from Dampier, will be the town for the nearby industrial and port towns; an eventual population of 25,000 is envisaged.
Marble Bar, said to be the most consistently hot town in Australia, is situated in rugged hill country which contains many minerals, including tin and manganese.

The main local attraction is the Marble Bar Pool, three miles west of the town, where a bar of coloured jasperlite rock has a marble-like appearance. The surrounding country has a rich flora and fauna which is concentrated along rivers, creeks, and waterholes.

Other Marble Bar features of interest are the State gold battery a mile from the town, a large tin-separating plant on the Nullagine road, and scenery along roads west of Nullagine.
Accommodation: hotel, caravan and camping park.
Newman, a new mining town 230 miles south of Port Hedland. Nearby at Mt Whaleback huge iron ore mining operations are under way. Guided tours of the mining operations can be arranged through the Walkabout Motel or at the Newman Mining Company's office.

Town facilities include swimming pool, motel, picture gardens.
Paraburdoo, south of Wittenoom and Mt Tom Price, is another mining town under construction.
Port Hedland, one of the older towns of the region, is situated on a small island and is reached over a built-up causeway across tidal mudflats. The town, particularly its business and industrial activities, has grown greatly with the exploitation of minerals further inland.

The country inland of Port Hedland is flat or slightly hilly, almost treeless, with spinifex; the main interest of this town is more as a stopping point en route to scenic areas of Wittenoom to the south or the Kimberleys in the north. Some places of interest at Hedland are: Finucane Island loading facilities (organized tours), Mt Goldsworthy iron ore mining (organized tours), Royal Flying Doctor base, and Pretty Pool, where there are Aboriginal carvings, and opportunity of swimming, collecting shells.
Accommodation: hotels, motel, several caravan and camping parks.
Roebourne, 1,000 miles from Perth, is an historic town on the north-west coastal highway, and centre of one of the oldest northern pastoral districts. Places of interest are:

Cossack, a ghost town eight miles from Roebourne, an important pearling port during the period 1866 to about 1885. The old buildings, beautifully designed and constructed of local stone, still stand basically intact.
Port Sampson, formerly important for export of asbestos.
Whim Creek, copper mine.
Accommodation: hotel, camping and caravan park.
Tom Price, located high in the Hamersley Ranges, is a new iron ore town with air-conditioned homes and suburban amenities such as swimming pool, community centre, supermarket and golf course. Permission to inspect iron ore workings should be obtained from the Hamersley Iron Pty Ltd office in Tom Price.
Wittenoom, at the foot of the Hamersley Ranges, is close to the spectacular gorge country of these ranges. The town was once important for asbestos mining, exists now mainly for the tourist trade, and may find new importance through iron ore. Places of interest are:

Wittenoom Gorge, Dale's Gorge, Yampire Gorge, Jubilla Gorge, Red Gorge, and Hamersley Gorge, all with incredible colours of deep red rock, white-trunked, bright green foliaged trees, all a bright colour contrast against the deep blue sky, and darker river pools.
Joffre Falls and Cascade Falls, are also near Wittenoom in the Hamersleys.
Mt Herbert, on the road from Wittenoom to Roebourne, gives panoramic views over incredibly-coloured rugged low ranges.
Python Pool, not far south-east of Mt Herbert, has a waterfall that drops to a deep rock pool.
Millstream, off the Wittenoom-Roebourne road, has a large river pool, dense riverside vegetation and trees, making a delightful cool green oasis in this hot dry area.
Accommodation: hotel, caravan and camping grounds.

THE KIMBERLEYS : WEST KIMBERLEY

The West Kimberley region comprises some 60,000 square miles of the most rugged, least-known country in Western Australia, as well as extensive grasslands used for production of beef cattle. Located in the tropical far-north, this region receives summer rains ranging from 15 inches per annum in the south to 40 inches or more along the northern coast.

About 1880 it was realized that the best quality pearlshell along the coast was obtained around Roebuck Bay, so a settlement at this spot, later known as Broome, became the headquarters of pearling.

For the tourist one of the main attractions of the Kimberleys will be the superb natural scenery, particularly of ranges and river gorges. West Kimberley towns are:

Broome, situated in Roebuck Bay, 1,370 road miles north of Perth, is best known as the home port of pearling luggers. At one time there were as many as four hundred luggers based here, until the use of plastics in place of pearlshell made pearling unprofitable. Now only a few luggers work from Broome, supplying oysters to the Kuri Bay cultured pearl industry, on the coast north of Derby. A large meatworks, designed to handle about 35,000 cattle a year, is now the main local industry.

Places of interest near Broome are:

Bedford Park, containing the War Memorial and Dampier's Chest.

Buccaneer Rock, in Roebuck Bay at the entrance of Dampier Creek, reputed to be the place where Dampier careened *Roebuck* in 1699.

Cable Beach, a good beach near Broome, named because it was the terminus of a cable under the sea to Java.

Dinosaur's tracks, imprinted in ancient sediments now hardened into sandstone, situated at the base of the cliffs of Gantheaume Point. The footprints were made by a dinosaur about 130 million years ago, and can be seen only at low tide.

Missions, at Beagle Bay and Lombadina; these are accessible only by four wheel drive.

Museum of firearms and convict irons, at the police station.

Pearling luggers, are often to be seen drawn up at the waterfront. A feature of interest is the 34 ft rise and fall of tides.

Accommodation: hotels, guest house, caravan and camping park.

Derby is situated in King Sound some 1,460 road miles north of Perth. The town's importance is due mainly to its beef producing hinterland. From 1949 to 1962 the much-publicised air-beef scheme was in operation, meat being flown across the King Leopold Ranges from Glenroy Station to Derby or Wyndham. This air beef scheme has been discontinued now that 'beef roads' have been constructed over the rugged King Leopold Ranges.

Places of interest around Derby are:

King Leopold Ranges, crossed by the Gibb River beef road approximately 90 to 100 miles north-east of Derby. The road climbs into the ranges and winds through narrow gorges for many miles, giving many views of this extremely rough country.

Fitzroy River, one of the biggest rivers in Australia, reaches the sea just south of Derby. Though it is only a chain of pools in the dry season it carries enormous flood during the wet. It is crossed by the Broome-Derby highway.

Mowanjum Aboriginal Mission, just south of Derby, where Aboriginal painting and carvings may be seen and purchased.

Windjana Gorge and Tunnel Creek, about 80 and 90 miles north-east of Derby; magnificent gorge of Lennard River through limestone ranges. Tunnel Creek flows through a huge cavern beneath the ranges.

Sport facilities include swimming pool, golf course, fishing in rivers and estuaries for barramuda.

Accommodation: hotel, motel and caravan park.

Fitzroy Crossing is a tiny settlement 170 miles east of Derby, where the Derby-Wyndham highway crosses the Fitzroy River.

Local features of interest are:

CARVED BOAB NUT, from the Mowanjum Aboriginal Mission near Derby ; depicts a dreamtime Wandjina.

Geikie Gorge National Park, about five miles from the town where the Fitzroy has carved a meandering gorge through the limestone ranges. A boat is an advantage here. There are permanent pools along the river through the dry season, containing freshwater crocodiles, barramundi, sawfish, stingrays. River trees and pools a great attraction for birds.

Accommodation: Hotel.

THE KIMBERLEYS : EAST KIMBERLEY REGION

The East Kimberley is the most northern part of Western Australia, and shares a common border with the 'top end' of the Northern Territory. With an area of 79,000 square miles it is almost the size of the State of Victoria, yet has a population of less than five thousand people. The greater part of this region consists of rugged ranges and plateaux, particularly in the north and north-western parts, while its eastern section has extensive grassland plains.

The ranges and plateaux, with flat tops and vertical cliffs, combined with jagged ridges and deep river gorges of red rock make spectacular scenery. Much of the northern Kimberleys is accessible only to four wheel drive vehicles, and even greater areas are accessible only by horseback or helicopter. Along remote northern rivers such as the Drysdale is scenery of river gorges, pools, lush tropical vegetation, wildlife, and Aboriginal paintings of the Wandjina type.

The climate is dry from April to October, with monsoon rains from December to March. April and May are probably the best months to visit the far north, before the country becomes too dry and dusty late in the dry season.

Wyndham, not far from the Northern Territory border, is the most northerly port in Western Australia, serving as the port for cattle export and for the Ord River farms. There is a large meatworks at the town. Places of interest near Wyndham are:

Button's Gap.

Crocodile Lagoon, Marlgu Lagoon, and Police Lagoon, have abundant bird life.

The Grotto, a deep rocky waterhole hear the town.

Sixteen-mile Billabong.

Spectacular scenery along road to Kununurra.

Sports include fishing, deep-sea fishing (boats can be hired). Accommodation: several hotels, caravan and camping park.

Kununurra, a modern town 66 miles south-east of Wyndham, is the administration and residential centre of the Ord River Scheme. The Ord plan involves storage of wet season floodwaters in a huge dam to irrigate 178,000 acres of potentially rich blacksoil plains. A diversion dam has been built, and construction is now proceeding on the main dam at a site about 30 miles further upstream. This main reservoir will cover 286 square miles; its main purpose is to keep the downstream diversion dam full during the dry season, and eventually to generate hydro-electricity.

Crops to be grown include cotton, safflower, linseed and sugar cane. Places of interest are:

Argyle Downs homestead, an historic building which will be flooded when the main dam eventually fills.

Cotton ginnery.

Kimberley Research Station.

Kelly's Knob lookout.

Middle Springs, and Thompson Springs.

Hidden Valley.

Aboriginal rock paintings.

Sports: fishing (most places require four wheel drive) and water skiing on diversion dam lake.

Accommodation: hotel, caravan and camping park.

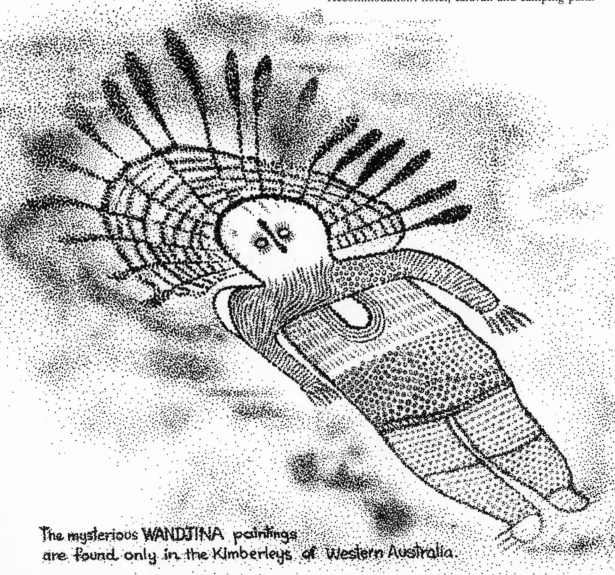

The mysterious WANDJINA paintings are found only in the Kimberleys of Western Australia.

Xantostemon paradoxus, a yellow-flowered tree of the Kimberleys

Victoria

FOOTBRIDGE, TARRA VALLEY, GIPPSLAND

THE LUCKY STATE

Victoria is perhaps the luckiest State in the Australian Commonwealth. It has little of the monotonous wasteland that fills much of the other Australian States. Its landscape, instead, is a rich aggregation of farm, bush and city; mountain, valley and plain; river, lake and coastal mixture of charm and grandeur.

Everywhere in Victoria there is wealth, or the potential for it—in the great forest lands, the rich dairy pasture and the huge brown coal deposits of Gippsland; in the fertile mountain valleys of the north-west; in the grazing, crop and cattle lands of the north-west; in the Western District, where the sheep was king and still clings determinedly to its tottering throne; in the wheatlands of the Wimmera and Mallee; and in great industrial complexes in Melbourne and decentralised areas like Geelong, Dandenong, Morwell, Shepparton and Warrnambool. Even the sea has produced wealth for the State in scarcely tapped oil and natural gas deposits.

So, Victoria is a most highly industrialised State, taking up only 3 per cent of the national area but carrying 28 per cent of the population (3,384,000 people) and making or growing one-third of the Gross National Product. The increasing output and value of its factory production has balanced the downturn of its rural production, but has added to the problem of increasing centralisation of population and activity on the capital, Melbourne, which sprawls now in untidy middle age on the undulating plain edged by the Dandenong Ranges and Port Phillip Bay.

Certain country centres are, at last, breaking away from the cultural and social stranglehold of Melbourne, recognising, perhaps, the benefit of living away from a city of such pace and momentum.

The Victorian is perhaps less overtly Australian than his countryman in other, harsher areas. His neighbours, and the devices of civilisation, are nearer at hand, and the time for elemental resourcefulness is long past. He is proud of his State, or at least happy with it, but in a mild and negative way that contrasts with the sometimes aggressive championing of other regions.

THE JAMIESON RIVER

MELBOURNE'S ARCHITECTURAL SCHIZOPHRENIA

Melbourne suffers from the architectural schizophrenia of all the big cities of the world . . . its classic Georgian and ornate Victorian buildings of the formative years when wool, gold and protected industry were its life blood, its wide tree-lined streets and the leafy avenues of approach which radiate from its centre vie now with high-rise columns of concrete and glass and the ersatz Americana of shopping malls, piped music and flashing signs.

The balance of old and new is a stimulating visual cocktail, but the fresh holes in the ground are there to indicate that the balance is swinging inexorably to the new.

But the trams still trundle on the grid pattern of streets, to the delight of tourists and the disgust of the strap hanging citizens; a grandly conceived square has given the city a much needed focal point, and the steely hand of authority and public opinion has kept the developer's blade from the magnificent encircling gardens which, with the River Yarra, are the city's main natural assets.

The river flows, albeit sluggishly, past the spot where, in 1838, John Batman proclaimed his village, and into the port which clusters around its mouth—a port receiving 3,000 vessels a year and loading about two-thirds of the cargo weight it receives—wool, wheat, beef, butter, fruit, and a vast range of manufactured goods.

It is this centralised factory production which has been mainly responsible for the city's phenomenal growth from the early 50's into an over populated enclave with a 15-mile radius of suburban density. Also responsible is the egalitarian Australian hunger for a house and a bit of land. At their best—in suburbs like Toorak, Kew, Malvern, Brighton, Beaumaris, Balwyn—the houses and their surrounds are magnificent. At their worst, they stretch south and east in flat monotony. A revitalisation of the old inner city suburbs and a fine, new cosmopolitan spirit in a city already noted for its restaurants and theatres does much to make up for the creeping conformity of suburbia, and matches Melbourne's new boast of internationalism.

BOTANICAL GARDENS, MELBOURNE

BOURKE STREET, MELBOURNE'S MAIN SHOPPING STREET

RAILWAY YARDS SERVING SUBURBAN NETWORK

THE SOUTH-EASTERN FREEWAY
LINE UP AT CAR PRODUCTION WORKS

THE PORT OF MELBOURNE

BANK BUILDING STATUARY
OLD CITY BUILDINGS REFLECT IN NEW GLASS HOUSE

CAPTAIN COOK'S COTTAGE
BOURKE STREET'S DAILY BUSTLE

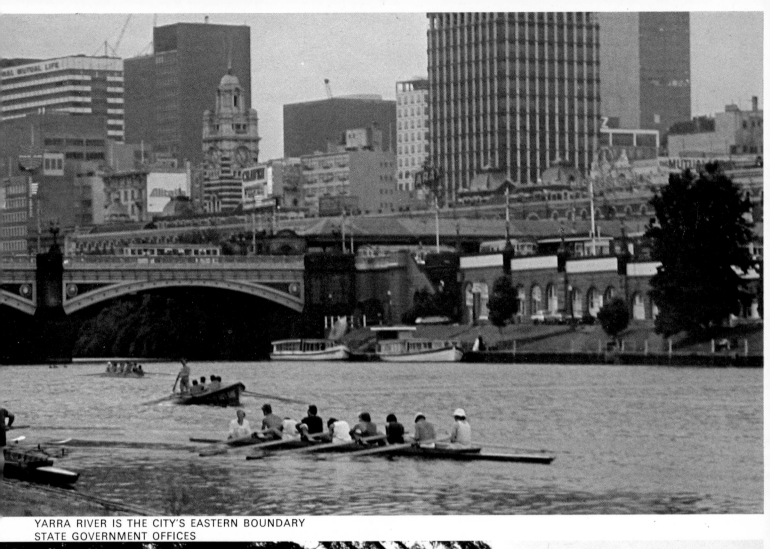

YARRA RIVER IS THE CITY'S EASTERN BOUNDARY
STATE GOVERNMENT OFFICES

A CITY OF EVENTS

Melbourne is a great city of events—its sporting, cultural and recreational fixtures are at the very core of the city's life, and the serious working world must make way for them.

Melbourne is the only city in the world which takes a day off for a horse race, but the Melbourne Cup classic at Flemington is no ordinary race. At its starting time of 3.00 p.m. on the first Tuesday of November, the whole nation stops work to listen to the race broadcast. For Melburnian's the whole Cup week is full calendar of race meetings and social gatherings.

A few weeks before is another, perhaps even more tumultuous highlight of the sporting year—the Victorian Football League Grand Final. Crowds of 120,000—plus pack the great stands of the Melbourne Cricket Ground to watch the heroes whose deeds have enthralled them through the winter months battle it out for the ultimate glory of the season.

The M.C.G. is also considered to be one of the great cricket grounds of the world. It has been host to the world record cricket crowd, and is always the biggest drawer of crowds to Test matches in Australia.

Perhaps this is because Melbourne, an Olympic city, is sports mad—every weekend in the appropriate season, the footballers, cricketers, lawn bowlers, tennis players, surfers, yachtsmen, athletes, golfers, etc. are out in the ample play areas of the city and suburbs.

One such place is Albert Park, two miles from the city centre. With a lake for rowing and sailing, two golf courses, cricket, hockey and football ovals, tennis and basketball courts and squash, badminton and table tennis centres, it is a sportsman's mecca.

But recreation in Melbourne is not all sport. It has Moomba, a successful annual festival of fun and culture, which culminates in a great city parade. It has in its Cultural Centre one of the finest art gallery complexes in the world, and other private galleries catering for a vigorous artistic interest. It is the home of the Australian Ballet Company, and is noted for its reception of both repertory and commercial theatre. It is the Melbourne audiences that guarantee the West End and Broadway musicals a profitable run in Australia.

Melbourne has been liberated from its archaic licensing laws, and has cast off its reputation of being a city of stay-at-homes—and even on Sundays, the pall of Victorian solemnity is no longer completely opaque.

ANNUAL OUTDOOR ART SHOW

LEAGUE FOOTBALL DRAWS BIG CROWDS

SUBURBAN BILLY CART DERBY
RETURN TO SCALE AFTER MELBOURNE CUP

INTERNATIONAL MOTOR RACE AT SANDOWN

A MOUNTAIN PLAYGROUND NEARBY

DANDENONG'S RESTAURANT
PICNIC IN DANDENONGS PARK

The blue hazed vista of the Dandenong Ranges hangs in Melbourne's eastern skyline, giving a physical focus and visual pleasure to the citizens on the undulating lowland below.

This is their other playground, and an autumn or winter day 'in the hills' is as familiar to them as a summer day on the beach.

There is much for them there—the roads wind through the picturesque mountain country, where great Eucalypts and ferny glades make a fine botanic confluence with introduced deciduous trees that blaze in an autumn display of gold and brown. The hill towns nestle picturesquely into the scene, studded with antique and curio shops, museums and galleries, chalet-style restaurants and gardens thrown open for Devonshire teas.

Picnic spots abound, and so do places of special interest—like the 100 acre Rhododendron garden at Olinda, Sherbrooke Forest, renowned for its Lyrebirds, the aboriginal sculptures in William Rickett's Sanctuary and the panoramic views of Melbourne from the highest point, Mt Dandenong.

Further into the hills at Belgrave is the famous Puffing Billy, a quaint old steam train running on narrow guage between Belgrave, Menzies Creek and Emerald.

Another mecca for tourists and Melbournians alike is the Healsville sanctuary, west of the main Dandenongs region. Here, in natural surroundings, are platypusses, kangaroos, wallabies, koalas, emus, peacocks, wombats, echidnas and a great array of other native animals and birds.

Nearby is the beautiful Maroondah dam, and the Acheron Way through great forests to the pretty town of Marysville.

To the north-east of Melbourne is the rolling Yan Yean hill country, with two picturesque satellite suburban towns in Eltham and Warrandyte. Stretches of farm and bush land roll further on to the fringing mountains of the Dividing Range, accompanied by the more pristine stream of the Upper Yarra.

SCULPTURE, WILLIAM RICKETT'S SANCTUARY
GARDEN'S AT THE MAROONDAH DAM, HEALESVILLE

DANDENONGS AUTUMN SCENE
PUFFING BILLY STARTS ITS WINDING TRIP THROUGH DANDENONGS

GIPPSLAND – *Heaped with Riches*

Victoria's eastern flank is the rich Gippsland region, notable at the tourist's first view for its solidly established country towns and the abundant pasture for cattle who reveal their contentment by giving forth dairy products in great quantities.

Gippsland is host, too, to some of Victoria's most valuable natural resources—the eucalypt forests in the far east region stand densely and majestically on a series of blue hazed mountains which spur across from the Great Dividing Range to the sea; offshore are the natural gas and oil wells of Bass Strait; further south, the world's largest commercially usable deposits of brown coal lie in the Latrobe Valley—200,000,000 tons have been scooped out of the open cut face—17,500,000,000 tons remain to generate most of the State's electricity.

The towns of Yallourn, Morwell, Moe, Traralgon, Drouin, Sale and Warragul handsomely support both the industrial complexes near this source of power, the agricultural wealth of the region and the surge of holiday makers which head for Gippsland's coastal resorts like Phillip Island, Lakes Entrance and Mallacoota.

Inland there is fascination for the tourist, too, in places like the old mining town of Walhalla, the vast limestone caves at Buchan, the Bulga and Tarra Valley national parks in rain-forest country and the Mt Baw Baw alpine village.

Gippsland is separated from northern Victoria by the high country of the Great Dividing Range, a great bulk of mountains carrying Victoria's sophisticated ski resorts —Mt Buller, Mt Buffalo, Mt Hotham, Falls Creek— and magnificent stretches of wild forest and straw country, which in season, from June until October, covers 800 square miles.

Few good roads cross the range from Gippsland, and they are for the skilled driver. But those who take them will be rewarded by the grandeur of great stretches of lonely mountain and forest scenery.

LATROBE VALLEY LANDSCAPE

DAIRY COWS ON RICH GIPPSLAND FARM
RIVER NEAR WALHALLA

CREAM PROCESSING PLANT, TRARALGON
OPEN CUT COAL MINE, YALLOURN

CONTROL ROOM, YALLOURN POWER STATION

EXCITING COASTAL SCENERY

In summer, when Victorians head for the beach in the expectation of fine weather, they have approximately 1,000 miles of coastline and a variety of resorts and aquatic environments from which to choose—inland estuaries, lonely ocean beaches, peaceful bay waters, popular surf strips and the near-at-hand city beaches of Port Phillip Bay.

Undoubtedly, the most popular resort is the Mornington Peninsula—a narrow, 40-mile long strip running from the outer Melbourne city of Frankston in a succession of headlands and sandy, ti-tree fringed bays facing Port Phillip Bay and, a few miles west behind a mountain ridge, in stretches of surf beach.

On the bay side the sea-front resorts merge into one vast holiday town, punctuated by identifying town signs— Dromana, McRae, Rosebud, Rye, Blairgowrie, Sorrento and Portsea—and by the changing degrees of domestic opulence. The simple holiday living and foreshore camping on much of the peninsula merges into the more fashionable resort areas of Blairgowrie, Sorrento and Portsea, where clifftop mansions are the weekenders of the city Establishment.

The surf side of the peninsula runs down to Westernport Bay, enclosed on the eastern side by Phillip Island. Here again, calm waters and the island's chain of beaches invite bathing, sailing and water skiing. Phillip Island is renowned for its colonies of Koala bears, seals, mutton birds and the dusk parade of thousands of fairy penguins to their beach side burrows at Penguin Beach. It is joined to the mainland by a bridge across a quarter-mile channel of water to the fishing town of San Remo.

Further east in Gippsland is the forbidding bluff of Wilson's Promontory, enclosed in a national park with a coastline of 100 miles and an area of 120,000 acres. Bushwalking tracks snake through this wild grandeur of scenery, accessible from the controlled camping reserve at Tidal River.

On the Gippsland coast, the Ninety Mile Beach runs in a magnificent stretch of wild, wind and sea swept beach, backed by the Gippsland Lakes—a vast and shallow estuary series which is ideal for boating. It meets the sea at Lakes Entrance—a picturesquely sited fishing and resort town on a flat strip of land between two lakes.

On the western side of Port Phillip Bay is the Bellerine Peninsula. Its main town of Queenscliff is two miles across water from Pt Nepean on the Mornington Peninsula, but as far as the motorist is concerned it is 150 miles away. The motorist, however, is usually more interested in the Great Ocean Road, which weaves its way west around the ocean front cliffs and through some of the State's premier surf beaches—Torquay, Anglesea, Lorne and Wye River. Further west, the road emerges from the mountains for a further wonder—cliffs carved by the sea into great caves, fiords and residual spires. They are the start of a fascinating trip through wild coastal country, where the journey can be broken at sleepy fishing villages or the larger coastal towns of Warrnambool and historic Portland.

ROCK FORMATION SOUTH WEST COAST

LAKES ENTRANCE BEACH
SURF CARNIVAL MARCH PAST, PORTSEA

EARLY MORNING, WILSONS PROMONTORY

SOLID RURAL REGION

The topography of Victoria is dominated by the Great Dividing Range, which begins with the isolated and beautiful Grampian range in the Western District and sweeps in a widening arc across the State to the snow and tall timber mountains of the north-east.

On the western and north-western plains, the rolling pasture and crop lands of the central and northern region, in the mountain valleys of the north-east and the rich watershed of Gippsland, the State's great business of agriculture goes on, despite the uncertainties of the world market which have plagued the once envied farmer in the late 60s and early 70s. The State produces a quarter of the nation's wheat, one-fifth of its wool, almost half of its butter, one-fifth of its beef, one-fifth of the fruits and two-thirds of its vine fruits.

The comparatively featureless plains of the south-west are sheep and beef cattle country, the home of the rural Establishment which, in past times, was a political power through landowners' seats of privilege in the State's Upper House. The Western District is studded with fine mansion homes, and handsome towns. Its major cities are on the coast—the deepwater port of Portland, where weathered bluestone buildings bear witness to its past as Victoria's first settlement; the thriving city of Warrnambool; and Geelong, an industrial city of 110,000 people which, although it is only 40 miles from Melbourne, styles itself as the Gateway of the Western District.

The central and north-west is hot, flat and dry country—the Wimmera and Mallee, where the bulk of the State's cereal crop are grown and which give way to sandplains and flat scrublands. Technically in the Mallee, too, is the Murray irrigation area around Mildura—intensively cultivated farmlands which produce a bounty of citrus orchards, vineyards and olive groves. The Murray Valley region winds with this greatest of Australian rivers across the north, which is rich in mixed farming and the tourism attracted by its river reaches, clear, sunny climate and the brilliantly conceived Swan Hill folk museum.

The central region, once the main area of Victoria's world famed gold fields, is agriculturally and industrially rich and varied. Its towns are rich in colonial architecture and historic association, the most notable being the gold 'capitals' of Bendigo and Ballarat.

The central north benefits from a wide irrigation system which waters apple, pear and stone fruit growing and rich pasture land. Here are the handsome, thriving centres of Shepparton in the Goulburn Valley, and Wangaratta in the Ovens Valley.

The north-east merges into the mountains in narrow and fertile valley corridors, carrying crops of tobacco and hops. Here are such magnificently scenic towns as Bright and Myrtleford, which blaze with the autumnal colours of introduced trees.

GOLDFIELD CITY OF BENDIGO

BLUE HAZED GRAMPIAN MOUNTAINS, CENTRAL WEST
A SNOWMOBILE ON FALLS CREEK RUN

GORGE IN THE GRAMPIANS
FARM IN GIPPSLAND BUSH

PART OF SWAN HILL FOLK MUSEUM
PADDLE STEAMER, MURRAY RIVER

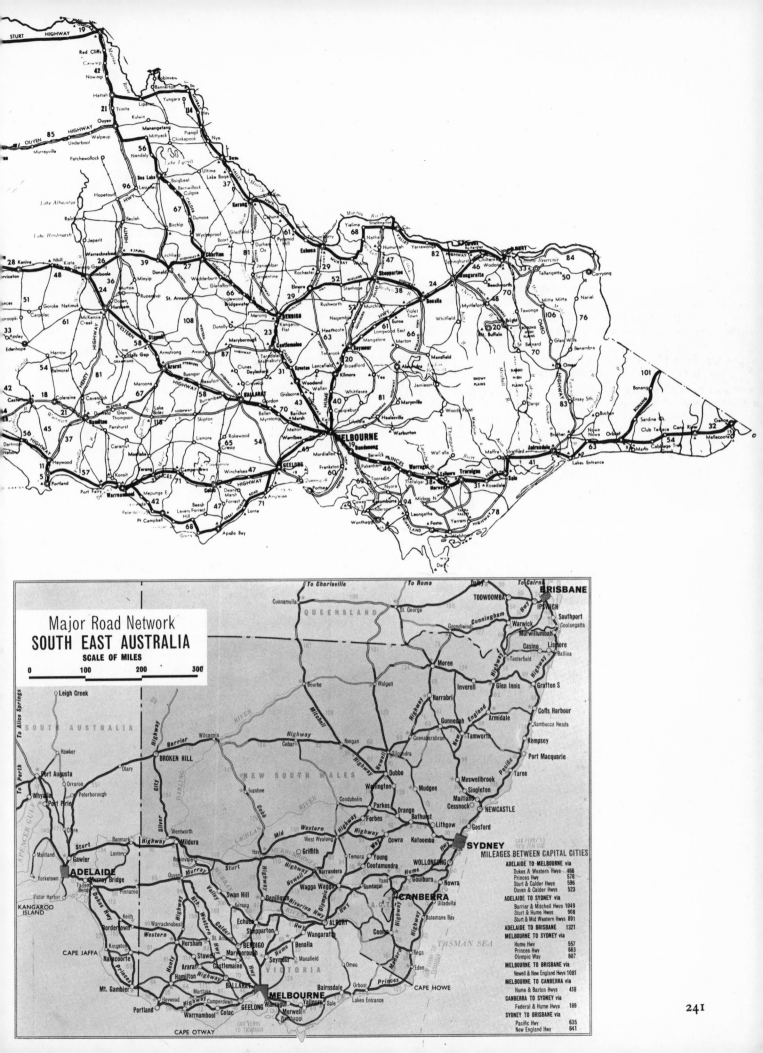

Major Road Network
SOUTH EAST AUSTRALIA

SCALE OF MILES

0   100   200   300

To Charleville   To Roma   Daley   To Cairns   **BRISBANE**

Cunnamulla   TOOWOOMBA   IPSWICH   Southport

QUEENSLAND   St. George   Coolangatta

Goondiwindi   Cunningham   Warwick   Murwillumbah

Leigh Creek   Moree   Casino   Lismore

Tenterfield   Ballina

Bourke   Walgett   Inverell   Glen Innis   Grafton S

To Perth   To Alice Springs   SOUTH AUSTRALIA   Narrabri   Coffs Harbour

Hawker   Wilcannia   Highway   Nyngan   Coonabarabran   Tamworth   Nambucca Heads

Barrier   Cobar   Gilgandra   Kempsey

Port Augusta   BROKEN HILL   Olary   NEW SOUTH WALES   Dubbo   Port Macquarie

Orroroo   Wellington   Muswellbrook   Taree

Whyalla   Peterborough   Ivanhoe   Condobolin   Mudgee   Singleton

Port Pirie   Parkes   Orange   Maitland   Cessnock

Wentworth   Forbes   Bathurst   Lithgow   Gosford   NEWCASTLE

Maitland   Renmark   Mildura   Mid   West Wyalong   Cowra   Katoomba

Gawler   Western   Highway   Griffith   Young   **SYDNEY**

ADELAIDE   Loxton   Narrandera   Temora   Cootamundra   WOLLONGONG

Murray Bridge   Ouyen   Murray   Swan Hill   Deniliquin   Wagga Wagga   Yass   Goulburn   Nowra

Tailem Bend   Pinnaroo   Gundagai   **CANBERRA**   Ulladulla

Victor Harbor   Keith   Warracknabeal   Echuca   Shepparton   ALBURY   Cooma   Batemans Bay

KANGAROO ISLAND   Bordertown   Western   St. Arn.   Benalla

CAPE JAFFA   Kingston   Naracoorte   Horsham   Maryborough   Mansfield   Bega

Ararat   Stawell   Castlemaine   BENDIGO   Seymour   Omeo   Eden   TASMAN SEA

Mt. Gambier   Hamilton   BALLARAT   **MELBOURNE**   Bairnsdale   CAPE HOWE

Portland   Mortlake   GEELONG   Warragul   Sale   Lakes Entrance

Warrnambool   Camperdown   Colac   Morwell   Yallourn   Wonthaggi

CAPE OTWAY   CAR FERRY TO TASMANIA

VICTORIA

MILEAGES BETWEEN CAPITAL CITIES

ADELAIDE TO MELBOURNE via

Dukes & Western Hwys	466
Princes Hwy	576
Sturt & Calder Hwys	596
Ouyen & Calder Hwys	523

ADELAIDE TO SYDNEY via

Barrier & Mitchell Hwys	1049
Sturt & Hume Hwys	908
Sturt & Mid Western Hwys	891

ADELAIDE TO BRISBANE 1321

MELBOURNE TO SYDNEY via

Hume Hwy	557
Princes Hwy	663
Olympic Way	607

MELBOURNE TO BRISBANE via

Newell & New England Hwys	1081

MELBOURNE TO CANBERRA via

Hume & Barton Hwys	410

CANBERRA TO SYDNEY via

Federal & Hume Hwys	189

SYDNEY TO BRISBANE via

Pacific Hwy	635
New England Hwy	641

241

PHYSICAL AND CLIMATIC FEATURES

Victoria can be divided into four main physical divisions—the Murray Basin plains, the central highlands, the southern plains and the southern uplands.

The Murray Basin plains comprise the Mallee and Wimmera areas in the north-west and the northern district plains. The central highlands cross the State in a generally westward direction from the New South Wales border to within 30 miles of the South Australian border. The eastern highlands contain the highest mountains in Victoria, the highest being Mt Bogong at 6516 feet. The southern plains embrace the western district plains and Gippsland plains. The southern uplands, between the plains and the sea, comprise the Otway Ranges, the Barrabool Hills, the South Gippsland highlands and Wilson's Promontory.

The principal inland rivers are the Murray, which flows for 1,203 miles along the northern boundary, the Goulburn (345 miles), Mitta Mitta (167 miles), Ovens (132 miles), Campaspe (155 miles) and Loddon (210 miles), which flow into the Murray. There are shorter coastal rivers and others terminating in lakes.

Climatically, the State is split into two parts by the Great Dividing Range. The range and the country to the south generally have a moderate to cool temperature, and good, evenly distributed rains. The northern and western plains are drier and experience greater heat.

A BRIEF HISTORY OF VICTORIA

In 1770, Lieutenant Hicks, in Captain James Cook's *Endeavour*, sighted the Victorian coast, at Point Hicks in Gippsland. A close survey of the coast was made in 1797–8 by George Bass and Matthew Flinders, and their discovery of the strait between Van Diemens Land (now Tasmania) and the mainland encouraged settlement of the south-eastern part of Australia.

Lieutenant J. Grant sailed the *Lady Nelson* into Port Phillip Bay in February 1802, and the following year, Lieutenant D. Collins was despatched by the Governor of New South Wales to settle the region. Collins chose a poor sandy site near the mouth of the bay, and when it proved unsuitable, reported unfavourably on the region and received permission to transfer to Van Diemen's Land.

Whaling and sealing ships continued to use coastal bases, but it was not until the early 1830s that Tasmanian immigrants began to explore the southern coast of the mainland for land more suitable than their Tasmanian holdings. The first permanent settler was Edward Henty, who settled on Portland Bay in 1834. A year later, the rival parties of John Batman and John Pascoe Fawkner explored the valleys of the Yarra and Maribyrnong rivers, at the head of Port Phillip Bay. Batman made his famous 'purchase' of 600,000 acres of land from aboriginals of the Doutta Galla tribe for an annual tribute of goods worth about $400. The transaction was repudiated by the British Colonial Office, but was later recognised as a *fait accompli*, and the Port Phillip district rapidly came under settlement.

In 1837, Governor Bourke visited the new town, named it Melbourne after the then British Prime Minister, and authorised James Hoddle to survey it to a convenient plan. The broad streets on convenient grid plan of today are due to Hoddle's foresight. In 1842, the City was incorporated and the first mayor and councillors appointed.

From its early days, the settlement sought independence from New South Wales. The settlers wanted to control their own destiny, and to have nothing to do with the convict system. Separation for the State of Victoria was achieved on 1 July 1851. Soon afterwards, a rich gold find was made at Buninyong near Ballarat, and a great gold rush began. The population of the State rose from 77,000 to almost 600,000 in five years. For a short time, the fields produced a third of the world's production, but the Victorian fields began to decline after 1860, and the gold immigrants stayed on to raise sheep, cattle and crops or enter the industry developing in Melbourne under the influence of a protectionist policy, which gave preferential aid to local industries.

The State prospered in both primary and secondary industries, and reached a boom period in the 1880s, in which superficial material progress was evidenced by the opulent buildings of the city and the fine homes of Melbourne's suburbs. Land speculation and vast borrowing for public works led to an inflation of values beyond reason.

The institutions which had their money tied in land began to founder; the huge building industry collapsed; public works ceased, and by 1891 a grim period of depression had begun. To escape the conditions, 161,000 people left Victoria between 1891 and 1910—20,000 more than the net immigration between 1861 and the bank crash.

The birth rate became alarmingly low, and this had an effect that lasted 60 years.

However, the economy found a sounder basis in rural expansion, with the Government playing a major part in revitalising agriculture, and population returned through immigration from Britain before and after the First World War.

Both world wars strongly stimulating the State's manufacturing industries, and migration from Europe since 1949 has considerably increased manpower.

In its secondary industry, Victoria produces 55 per cent of Australia's textiles, 50 per cent of its rubber products, 40 per cent of its clothing, 35 per cent of its chemicals and 30 per cent of its industrial metals, machines and vehicles.

TRAVELLING IN VICTORIA

Victoria is well served by a network of good, all-weather roads. There are few parts of the State of interest to tourists that cannot be reached in comfort, although the weather and likely state of roads should be considered on any trip to the snow fields, and chains fitted if necessary. Train and road coach services provide a thorough network of the State. Intra-state air services run between Melbourne and the major provincial centres on the Murray, in the Western District and in Gippsland.

Fast and modern interstate trains link Melbourne with Sydney, Adelaide and points beyond daily, and there are scheduled daily air services between the capitals, with Sydney flights being the most frequent. For rail enquiries, ring 62 0311. All planes for overseas and interstate leave from the Tullamarine terminal. Interstate operators are Ansett Airlines of Australia (34 0291) and T.A.A. (34 0411).

The Melbourne transport service is established around the efficient tram and electric train services, with bus links in outer areas and across routes. Taxis and hire cars charge 23 cents flag fall and 22 cents per mile. Hire-drive cars are available at many locations.

Motorists should beware of one-way traffic in Melbourne's 'little streets', where traffic can proceed from east to west only, except Little Lonsdale Street, which runs west to east. The Royal Automobile Club of Victoria extends advisory services to visiting members of motoring organisations and overseas motorists (60 0251).

NATIONAL PARKS AND WILDLIFE SANCTUARIES

Victoria is well served with national parks and sanctuaries which are easily within access of Melbourne and settled country areas, and which cover the spectrum of Victorian scenery, from snow capped ranges through luxuriant forests, lush fern gullies, downland and desertland.

The main Victorian parks include:

Mt Buffalo (north-east): mountain landscape views, spring wildflowers, winter snowfields, walking trails.

Fraser National Park (north-central): on shores of Eildon Reservoir; water sports and accommodation; kangaroo and bird sanctuary.

Wilson's Promontory (south-east): mountainous, magnificent coastal views, granite bluffs, sweeping beaches, fern valleys.

Hattah Lakes (north-west): the lakes and marshes are a sanctuary for prolific and varied bird life—ducks, geese, pelicans, black swans, brolgas.

Wyperfield (north-west), **Little Desert** (central-west): Mallee eucalypt scrublands, the habitat of a variety of animal and bird life, including the Mallee fowl.

Ferntree Gully (central-south): lush fern and mountain ash vegetation, superb mountain scenery, home of superb lyrebird.

Tara Valley and **Bulga** (south-east): in Strzlecki ranges; fern vegetation and giant mountain ash.

Port Campbell (south-west): golden cliffs, with residual wave cut spires, arches and gorges.

Mt Eccles (south-west): volcanic crater and crater lakes.

Grampians (south-west): superb mountain scenery and walks, bird and animal life; wildflowers.

Mallacoota (south-east): deep estuary surrounded by heavy forest land; birds and wildflowers.

MELBOURNE

Melbourne is sited at the mouth of the Yarra River at the head of Port Phillip Bay, an almost land locked stretch of water extending north from Bass Strait.

The terrain of the city area is mostly flat or gently undulating, with the hilliest areas following the generally north-eastern course of the river. The southern bay suburbs, with their indented foreshores, and the river and its tributaries break up the grid patterns of the streets. The suburbs extend up to 20 miles from the city, with movement mainly to the south and east. The northern and eastern suburbs are within sight of the Great Dividing Range and the Dandenong Range.

Attractions in the city and suburban area include:

PARKS AND GARDENS

Without spectacular natural characteristics, Melbourne has compensated by creating and preserving wide tree-shaded streets and avenues and magnificent parks and gardens, which mainly cover a wide belt in the south and east of the city. They include: **The Royal Botanic Gardens and National Herbarium** (off St Kilda Road): 105 acres of flower beds, plantations, lakes and lawns, superbly planned and tended, and regarded by experts to rank with the finest gardens in the world. A great variety of tropical, sub-tropical and temperate zone flora can be seen. The 62 acre gardens of Government House are adjoining.

King's Domain (St Kilda Road): Undulating, tree-shaded lawns, containing the Shrine of Remembrance, old Observatory and Governor Latrobe's cottage.

Alexandra and Queen Victoria Gardens (St Kilda Road or Alexandra Avenue): 320 acres of gardens, containing the Sidney Myer Music Bowl, where 60,000 people can watch concert performances.

Treasury and Fitzroy Gardens (Spring Street): Near city centre and Government offices. Fitzroy Gardens were laid out so that the avenues of trees described the pattern of the Union Jack. The gardens contain **Captain Cook's cottage,** transported from the famous navigator's native Yorkshire, and a model **Tudor village.**

Flagstaff Gardens (William Street): In the west of the city and Melbourne's first public gardens. Originally a signalling station to inform settlers of the arrival and departure of ships at Williamstown.

Exhibition Gardens (Exhibition Street): Containing the impressive, domed **Exhibition Building,** erected for the Great Exhibition of the 1880s and the first Federal Parliament House for 27 years. The 60 acres of flowers, lawns and trees contain fountains, statuary and an ornamental lake.

Melbourne Cricket Ground (Brunton Avenue): The stadium which can accommodate 120,000 people is in Victoria Park, which also contains the Richmond Cricket Ground. Nearby is the **Olympic Park** complex, containing several ovals and the Olympic Swimming Pool.

Royal Park (off Royal Parade): A largely open and recreational parkland, containing several ovals, and the Zoological Gardens of 50 acres, which have recently been improved with open reserves for many animals.

Albert Park (Queens Parade): A large sporting area, containing two football stadiums, golf courses, ovals, indoor sports centres and a lake for rowing and boating.

BEACHES

Port Phillip Bay beaches closest to Melbourne are: (east)—St Kilda, Brighton, Elwood, Black Rock, Hampton, Sandringham, Aspendale, Edithvale—(west)—Williamstown, Altona. All beaches are in sheltered bay waters. Active yachting clubs operate from many beach areas, and boat hire for fishing and sailing can be arranged (consult classified telephone directory).

POINTS OF INTEREST

Arts Centre of Victoria (National Gallery): A magnificent bluestone and concrete building, designed around three vast courtyards and containing the famous Great Reception Hall, with its stained glass ceiling by Leonard French. Part of the $7\frac{1}{2}$-acre centre, when completed, will also have auditoria for music and theatre, an art school, restaurant and administrative offices. The Gallery has a fine permanent exhibition, and is vigorous in its presentation of special exhibitions. Closed Mondays.

State Library (Swanston Street): Contains over 800,000 volumes and manuscripts, including a notable collection of Australiana in the Latrobe Library.

National Museum (Swanston Street): Contains a fine section of aboriginal and Pacific Island artifacts, and many fascinating general exhibits, including the famous Phar Lap.

Como (Como Avenue, South Yarra): Century-old mansion house in superb grounds, furnished in Victorian style. Open 10.00 am–5.00 pm daily.

Cathedrals: St Patrick's (Roman Catholic) in Gisborne Street, and St Paul's (Anglican) in Flinders Street are magnificent Gothic cathedrals.

Panoramic views: From the observation deck, National Mutual Centre (Collins Street) and the panoramic deck (I.C.I. building), Nicholson Street. Open weekdays.

Tram rides: The best tram ride is the number 15 from Swanston Street, along St Kilda Road to St Kilda beach.

River cruises: Available daily from Princes Bridge or from Studley Park boat house, Kew.

Shrine of Remembrance (King's Domain, St Kilda Road): The war memorial of Victoria dominates the Melbourne skyline. Contains the Rock of Remembrance. At 11.00 am on November 11 each year, a ray of light shines through the roof onto the rock. Open weekdays and 2.00 pm–5.00 pm, Sunday.

State Parliament House (Spring Street): Open on weekdays, and in session.

Railway Museum (Champion Road, North Williamstown): An outstanding collection of steam trains. Open for inspection Saturdays and Sundays (2.00 pm–5.00 pm).

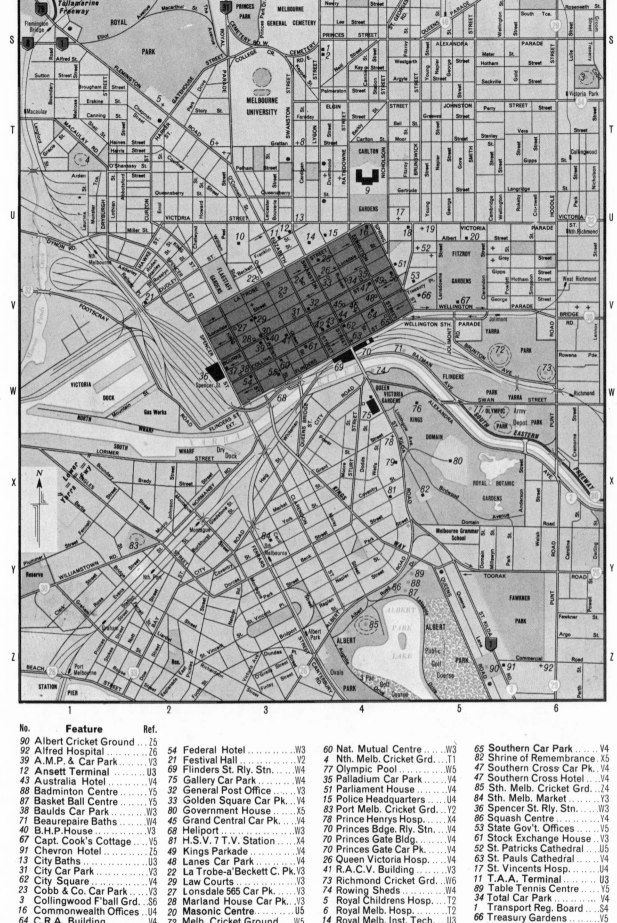

No.	Feature	Ref.
90	Albert Cricket Ground	Z5
92	Alfred Hospital	Z6
39	A.M.P. & Car Park	V3
12	Ansett Terminal	U3
43	Australia Hotel	V4
88	Badminton Centre	Y5
87	Basket Ball Centre	Y5
38	Baulds Car Park	W3
71	Beaurepaire Baths	W4
40	B.H.P. House	V3
67	Capt. Cook's Cottage	V5
91	Chevron Hotel	Z5
13	City Baths	U3
31	City Car Park	V3
62	City Square	V4
23	Cobb & Co. Car Park	V3
3	Collingwood F'ball Grd.	S6
16	Commonwealth Offices	U4
64	C.R.A. Building	V4
72	Melb. Cricket Ground	W5
7	Dental Hospital	T3
24	Downtown Car Park	V3
18	Eastern Hill Fire Stn.	U4
9	Exhibition Buildings	U4
19	Eye & Ear Hospital	U5
54	Federal Hotel	W3
21	Festival Hall	V2
69	Flinders St. Rly. Stn.	W4
75	Gallery Car Park	W4
32	General Post Office	V3
33	Golden Square Car Pk.	V4
80	Government House	X5
45	Grand Central Car Pk.	V4
68	Heliport	W4
81	H.S.V. 7 T.V. Station	X4
49	Kings Parkade	V4
48	Lanes Car Park	V4
27	Lonsdale 565 Car Pk.	V3
28	Marland House Car Pk.	V3
20	Masonic Centre	U5
44	Melb. Town Hall	V4
2	Motor Registration Br.	S4
25	Museum & Pub. Library	U4
76	Myer Music Bowl	W5
60	Nat. Mut. Car Park	W3
60	Nat. Mutual Centre	W3
4	Nth. Melb. Cricket Grd.	T1
77	Olympic Pool	W5
35	Palladium Car Park	V4
51	Parliament House	V4
15	Police Headquarters	U4
83	Port Melb. Cricket Grd.	Y2
78	Prince Henrys Hosp.	X4
70	Princes Bdge. Rly. Stn.	W4
70	Princes Gate Bldg.	V4
70	Princes Gate Car Pk.	V4
26	Queen Victoria Hosp.	V4
41	R.A.C.V. Building	V3
73	Richmond Cricket Grd.	W6
74	Rowing Sheds	W4
5	Royal Childrens Hosp.	T2
6	Royal Melb. Hosp.	T2
14	Royal Melb. Inst. Tech.	U3
8	Royal Womens Hosp.	T3
37	Savoy Plaza Hotel	W3
46	Scots Church	V4
55	S.E.C. Building	W3
30	SHELL CORNER	V3
65	Southern Car Park	V4
82	Shrine of Remembrance	X5
47	Southern Cross Car Pk.	V4
47	Southern Cross Hotel	V4
85	Sth. Melb. Cricket Grd.	Z4
84	Sth. Melb. Market	Y3
36	Spencer St. Rly. Stn.	W3
86	Squash Centre	V4
53	State Gov't. Offices	V5
61	Stock Exchange House	V3
52	St. Patricks Cathedral	U5
63	St. Pauls Cathedral	V4
17	St. Vincents Hosp.	U4
11	T.A.A. Terminal	U3
89	Table Tennis Centre	Y5
34	Total Car Park	V3
1	Transport Reg. Board	S4
66	Treasury Gardens	V5
79	Victoria Barracks	X4
10	Victoria Market	U3
75	Vic. Arts Centre	W4
42	Vic. Govt. Tour. Bureau	V4
50	Windsor Hotel	V4

SHELL guide to MELBOURNE CITY OUTLETS

SCALE OF MILES

0   ¼   ½   1

PLACES OF INTEREST NEAR MELBOURNE

SPORTS

Dandenong Ranges: The ranges, which are blue-hazed when seen from a distance, carry a dense cover of native and exotic vegetation. They are fairly closely settled and well served by good, if winding roads. European trees have been extensively introduced, and blend superbly with the natural bush and tall Eucalypt trees. Notable attractions are:

Sherbrooke Forest: a magnificent, natural forest, unspoiled despite the visits of tens of thousands of people every year, and a sanctuary for native animals and prolific bird life, which includes the elusive lyrebird.

William Rickett's Sanctuary: near Mt Dandenong, where the work of the noted sculptor of aboriginal themes is displayed.

Rhododendron Garden: a superb 100-acre garden at Olinda.

Silvan Reservoir: in an immaculate parkland setting; the shores of the magnificent lake contain an established picnic ground.

Puffing Billy: runs between Belgrave and Emerald, via Menzies Creek, three times a day at weekends all the year, with extra trips on public and school holidays. The railway is narrow guage, and the train's progress through the wooded hills is delightfully slow and cantankerous.

Sir Colin McKenzie Sanctuary: at Healesville, 36 miles from Melbourne. A 78-acre reserve contains many tame native animals and Platypus Research Station. First platypus was bred in captivity here in 1948.

Healesville: (36 miles) a resort town, popular with weekend drivers and set in superb mountain country. Here, the Maroondah Reservoir is in a picturesque woodland setting. Splendid bush walking country.

Mt Macedon: (38 miles) with superb views from the summit, beautiful gardens and fine homes.

Acheron Way: a fine road, deep into mountain country and to the picturesque towns of Warburton (49 miles) and Marysville (552 milles).

Emu Bottom: At Sunbury (15 miles), is Emu Bottom homestead, recreated in 19th century period, with demonstrations of pioneer life, shearing, sheep dog work, etc.

Montsalvat: at Eltham (14 miles)—with a great hall, and the mud and stone cottages of the artists' colony. Grounds and some areas open for inspection.

Lion Safari: (36 miles) lions roam in natural setting, 3 miles past the township of Bacchus Marsh. Nearby is the **Werribee Gorge National Park** and **Lederderg Gorge.**

Horse Racing: Flemington, Sandown, Caulfield and Moonee Valley racecourses. Every Saturday, and holidays. Weekday meetings in country areas.

Night Trotting: (summer) At showgrounds, Ascot Vale.

Dog Racing: Olympic Park, Sandown Park.

Cycling: The Velodrome, Olympic Park.

Motor Racing: Sandown Park, Calder Raceway.

Cricket and **Australian Rules Football:** MCG and suburban stadiums.

Soccer: At Olympic Park and suburban grounds.

Swimming: Olympic Pools, Batman Avenue and Olympic Park (indoor); City Baths (indoor). Most suburbs have Olympic pools.

Ice Skating: Glaciarium, St Kilda; Ringwood Rink.

Boxing and **Wrestling:** Festival Hall.

Golf and **Tennis:** numerous public courses and courts. World class private golf courses where visitors can often arrange a game by contacting club secretaries.

Lawn Bowls: Visitors are welcome at most lawn bowling rinks after contacting club.

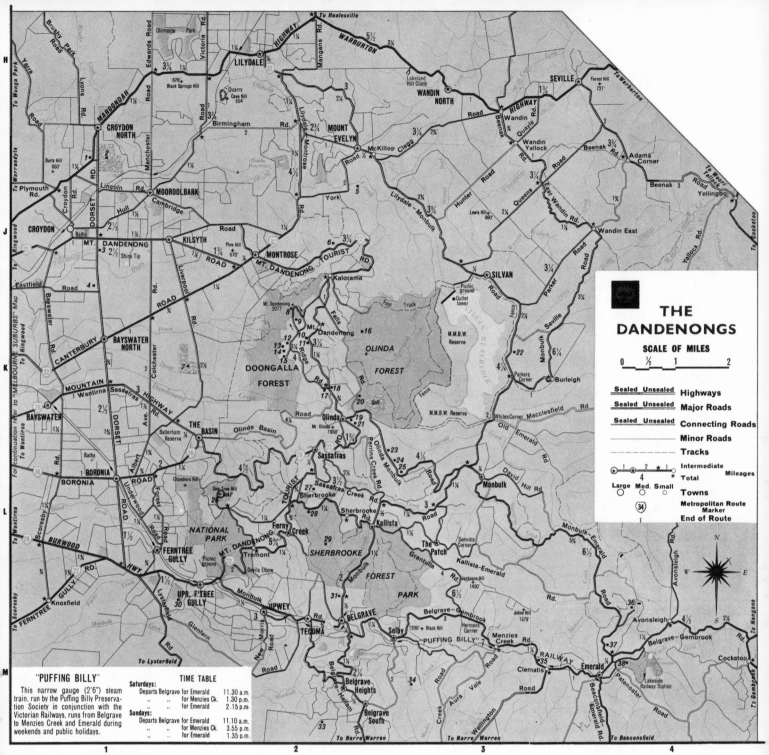

THE DANDENONGS

SCALE OF MILES

0   ½   1   2

Sealed	Unsealed	Highways
Sealed	Unsealed	Major Roads
Sealed	Unsealed	Connecting Roads

Minor Roads
Tracks

Intermediate Mileages
Total

Large   Med.   Small   Towns

(34)   Metropolitan Route Marker
★   End of Route

"PUFFING BILLY"

This narrow gauge (2'6") steam train, run by the Puffing Billy Preservation Society in conjunction with the Victorian Railways, runs from Belgrave to Menzies Creek and Emerald during weekends and public holidays.

TIME TABLE

Saturdays:
Departs Belgrave for Emerald .... 11.30 a.m.
" " for Menzies Ck. ... 1.30 p.m.
" " for Emerald .... 2.15 p.m.

Sundays:
Departs Belgrave for Emerald .... 11.10 a.m.
" " for Menzies Ck. ... 3.55 p.m.
" " for Emerald .... 1.35 p.m.

INDEX TO THE DANDENONGS

ACCOMMODATION

Good accommodation is available throughout the State, with country highways and towns now well served by hotels.

Among hotels and motels recommended in and around Melbourne are:

HOTELS
Australia Hotel, 266 Collins Street, 63 0401
Graham Hotel, 69 Swanston Street, 63 7011
Hosies Hotel, 1 Elizabeth Street, 62 5521
Old Melbourne Motor Inn, 5–17 Flemington Road, North Melbourne, 329 9344
Racecourse Hotel-Motel, Epsom and Ascot Vale Roads, Flemington, 33 0337
Southern Cross Hotel, 131 Exhibition Street, 63 0221
Windsor Hotel, 115 Spring Street, 63 0261

MOTELS
John Batman TraveLodge, 69 Queens Road, Melbourne, 51 5233
Brighton Savoy, 150 The Esplanade, Brighton, 92 8233
TraveLodge Chadstone, Dandenong Road, Chadstone, 569 0656
Commodore, Kingsway and Queen's Road, 26 2411
Commodore Downtowner, Carlton, 34 9101
Crossley Lodge, 34 Crossley Street, Melbourne, 662 2500
Caravilla De Ville, 461 Royal Parade, Parkville, 38 6771
Diplomat, 5 Eildon Road, St Kilda, 94 0422
Motel Domain, 52 Darling Street, South Yarra, 26 3701
Executive, 239 Canterbury Road, St Kilda, 94 0303
Lygon Lodge, 204 Lygon Street, 34 9334
The Leicester Square, 15 Acland Street, St Kilda, 94 0673
Sandown Park, 438 Princes Highway, Noble Park, 546 9394
Koala Park Top, 94 Flemington Road, Melbourne, 329 6077
Parkroyal, 441 Royal Parade, Melbourne, 38 9221
Parkville, 68 Park Street, Brunswick, 38 6701
President Motor Inn, 63 Queens Road, 51 8411
Princes Park, 2 Sydney Road, Brunswick, 38 6891
Prince Mark, Princes Highway, Dandenong, 2 9725
Koala Queenslodge, 81 Queens Road, 51 8581
St Kilda Caravilla, Canterbury Road, St Kilda, 94 0591
St Kilda TraveLodge, cnr Albert Road and Park Street, 69 0420
St Kilda Beach Car-O-Tel, 4–6 Carlisle Street, St Kilda 94 0781
St James, 35 Darling Street, South Yarra, 26 4455
Tullamarine TraveLodge, Melbourne Airport, 338 2322
William Hotham, 250 Dandenong Road, East St Kilda, 51 8791
Sheraton, 13 Spring Street, 63 9961

THEATRES AND RESTAURANTS

Melbourne has over 20 commercial cinemas, several commercial theatres, repertory and experimental theatres. Consult current hotel and newspaper directories when visiting.

Melbourne has become a city noted for the variety and quality of its restaurants, coffee houses, carvery bars, etc. Just out of town, Toorak Road, South Yarra has become a night life centre—but there are fine restaurants in other suburban areas.

Among Melbourne's recommended restaurants are:

Beefeater, Carlisle Street, Balaclava, with the atmosphere of the old English inn.
Frenchy's, Jolimont Street, Jolimont. Provincial French meals.
The Southern Cross, Exhibition Street, with a selection of four restaurants, each with individual, elegant decor.
The Black Knight, Hawthorn, in a mediaeval setting.
The Stagecoach Inn, in Queen's Road.
Geoff Brooke's Steak Cave, Queen Street. An elegant cellar atmosphere.
Fanny's, Lonsdale Street. Bistro and restaurant.
The Pickwick Restaurant, Toorak Road, South Yarra, has a graceful, old world Edwardian atmosphere.
Maxim's City, 100 Bourke Street.
Oyster Bar, 76 Bourke Street.
The Spanish Cellar, 131 Collins Street.
Lazy Leprechaun, 290 Exhibition Street.
Gina's Bistro, Lygon Street, Carlton.
The Walnut Tree, William Street.
Balzac, Wellington Parade, East Melbourne.
Beachcomber, on the St Kilda Beach front.
The Blue Dragon Restaurant, Camberwell Road, Hawthorn East. Indonesian cuisine.
Florentino, 80 Bourke Street. Has a restaurant, Bistro Grill and Bistro Cellar.

MORNINGTON PENINSULA

The Mornington Peninsula is a boot shaped promontory which separates Port Phillip from Westernport Bay. Its closer towns are now busy centres, catering for holiday home owners and city commuters, but the inland is still rural in character and the Westernport side is not so densely settled.

The Port Phillip Bay foreshore is indented into a series of attractive bathing beaches in calm 'safe' water, while good surfing beaches are on the heel of the 'boot', which faces the ocean.

Towns and points of interest include:

Arthur's Seat: A high (1100 feet) feature at Dromana, commanding panoramic views of Port Phillip and Westernport. A chairlift operates throughout the year, and there is a restaurant at the summit.

Dromana: In the summer holiday season, this is the camping centre of Victoria, with regulars setting up the most elaborate camps along the foreshore in eight reserved areas.

Sorrento: At the head of Port Phillip, this attractive town is closely associated with early settlement. In October 1803, David Collins established temporary settlement here with 50 marines, 31 civilians, 299 convicts and 71 wives and children. Graves and a memorial to them are on the site. Early buildings of limestone are also interesting. During the season, a ferry operates between Sorrento and Queenscliff, on the other side of the bay.

Portsea: Two miles west of Sorrento, this is a holiday centre noted for its superb beach mansions, many commanding clifftop positions. The back beach is the best of the peninsula surf beaches, with a chairlift operating from the sandhills above. Nearby is *London Arch*, an impressive rock formation where the ship, Sierra Nevada was wrecked in 1900.

Flinders: On the south coast of the peninsula, it is near the Cape Schank lighthouse, the blowhole and Elephant Rock.

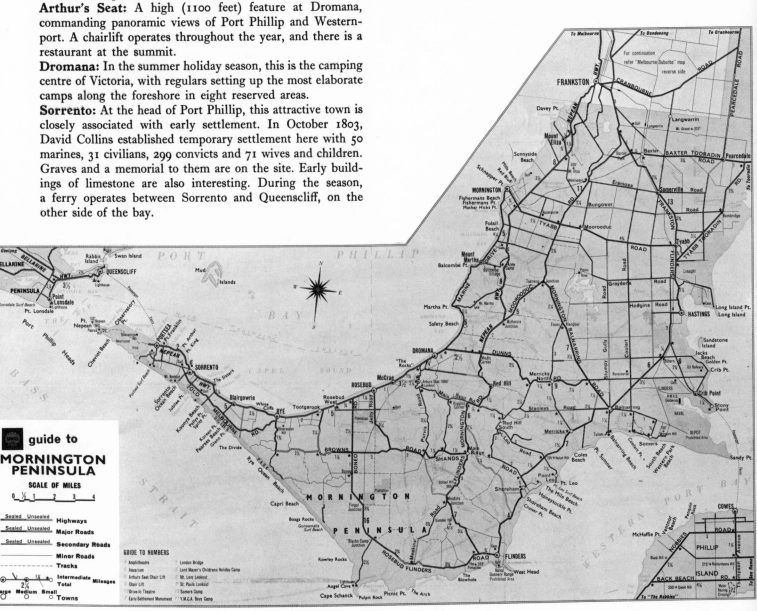

GEELONG AND WESTERN DISTRICT

The volcanic plains of the Western District—in reality the south-western corner of the State—carry about one-third of the sheep and beef cattle population, although its area is only about one-sixth of the State's total.

The plains are mostly flat, monotonous country, which have been cleared of timber for pasture improvement. The south-western coast, however, is rugged and scenically magnificent. From Cape Otway to the Bellarine Peninsula, it is traversed by the Great Ocean Road which winds along cliff faces and through the wooded mountains behind the sea. From it, a number of roads wind north into mountain country, to connect with the Princes Highway. The main towns of the south-west are the old town of Portland, where a recently built artificial harbour has made it a major shipping centre, and the commercial-industrial centre of Warrnambool.

Geelong, Victoria's second city with a population of 120,000, is only 45 miles from Melbourne, sited on Corio Bay. But it is styled the 'Gateway to the Western District', and the plains inland from it are indeed typical of the country further west. Its rural character, with fine buildings and parks and gardens, must now compete with the less attractive trappings of heavy industry.

Among the towns and places of interest in the Western District are:

Geelong

Historic buildings include: **Merchiston Hall** (Gordon Street), an eight-roomed stone house built in 1856 for James Cowie, the first settler.

Customs House (Brougham Place), built in 1855-6.

Christ Church (Moorabool Street), with foundation stone laid in 1843.

The Hermitage school (Pakington Street), built 1859-60 for George Armytage.

Industry: The city's secondary industries include nine major woollen mills, automotive works, an oil refinery and petro-chemicals plant, engineering works, phosphate fertilizers plant and many factories. Arrangements can be made for inspection of many of these works.

Schools: Geelong is noted for its select independent schools—Geelong Grammar School and Geelong College (boys) and Morongo and The Hermitage (girls).

Port: The port comprises 17 shipping berths, a bulk grain terminal, an oil wharf and extensive cool storage.

Wool: Geelong is the wool selling centre for the Western District. The wool research laboratories of the C.S.I.R.O. and the Gordon Institute of Textile Technology are situated in the city.

Parks and Gardens: About 40 per cent of the city area has been reserved for parks, gardens and sports grounds. The Barwon River, which is flanked by park reserve, is the scene of the annual public schools' Head of the River regatta each April.

Nearby places of interest:

Brownill observation tower (Ceres) south-west of town;

You Yang Wildlife Sanctuary (in volcanic range) north of city;

Twin Lakes Fauna Sanctuary (12 miles from city) a breeding place for wildfowl, kangaroos, koalas, etc.

Fairy Park (behind You Yang ranges) an extensive miniature village for the amusement of children.

BELLARINE PENINSULA

Jutting south-east of Geelong, the peninsula's rolling country and picturesque seaside resorts make it a major Victorian holiday area.

Small resorts include Portarlington, Indented Head, St Leonards, Ocean Grove, Barwon Heads and Point Lonsdale. The southern side of the peninsula and nearby coastline has the finest surf beaches in the State. **Queenscliff** on the western headland of Port Phillip Bay, was established as a fishing centre in the 1850s. The Australian army's staff college is situated at the old fort in the town.

SOUTH-WEST COAST

Torquay; 58 miles from Melbourne, has an excellent surf beach at which interstate carnivals are held.

Anglesea is one of the most attractive south-west coast towns. It has a fine surf beach and there are bush walks along the Anglesea River and in nearby hills.

Lorne; 83 miles from Melbourne, is an extremely popular surf resort. It is sited at the foot of rugged mountains of the Otway Ranges. There are nearby waterfalls and an ocean panorama from **Teddy's Lookout.**

Apollo Bay; a fishing, dairying, timber and tourist town. The rugged coast nearby was the scene of many shipwrecks in sailing days.

Port Campbell; a small town, 150 miles from Melbourne. It is close to superb coastal scenery of wave cut cliffs and residual spires and formations.

Warrnambool; a regional commercial centre for the Western District, grazing lands and coastal dairying country. Nearby is **Tower Hill,** a volcanic cone overlooking one of the largest lava plains known to geologists. Its original flora and fauna have been re-established in an intensive programme by the Victorian Wildlife and Fisheries Department.

Port Fairy; a fishing village and the second oldest town in Victoria. It was originally a whaling station. The old fort and signal station are on the Mayne River.

Portland; Victoria's first settlement (1834), has many fine stone buildings. It has the only deepwater port between Melbourne and Adelaide, and is developing as an industrial base. Historic places of interest include Kurtze's museum (1854), in the homestead of the first settler Edward Henty; the Court House (1850) and Maretimo Homestead (1854).

WESTERN DISTRICT

The main inland towns of the Western District are Hamilton, Colac, Camperdown and Ararat. The region is noted for its fine homesteads, established by the pioneering grazing families. Near Ararat are the **Great Western Vineyards,** producing some of the finest dry red and champagne wines in Australia. Tours of the cellars and winery can be arranged with the proprietors, Seppelt and Sons.

WIMMERA AND MALLEE

The Wimmera is the central-western part of Victoria. Apart from the Grampian mountains in its south-east corner, it is relatively flat, scenically uninteresting and dry. Considerable areas are irrigated and the bulk of Victoria's cereal crops are grown there. The Mallee is the extreme north-western corner, comprising mainly flat, semi-arid sand plains which were originally covered with eucalyptus mallee scrub. The light soil is fertile after rain, and produces the State's second largest grain harvest.

Places and points of interest in the Wimmera and Mallee include:

Horsham; 187 miles west of Melbourne, is the main town in the Wimmera, a stock selling, administrative and commercial centre. Nearby is Pine Lake and the **Longerenong Agricultural College**, with its Cereal Research Centre (inspection by arrangement).

Warracknabeal; centre of the Wimmera wheatlands. Nearby is **Lake Hindmarsh,** the largest natural fresh water lake in Victoria. **Jeparit,** near the lake shore, is the birthplace of the Australian statesman, Sir Robert Menzies.

Wyperfield National Park, Victoria's largest wildlife reserve, comprises 140,000 acres of arid mallee country carrying abundant bird and animal life.

Stawell; east of the Grampians, an agricultural and manufacturing town. The Stawell Athletic Club stages an Easter carnival every year, during which Australia's best known professional footrace, The Stawell Gift, is run over 130 yards. **Bunjil's Cave,** south of the town, contains aboriginal paintings in ochre. Big Hill, where gold was first discovered in the district, is a Stawell landmark, **Tottington Woolshed,** 34 miles north-east, is an example of traditional mid-19th century woolshed construction.

THE GRAMPIANS

The spectacular, 60-mile long ridges of sandstone, are the western extremity of the Great Dividing Range. Rising to peaks of 3,500 feet, the mountains have long sweeping slopes on one side, and almost vertical faces on the other. Rock formations are eroded into fantastic shapes. The mountains are particularly beautiful in the spring wildflower season, when thousands of acres of flowering plants—heaths, wattles, wild fuschias, boronia, flowering peas—are in bloom. Over 700 species of flowering plants have been catalogued in the area—over 100 species of birds, koalas, kangaroos, platypusses and deer. The tourist centre of the Grampians is Hall's Gap, a small, beautifully sited settlement.

Nhill, Sea Lake and **Ouyen** are the main towns in the comparatively featureless Mallee area.

GIPPSLAND

Gippsland is the south-eastern section of Victoria, following the coast between the Great Dividing Range and Bass Strait and the Tasman Sea. The coastal plains are well watered dairy lands. The mountains are the base for important forest industries. Gippsland's economic importance is also built around its enormous deposits of Latrobe Valley brown coal which generates two-thirds of the State's electricity, the industry that has been attracted to this power source, and the newly found deposits of natural gas in Bass Strait.

Gippsland is traversed from east to west by the Prince's Highway, from which radiates roads into the coastal farming lands and into the mountains. Its main towns are along the highway, and are a solid declaration of the affluence and attractiveness of the region.

Places and points of interest in Gippsland are:

CENTRAL GIPPSLAND
Morwell, an industrial town in the heart of the Latrobe Valley coal fields, 92 miles south-east of Melbourne. The State Electricity Commission mining projects, briquette works and power plants are open daily for inspection. Arrangements can be made to inspect the Gas & Fuel Corporation's gas plant.

Yallourn: planned and built by the S.E.C. for its brown coal workers, the model settlement has wide streets with lawns and tree plantations, well designed public buildings and an attractive shopping area.

Moe, another Latrobe Valley industrial town. A fine scenic road leads to the gold mining ghost town of Walhalla, magnificently sited in a deep valley. The town has interesting brick and stone ruins and the remnants of the miners' houses of the boom era.

Traralgon, 103 miles from Melbourne, is the centre of the paper making industry, drawing on the forest resources of the mountains to the north.

Warragul, Drouin and **Trafalgar** are solid dairying towns closer to Melbourne. From Warragul, the Grand Ridge Road leads through the superbly scenic Strzlecki Ranges. The road north from Drouin to Noojee and Warburton is also a fine scenic drive. Trafalgar is well situated for trips north to the Upper Latrobe and Tanjil River valleys in the mountains. Other scenic spots near Trafalgar are Trafalgar South lookout, Narracan Falls and Hendersons gully.

EAST GIPPSLAND
Sale, the administrative centre of Gippsland, is 134 miles from Melbourne. Sale is the centre of a productive pastoral district. It is a good base for excursions—to the large Glenmaggie Reservoir favoured by speedboat enthusiasts, across the Dargo High Plains Road to the Alpine Highway at Mt St Bernard, or south to the ninety-mile beach resort of Seaspray. A canal connects Sale with the Gippsland Lakes. Nearby is the Lake Guthrie bird sanctuary and the Lake Wellington Wildlife Sanctuary.

Bairnsdale: an attractive town, 177 miles east of Melbourne, Bairnsdale is the commercial centre of an important dairying, wool and timber district, and the 'gateway' to the **Gippsland Lakes.**

The Gippsland Lakes are an interconnecting chain of shallow lakes, separated from the sea by a narrow ridge of dunes and hummocks, and stretching for 50 miles parallel to the Ninety Mile Beach. They are ideal for boating in sheltered water.

Lakes Entrance: the major tourist resort on the lakes, sited on a finger of land between two lakes and with a pedestrian causeway across a lake to the surf beach. A panoramic view of the town and lakes can be had from Jimmy's Point on the high forested ridge behind the lakes. Other towns are **Paynesville** and **Metung,** the former offering both boating and surfing, and the latter being a picturesque boat haven and resort.

Buchan: 58 miles north-east of Bairnsdale, Buchan is set in fine mountain scenery. Its main attraction is a series of limestone caves—the best in Victoria—lit by electricity. Conducted tours twice daily.

Omeo: in the heart of the Victorian alps at 2,108 feet, Omeo is a base for winter traffic approaching the snow resort at Mt Hotham from the south, and for summer bushwalking and fishing expeditions to the Bogong High Plains. There are fine trout streams and interesting caves to explore.

Orbost: sited near the mouth of the Snowy River, Orbost is the last major town before the East Gippsland and southern New South Wales mountain country. From it, the Bonang Highway leads through the densely timbered mountains to join the Monaro Highway in New South Wales, and the Princes Highway continues to meet the coast again at the New South Wales fishing resort of Eden.

Mallacoota: on a deep inlet near the Victorian border and 15 miles from the highway, Mallacoota is a popular holiday resort, with excellent fishing. Also, off the highway is the fishing resort of Bemm River and Winjan, Lind and Alfred National Parks.

SOUTH GIPPSLAND
Wonthaggi: a black coal mining, industrial, pastoral and agricultural town. Nearby beach resorts are Inverloch, Walkerville and Anderson's Inlet, all comparatively secluded and offering good coastal scenery.

Phillip Island: 50 miles south-east of Melbourne (or 87 road miles), Phillip Island stands at the entrance of Westernport Bay, separated from the mainland on the south side by a narrow channel which is crossed by a bridge to San Remo. The island, 14 miles wide and 16 miles long, has impressive coastal scenery and is a popular holiday centre, with sheltered bay beaches, and a number of excellent surf beaches. Its main settlement of Cowes is a crowded resort in summer, and there are smaller settlements at Rhyll and Newhaven. Places of interest include the **Koala Sanctuary** on the main Cowes road; the **Penguin colony** at Summerland beach, where the birds come ashore after a day's fishing in the summer nesting season and parade to their burrows in the tussocky dune land behind the beach; **Seal rocks** offshore from the Nobbies and Pyramid rock, spectacular formations at the western end of the island. A ferry brings visitors across to the island from the Mornington Peninsula town of Stony Point and also takes excursions from Cowes to French Island, Seal Rocks and Newhaven.

Wilson's Promontory: a wild desolate headland in a national park of 103,000 acres, 'the prom' has been closely reserved and sustains much wildlife. A number of walking tracks have been cleared from Tidal River, the park authority controlled tourist centre. The beaches, fishing and coastal scenery are superb.

Korumburra, Leongatha, Foster and **Yarram** are small, attractive towns in the attractive, hilly South Gippsland farming country. Yarram is close to beauty spots in the Strzlecki Ranges. **Tarra Valley** and **Bulga** National Parks are both 17 miles from town. **Port Welshpool** and **Port Albert** are tiny fishing settlements, both with old buildings and historic atmosphere.

CENTRAL AND NORTHERN VICTORIA

The central and central northern regions of the State are mostly rolling pastoral country, interspersed with wooded hills and ranges. It is a large and solidly productive region, particularly where irrigation has enabled diversification of produce. Its cities and towns have the solidity of long establishment, and many of them are pleasant, well planned and architecturally interesting.

Among towns and places of interest are:

Ballarat is Australia's largest inland city, with a population of approximately 60,000. It serves a productive agricultural and pastoral district, and has more than 300 factories in the Greater Ballarat area. The city, 70 miles from Melbourne, preserves the atmosphere of the 1860s and 1870s, when many of its impressive public buildings were built. It has many tree-planted streets and fine public parks and gardens. Ballarat was the main centre of alluvial mining from 1851, and had a population of over 20,000 in 1853. It was the scene of the Eureka Stockade uprising in 1854.

The Sovereign Hill museum recreates Ballarat's mining days and is a major attraction. Historic houses include Adam Lindsay Gordon's cottage, where the famous poet lived for some years; Ercildoone homestead and Smeaton House, two fine homesteads; the old oatmeal mill and water wheel; the Charles Napier Theatre and the St John of God hospital.

Near the city is **Lake Wendouree,** a swamp developed into a lake and now a major aquatic venue. The 100 acre **Botanic Gardens** adjoin Lake Wendouree, and are the focus of the annual Begonia Festival in March.

The Victory Arch and **Avenue of Honour,** 14 miles long on the Burrumbeet road, contains 3912 trees, one for each man and woman who enlisted in the First World War. The **Eureka Stockade** memorial is on the site of the original stockade in East Ballarat.

Daylesford: a small town in picturesque country, 76 miles from Melbourne, noted for the nearby **Hepburn Springs** which have waters reputed to possess high therapeutic value.

Bendigo: the second major city of Victoria's central highlands, Bendigo was also a product of the gold rush. The first find was in 1851, and eventually the 'field' extended over 14 square miles. Many of its buildings are well-preserved examples of the ornate neo-classical style of mid-19th century architecture. They include the **Post Office** and **Shamrock Hotel, State Public Offices, Capital Theatre** and the **Art Gallery.**

Other *historic gold towns* of the central region include **Castlemaine, Clunes** and **Maldon.** Maldon has the distinction of being the only town declared as notable in its entirety by the National Trust. Its fine buildings, mainly of local stone, include Maldon Hospital; the post office, where the famous novelist, Henry Handel Richardson, lived as a child; St Augustine's Church; the old Council offices, now converted into a folk museum; and 'Dabbs General Store'.

Shepparton: A fine, modern city, Shepparton (112 miles from Melbourne) is the hub of the highly productive agricultural and fruit growing area, irrigated by the Yarrawonga and Eildon reservoirs. Shepparton won Victoria's 'premier

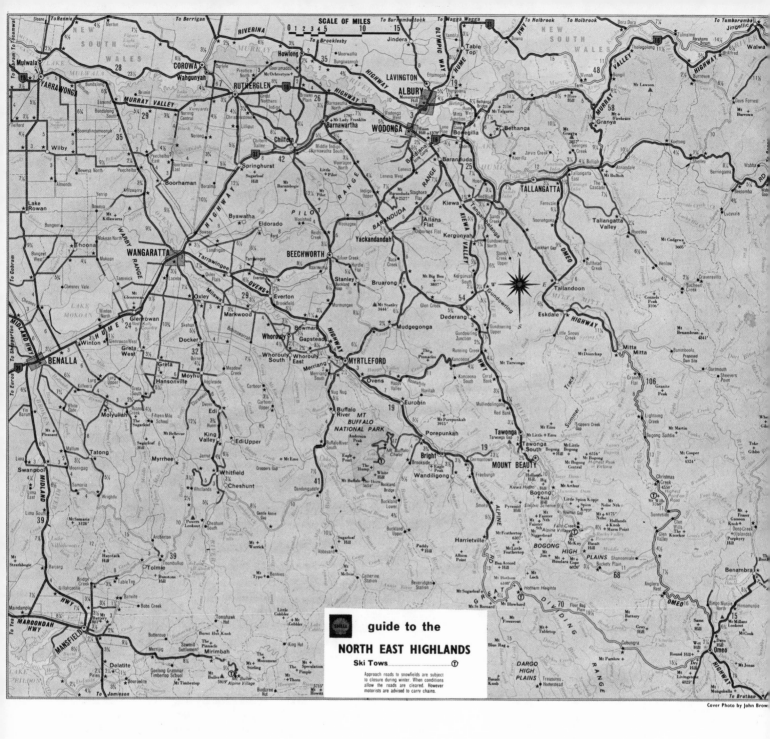

guide to the
NORTH EAST HIGHLANDS
Ski Towns..................T

Approach roads to snowfields are subject
to closure during winter. When conditions
allow the roads are cleared. However
motorists are advised to carry chains.

Cover Photo by John Brow

town' contest in 1961. Its modern shopping centre is surrounded by parkland, an open air music bowl, public library and art gallery.

Eildon: The flourishing holiday town of Eildon is on the south-western shore of the great reservoir, with a shoreline of about 50 miles. The reservoir has become Victoria's major inland aquatic centre. Nearby are the Snobs Creek fish hatchery, where two million brown and rainbow trout are bred every year, a **fauna sanctuary** on the way to the hatchery, **Snobs Creek Falls, Morris' lookout,** with a view of the lake, and **Mt Pinniger,** with its panorama of Mt Buller and the alps. Fraser National Park is on Eildon's western shores.

Mansfield: Nearest town to Eildon, Mansfield is becoming a popular inland resort. It is also on the way to the Mt Buller snow field. Other attractive towns in the Eildon region are **Jamieson, Taggerty** and **Alexandra.**

Euroa: on the Hume Highway, 95 miles from Melbourne, became famous in 1878 for the bank robbery in which Ned Kelly and his gang rounded up 50 people, locked them in the local police station and left with £2,200.

Yea: a delightfully situated town, 64 miles north-east of Melbourne, giving access to the south to the **Kinglake National Park,** with several beautiful waterfalls and **Ned Kelly's lookout.**

NORTH-EASTERN VICTORIA

In the north-east, the characteristic rolling country merges, sometimes through long and tranquil valley, sometimes with an abrupt topographical change, into the foothills of the Great Dividing Range. The towns of the north-east have a richness and variety of character in keeping with the varying moods of the country.

Among the main places and points of interest are:

Wangaratta: one of the most attractive provincial cities in Victoria, in a district producing wool, wheat, hops, oats, wine and table grapes, dairy produce, tobacco and flax. 10 miles south-west is Glenrowan, a small township which was the scene of Ned Kelly's last stand.

Rutherglen: 25 miles north of Wangaratta, Rutherglen is the centre of an important vine growing area. It produces full bodied dry red table wines, many delicate white wines, and sherries, ports and muscats of distinction. The cellars of **All Saints Estate** are classified by the National Trust.

Beechworth: magnificently sited on the edge of the Victorian alps, Beechworth's public buildings and old shop fronts and dwellings have been carefully preserved and restored to a point where the town's mining heyday of the 1850s—it had 61 hotels—has almost been recreated. Places of historic interest include the Post Office; the **Powder Magazine,** built of local granite; the **Government buildings;** the **Robert O'Hara Burke memorial museum,** with relics of gold rush days; Kelly's lookout, overlooking the Woolshed Creek alluvial field; the Chinese funeral ovens at the Beechworth cemetery.

Other attractive towns in the scenically exciting mountain foothills are Bright, Myrtleford, Harrietville, Mt Beauty and Towonga.

SNOW FIELDS

Victoria's snowfields cover an area of approximately 800 square miles. The first heavy falls usually occur towards the end of May or early June, and ski runs usually remain in good condition until mid-October. Australian snow is usually 'wetter' than that of Europe because of relatively moderate winter temperatures, and the best skiing is usually in August and September, when it has compacted and formed a firm crust. The major resorts have been established above 6,000 feet, in terrain which provides a wide variety of ski runs and maximum of shelter.

The resorts are now comfortable and well equipped for the visitor as well as the regular, accommodation being in hotel-style chalets, club 'huts', flats or private lodges. All resorts have chair lifts, hire and tuition services. The ski resort life is generally informal, high spirited, with bright life mixed exhaustingly with maximum skiing. The main resorts are:

Mt Hotham: the best for snow, but the most difficult to reach. It is 232 road miles from Melbourne.

Mt Buller: only 160 miles from Melbourne and the most developed of the Alpine tourist villages.

Falls Creek: protected by high mountains and safe in any weather.

Mt Buffalo: an attractive resort in summer as well as winter, with bush walking, trail riding, boating and swimming replacing skiing. The snow is unpredictable, but is satisfactory after good falls.

Mt Baw Baw: 119 miles from Melbourne, but relatively undeveloped. Private lodges only.

Lake Mountain and **Mt Donna Buang:** are close to Melbourne (76 and 60 miles), but have pleasure snow only. Skiing is possible after very heavy falls.

MURRAY VALLEY

The Murray River, which forms the northern boundary of Victoria, gives a scenic focus to the region, which follows the river eastwards from Mildura to its beginnings in the watersheds of the Great Dividing Range.

It is a region made rich by irrigation, which has led to intensive vine, fruit and crop cultivation, and close pastoral activity. The attractive autumn and winter climate, and the enterprise of the tourist conscious citizens of the Murray Valley towns have added a further dimension in prosperity. Now houseboats and speedboats ply where once the paddle steamers that were the backbone of Australia's transport system threaded their way along the river's course.

Main places and points of interest are:

Mildura: The centre of the earliest irrigation area in Australia, the attractive town, 356 miles from Melbourne, is surrounded by nearly 50,000 acres of citrus orchards, vineyards, olive groves and croplands. It is a popular resort for those attracted by its peace, dry and sunny climate, fishing and water sports. Nearby, in the district known as Sunraysia, are the towns of Redcliffs, Irymple and Merbein.

Swan Hill: 222 miles north-west of Melbourne, Swan Hill is the market centre for the Southern Riverina, and a growing tourist centre. Its main attraction is the famous Swan Hill Folk Museum, and living recreation of Australia's pioneering past, with demonstrations of the skills and working practices of early life. It is set in riverside parkland, with an old paddle steamer, *Gem*, in its floating dock, as the museum entrance and restaurant. Swan Hill and **Echuca**, 128 miles from Melbourne, were the main ports of the Paddle Steamer era. Other Major Murray River region towns are **Kerang, Kyabram, Yarrawonga** on Lake Mulwala, and **Wodonga** which is contiguous with the city of Albury in New South Wales, and is the largest stock and rail-trucking centre in Australia, being the border point for the Hume Highway between Melbourne and Sydney, and the inter-State railway.

The broad tranquil reaches of the Murray River itself are popular for boating and fishing, and there are numerous camping reserves on its banks. The district abounds in river-fed lakes and reservoirs, many of them haunts for water birds, particularly the marshes of the Kerang district, where ibis abound.

SHERBROOKE FOREST GUMS, DANDENONG RANGES

Canberra

FULFILLING A VISION

'More and more is the word *Canberra* becoming a symbol of the Commonwealth. And it is undoubtedly an integrating force in a country that has a longer period of disunion behind it than of union. Canberra is more than a city, it is an idea; and as the city grows, the idea grows with it.'

So spoke Sir Robert Garran, one of the fathers of Australian Federation.

Strange irony that Canberra, a city born of disunion and jealousy, should come to fill that role. Its very existence sprang from the fact that neither of the biggest two of the federating colonies would bring itself to trust a government headquartered in the other. So a piece of (relatively) neutral ground was found, and a new capital built up from the plains.

For decades Australia's capital was a national joke, where parliamentarians met in the bush, a long way from the affairs of the nation. Two wars and a Depression slowed down a development task which seemed to many to be futile at best, irresponsible at worst.

Suddenly, in the 1960s, Canberra seemed to blossom, and Australians began going there in droves, more than half a million of them every year to see the developing city.

Walter Burley Griffin had designed his future city to make full use of the natural features on which it was to be sited.

He envisaged a land axis from about the site of the present (temporary) Houses of Parliament to a major national monument below the commanding forested peak of Mt Ainslie, the site now occupied by the Australian War Memorial. The two buildings are connected by a vista across Lake Burley Griffin and along the wide ceremonial marching route of Anzac Parade. The new Parliament House will eventually be built on Capital Hill, Griffin's original choice. His land axis will thus be preserved.

The creation of Lake Burley Griffin by the damming of the Molonglo River in 1964 finally gave Canberra a water axis.

For all its hesitation, for all its uncertainty, Canberra is beginning to fulfil Griffin's original vision.

WATERFRONT, LAKE BURLEY GRIFFIN

PARLIAMENT HOUSE, CANBERRA

YARRALUMLA, THE GOVERNOR GENERAL'S RESIDENCE AT CANBERRA

AN AUSTRALIAN LANDSCAPE

Australia has many landscapes, from tropical jungle to snow covered Alps. Yet if the Australian landscape has a popular image, it is one of rolling plains, of weather worn hills and creeks lined with eucalypt trees.

In such a landscape the planners chose to site the Australian Capital Territory, the 910 square miles of Australia that insulates the nation's capital from the rest of the country. Fittingly, its main industry, apart from Government, is wool growing.

The ACT, as it is called, (never 'The Territory' which means the Northern Territory), has its own private slices of some of Australia's physical features. The 1,800 feet high undulating plains on which the city of Canberra stand rise to the Great Dividing Range along the southern and western boundaries of the ACT, reaching the 6,274 feet of Mt Bimberi.

And the Murrumbidgee, that archetype of Australia's inland rivers, meanders across the ACT on its journey westwards to join the Murray. The Molonglo, which keeps Lake Burley Griffin full, the Cotter, which provided Canberra's first water supply, and the Murrumbidgee, are the ACT's three rivers.

With such a growing population, and such a constant stream of visitors, Canberra is beginning to appreciate the recreational potential of its rivers and mountains. Cotter Reserve, near the junction of the Cotter and Murrumbidgee, has become a favourite spot for such unsophisticated but pleasant pursuits as swimming, picnicking, or merely admiring the many groups of casuarinas (she-oaks) and giant poplars that line the rivers.

Such delightfully rural touches as a one way timber bridge over the Murrumbidgee are still to be found within a few miles of Canberra. At Casuarina Sands, on the Murrumbidgee, Canberra even has its own version of something that is dear to the heart of most Australians— a beach.

To the south and south-west, the ACT makes its own contribution to Kosciusko National Park, a region of impressive mountain scenery.

In the spaciousness of the countryside around Canberra, there was even room to set aside 12,000 acres for Tidbinbilla Fauna Reserve.

Only a little industry disturbs all this tranquility, and it is mostly noiseless, smokeless industry at that. Wool we have already mentioned. Dairying and market gardening takes place along the Molonglo flood plain and terraces. *Pinus radiata* trees grow quietly to maturity in the Cotter catchment and along the slopes now mirrored in the lower end of Lake Burley Griffin. At Fyshwick, Canberra has a developing industrial suburb, just like a real city.

PINE FOREST NEAR CANBERRA

A PARKLAND FOR WORKING AND LIVING

Politics rather than environment dictated the site of Canberra. With few natural advantages, it was not the place where a city might grow up naturally.

Even trees were scarce on the grazing land of the Limestone Plains. In the early years of development, high priority was given to planting shelter-belts of trees to temper the winds that swept down from the nearby ranges. While building lagged through two wars and a depression, these trees continued to grow.

There was a time when cynics said you couldn't see Australia's Capital for the forest in which everyone seemed to be permanently lost.

Canberra already had some buildings that merged into the new city. Yarralumba, destined to become the residence of the Governor General, was built in the 1890s, taken over by the Government in 1913, and first occupied by Lord Stonehaven in 1927.

The Church of St John the Baptist, begun in 1841, records on its tombstones and other memorials much of Canberra's early history. Blundell's Farmhouse, originally built in 1858 by pioneer Robert Campbell, survives.

Grander buildings began to join them. There was something tentative about the first of them. Parliament House is still temporary, although nearing the completion of its first half century of service. The National Library, completed in 1968, is typical of a more confident new generation of Canberra buildings.

As the buildings began to take their place, it became apparent that there had been method in all the tree planting. Careful admixture of native and exotic species had resulted in a succession of beauty throughout the seasons.

At Canberra's opening ceremony in 1913, Prime Minister Andrew Fisher expressed the hope that the city would become a centre of learning as well as of government. The buildings of the Australian National University, the Institute of Anatomy, and the Australian Academy of Science are the physical evidence that his hope was not in vain.

Canberra's role as the national capital has given it an impressive array of embassies since the United Kingdom built the first of them in 1936.

SPRING BLOSSOMS, CANBERRA

QUEEN ELIZABETH MEMORIAL, CANBERRA
PART OF CANBERRA'S COMMERCIAL CENTRE

ST JOHN'S CHURCH, CANBERRA

CONTROLLED SUBURBIA

Australia is a nation of minor capitalists. Per capita, no nation owns more private housing. Ownership of a five roomed house on its own plot of earth is the great Australian dream, although it is to urban planners nothing short of a nightmare. Left to the whims of their inhabitants, Australian cities become one massive sprawl.

Since Canberra was to be a planned city, such undisciplined behaviour was not to be permitted. It was, one writer has said, a product of artificial insemination.

So Canberra's early citizens found themselves denied the great Australian dream. Bureaucrats had rather more say in where they lived, what kind of house they lived in. Leasehold rather than freehold was the common basis of occupation. But the formula of every dwelling to its own plot of earth was substantially preserved, and finally Canberra suburbs came to look not too different from those of other Australian cities.

The circles, radii, boulevards and vistas of Griffin's original vision failed to develop beyond the inner suburbs, but the layout of Canberra's suburbs has never quite degenerated into the gridiron pattern so beloved of surveyors responsible for other Australian cities. Crescents and flowing patterns do avoid monotony in Canberra's suburbs, and make at least some concessions to the contours.

Canberra's more recent suburbs even make concessions to the era of the motor car, with cul-de-sacs leading to feeder roads for major expressways, with some rear-serviced houses and pedestrian enclaves to keep cars and pedestrians apart.

Canberra is already developing satellites, such as Woden, its first new town, six miles south-west and the home of 30,000 people, many of them employed in the Woden Town Centre, developed to become the focal point of the Valley.

Belconnen is another satellite, planned for 120,000 people, six miles north-west. In a significant contribution towards decentralisation, Canberra's College of Advanced Education, was sited at Belconnen.

A NEW CANBERRA SUBURB

CANBERRA

Australia at the end of the nineteenth century was divided into six separate colonies, each politically independent of the others. In the 1890s there were strong movements towards Federation, which was accomplished with the coming into existence of the Commonwealth of Australia on 1 January 1901.

Many and varied were the problems that had to be resolved between the parties that went to make up the new nation, the first to have a whole continent to itself.

Not the least of them was the choice of the Federal capital. Sydney, as capital of the senior colony, may have felt entitled, but Melbourne, capital of Victoria, was unlikely to agree to that. Drafters of the constitution ducked the issue by leaving it to the future Parliament to resolve. When the voters of New South Wales rejected the proposed constitution in 1899, Victoria agreed to give a little, and accepted the notion of a capital city within New South Wales, but at least 100 miles from Sydney, in territory to be ceded to the Commonwealth. New South Wales agreed to this, and to the use of Melbourne as a temporary capital—'temporary' in this case finally being for 27 years.

Various sites for the new capital were proposed. In 1908, Canberra was finally chosen. In 1911 a worldwide competition for the design of the future capital was launched. It was won by a young Chicago architect, Walter Burley Griffin, who came to Australia to assist with implementation of his plan.

Work began in 1913, but proceeded at a slow rate, due partly to feuding between Griffin and the public servants with whom he had to work. Outbreak of war in 1914 added to the problems, for money was needed more urgently elsewhere.

After the war, Griffin finally left the project. Not until 1927 was Canberra ready for occupation by the Commonwealth Parliament. On 9 May, the Duke of York, son of the reigning King George V, opened the first Federal Parliament there, 27 years to the day since his father had opened the first Parliament of the Commonwealth of Australia in Melbourne.

The job of transferring the machinery of government from Melbourne, along with records, archives and staff, begun in 1927, is still going on, with some departments showing a marked reluctance to leave the comforts of Melbourne for Canberra, which some people still regard as an artificial creation, without any real ethos.

Once Federal Parliament had moved to Canberra, there seemed to be hope that the rapid development of the capital was assured. But the cold winds of the Depression came, then World War II. During the war, Federal cabinet found itself meeting in three places—Canberra, Melbourne and Sydney—often in as many weeks.

After the war, the building of Canberra was resumed, the process being greatly accelerated by establishment of the National Capital Development Commission in 1957. So rapid has been recent development that the population of 100,000 in 1967 is expected to have grown to 250,000 by 1980.

OPENING OF PARLIAMENT HOUSE, CANBERRA, ON 9 MAY 1927

CANBERRA POINTS OF INTEREST

Regatta Point Development Display
The kiosk in Commonwealth Park—near the northern end of Commonwealth Bridge—houses a collection of models, diagrams and pictures showing the present and future development of Canberra. Open 9 am to 12.30 pm and 1.30 to 5 pm each day; school and public holidays 9 am to 5 pm.

Parliament House
'The House' is the focal point of Canberra and the home of Commonwealth Parliament. Laws are made here and national issues debated. An attractive white building set among trees, lawns and rose gardens, it faces Lake Burley Griffin up the broad sweep of Anzac Parade to the Australian War Memorial. Inside is the Senate Chamber, the House of Representatives and related offices. In recess, the House opens Monday to Sunday 9 am to 12.30 pm (last tour starts at noon) and 1.30 to 5 pm (last tour at 4.30 pm). On Good Friday and Anzac Day the House opens 1.30 pm to 4.30 pm. During Sessions there are no conducted tours if either House is sitting but King's Hall and both visitor's galleries are open to the public. When neither House sits in the morning, the usual pre-lunch tours operate and, on non-sitting days and Sundays, tours are conducted as in recess.

Australian War Memorial
Erected to commemorate the men and women of Australia who gave their lives in the service of their country, this impressive memorial houses a huge collection of relics and paintings from all theatres of war. Its cloisters, Pool of Reflection, Hall of Memory and many galleries of war relics, provide an unforgettable experience. Open from 9 am to 4.45 pm each day; 9 am to 6 pm between December 26 and January 31.

Anzac Parade
This broad avenue, sweeping down from the Australian War Memorial to Lake Burley Griffin, was completed in 1965 to mark the 50th anniversary of the landing at Gallipoli. It is bordered with Australian Blue Gums and New Zealand shrubs. The first of the statuary to be erected on Anzac Parade is the Desert Mounted Corps Memorial replica, situated near St John's Church.

Royal Australian Mint
Plate glass windows in the visitors' gallery give excellent views of production floor processes in working rotation. The Mint (off Kent Street, Deakin) opens 9 am to 4 pm. Monday to Friday (work stops 12—12.40 pm), and 1.15 to 4.30 pm Sundays and holidays only from December 26 to January 31 and on Easter Sunday and Monday (no production these days).

A.C.T. Law Courts
Situated on the western side of London Circuit, the Law Courts building is faced with polished grey marble and has replicas of the Australian Coat of Arms above its two entrances. The ground floor court rooms are panelled with native timbers donated by six Australian States. Opens Monday to Friday 8.30 am to 4.51 pm, Saturdays 10 am to noon, holidays 10 am to 4 pm. Closed Good Friday and Anzac Day.

National Library of Australia
Sited in the heart of Canberra, overlooking the lake, the five-storey Library houses more than a million volumes and maps, plans, pictures, prints, photographs and cine films. Such historic manuscripts as Captain Cook's Journal, diaries from the Burke and Wills expedition and the papers of Australia's first Prime Minister are included. Open Monday to Friday 9 am to 10 pm, Weekends and public holidays 9 am to 4.45 pm.

Civic Square and Theatre Centre
With its large fountain flanked by two government offices, the Square forms the civic heart of Canberra. The statue of Ethos by sculptor Tom Bass symbolises the spirit of the community. At the head to the Square, the Canberra Theatre Centre consists of two buildings linked by a covered way. The larger building—Canberra Theatre—seats 1,200 people and is designed for symphony concerts, ballet, opera and stage shows. The smaller building—The Playhouse, seating 312—is used for more intimate productions.

Lake Burley Griffin
The Lake, named after Walter Burley Griffin, who designed the original Canberra plan, is a major ornamental feature of the City and an increasingly popular trout fishing and wildlife area. At the western end, near Government House, Scrivener Dam holds back the waters of the Molonglo River to form the Lake. Numerous picnic areas (with barbecues), and launching points for sailing boats dot the 22 miles of foreshore. The character of the Lake changes noticeably from the formal central region to natural areas at the western end where wildlife, trees and grassy banks delight picnickers and fishermen alike. Commonwealth Park, on the north-eastern shore of Central Basin (between the two bridges) is being developed as a completely landscaped area including a series of Marsh Gardens and a Children's Play Area. The jetty in West Basin is the departure point for lake cruises and a depot for hiring rowing boats, canoes and pedlos. Power boats are not permitted.

Carillon and Water Jet
The Carillon, a gift from the U.K. Government to mark Canberra's 50th Jubilee, is situated on Aspen Island near Kings Avenue Bridge. Its 53 bells play a selection of Australain, English and Scottish tunes. The Water Jet and associated lakeshore Terrestrial Globe is in central Lake Burley Griffin near Regatta Point. Built as a memorial to mark the bi-centenary of Captain Cook's discovery of Eastern Australia, it can send a water column 450 feet above the Lake. For Carillon recital times and Water Jet operating hours, enquire at Tourist Bureau.

Lookouts
Black Mountain, 2,664 feet above sea level, Mount Ainslie (2,762 feet), Red Hill (2,368 feet) and Mount Pleasant (2,175 feet) provide fine views of Canberra and surrounding districts. Good roads lead to each.

Royal Military College, Duntroon
The College, Australia's best known military academy, trains officers for the Regular Army. Conducted inspections of the grounds may be made at 2.30 pm Monday to Friday, except during December and January and on public holidays.

Institute of Anatomy
This centre of research into nutrition has a series of displays showing the functions of various body organs. In one wing are interesting ethnological displays about the life and culture of the Australian Aborigine. Open Monday—Saturday 9 am to 5 pm, Sunday 2 to 5 pm and holidays 10 am to 4.30 pm. Closed on Good Friday.

Australian Academy of Science
The Academy, founded by Royal Charter in 1954, aims to promote scientific knowledge. One of Canberra's landmarks, the building is a copper covered shell concrete dome, 150 feet in diameter, resting on arches set in an annular pool. Inside is a central lecture chamber and the offices of the Academy. Not open for public inspection.

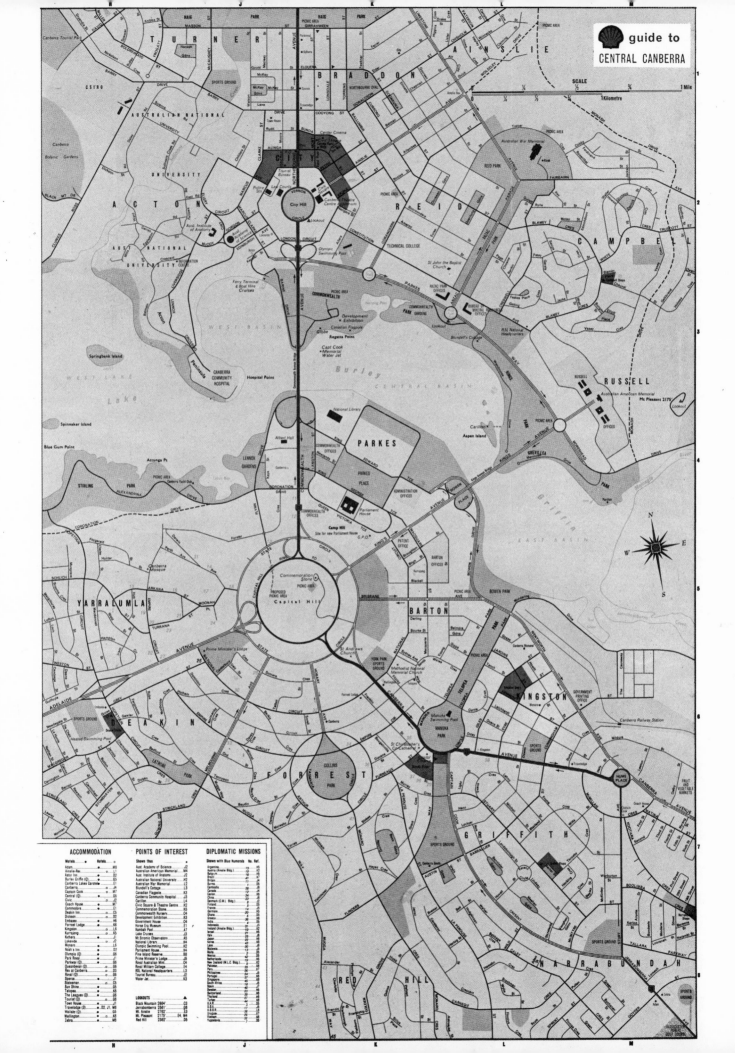

The Australian National University

The University comprises the School of General Studies which undertakes the usual teaching and research functions of a university and the Institute of Advanced Studies, devoted entirely to research and the training of research students. The School of General Studies has Faculties of Arts, Economics, Law, Oriental Studies, and Science. The Institute comprises the John Curtin School of Medical Research, Research Schools of Physical Sciences, Social Sciences, Pacific Studies, Chemistry, and Biological Sciences. A conducted car convoy tour leaves the main entrance of University House at 3 pm Monday to Friday, except public holidays and the period December 25 to January 1 inclusive.

Government House

The official residence of the Governor-General is at the end of tree-lined Dunrossil Drive running off the Cotter Road, just beyond the suburb of Yarralumla. Neither grounds nor House are open for inspection but there is a good view of the building from a look-out on Lady Denman Drive between the Cotter Road and Scrivener Dam.

Prime Minister's Lodge

The official residence of the Prime Minister is in Adelaide Avenue, Deakin. Neither the residence nor the grounds are open to the public.

Diplomatic Missions

There are nearly 50 countries with diplomatic representation in Canberra. The growth of the Diplomatic Corps has brought an interesting and international flavour to the City's architecture. Most of the embassy buildings are in the suburbs of Red Hill, Forrest and Yarralumla. A pamphlet giving addresses of all embassies is available from Canberra Tourist Bureau.

Churches

Canberra's churches provide fascinating contrasts in architecture. The Church of St John the Baptist, begun in 1841, records on its tombstones and other memorials much of Canberra's early history. The adjacent Schoolhouse houses relics of Canberra's early history. Open Wednesdays 10 am to 12 noon, Saturdays and Sundays 2 pm to 4 pm. Admission 10c per adult. All Saints Church, Ainslie, is built from carved masonry previously forming the Mortuary Station at Rookwood, Sydney, erected in 1868. Many newer churches are of unusual contemporary design. Details of services can be obtained from the Tourist Bureau.

Blundell's Farmhouse

Originally built in 1858 by pioneer Robert Campbell for his ploughman, the rear portion was added in 1888. The Canberra and District Historical Society has furnished three rooms with pieces contemporary to its early history. Open daily from 2 to 4 pm and 10 am to 12 noon Wednesdays.

Australian-American Memorial

A 258 feet aluminium shaft, surmounted by an eagle, commemorates the contribution made by the people of the United States to the defence of Australia in World War II. It stands in the centre of a complex of buildings housing the Defence departments at Russell.

New Districts

Twelve of twenty new residential suburbs with a total population of about 95,000 are nearing completion in the Woden Valley, south-west of Canberra City. At Belconnon, to the north-west, work has begun on another 25 suburbs which will eventually house some 120,000 residents. Each district will have its own Town Centre.

Swimming Pools

The Canberra Olympic Pool (City) has a 50 metre pool, one for diving and a children's pond. Other pools at Dickson, Manuka and Deakin open daily October to March. A heated, indoor training pool at Deakin has sauna baths and a gymnasium. Some hotels and motels have private pools.

Mt Stromlo Observatory

The large silver domes and buildings on Mt Stromlo, 10 miles west of Canberra, house the telescopes and other instruments of the Department of Astronomy of the Australian National University. The observatory is one of the largest in the southern hemisphere. A visitors' centre at the 74-inch telescope opens from 9.30 am to 4 pm each day.

Tracking Stations

Space tracking stations at Tidbinbilla (25miles), Honeysuckle Creek (31) and Orroral (36) are among the most advanced in the world. They open for inspection as follows: Honeysuckle Creek, Monday–Tuesday 2 pm sharp; Tidbinbilla Wednesday and Friday 3.30 pm sharp; both closed public holidays; Orroral, Thursday, Saturday, Sunday, 2 pm sharp. Inspection subject to operational requirements. Enquire at Tourist Bureau.

Tidbinbilla Fauna Reserve

Twelve thousand acres in the Tidbinbilla Valley, 25 miles southwest of Canberra, are being developed as a reserve to enable visitors to see Australian flora and fauna in natural surroundings. Picnic facilities and walking tracks are being established. Animal enclosure opens 11 am to 4 pm daily. Dogs, cats, firearms prohibited.

Cotter Dam

The city's original water supply, 14 miles west of Canberra, is reached by crossing the Murrumbidgee and Cotter Rivers. There are pleasant picnic and camping areas, swimming pools, children's playgrounds and a light refreshment kiosk near the Dam.

Picnic Spots

Canberra's parks and lakeside areas provide convenient picnic facilities while, further afield, the Murrumbidgee and other A.C.T. rivers and streams are attractions. Favourite spots are Weston Park on Lake Burley Griffin, near Commonwealth Nursery, Casuarina Sands (12 miles), Kambah Pool (13), Cotter Reserve (14), Uriarra Crossing (15), Point Hut Crossing (16), Pine Island (17) and Gibraltar Falls (30). Further information from the Tourist Bureau.

The Mountains

The Brindabella-Bimberi Ranges forming the Territory's western boundary have a number of peaks between five and more than six thousand feet. The best known is Mount Franklin, 5,400 feet, 45 miles from Canberra where there is skiing in winter and pleasant picnic places at other times.

GOLD ARROW CAR TOUR

Visiting motorists with limited time can see most of the city's points of interest in the 19 mile Gold Arrow Tour, which takes about three hours, allowing short stops at major points of interest.

The Gold Arrows on signposts indicate a route that takes in the Parliamentary Triangle, Regatta Point Development Display, Parliament House, National Library, Australian War Memorial, Canberra Carillon, Blundells Farmhouse, the Australian-American Memorial, the Defence complex at Russell, Civic Square, two lake crossings, the Embassy area and Red Hill Lookout.

An extension of time would permit a call at the Anglican Church of St John the Baptist (1845) or a longer stopover at the War Memorial.

A pamphlet, available from the Canberra Tourist Bureau, cnr London Circuit and West Row, Canberra City (P.O. Box 744 Telephone 49 7555) describes the route of the Gold Arrow Route in detail.

DO-IT-YOURSELF CAR TOURS

The suburbs and countryside around Canberra offer many opportunities for do-it-yourself car tours. A pamphlet detailing eleven of these, including the Gold Arrow Tour described above, is available from Canberra Tourist Bureau.

Tours included are: 1. Gold Arrow Tour. 2. Lakeside Parks and Gardens. 3. The Developing City. 4. Woden Valley, Mugga Way, Red Hill. 5. North of the Lake. 6. Australian National University. 7. Tidbinbilla Fauna Reserve and Space Tracking Station. 8. The Three Rivers. 9. Cotter Dam, Casuarina Sands, Mt Stromlo Observatory. 10. Molonglo Gorge and Queanbeyan. 11. Snowy Mountains.

INFORMATION SERVICES

Literature of Canberra and the Australian Capital Territory is plentiful but not as well distributed as perhaps it should be. The only office of the Canberra Tourist Bureau is in Canberra itself, at the corner of London Circuit and West Row, Canberra City. Telephone 49 7555. Provided you don't mind waiting until you actually get to Canberra, you'll find all the help you are likely to need there.

If you like to plan ahead, you can usually get some literature on Canberra at the local office of the New South Wales Government Tourist Bureau, or from the various motoring organisations. Canberra Tourist Bureau is also happy to send material by mail. Their postal address is P.O. Box 744, Canberra City, A.C.T. 2601.

The Canberra office of the National Roads and Motorists Association is at 92 Northbourne Ave, Canberra City. Telephone 49 6666. (For 24 hours emergency road service after hours 49 6423).

This Week in Canberra, available at most hotels, motels, etc., has up to the minute information about Canberra's current attractions.

EMBASSIES IN CANBERRA

As Australia's Federal Capital, Canberra has a large number of foreign embassies. They have added distinction and variety to the architecture of Canberra.

The United States embassy, with its distinctive Virginian Colonial style stands high on a hill in the suburb of Yarralumla. It contrasts with the Cape Dutch architecture of the nearby South African official residence, and the contemporary design of the Embassy of the Philippines.

The nearby Belgian Chancery is a combination of modern and Flemish styles, and not far away the German Embassy, standing among fine gardens, is in the modern style of German architecture.

The residence of the Japanese Ambassador in Yarralumla is a fine example of modern Japanese architecture, blended with elements of the styles of the 10th and 13th centuries.

There are some exceptions, but most Embassies and diplomatic residences are in an area near the Prime Minister's Lodge in Forrest, and the neighboring divisions of Yarralumla, Deakin and Red Hill.

They have become a distinct tourist attraction. They are only open for public inspection on special occasions, but thousands of people seem to be prepared to drive around the Embassy areas just to look at the buildings. Several of them are on the do-it-yourself Gold Arrow Tour.

A pamphlet 'Embassies in Canberra', giving the full address of all embassies, is available from the Canberra Tourist Bureau, cnr London Circuit and West Row, Canberra City, (P.O. Box 744, Telephone 49 7555).

DINING OUT IN CANBERRA

Canberra's hotels and motels usually have good dining rooms and restaurants, several of them with dancing.

Dinner dances are Friday and Saturday night features at the Commodore and the Canberra Rex. On Saturday nights, they are joined by the Coach House, the Embassy Motel, and the Four Festivals Restaurant at the Parkroyal Motor Inn.

Supper dances are held on Wednesdays, Thursdays, Fridays and Saturdays at Deakin Inn, and on Thursdays, Fridays and Saturdays at the Hotel Dickson and the Civic.

Restaurants with dancing include the Balcony Room (six nights a week), the Lobby, and the Lotus (both on Fridays and Saturdays). Gus' Alouette, open seven nights a week, has gypsy music as well as music for dancing.

Steaks are likely to be good at any Canberra restaurant or hotel. Establishments which specialise in grills include the Bacchus Tavern, Hobart Place, Civic, which serves French cuisine as well as finest steaks from the charcoal broiler. The Charcoal Restaurant naturally enough specialises in steaks and aged beef, as does the Hotel Dickson, which also offers fine seafood.

The Lobby, diagonally Parliament House, is about as close as ordinary folk can hope to get to eating in the corridors of power. As befits its name, it has intimate decor.

French and international cuisine is offered by the Chantilly Restaurant. Noah's, at the Town House Motel, claims to make the best Crepes Suzette outside Paris. Neptune's Tavern is Canberra's first all-seafood restaurant, with rare seafoods and recipes culled from all parts of the world.

Chinese restaurants in Canberra include the Lotus, with authentic Peking, Cantonese, Szechuan and Shanghai dishes. Happy's Chinese Restaurants are in Garema Place and in Queanbeyan.

The Carousel Restaurant, at the top of Red Hill, provides a view of Canberra while you dine.

Other recommended spots for dining out in Canberra include Charlie's, the Mogambo, Zorba's, Taverna, Hotel Wellington, Spero's Motel, Homestead Hotel, Canberra Hotel, The Red Door (at Travelodge).

ACCOMMODATION
RECOMMENDED CANBERRA ACCOMMODATION IS LISTED BY SUBURB.

Acton	Canberra Hotel, Commonwealth Ave. 7 2251
Braddon	Canberra Rex Hotel, Northbourne Ave. 4 5311. Ainslie Rex Hotel, Ainslie Ave. 4 3351. Parkroyal Motel, 102 Northbourne Ave. 49 1411. Kythera Motel, Northbourne Ave. 4 1239. Speros Motel, 82 Northbourne Ave. 49 1388.

Canberra City	Civic Hotel, Northbourne Ave. 4 1241. Travelodge Canberra City, cnr. Northbourne Ave. and Cooyong St 49 6911. Town House, 12 Rudd St 4 0303.
Curtin	Statesman Hotel, Strangeways St 81 1777.
Deakin	Deakin Inn, Kent St 81 0111. Embassy Motel, cnr Hopetoun Circuit and Adelaide Ave 81 1322.
Dickson	Dickson Hotel, Anthill St 49 6848. Astor Inn, Northbourne Ave 4 2321.
Forrest	Wellington Hotel, cnr National Circuit and Canberra Ave 7 1313. Forrest Motor Lodge, 30 National Circuit 73 2513. Telopea Motor Inn, 16 New South Wales Crescent 73 2557.
Griffith	Coach House Motor Inn, McMillan Circle 9 0074. Kingston Hotel, Canberra Ave 9 0123. Manuka Travelodge, cnr Canberra Ave and Burke Cres 9 0481.
Kingston	Monaro Motel, 27 Dawes St 95 0370.
Lyneham	Travelodge, Barton Highway 4 5353. Canbery House, 39 Barton Highway 49 6855.
Narrabundah	Zebra Motel, Jerrabomberra Ave 9 0174.
Watson	Commodore Motel, Federal Highway 49 8844.

PARKS AND GARDENS

Nobody is ever far from a park in Canberra. Parks and gardens of particular note are:

Parliamentary Rose Gardens.

Two identical gardens each with more than 20 beds set in a circular formal design. The gardens contain about 2,500 roses of many varieties. They flower in spring and summer.

Commonwealth Park.

Lakeside picnic spot surrounging the Nerang Pool, in which grow an outstanding selection of water-lilies.

Haig Park.

Some of the oldest tree plantings in Canberra are in this belt of parkland, which extends in an axis across the northern suburbs of Turner and Braddon.

Cotter Reserve.

Near the junction of the Cotter and Murrumbidgee Rivers, 13 miles west of Canberra. A popular swimming and picnicking resort for Canberra people and a favoured camping ground for visitors, the area is noted for its many large groups of giant poplars and casuarinas (she-oaks).

Woden Valley.

In Hughes, the first of the neighbourhoods of the Woden Valley, there is a new style of street planting. Informal group plantings of trees of mixed species have been developed in contrast with the more conventional avenues of a single species in the older areas.

Weston Park.

This pleasant park is on the northern boundary of the Yarralumla Nursery and overlooks a quiet corner of Lake Burley Griffin. Groups of identified trees are a feature. There are established fireplaces and barbecues. The area is favoured by waterbirds: curlews, wood ducks, cormorants, silver gulls and smaller birds often take the sun there.

Black Mountain Peninsula.

Black Mountain Peninsula, on the opposite side of the lake, is another waterside picnicking area.

Telopea Park.

Telopea Park has outstanding examples of eucalypt trees, as well as elms, poplars and blossom trees. There is a swimming pool at the southern end of the park, and from the northern end, a superb view across the lake towards the Australian-American memorial and the Defence buildings complex.

Duntroon Park

Is a riverbank park on the backwaters of the Molongo River, which feeds Lake Burley Griffin. Mature willows which line the bank recall the appearance of the Molonglo before Scrivener Dam backed up the river to form the lake. The park is a favourite fishing spot with Canberra anglers.

Anzac Parade,

Leads up to the Australian War Memorial, is flanked by Australian blue gums with the centre beds planted with varieties of New Zealand veronica. Together they symbolise the word Anzac—Australia and New Zealand Army Corps.

Yarralumla Nursery.

This 70 acre government nursery has produced all the trees and shrubs growing in Canberra's streets, reserves and public parks, as well as a large proportion of those growing in private gardens. Visitors are welcomed daily between 8 am and 4 pm.

Botanic Gardens.

Devoted entirely to Australian native plants, these gardens are being developed on about 100 acres of the lower slopes of Black Mountain with entry from Clunies Ross Street. The gardens are planned to promote scientific and educational interest, not as a picnic area or playground. Open 9am to 5pm each day. One hour guided tours Monday to Friday, 11.30am, Saturday and Sunday 2.30pm.

TREES

That trees would have an important place in Australia's future showplace capital was accepted from the very earliest stages of planning. Planting began in 1915 and has continued ever since.

In selecting trees for Canberra, a careful balance was struck between native Australian species and exotic species from overseas.

Many of the native species belong to the genus Eucalyptus, members of the Myrtaceae (Myrtle) family of trees. There are about six hundred species of Eucalypt, nearly all of them originally restricted to Australia and New Guinea, but today widely spread throughout the world, notably to California. About 95 per cent of Australia's natural forests are covered with Eucalypts.

They range in size from the 300 feet Mountain Ash (Eucalyptus regnans) down to Eucalyptus dumosa, the dwarf mallee. They are often called gums, because of the sticky resin they sometimes exude. Only species suitable as street and park trees have been planted in Canberra.

Other indigenous species include members of the genus Acacia, in the Mimosaceae family. Known collectively as wattles, the six hundred species of Acacia that grow in Australia produce masses of golden blossom, Australia's national floral emblem. Casuarinas are another genus of native Australian trees represented at Canberra. Casuarina cunninghamiana, the River She Oak, for instance, is to be found there, as well as along the banks of many rivers in the east and north of the continent.

Introduced trees include not only such classic types as cedar, cypress, ash, liquidamber, Monterey pine, plane, poplar, cherry, prunus, oak, weeping willow and elm, but also walnuts from Arizona and Europe, olives from the Mediterranean, deodars from India, pepper trees from Peru, silk trees from China.

A short list of trees to be seen in Canberra is reproduced from. 'Canberra—City of Parklands', available from Canberra

Tourist Bureau. In the pamphlet the individual species are keyed to a map.

Detailed information is contained in a 127 page book 'Trees in Canberra' by L. D. Pryor, Professor of Botany at the Australian National University, Canberra.

TRANSPORT SERVICES

City and suburbs. Canberra's public transport is provided by a fleet of buses. They cater for local residents' needs rather than those of tourists. There is no city or suburban railway system.

Taxis are readily available at 20 cents flagfall, 20c mile, 10c radio booking fee. Out of town, the mileage rate is 14c. Waiting time $2.50 an hour. Telephone 49 8411. Hire cars, with driver, are available. Telephone 95 7750   48 5381   48 6638   49 6748   49 9132. Drive yourself cars are available from Avis 49 6088 and Rumbles Rent-A-Car 95 0019.

INTERSTATE

Both Australia's domestic airlines service Canberra with frequent flights. Ansett Airlines of Australia 49 7333. Trans Australia Airlines 48 8433.

RAIL

Rail services out of Canberra are operated by New South Wales Government Railways, which provides direct services to Sydney, and overnight sleeper services to Melbourne.

INTERNATIONAL

There are no direct flights from Canberra to overseas destinations. Domestic services connect with overseas flights at Sydney and Melbourne. Qantas, Australia's overseas airline, has an office in Canberra. Telephone 48 1411.

AUSTRALIA'S GOVERNMENT

Since 1 January 1901, Australia has been a Federation of six states: New South Wales, Queensland, South Australia, Tasmania, Victoria and Western Australia. Canberra is where the Federal Government meets. Government is in accordance with a written constitution.

The Parliament consists of two houses, the House of Representatives and the Senate.

The House of Representatives has 121 members representing the various States in proportion to population, plus two members with restricted voting rights to represent the Australian Capital Territory and the Northern Territory. All members of the House must stand for re-election at least once in every three years. Of the two houses, the House of Representatives is the more powerful. The Prime Minister, for instance, must be a member of the Representatives. This pre-eminence of the 'lower' house is in accordance with British practice.

The Senate has sixty members, ten from each State. A Senator's term is six years, half the members standing for re-election each three years.

Although the composition of the two Houses is very similar to those in the United States, nearly all the forms and procedures of Australian parliamentary practice follow British methods of Responsible Government. The Prime Minister and all Cabinet Ministers must be either Representatives or Senators, and take part in the making of the law as well as in its execution. A government may be removed at any time if it loses the confidence of the Parliament, particularly of the House of Representatives. The Government is chosen from the party or alliance of parties which can command a majority in that House.

AUSTRALIAN WAR MEMORIAL

One feature of Canberra that invariably impresses visitors is the Australian War Memorial, set at the foot of Mount Ainslie, on a site Walter Burley Griffin designated for a great national monument, some years before he could have realised just how soon the basis of such a memorial would develop.

Most people leave the War Memorial feeling that they should have allowed much more time than they did. A whole day can easily be spent there. In exhibits, models, dioramas, paintings and relics, it tells of Australia's part in several wars.

The War Memorial today has three main functions: commemoration, exhibition galleries and library.

The purely commemorative features stand on either side and at the far end of the open quadrangle or courtyard into which visitors first pass from the main entrance. To left and right and above the Pool of Reflection, in the arcaded galleries, are the bronze panels of the Roll of Honour, containing the names of more than 100,000 men and women who died in the service of Australia. They are assembled alphabetically in the unit or branch of the service to which they belonged, without distinction of rank, status or decoration. On the left or western wall is the Roll of Honour of the 1914–18 and earlier wars; on the right or eastern wall that of the 1939–45 and later wars.

At the far end of the courtyard is the Hall of Memory, designed as the focal point of the building. In statuary, stained glass window and more than six million pieces of mosaic tile, it depicts symbolically the qualities—social, personal and martial—said to have been outstanding in the Australian servicemen and women.

In the wings to each side of the commemorative area are the exhibition galleries. Those on the western side of the building relate generally to the 1914–18 and earlier wars; those on the eastern side to the 1939–45 and to Korea and Vietnam. The galleries contain a collection of relics, paintings, statuary and dioramas—unforgettable picture models, vividly recreating famous battles or everyday scenes in the life of the soldiers—that is unsurpassed.

Separate galleries commemorate the work of the Australian navy and air force and of the medical and women's services.

On the lower floor, at ground level, are galleries containing historic pieces of heavy ordnance—tanks, guns, torpedoes, landing craft; display windows, showing among other things, aspects of the work of religious orders and philanthropic organisations; and show cases displaying ships models, small arms, sidearms and other technical exhibits as well as documents relating to each of the wars.

Visiting hours at the Australian War Memorial are 9am to 4.45pm daily except Christmas Day, when the Memorial is closed.

WALTER BURLEY GRIFFIN

Walter Burley Griffin, whose fundamental plan for Canberra has survived generations of officialdom, was born in Maywood, Illinois, in the United States, in 1876.

Educated at the University of Illinois, he worked under Frank Lloyd Wright, and on his own. It was in collaboration with his future wife, Marion Mahoney, that he won the international competition for a plan for Australia's new Federal Capital.

The Griffins came to Australia, and lived in Melbourne,

the temporary capital. He was director of the board controlling Canberra's development, but had many disputes with official-dom. Fortunately his basic plan was completed before he resigned in 1921, frustrated and disgusted.

In private practice, he designed some notable Melbourne buildings, including the Capitol Building in Swanston Street, Newman College at Melbourne University, and several Toorak houses, as well as laying out the Sydney suburb of Castlecrag and the town of Griffith, in the Murrumbidgee Irrigation Area of New South Wales.

Some of his best houses, aimed at providing space, privacy and unobtrusive building, are at Castlecrag. They were low stone or concrete flat roofed houses. After leaving Melbourne in 1928, he lived for a time in one of the Castlecrag houses.

The Griffins left Sydney in 1933 for Lucknow, there to design university buildings. It was there, in 1937, that Walter Burley Griffin died.

GALLERIES

Australian Sculpture Gallery, 1 Finniss Cres., Narrabundah. Permanent exhibition of sculptures by Australian artists, Aboriginal art, ceramics, jewellery, New Guinea artifacts.

Greta Daly. The Australian Gallery, 3 Grant Crescent, Griffith. Authentic Aboriginal artifacts, including boomerangs, shields, woomeras, spears. Bark paintings from the Centre and Arnhem Land.

The Curiosity Shop, Civic Arcade, Garema Place and Kennedy St, Kingston. Furniture, bronzes, porcelain (English and French), candlesticks and sterling silver.

Macquarie Galleries, Macquarie House, 23 Furneaux St, Forrest. Comprehensive collection of work by leading artists and potters on display at all times in addition to regular exhibitions.

Theatre Centre Gallery, Civic Square, London Circuit.

Antique Centre, 29 Bougainville St, Manuka. Antiques. Collectors items from all over the world. Old and contemporary paintings.

Narek Craft Galleries, 66 Carnegie Cres., Narrabundah. Continuous exhibition of Australian handcrafts of leading craftsmen including pottery, weaving (rugs, ties, wall hangers), batik, tie dye, furniture, jewellery.

DO-IT-YOURSELF CAR TOURS

The suburbs and countryside around Canberra offer many opportunities for do-it-yourself car tours. A pamphlet detailing eleven of these, including the Gold Arrow Tour described above, is available from Canberra Tourist Bureau.

For the benefit of motorists without the pamphlet, brief details are given here.

Tour 1 Gold Arrow Tour (see above).

Tour 2 Lakeside Parks and Gardens. Botanic Gardens, Black Mountain Summit, views of Yarralumla (Governor-General's Residence), Scrivener Dam, Regatta Point Development Display. Possible diversions along the way include Commonwealth Park (Stream Valley cascades and Marsh Gardens) Royal Australian Mint, Government Nursery, Parliament House, Blundell's Farmhouse, National Library, Institute of Anatomy. Basic tour of 25 miles takes about 3 hours.

Tour 3 The Developing City. Planned to show something of Canberra's pre-war suburbs, urban development in the early 1960s, and current construction of the Belconnen satellite city north-west of Black Mountain. Tour takes in the Old Schoolhouse and St John's Church, a drive to Mount Ainslie Lookout, All Saints Church, Dickson Regional Shopping Centre, Horse Era Museum, and a drive along Belconnen Way with its 'Beware of Kangaroos' signs. 30 miles, about 2½ hours.

Tour 4 Woden Valley, Mugga Way, Red Hill. Woden, Canberra's first satellite city, is in the Woden Valley, south-west of the city proper. Tour includes a visit to the Royal Australian Mint, brief glimpses of the Embassy Area, the elite Mugga Way, views of the old and the new Canberra from Red Hill. 26 miles, about 2½ hours.

Tour 5 North of the Lake. A visit to the Australian War Memorial and the Royal Military College at Duntroon, the Russell Defence Complex, Australian-American War Memorial and a drive to the summit of Mount Ainslie. Possible diversions include the Regatta Point Development Display, the Old Schoolhouse and the Anglican Church of St John the Baptist (1845), Blundell's Farmhouse (1858), and Commonwealth Park (Stream Valley cascades and Marsh Gardens). Basic tour is 14 miles, takes about two hours including one hour at the Australian War Memorial.

Tour 6 Australian National University. 5 miles. 1½ hours. See notes on the University, in 'Points of Interest'.

Tour 7 Tidbinbilla Fauna Reserve and Space Tracking Station. 66 miles. Driving time 3 hours. See notes on Fauna Reserve and Tracking Stations, in 'Points of Interest'.

Tour 8 The Three Rivers. A round trip through pastoral and Brindabella foothill country, with extensive views of the Murrumbidgee Valley, to picnic grounds at Coppins Crossing (Molonglo River), Uriarra (Murrumbidgee), Cotter River and Dam (Cotter River) and Casuarina Sands (Murrumbidgee). Four river crossings are involved, one affording a view of the Murrumbidgee and Cotter River Junction. Possible variations include the satellite city of Belconnen, to Mt Stromlo Observatory and Royal Australian Mint. Basic tour is 45 miles, driving time 2 hours.

Tour 9 Cotter Dam, Casuarina Sands, Mt Stromlo Observatory. South side Embassy Area, Cotter River picnic grounds, Casuarina Sands (Murrumbidgee) swimming beach, Mt Stromlo Observatory, short forest drive. Possible diversions include Royal Australian Mint, Woden Valley, Black Mountain Summit, Botanic Gardens. Basic tour is 40 miles, driving time 1½ hours.

Tour 10 Molonglo Gorge, Queanbeyan. This short tour embraces Canberra Airport, the 1940 Air Disaster Memorial in Fairbairn Forest, Molonglo Reserve and Gorge River Walk along the ACT border, with a return via Queanbeyan (NSW border town) Harman Naval Station, and Fyshwick, Canberra's industrial centre. 26 miles. Driving time 1¼ hours.

Tour 11 Snowy Mountains—By making an early start it is possible to see some of Australia's Snowy Mountains and Snowy Mountains Hydro-electric Scheme in a day trip from Canberra. A variety of routes is suggested in the Canberra Tourist Bureau pamphlet.

South Australia

THE THIRSTY STATE

Four times as large as the United Kingdom, South Australia is home to only a million and a quarter people, less than half the population of Wales.

Although the South Australians have 380,070 square miles at their disposal, they cluster together in the south eastern corner of the State, for more than four-fifths of South Australia gets less than ten inches of rain a year.

As if to make up for such neglect, nature has smiled upon the area around the two gulfs—Spencer and St Vincent. In Adelaide, the State capital, 21 inches of rain, seven hours of sunshine for every day of the year, and temperatures that vary between averages of 23°C in summer and 12°C in winter, provide an ideal climate for the outdoor kind of living for which Australia at large is reputed.

Surveyor General Colonel Light picked a billiard table site for South Australia's capital city, halfway between the Mount Lofty Ranges and a 20 mile sweep of white, sandy beaches on Gulf St Vincent.

South Australia's agricultural areas are never far from Adelaide. The early settlers spread out rapidly and went too far, convincing themselves in their hunger for land that 'rain follows the plough'. But it did not, and they learned to their sorrow that Goyder's Line, drawn in 1865 to show the end of the ten inch rainfall area (and therefore the limit of agriculture) was no imaginary line.

South Australia's tourist venues are beginning to enjoy the support they deserve.

Adelaide itself has its charm, as do its nearby hills, and and the Barossa Valley. The last 400 miles of the Murray River are in the State, and it has 2,400 miles of coastline, with every kind of beach and swimming water.

The ancient volcanic country of the south east of South Australia, around Mount Gambier, features such attractions as the mysterious Blue Lake, and Naracoorte's fascinating caves.

South Australia has figured largely in the growing fascination of Australians with their Outback. No capital is closer than Adelaide to the 'real Australia' of the inland.

CATTLE MUSTER NEAR MT GAMBIER
B.H.P. IRON QUARRY, IRON PRINCE, NEAR WHYALLA

300 FT HIGH CLIFFS OF THE GREAT AUSTRALIAN BIGHT
SEAVIEW ESTATE VINEYARDS AND WINERY

ADELAIDE'S EARLY PLANNING PAYS OFF

Right from the start Colonel Light's vision of a city on the banks of the Torrens had its critics. Time, he said, would prove he was right. And to the 800,000 people who call Adelaide home, so it has. In the city proper they enjoy wide streets and an abundance of beautiful and well preserved commercial and public buildings and churches.

In the major part of his city Light put five squares, including the central one where he intended a cathedral to rise up and contemplate a government house at the end of the wide thoroughfare that became King William Street. Neither the cathedral nor the government house were built where Light intended, which at least gave Adelaide enough flexibility to cope with the motor car age.

Judicious rearrangement of Victoria Square provided the sweeping curves the motor cars seemed to demand, while extension of King William Street into King William Road provided a way out of town for the twentieth century's favourite form of transport.

Long turned over to pasturing cows, the Adelaide Parklands are today very much in use. Many an Adelaide office worker stops off for a few holes of golf as he crosses the Parklands on the way from suburb to city. Children go boating in the lake in Rymill Park, or wade in the East Parklands. Others just stroll, enjoying the peace and tranquillity with which Adelaide's parklands surround the city. The sense of well being extends into the suburbs. There are none of the depressed areas of the larger capitals, and the suburbs have an agreeable proportion of well bred stone houses and quiet, leafy streets.

Every second year, in the years of even number, Adelaide turns on its Festival of Arts. For sixteen days, the city offers a feast of music, opera, ballet, theatre, art, literature and light entertainment. Adelaide has proved itself an ideal venue for such a festival—large enough to provide good audiences, small enough to establish a sense of unity, for artists and audiences to become acquainted.

The Festival and the liberalisation of licensing laws are factors in the change in Adelaide from a staid and socially stratified city to one with a more lively and spontaneous atmosphere.

THE STATUE OF ADELAIDE'S PLANNER, COLONEL LIGHT, SURVEYS THE CITY
BOATING ON THE TORRENS RIVER IS POPULAR

AERIAL VIEW OF ADELAIDE SUBURBS
BONYTHON HALL, ADELAIDE UNIVERSITY

KING WILLIAM STREET, ADELAIDE

ADELAIDE HILLS SCENE
HOMESTEAD NEAR STRATHALBYN. SOUTH OF ADELAIDE

AUSTRALIA'S VINEYARD

Wining and dining has become very much a part of the Australian scene, and the people of the Barossa Valley have helped to make it so. From this small vale, about 18 miles long and 5 miles wide, comes about a third of all the wine produced in Australia.

The valley has a German flavour to it. Freedom to practise their Lutheran religion was what its first settlers sought. Led by Pastor Kavel, they arrived in 1838, from Silesia, and settled at Bethany.

Any trip through the Barossa Valley shows that many of the vineyards and businesses are owned by people with German names—Gramp, Seppelt, Hoffman, Liebich and Henschke. You see the German influence too in the Lutheran Churches that grace every town.

Solid stone houses and old German cottages, together with carefully cultivated gardens in scrupulously clean and neat tree lined streets, characterise the valley towns. And not far from each of them, several wineries are to be found.

One of the largest is at Seppeltsfield, which dates from 1850. In that year, Joseph Seppelt arrived from Germany, and planted grape vines and tobacco plants. The grape vines flourished, so he concentrated on them.

Other Barossa Vineyards and wineries are much more recent. Chateau Yaldara is owned by a German migrant who came to the Valley in 1947, worked for wages for a year, then set up on his own. Now, a mere twenty years later, Thumm's Chateau Yaldara has taken its place among the sources of well known Australian wines.

The Barossa Valley was given its name by Colonel William Light, who was sent to survey the new colony. It reminded him of a valley in Spain, where he had been in the Peninsular War. Somewhere along the way, the spelling changed. The Spanish Barrosa became the Australian Barossa.

SEPPELTSFIELD WINERY BUILDINGS

CELLARS AT SEPPELTSFIELD

MURRAY RIVER – *the Fountain Head*

For 400 miles, a quarter of its length, the Murray flows through South Australia. Australia's noblest river, it is South Australia's only large watercourse.

Three main sectors of the Murray may easily be identified in South Australia.

From the border to Overland Corner it flows by such irrigation settlements as Renmark, Berri, Loxton, Barmera and Waikerie. These centres owe their origin to the industrious Chaffey brothers, irrigation specialists from Canada and California, who established Renmark in 1887. (Victorians and New South Welshmen tend to know the Chaffeys better for their work at Mildura.) Oranges and grapes thrive when the magic touch of the river's water gets together with the richness of the soil and the warmth of the climate.

At Overland Corner the Murray makes a great curve to the south, entering a gorge which is rarely more than a mile wide. Limestone cliffs are hundred feet high some times close in upon the river. Elsewhere it is flanked by narrow swamp lands, many of them reclaimed to provide pasture for a dairy industry.

It was on this stretch of the Murray that South Australia provided the initiative for the river boat trade that grew up in the second half of the nineteenth century.

Soon after Captain Charles Sturt's great whaleboat journey down the Murray in 1830, some observers realised that the river could become the 'Mississippi of New Holland'.

Eventually there were hundreds of paddle steamers making their way up and down the Murray. In South Australia, Morgan, Mannum and Goolwa were major ports, with Morgan really coming into its own once the railway reached it in 1878.

The third and final segment of the Murray in South Australia is the region of the lakes—Alexandra and Albert—into which the river spreads before finding its way into the sea near Goolwa, where five barrages across the river mouth prevent the intrusion of salt water into the lakes and river.

RAILWAY AND ROAD BRIDGES AT MURRAY BRIDGE, SOUTH AUSTRALIA

GRAPE HARVEST, RENMARK
IRRIGATED FARMLANDS, MURRAY RIVER DISTRICT

FLINDERS – NATURE LAID BARE

That was how South Australian painter Sir Hans Heysen described the Flinders Ranges. Nature has had ample time to lay bare her bones, for geologists estimate that the ranges were thrown upwards by earth movements in tertiary times, beginning 60 million years ago and reaching their maximum height about two million years ago.

The great hardened sandstone formations known as quartzites were left exposed by the heavier rainfall of those times and it is to these that the Flinders Ranges owe their scenic grandeur.

Wilpena Pound is among the best known features of the Flinders Ranges. The aboriginal word Wilpena means 'place of bent fingers'; the pound resembles the palm of the hand with the fingers bent into a shallow depression. Advancing pastoralists gave it the name Pound, for its enclosing mountains made it a good place to keep cattle.

Hardy souls climb the 3,900 feet of St Mary Peak, the highest point in the mountains that surround the Pound. Others prefer to do their exploring by car, over roads which are good enough to be trafficable, but not so good as to be uninteresting.

One road leads into the lovely, large wide grassy Bunyeroo Valley. Suddenly it is in Bunyeroo Gorge, where the road and the creek bed are often the same. On it goes through Brachina Gorge before emerging into the comparatively open country through which passes the railway to Alice Springs.

The round trip to Wilpena Pound goes back through Parachilna Gorge, through the old copper mining town of Blinman and skirts the Great Wall of China.

In spring, square miles are covered with the blue flowering plant variously known as Pattersons Curse, Salvation Jane, or *Lycopsis plantagineum*. It gets vigorous competition from another introduced species, rosy dock, also called native hops and *Rumex vesicarius*. But there is nothing imported about *Eucalyptus camaldulensis*, the red river gums, which line the creekbeds that have carved their way between the mountains of the Flinders Ranges.

WILD HOPS GROWING IN THE FLINDERS RANGES

A FLAT, FORBIDDING INLAND

'South Australia is a land of generally low relief, the inland area being largely covered by featureless plains or sand and gibber deserts.' In such matter-of-fact phrases, the South Australian Year Book disposes of most of the state's 'physical features'.

Anybody who has driven across the Nullarbor Plain, north to Alice Springs, or along the fabled Birdsville Track, knows the featureless feeling well enough.

Half the State is less than 500 feet above sea level, four-fifths of it less than a thousand feet. Mt Woodroffe, the State's highest point, in the Musgrave Ranges of the far north, is only 4,723 feet high.

Nowhere does the featureless quality show itself quite so much as in the Nullarbor Plain, where not even a tree breaks the skyline. Yet such country has its pull, and 'crossing the Nullarbor' is still a great Australian achievement, though it's usually done in a modern car on the Eyre Highway, between Port Augusta and Norseman (in Western Australia). To call this 'crossing the Nullarbor' is to handle the truth loosely, for only twenty of the highway's 1,063 miles are on the Nullarbor at all.

Train passengers such as those in the Sydney–Perth 'Indian Pacific', get a better look at the Nullarbor. Instead of hugging the coast, the builders of the railway plunged into the plain, headed directly for their goal at Kalgoorlie.

'Because it is there' is the only reason offered by the steady stream of hardy tourists who follow in the steps of Torrens and Eyre to see the desolation that is Lake Eyre. Here the land of generally low relief excels itself, and sinks to 39 feet below sea level.

Lake Eyre glares in the sunlight, the searing white of its salt-encrusted surface mocking the cool blue the map-makers use to show its location. A trip to the interior should be compulsory for all such innocents. Around here, the ten inch annual rainfall of the Nullarbor seems like one continuous deluge. Five inches is a wet year at Lake Eyre.

ROCKET LAUNCH AT WOOMERA RANGE

A LITTLE JOKE IN DESOLATE COUNTRY NEAR LAKE EYRE

THE OPAL TOWN OF COOBER PEDY
LAKE EYRE

POLISHED AND NATURAL OPAL

HORSES ON KOONALDA STATION
GOANNA IN THE SOUTH AUSTRALIAN DESERT

FACTS & FIGURES

South Australia is a State of the Commonwealth of Australia, third largest in size, fourth in population.

SIZE AND LOCATION

The State's total area of 380,070 square miles (one-eighth of the Australian continent) is bounded on the north by the 26th parallel of south latitude, on the west by the 129th meridian of east longitude. (When the colony was first defined, in 1834, this boundary was set at 132 degrees, but it was subsequently moved westwards to correspond with the previously defined boundary of Western Australia.) The eastern boundary north of the Murray River is the 141st degree of longitude. South of the Murray, the boundary should have followed the same meridian, but bungling surveyors set it out two miles to the west, and so far South Australia's efforts to get this piece of territory back from Victoria have been unfruitful.

At the northern boundary, (with the Northern Territory) South Australia is 746 miles from east to west. At the head of the Great Australian Bight this distance has been reduced by the curvature of the earth to 710 miles. From north to south, the State measures 391 miles along the border with Western Australia, 823 miles along the eastern border with Queensland, New South Wales and Victoria.

PHYSICAL FEATURES

Five main geographical areas may be identified in South Australia.

The Murray River Basin, in the south east, is the most fertile part of the State. Indeed, the Murray is its only major river. It irrigates the State's orchards, vineyards and pastures, and makes a major contribution to the water supply of Adelaide and other South Australian cities. Associated with the Murray River Basin are the fertile volcanic plains of the Mount Gambier region.

The Highland Chain formed by the Mount Lofty and Flinders Ranges, runs north from the region of Adelaide for several hundred miles. Its highest point is the 3,900 feet of St Mary Peak, on the rim of Wilpena Pound. This highland chain influences the climate of the fertile coastal plains on which Adelaide stands.

The Great Artesian Basin extends from Queensland and the Northern Territory into the north-east corner of South Australia. Because of its underground water, the basin is an important factor in South Australia's beef cattle industry.

The Western Plateau, which accounts for most of the States' land area, covers most of the territory between the Eyre Peninsula and the northern and western boundaries.

It is an area of low rainfall, sparse population and minimal economic value. Much of it is set aside as a reserve for aborigines and for the Woomera Rocket Range.

The Eucla Basin, in the south west of South Australia, includes the Nullarbor Plain. It is a treeless, unproductive area.

POPULATION

At the 1971 census, South Australia had a population of 1,172,774 of whom 842,611 lived in Adelaide. Other important urban centres were: Whyalla (32,085), Mt Gambier (17,867), Port Pirie (15,506) and Port Augusta (12,095).

PLACES OF INTEREST IN ADELAIDE

Adelaide is a planned city, its central area one mile square and surrounded by parklands. This central square mile is quartered by four wide streets which join with Victoria Square. Symetrically placed within the quarterings are other smaller garden squares—Hindmarsh, Hurtle, Whitmore and Light Squares.

The River Torrens and North Parklands separate Adelaide from its original residential suburb, North Adelaide.

CITY STREETS

King William Street is the widest main street (132 feet) of Australia's state capitals. Famous landmarks are the two clock towers, one on Adelaide Town Hall, one on Adelaide General Post Office opposite.

Victoria Square, besides dominant new buildings, the Commonwealth Reserve Bank and the State Administration Centre, has some noted early examples of early Adelaide architecture around it—Treasury Building, St Francis Xavier's Cathedral, the Magistrates Court House, and the Supreme Court.

The modern cast aluminium **Victoria Square Fountain** was designed by Adelaide sculptor, John Dowie, and has as its theme three of South Australia's rivers—Torrens, Onkaparinga, and Murray.

Rundle Street, Adelaide's busiest thoroughfare, has department stores, fashion shops, cinemas, cafes and restaurants, all within a compact quarter mile. Four arcades—City Cross, Adelaide Arcade, Regent Arcade and Richmond Arcade—have entrances from Rundle Street.

Hindley Street, sometimes called 'Little Europe', is the city's cosmopolitan corner. Restaurants serve international cuisine; expresso bars offer inexpensive continental snacks. 'In gear' for trend setters is displayed under colonial wrought iron balconies.

Grote and Gouger Streets have numerous retail shops on either side of the Central Market, where there is a fascinating array of produce—open Tuesday 7 am to 6 pm, Friday 7 am to 10 pm, and Saturday 7 am to 2 pm. In the arcades leading to the market, just about anything can be bought or sold.

North Terrace is a treelined boulevard bordered by a unique concentration of cultural and public buildings, best explored on foot. Travelling from west to east:

Holy Trinity Church of England, built in 1838, is the oldest church in South Australia. The beautiful clock in its tower was made by the clockmaker to William IV.

The Grosvenor, Adelaide's largest hotel.

Adelaide Railway Station, the city rail terminal.

Parliament House, built of South Australian marble from Kapunda and grey granite from Victor Harbour. A plaque on Parliament House commemorates Edward Gibbon Wakefield, whose system of land sale colonisation formed the basis upon which South Australia was founded. On the building is a portion of the Royal Coat of Arms presented to South Australia by the Houses of Parliament, London.

Government House, the vice-regal residence, set in $5\frac{1}{2}$ acres of lawns and gardens.

State National War Memorial, a bronze group by G. Rayner Hoff, set against Macclesfield marble and erected in 1931.

Institute Building, housing the Adelaide Circulating

Library, Newspaper (Australian and Overseas) Reading Room, and the Royal S.A. Society of Arts Gallery.

State Library, with about 200,000 volumes—open from Monday to Saturday, 9.30 am to 9.30 pm, Sunday 2 pm to 5.30 pm. There is a Children's Library and an Archives Section.

S.A. Museum containing the largest aboriginal collection in the world, a very important Melanesian collection, a rock, mineral and meteorite section with the world's largest collections of Australites, and an extremely comprehensive collection of New Guinea Amphibia. Open Monday to Saturday 10 am to 5 pm, and Sunday 2 pm to 5 pm. Holidays 10 am to 5 pm (except Christmas Day and Good Friday).

Bonython Fountain—commemorates one of Adelaide's famous citizens.

Art Gallery of South Australia, which has displays of paintings, drawings, ceramics, sculpture, glassware, furniture and Australia's finest coin collection. Open Monday to Saturday 10 am to 5 pm, Sunday and holidays 2 pm to 5 pm.

University of Adelaide with various faculties housed in fine buildings occupying about 27 acres. Open to the public. Union Hall is within the grounds.

Adelaide Teachers College in Kintore Avenue, next to the University. It has Scott Theatre in its grounds.

Bonython Hall, the great hall of the University, named after its donor, Sir Langdon Bonython.

S.A. Institute of Technology which conducts courses for a number of trades and professions. Some faculties are already at its new site, The Levels, Main North Road.

Royal Adelaide Hospital, the city's largest hospital.

East Terrace is Adelaide's only 'crooked' street. Legend has it that the terrace originally followed a creek, resulting in its present character. Gracious old Adelaide is well represented by bluestone, slate, bay windows and cast iron trimmed verandahs. East End Market opens early every day with main trading activity between 6 am and 8 am on Monday, Wednesday and Friday. Interesting old hotels in this area serve extremely cheap counter meals. Rymill Fountain is pleasantly sited on the lawns.

South Terrace has a number of charming cottages and mansions, fine examples of early town houses, that face the parklands.

The main exit roads to the beach suburbs lead off **West Terrace.**

ACCOMODATION

Good accommodation is available in Adelaide and throughout the settled areas of South Australia. In the remote areas it can be scarce or non-existent and sometimes of indifferent standard. Enquiries and bookings can be made at offices of the South Australian Government Tourist Bureau, independent travel bureaux, or direct with the accommodation itself.

Recommended accommodation in Adelaide includes:

HOTELS

Arkaba Hotel, cnr Glen Osmond and Fullarton Roads. 79 3614
Australia Hotel, 62 Brougham Place, North Adelaide. 67 3444

Criterion Hotel, 137 King William Street. 51 4301
Earl of Zetland Hotel, 158 Gawler Place. 23 5500
Grosvenor Hotel, 125 North Terrace. 51 2961
Hotel Enfield, 184 Hampstead Road. 62 3944
Family Hotel, 1 Seawall, Glenelg. 94 1222
Feathers Hotel, Glynburn Road, Burnside. 31 3151
Highway Inn, Anzac Highway, Plympton. 53 6155
Pier Hotel, 2 Jetty Road, Glenelg. 95 4116
Hotel Richmond, 128 Rundle Street. 23 4044
St Vincent Hotel, 28 Jetty Road, Glenelg. 95 9511
South Australian Hotel, 150 North Terrace. 51 1221
Hotel Strathmore, 129 North Terrace. 51 4456

MOTELS

Adelaide Travelodge, 223 South Terrace. 23 6177
Airways Beach Motel, opposite Airport entrance. 57 3561
Anzac Highway Motel, 626 Anzac Highway, Glenelg East. 94 1344
Arkaba Court, 232 Glen Osmond Road. 79 1645
Commodore Motel, 373 Glen Osmond Road. 79 1601
Flinders Lodge, 27 Dequetteville Terrace, Kent Town. 31 3131
Glen Osmond Motel, 592 Portrush Road, Glen Osmond. 79 1741
Haven Motel, 7 Adelphi Terrace, Glenelg. 94 1555
Hilton Motel, 176 Greenhill Road, Parkside. 71 0444
Regal Park Motel, 44 Barton Terrace, North Adelaide. 67 3222

ADELAIDE HILLS

The Mount Lofty Ranges are a beautiful background to the city scene and they have many vantage points overlooking the complete Adelaide panorama to the sea.

Driving into the hills, in any direction, leads to delightful scenery. You can follow a map and travel a number of well known routes or you can take pot luck and get pleasantly lost. Main roads and back lanes wind through valleys and over slopes covered, in turn, by scrub, forests, pastures, market gardens and orchards—cherry, apple, and pear. Native evergreens harmonise with maples, birches and oaks.

Small hamlets and larger 'hills towns' retain charm from the times when they were settled, 130 years ago. Those people, who delight in the discovery of old buildings, find the Adelaide hills particularly exciting, as stately homes in spacious grounds, little cottages, rambling farm houses, historic mills and barns are scattered throughout the ranges.

FROM ADELAIDE BY THE MAIN NORTH EAST AND LOWER NORTH EAST ROADS

Both roads offer pleasant ways to Para Wirra National Park—through to Modbury on the Main North East Road, then by the Golden Grove Road as far as Golden Grove, and turn right to Para Wirra National Park, by way of Sampson Flat.

The Lower North East Road passes Happy Valley Reservoir and goes on through Highbury to join the scenic road to One Tree Hill, an attractive way to Para Wirra National Park.

The Main North East and Lower North East roads meet at Inglewood and continue round Millbrook Reservoir to Chain of Ponds.

Para Wirra National Park, 3,127 acres of well wooded plateau with steep gullies is cut by the South Para Gorge. It has picnic areas with barbecue points and tennis courts and ovals are for hire. Wildlife—kangaroos and emus—roam free in the park and opposite the kiosk, is a wildlife enclosure.

Millbrook Reservoir, capacity 3,647 million gallons, is in a picturesque setting, possibly best described by the name of the old town 'Chain of Ponds'.

Taking the road north-east of Chain of Ponds you can make it a forest and reservoir day, visiting Kersbrook and Mount Crawford forest and sightseeing around South Para, Warren and Barossa Reservoirs.

South Para Reservoir, capacity 11,300 million gallons, has a beautiful setting in a system of valleys. There are parking and garden areas to allow easy viewing of its various aspects.

Warren Reservoir, capacity 1,401 million gallons, has a pleasant setting close to Mount Crawford Forest.

Barossa Reservoir, capacity 993 million gallons, receives the overflow from South Para Reservoir. It is noted for its Whispering Wall. The lightest gossip is carried with perfect fidelity from one end to the other of its concrete arch dam.

FROM ADELAIDE BY THE TORRENS GORGE ROAD

By Castambul and over the spectacular Gorge Road, above Kangaroo Creek, South Australia's most recently constructed reservoir, and following the Torrens Valley past the Gorge Wildlife Park, with pleasant scenery all the way to Chain of Ponds or to Cudlee Creek, on the road to Mount Torrens.

The Gorge Wildlife Park, with Australian and exotic fauna, and a snake collection, is open daily 9 am to 5 pm. Adult 35 cents, child 15 cents.

FROM ADELAIDE BY BLACK HILL ROAD

A byway on an attractive 'dead end road' leads through the little village of Montacute. The main road follows along the ridge past Marble Hill to Ashton.

FROM ADELAIDE BY THE NORTON SUMMIT AND OLD NORTON SUMMIT ROADS

By way of Norton Summit, Ashton and Basket Range to Lobethal. Delightful little villages on hillsides are surrounded by hills and valleys where pastures, market gardens and orchards meet bushland, dark pines and tall stands of stringy bark. From Lobethal, you can turn south to return through Woodside and Balhannah or travel on through towns like Birdwood, Mount Pleasant, Springton, Eden Valley and Keyneton to Angaston—one of the pleasant routes into the Barossa Valley.

FROM ADELAIDE BY GREENHILL ROAD

At Hazelwood Park, Waterfall Gully Road leaves Greenhill Road to lead through an attractive valley into Waterfall Gully Reserve. Greenhill Road continues over the ranges past Cleland National Park, through Summertown, Uraidla, Carey Gully and Oakbank to Woodside.

Cleland National Park on the slopes of Mount Lofty contains a native fauna reserve. The reserve is divided into six areas. Within four of the areas Australian animals roam freely; the fifth area is left as natural bushland and in the sixth there is a kiosk and a toilet block. Barbecue points are in a woodland setting before the park entrance. A walking track connects the park with Waterfall Gully Reserve.

Entrance is from Summit Road between Greenhill Road and Princes Highway (diverging at Crafers). Entrance Adult 30 cents, child 10 cents.

Oakbank is noted for the famous Easter Onkaparinga Race Meeting, the highlight of which is the Great Eastern Steeplechase.

At Summertown there is a charming byway through market gardens of Piccadilly Valley, with a patterned landscape reminiscent of Van Gogh and Cezanne. As you travel through the little town of Piccadilly, you are likely to see brightly clad workers, the men wearing broad hats and the women with kerchiefs over their heads, further reminders of the Mediterranean climate.

FROM ADELAIDE BY PRINCES HIGHWAY (HIGHWAY 1)

This, one of the main highways to the eastern states, goes through some of the most beautiful of the Adelaide Hills, passing a mile south of Mount Lofty Summit. It leaves the city by the Old Toll House at Glen Osmond. On the hill just north of the Toll House is the ventilation shaft for the old Glen Osmond silver mines, the oldest in Australia. The road below the chimney commands magnificent views over Adelaide. The highway becomes the South East Freeway just past the old hotel 'Eagle on the Hill', with access to the Mount Lofty Summit, Crafers, Stirling, Aldgate and Hahndorf.

Mount Lofty Summit (2,334 ft), the highest point of the ranges, commands fine panoramic views of the foothills and city and, in another direction, the colourfully patterned Piccadilly Valley. Flinders' Monument, a tower on the summit, commemorates the sighting and naming of Mount Lofty by Captain Matthew Flinders in 1802. A restaurant, with a kiosk, serves Devonshire teas and meals.

The hills towns have antique shops, galleries, and interesting restaurants. They are rich in old and modern architecture in unusual bushland settings, with many European trees amongst the native evergreens. The town of Aldgate celebrates the fall with an Autumn Leaves Festival, in April.

Bridgewater Mill is an old mill, now owned by Hamilton's Ewell Vineyards Pty Ltd., complete with a water wheel, which is being restored to working order by the Mount Lofty branch of National Trust. It has a very attractive setting.

Mount Barker Mill is a Dutch style flour mill, restored complete with sails, standing on top of a hill near the road to Mount Barker.

Hahndorf Mill Restaurant is yet another old mill and, here, waitresses in German costume serve fine food in authentic historic surroundings of brick floors, solid furniture and stout wooden beams.

Hahndorf Academy Museum is a museum and art gallery with a changing exhibition and permanent exhibitions including works by the late Sir Hans Heysen, famous for his paintings of great gums in the country around Hahndorf. Open every day (including public holidays) 10 am to 5.30 pm. Entrance adult 30 cents, child 5 cents.

Just before Littlehampton there is a turnoff to Mount Barker. The summit of the mount, which is a pleasant bushland park with marked walks, is off the road to Callington.

From Adelaide by Belair Road (continuation of Unley Road) or Upper Sturt Road (off Belair Road) Shepherd's Hill Road (meets South Road at Bedford Park) or Happy Valley Road (from the main South Road at O'Halloran Hill).

Upper Sturt Road leads to Belair National Park. It leaves Belair Road about a mile past Windy Point.

BELAIR NATIONAL PARK

More than half of this 2,065-acre park is reserved for native flora, to cater for those interested in scientific studies, bush walking or bird watching. In the remainder of the park are tennis courts, cricket ovals, an 18-hole golf course and numerous shelter sheds and arbours. Many water points and fireplaces are provided and there are kiosks at either end of the park. 'Old Government House', once residence of colonial governors, is within the park. Now a museum with many exhibits, it is open for inspection in the afternoon from Wednesday to Sunday and public holidays. Entrance adult 50 cents, child 10 cents. The park is open daily from sunrise to sunset.

Shepherd's Hill Road and Belair Road meet at Blackwood to become the way through the Coromandel Valley. It is joined by Happy Valley Road just before Clarendon, a delightful town surrounded by interesting old buildings. Clarendon Weir on the Onkaparinga River is in an attractive setting, notable for its tall poplars. Just after Clarendon is the turnoff to Mount Bold Reservoir.

Mount Bold Reservoir, capacity 10,414 million gallons, is a very popular place particularly after heavy winter rains when water is flooding over the spillway. After Mount Bold turnoff the road goes on through Kangarilla, Meadows and Macclesfield, or, in another direction, by Ashbourne to Strathalbyn.

This suggests an interesting round tour. One way through the Coromandel Valley and by Ashbourne to Strathalbyn, the other by Macclesfield, Echunga and Aldgate.

Roads south lead through delightful orchards, vineyards, woodland and pastoral country of the Southern Vales of Fleurieu Peninsula and the coast—from Kangarilla through McLaren Flat, from Meadows past Kuitpo forest and Dingabledinga, from Ashbourne past Mount Magnificent National Park—many scenic roads, vivid with wildflowers in spring.

SOUTHERN VALES

The Southern Vales begin at O'Halloran Hill, 12 miles south of Adelaide and cover some 13 miles down Fleurieu Peninsula to Willunga.

The district's gently rolling hills close to the sea and its type of soil are likened to those of Bordeaux, France, and the dry red wines of the area have many of the characteristics of their French counterparts. There are 16 wineries in the vales. Cellar door buying, on weekdays only, is an intriguing experience two gallon minimum).

Reynella was named after John Reynell whose family were the first in South Australia to grow grapes commercially for wine making. The first vintage was in 1842 and, although the industry has grown considerably since then, the town has remained a delightful hamlet.

Morphett Vale—Although the southern suburbs now extend into Morphett Vale there are still areas where vineyards flourish and gums provide shade. In the town itself, a modern shopping centre contrasts with the old hotel and nearby churches. The Catholic Church built in 1845, is the oldest in South Australia.

Noarlunga sits snugly in a deep bend of the Onkaparinga River. The Anglican Church of St Phillip and St James has overlooked the township for more than 120 years. The 'church on the hill', with its weather vane, is a familiar landmark to travellers on the South Road, as they drive around the 'horse shoe'. On the northern side of the town is a major meat works.

McLAREN VALE AND McLAREN FLAT

The densest concentration of wineries in the Southern Vales occurs around the towns of McLaren Vale and McLaren Flat. Many of these wineries are of recent origin, but there are others, such as Thomas Hardy's Tintara, that have built up many traditions. The Barn on the main street of McLaren Vale, a quaint thatch roofed building that was once a wayside inn, is now a bistro-wine cellar-art gallery. It also sells wines to take away and the wines of the district are readily available at the Southern Vales Co-operative Winery on the main road.

Willunga, at the end of the vales, is the centre for Australia's almond industry. South Australia has 6,000 acres of almond orchards, 98% of Australia's total, and 4,000 acres grow around Willunga. In early spring there is an Almond Blossom Festival and coach tours of the district are conducted.

In 1839 slate was discovered and quarried by Cornish settlers. Many early buildings survive, some with slate roofs, paths and walls. The old courthouse has been carefully restored as a National Trust Museum.

FLUERIEU PENINSULA

ADELAIDE'S SOUTH COAST

This is an area to the south of Adelaide where the Mount Lofty Ranges meet the sea. Along this coast are some of South Australia's principal country seaside resorts, the furthest only two or so hours driving from Adelaide.

It is a coast of contrast. Sandy beaches and rugged headlands alternate along the sheltered shores of Gulf St Vincent. Further south the coast faces the Southern Ocean. Here are surfing beaches and, protected by rocky promontories, more calm bays.

Inland, a network of sealed main roads and gravel byways wind through wooded hills and pastures.

It is a popular area for a day or half day trip from Adelaide or for a seaside holiday.

Christies Beach and Port Noarlunga are close enough (20 miles) to Adelaide to be home for many city workers. They are twin seaside resorts, separated by a headland. Their long beaches, protected by an offshore reef, are ideal for bathing. Fishing is good from the jetty, the reef and the estuary of the Onkaparinga River.

Moana is a good surf beach, where cars can drive on to a mile of firm sand. Near the kiosk is mounted a ship's anchor, relic of the migrant vessel 'Nashwauk' which was wrecked in 1855.

Myponga Dam, a reservoir completed in 1962, has a capacity of 6,000 million gallons. A deviation loop off the main road passes over the dam wall.

Myponga township is the centre for a large dairy industry. Cheeses can be bought at the factory in the main street.

Yankalilla is sheltered on three sides by rolling hills. The Bungala River springs from these hills and winds through the town. In the district are prosperous dairies and stud farms.

Normanville is more or less continuous with Yankalilla. Mile long Jetty Road leaves the Main South Road to follow the course of the Bungala River to two miles of wide sandy beach, a break in an otherwise rugged coastline. Only a short remnant of jetty juts into the sea, to recall the sailing days when this was a port for the export of grain.

Second Valley—A road winds down the unusual valley from

a little hamlet, with old houses and a particularly fine old barn, to where the rolling hills tumble into the sea around a small sandy cove, with a little jetty and a high reef, popular with fishermen.

Rapid Bay makes another break in the hills as they meet the sea on a generally rugged coast. It has a sandy beach and deep water offshore. Leading far out into the bay is a 1,600 ft jetty, equipped with a conveyor belt over which crushed limestone, quarried from the adjoining headlands, is carried to ships for transport to New South Wales, where it is used in making steel. There is good fishing from the jetty.

Cape Jervis is at the end of the coast road. Kangaroo Island is only 10 miles away across Backstairs Passage (the main shipping route between Adelaide and Melbourne). From the small jetty, boats go out to fish the often turbulent but fruitful grounds offshore.

Glacier Rock tea rooms, in a pleasant setting 8 miles from Victor Harbour on the Yankalilla road, are alongside some interesting examples of glacial erosion.

Victor Harbour, within two hours easy drive of Adelaide, is the largest of the South Coast seaside resorts. Surrounding the mouths of the Hindmarsh and Inman rivers, it is sheltered by Granite Island and the Bluff. It faces Encounter Bay, historic meeting place of the English and French explorers, Matthew Flinders and Nicolas Baudin, in 1802.

There is a half-mile long causeway between Victor Harbour and Granite Island. From November to May a tractor train takes visitors to and from the island, which has a chair lift.

There are fine bowling greens and tennis courts on the foreshore, a first-class golf course overlooking the harbour, sheltered swimming beaches and a good surf beach at Chiton Rocks, a mile from the town.

The Museum of Historical Art, commands a magnificent view from Porters Hill. It has a collection of coins, medals, minerals, birds' eggs, sea shells and weapons, and souvenirs for sale.

The Cornhill Museum and Art Gallery, in Cornhill Road, has collections of mineral specimens, coral and sea shells, Australian butterflies, paintings, artifacts and antiques.

'Whalers' Haven', a private museum with a collection of relics from early South Australian history with emphasis on whaling, is at Rosetta Bay, on the road from Victor Harbour to the Bluff. A modern, licensed dining room 'Whalers' Inn', adjoins the museum. The Whalers' Inn Gallery displays paintings by Ainslie Roberts.

The Hindmarsh Falls are in picturesque, thickly wooded country a quarter of a mile off the road from Victor Harbour to Myponga via Hindmarsh Valley.

Port Elliot was the first port to be established on Encounter Bay. When the Murray was a busy commercial waterway, Australia's first public railway linked Port Elliot and Goolwa (in 1854).

It is now a charming seaside resort on sheltered Horseshoe Bay, a smaller harbour within Encounter Bay, one of the safest and prettiest bathing beaches in South Australia. Walking paths lead around a rugged promontory to Rocky Bay, Green Bay and Boomer Beach.

The workroom and showroom of the Port Elliot Art Pottery are open for inspection.

Goolwa, an historic little town on the shores of Lake Alexandrina, is about 7 miles from the mouth of the River Murray. A road leads from the town along the shores of the lake to a barrage, one of the five barrages across the river's estuary, preventing the intrusion of salt water into the lake and river.

South Lakes golf course is by the lake about two miles from Goolwa. The M.V. Aroona cruises from South Lakes jetty to the Murray Mouth, Point Sturt and Loveday Bay.

Many fishing boats, pleasure launches, speedboats and water skiers use the lake, which is a sanctuary for waterfowl.

The first railway passenger vehicle to run in South Australia is exhibited in the town.

A ferry carries cars to Hindmarsh Island, over which a road leads to a point where there is a view of the mouth of the Murray.

ELIZABETH

Elizabeth is a new city, commenced in 1955, and developed by the South Australian Housing Trust. Officially classified as part of the Adelaide metropolitan area, it is a self-contained city, population 50,000 with a main town centre which includes a modern shopping complex and Octagon and Shedley Theatres to provide a wide range of recreational and cultural activities.

Ample provision has been made for schools, churches and service organisations and large areas of land have been made available for recreational purposes. Fourteen thousand acres have been set aside for garden reserves and many of the 250,000 trees and shrubs, which have been planted, are approaching full growth.

The suburban areas have been planned to be separated from but convenient to industrial sites. Smaller shopping centres cater for suburban needs.

General Motors-Holden's largest plant in Australia is at Elizabeth.

Elizabeth, on Sturt Highway, is often included by visitors in a round trip to the Barossa Valley.

BAROSSA VALLEY

About 40 miles north of Adelaide, the Barossa Valley, with many miles of vineyards and twenty-five wineries, is a famous wine region and a wonderfully interesting place for sightseeing.

Settlement of the valley was commenced in 1842 by Lutherans from Prussia and Silesia, who migrated so that they could practice their religion free from interference.

Solid stone houses and old German cottages, with carefully cultivated gardens in scrupulously clean and neat tree-lined streets, characterise the towns of the valley. German names still largely prevail amongst shop signs.

Besides Tanunda, Angaston and Nuriootpa, which are the main towns, there are a number of smaller settlements such as Lyndoch, Bethany, Rowland Flat, Greenock, Marananga and Light's Pass. Altogether, there are some twenty small communities within a radius of twenty miles of Tanunda.

Seppeltsfield, 4 miles off the main road leading through the Barossa Valley, is an unusual example of a complete village built around a single winery. Gramp's Orlando at Rowland Flat, Thumm's Yaldara near Lyndoch, Smith's Yalumba at Angaston and Kaiser Stuhl and Penfolds at Nuriootpa are other wineries that vie with the towns in dominating surrounding vineyards.

Tanunda is a thriving town with nine wineries within a three-mile radius. The largest is on the edge of the town—the picturesque Chateau Tanunda, styled on a French chateau.

Two of the oldest Lutheran churches in the valley, the Langmeil and the Tabor, are just off the long, shady main street. Each November the Tanunda 'Brass Band Competitions' attract thousands of spectators.

The Barossa Valley Historical Museum, Murray Street, is open Monday to Friday 1 pm to 3.30 pm, Sunday 2 pm to 4.30 pm.

Nuriootpa is an aboriginal name meaning meeting place; the town, besides being near the meeting place of the Angaston Creek and the North Para River, is in the heart of the valley, at the junction of the main highway. It is noted for community activities.

Coulthard House Museum and Gallery is open for inspection daily.

Angaston, nestled in low hills on the eastern edge of the valley has tree-lined streets and a fine park. As well as vineyards and the attractive Yalumba winery, Angaston has many stone fruit orchards and several dried fruit packing sheds. Some of the surrounding hills are almost pure marble—used in many fine Adelaide buildings. Local marble is the basis of a large cement industry near the town.

Mengler's Hill Road, a direct link between Angaston and Tanunda, provides excellent views of the entire valley.

'Sightseeing Guide to the Barossa Valley' lists winery visiting times. Available from the South Australian Government Tourist Bureau.

MURRAY RIVER

For the last 400 miles of its 1,600 mile course, the Murray River flows through South Australia. By this stage of its journey from the mountains to the sea, it is slow flowing and stately. In its last hundred miles, it has a fall of only one inch to the mile.

The upper reaches of the Murray in South Australia flow through extensive irrigation areas, developed since 1887 when the Chaffey brothers, irrigation experts from California, founded Renmark. Towns here tend to be surrounded by orchards and vineyards. Most of them offer good accommodation for visitors, often in community run hotels. They usually have attractive riverside gardens and drives. Packing sheds and wineries welcome visitors. Wildlife sanctuaries abound along the river, where birdlife is plentiful. Monuments to Captain Charles Sturt, who explored the Murray in 1830, are to be found in most towns. Locks across the Murray are another frequent point of interest.

Towns in the Riverland Irrigation Area include Renmark, Berri, Loxton, Barmera, Waikerie.

Near Morgan, the Murray swings in a great bend to the south and heads for Lake Alexandrina and the sea.

Morgan was during the latter part of last century Australia's busiest river port. Just past the railway station are the remains of the 400 feet of wharves which were once hardly adequate to handle the riverboat trade. From here, paddle steamers ventured far up the Murray and Darling systems, tapping the trade to and from inland Victoria and New South Wales and channelling it over the short railway to Adelaide.

Points of interest in Morgan include the old wharves, customs house, court house and old buildings, the inevitable memorial to Captain Sturt, the pumping station, and the commencement of the pipeline that takes Murray water from Morgan to Whyalla.

Mannum is another centre closely involved in the history of the riverboat traffic. It was here in 1852 that Captain William

Randell launched 'Mary Ann', first of the hundreds of steamboats to ply the Murray. Relics of 'Mary Ann' are displayed on the riverfront recreation reserve, along with a replica of Captain Sturt's whaleboat. A museum of the old Murray days is housed in the paddlewheeler 'Marion', now in permanent dry dock at Mannum.

Between Morgan and Mannum, the Murray passes Blanchetown, site of the first of the 26 locks across the river, and only 12 feet above sea level, although still 170 miles from the mouth. Swan Reach is another sleepy town along this part of the river.

Murray Bridge, biggest town on the Murray in South Australia, is where both main Melbourne–Adelaide road routes and railway line cross the river. The paddle steamer 'Coonawarra' may be seen here on Saturdays and Sundays. On weekdays it is away on a five day cruise, taking passengers along the river. Murray Bridge has a good privately run museum, with many relics of the old paddleboat days, including fascinating roll charts of the rivers.

Motorists driving between Adelaide and Melbourne by both the Princes and Western Highways follow the river closely between Murray Bridge and Tailem Bend.

Goolwa, on Lake Alexandrina, was the last port of call for the riverboats. Cargo from here went cross country a few miles by train for transhipment to ocean going vessels at Port Elliot or Victor Harbour.

Goolwa is an excellent starting point for exploring Lakes Alexandrina and Albert, the extensive lakes into which the Murray spreads before finally entering the sea. Barrages at Goolwa, built to keep salt water out of the lakes and the river are worth inspection. The 50 passenger 'Aroona' cruises round Lake Alexandrina and to the Murray Mouth. The mouth of the river can also be reached (almost) by road or on foot, but this is a project to be entered into only by the hardy.

Drive yourself houseboats: Anyone who can drive a car can drive a houseboat, available in various sizes at Renmark, Berri, Morgan, Blanche Town, Mannum, Murray Bridge and Goolwa. Sample rates: 5 berth, $16 per day, $105 per week, 8 berth, $24 per day, $168 per week. Minimum hiring is 2 days. Houseboats have gas cookers, refrigerators, and hot water, electric light, shower and toilet.

FLINDERS RANGES

The Flinders Ranges are a rugged series of ranges which rise between Crystal Brook and Peterborough, about 120 miles north of Adelaide. They run north from here, petering out about 100 miles to the east of Marree.

There are four main routes from Adelaide to the Flinders Ranges. 1. The most interesting way, scenically, is via Clare, Wilmington, Quorn and Hawker. The road is sealed for most of the way to Wilpena Pound. 2. A shorter route after leaving Clare is by way of Jamestown, Orroroo and Hawker. 3. A third route, branching off three miles past Tarlee, goes through Burra, Peterborough and Hawker. 4. The route through Port Wakefield, Port Pirie, and Port Augusta follows Route No 1 as far as Port Augusta. It offers the easiest driving, and the least interesting. Some people prefer it for the return journey.

Wilpena Pound is probably the best known formation in the Flinders Ranges, a great dish enclosed by mountains on all sides, with only one narrow entrance.

Wilpena Pound makes an excellent base for exploring the Flinders Ranges. Walking trips, mountain climbing expeditions and car trips can be planned around the Pound. It has an excellent camping ground and a first class licensed motel with a swimming pool. As a general rule, accommodation in the Flinders Ranges is not plentiful; careful planning and advance bookings are recommended.

Even casual visitors to Wilpena Pound, with no great yen for marathon walks, usually bestir themselves sufficiently to take the short track across Sliding Rock and through the narrow gorge, to the only entrance. The Parklike floor of the Pound covers 32 square miles, and it is completely encircled by a huge rock wall. Big river gums mark out creeks and lower areas, while higher parts are covered by native pines.

Clearings in the Pound date from 1902–1904 when John Hill and family grew wheat there. The stone house in which they lived still survives. Signs near the house show the way to a lookout area on the inside slopes and to tracks through the Pound. A day can be spent in climbing the 3,822 feet of St Mary Peak.

Quorn is a historic town in the Flinders Ranges, once the junction station of the east–west and north–south railways, a role it lost when the direct link from Port Augusta to Port Pirie was established. The three storey Quorn Mill, which had a very short career as a flour mill, is now an art gallery, museum, motel and restaurant.

Willochra Plain, north of Quorn, was for a time the main hope of wheat farmers spreading northwards in the mistaken belief that rain would follow the plough. They arrived in a good season, got one or two successful crops, then only heartbreak, as the remains of deserted towns like Gordon and Wilson attest. Kanyaka ruins, those of a substantial early homestead, are near the Quorn–Hawker road.

Arkaroola is in the Mount Painter country, the rugged red-brown mountains of the northernmost Flinders. Some 80 miles east of Copley, nestled in these mountains, are the 20 unit Greenwood Lodge and Mawson Motels, with swimming pool, and Wywhyana Caravan Park. Low cost bunkhouses are available for school, club or society groups.

They are in a sanctuary where kangaroos, euros, wallabies and native birds are seen in outback terrain. Four wheel drive tours explore spectacular mining tracks over the mountains. Roads suitable for conventional vehicles lead over heights, into gorges, and to beautiful rock pools. This is richly mineralised country, a paradise for rock hounds.

EYRE PENINSULA

Eyre Peninsula is that triangular shaped piece of land between Spencer Gulf and the Great Australian Bight.

The Eyre Highway skirts it in the north, between Port Augusta and Ceduna, on its way from Adelaide to Perth. From Port Augusta to Port Lincoln, the Lincoln Highway hugs the east coast of Eyre Peninsula (that is, the west coast of Spencer Gulf). The Flinders Highway completes the triangle by following the coast of the Great Australian Bight from Port Lincoln to Ceduna.

Eyre Peninsula has many pleasant beaches, a major holiday resort at Port Lincoln, one of Australia's greatest iron mines at Iron Knob, and an important iron ore exporting, shipbuilding, iron and steel producing centre at Whyalla, South Australia's second biggest city.

PORT AUGUSTA

204 miles from Adelaide at the head of Spencer Gulf, is where motorists coming from the east usually enter Eyre Peninsula. One of Australia's most important crossroads, it is where the major east–west transport axis meets the major north–south transport axis, a gathering place for tourists, truckies and train men, resting up from the stretch behind them, or marshalling their strength for the stretch in front of them. The Indian-Pacific, the train that crosses Australia, from Sydney (on the Pacific Ocean) to Perth (on the Indian Ocean) passes through Port Augusta twice a week.

The Thomas Playford Power Station at Curlew Point (3 miles south of Port Augusta) generates more than half South Australia's power, using sub-bituminous coal brought 174 miles from the open cuts at Leigh Creek in what must be Australia's most enormous trains. Public inspection at 9 am, 11 am, 2 pm daily.

From its Port Augusta base, the Royal Flying Doctor Service maintains radio contact with almost three hundred outback outposts. A School of the Air is conducted for outback children. Inspections, weekdays only, 9.30 am to 11 am, 12 noon to 2 pm, 3 pm to 4 pm.

WHYALLA

Seeing the BHP steelworks and shipyards are popular visitor activities in Whyalla, 45 miles down the coast from Port Augusta. The main BHP installations are on the left of the northern approach to the city.

Steelworks tours commence at the visitors reception centre, Mondays to Fridays, at 9.30 am. Visitors are also given a brief talk and shown a film. For safety reasons, no open footwear is allowed.

Shipyard tours begin at the shipyard main gate at 2 pm daily.

IRON KNOB

Iron Knob, rising out of the salt bush plain, 32 miles from Whyalla, was the original source of iron ore for all BHP's steelmaking activities. No longer worked, it has been passed over in favour of nearby Iron Monarch and Iron Prince, where iron ore is quarried in enormous open cuts.

Iron Monarch visiting hours are 10 am to 11 am and 2 pm to 3 pm Monday to Friday. Enquire at the BHP Town Office at Iron Knob.

PORT LINCOLN

Port Lincoln offers holidaymaker a Mediterranean climate which goes well with the clear, intensely blue waters of the harbour. Calm inner waters are suitable for swimming and water skiing; southern ocean beaches offer the steep slopes of long ocean waves. Yachting is popular, a variety of conditions being available.

Lincoln National Park, covering 35,000 acres, a few miles south of Port Lincoln, has rugged bushland of dense Mallee, sheoak on limestone rises, sandhills, fine coastal scenery. Spring brings wildflowers to the country around Port Lincoln.

STREAKY BAY

Streaky Bay is the spot where Peter Nuyts, a high official of the Dutch East India Company and Thijssen, master of the *Gulden Zeepard*, in 1627 decided to turn back and abandon their exploration of the Australian coast. Nuyts Beacon, erected by Streaky Bay Council in 1927, commemorates the tri-centenary of their voyage.

The town is actually on Blanche Port, a sheltered inlet at the southern end of Streaky Bay. The caravan park is close to a good swimming beach for children. The water is deeper nearer the town.

Streaky Bay jetty is reputed to be one of the most rewarding in South Australia for fishermen, with good catches of whiting, tommies, gar, snapper and ten other varieties. Good fishing grounds around the coast are at Speeds Point, Baird Bay, Smooth Pool and Perlubie Beach.

The shark proof swimming enclosure beside the jetty is recommended.

CEDUNA

Ceduna is where motorists taking the Eyre Highway, National Route No 1, direct from Adelaide to Perth, first see the Great Australian Bight.

A much photographed sign on the Perth side of town warns of limited water supplies between Ceduna and Norseman, in Western Australia.

The Overseas Telecommunications Commission Earth Station, 23 miles north-west of Ceduna, sends and receives signals from its 97 feet dish to Intelstat III, over the Indian Ocean. Open to visitors 10 am–12 noon, 2 pm to 4 pm Monday to Friday.

THE SOUTH EAST

Many Victorians and New South Welshmen who have never quite made it to Adelaide have had a taste of South Australia by crossing the border into the South East. Once you're in South Australia it's only 13 miles to Mount Gambier, which used to be South Australia's second biggest city, until Whyalla took over that role.

Mount Gambier's main claim to fame, of course, is its Blue Lake, and the mystery of why it suddenly changes colour every year at the end of November, throwing off its sombre grey overnight in favour of intense blue. Between March and June it slowly reverts to its delicate winter grey. As well as pleasing the tourists and puzzling the scientists, the lake serves the very practical function of providing Mount Gambier's city water supply.

The Blue Lake is one of four crater lakes, all near each other and linked by a scenic drive. The others are Leg of Mutton Lake, Browne Lake and Valley Lake.

In the Cafpirco area, seven miles west of Mount Gambier, the quarrying of Mount Gambier stone (coralline limestone) may be inspected. A visit to the Cave Garden Reserve, built round a natural cave in the centre of the city, is usually expected of tourists in Mount Gambier. It is lit at night.

Mount Gambier is also proud of its sawmills. The State Sawmill, largest softwood mill in the Southern Hemisphere, may be inspected only on Tuesdays at 2 pm, but various other mills are more receptive to visitors, as follows: Mt Burr, Monday to Friday 10 am to 4 pm. Nangwarry, Monday to Thursday 10 am to noon, 2 pm to 4 pm. Penola Timbers and Coreboard, Mount Gambier, Tuesday and Thursday afternoon.

A popular drive from Mount Gambier is to head south through Port MacDonnell, over the border to Nelson in Victoria, then back to Mount Gambier. This drive passes Dingley Dell, once the home of poet Adam Lindsay Gordon. In a room at the cottage is a museum where relics of Gordon's life are displayed.

Coastal resorts in the South East include:

Port MacDonnell, where the surprisingly large post office is not a monument to the verbosity of the locals, but a converted customs house, used during the days when Port MacDonnell was a thriving port handling large quantities of wool and grain; **Beachport,** notable for a customs house that has been turned into a museum, a penguin sanctuary on Penguin Island which can be reached in boats that are for hire, and the Pool of Siloam, a lake so salty that it's almost impossible to sink in it; **Southend,** (*Grey*) a crayfishing village which provides access to the 22,000 acre Canunda National Park; **Robe,** on Guichen Bay, which was chief port of entry for Chinese on their way to the Victorian gold diggings, where visitors can sleep in the hotel room where Adam Lindsay Gordon was nursed back to health by Maggie Parke, the 15 year old girl he was later to marry, and where Hoopers Beach and Long Beach are popular places for swimming and surf fishing; and **Kingston,** a good spot for catching mullet, snook and whiting, or for watching the comings and goings of the crayfishing fleet.

The Coorong, a 90 mile lagoon, separated from the ocean by low sandhills known locally as the Hummocks, is visible from the Princes Highway south of Meningie. Large formations of pelicans, black swans and ducks are often seen.

There is a road into the 90-mile beach which fronts the ocean, being separated from the Coorong by Younghusband Peninsula. It leaves the Princes Highway about two miles on the Meningie side of Kingston. But motorists need to watch for high tide, which covers the firm sands.

Naracoorte Caves, a National Pleasure Resort with a caravan and camping ground, are near the main road to Mount Gambier, south of Naracoorte. Visitor interest is concentrated on three of the ten caves: Alexandra, Blanche and Victoria, the latter leading to the Fossil Cave, discovered in 1969 and containing some of the world's most important deposits of extinct marsupial remains in the world.

INFORMATION SERVICES

Pamphlets and information about every aspect of tourism in South Australia may be obtained from the South Australian Government Tourist Bureau at addresses listed below. Bookings for travel and accommodation may also be made there.

27 King William Street, Adelaide, 5000. (51 3281)
8 Royal Arcade, Melbourne, 3000. (63 2760)
402 George Street, Sydney, 2000. (25 2641)

Royal Automobile Association of South Australia, with headquarters at 41 Hindmarsh Square (23 4555) also provides information to visiting motorists with accreditation from their home body. Their literature is also available from offices of interstate affiliated bodies.

This Week in Adelaide is an informative booklet published every week with lots of information about current events, shopping and restaurants. Free from most hotels and travel offices.